D1590175

CHURCH AND SOCIETY
IN THE MEDIEVAL NORTH OF ENGLAND

CHURCH AND SOCIETY IN THE MEDIEVAL NORTH OF ENGLAND

R.B. DOBSON

THE HAMBLEDON PRESS

LONDON AND RIO GRANDE

Published by The Hambledon Press 1996
102 Gloucester Avenue, London NW1 8HX (UK)
PO Box 162, Rio Grande, Ohio 45674 (USA)

ISBN 1 85285 120 1

A description of this book is available from
the British Library and from the Library of Congress

Typeset by The Midlands Book Typesetting Company
Printed on acid-free paper and bound in Great
Britain by Cambridge University Press.

Contents

Acknowledgements

The essays in this volume first appeared in the following publications and are reprinted by the kind permission of the publishers.

1   *Northern History*, 19 (1983), pp. 15–44.

2   *Ampleforth Journal*, 64 (1969), pp. 161–76.

3   Durham Cathedral Lecture (1972).

4   A. Goodman and A. Tuck (eds), *War and Border Societies in the Middle Ages* (London, 1992), pp. 124–54.

5   *Scottish Historical Review*, 46 (1967), pp. 1–25.

6   *Transactions of Cumberland and Westmorland Antiquarian and Archaeological Society*, new series, 65 (1965), pp. 182–221.

7   P.R. Coss and S.D. Lloyd (eds), *Thirteenth-Century England*, 3 (1991).

8   *Bibliothèque de la revue d'histoire ecclésiastique*, 72 (1987), pp. 181–91.

9   *Journal of Ecclesiastical History*, 30 (1979), pp. 145–74.

10   R.A. Griffiths and J. Sherborne (eds), *Kings and Nobles in the Middle Ages* (Gloucester, 1986), pp. 130–54.

11   *Studies in Church History*, 4 (1967), pp. 22–38.

12   D. Abulafia, M. Franklin and M. Rubin (eds), *Church and City, 1000–1500: Essays in Honour of Christopher Brooke* (Cambridge, 1992), pp. 311–32.

13   I. Wood and G.A. Loud (eds), *Church and Chronicle in the Middle Ages: Essays Presented to John Taylor* (Hambledon Press, London and Rio Grande, OH, 1991), pp. 201–18.

To Theo

Introduction

The thirteen essays collected in this volume are all concerned, albeit in very different ways, with the history of the Christian church in northern England between the Norman Conquest and the Reformation. More precisely still, they tend to focus on the period between the accession of Richard II (1377) and the death of Richard III (1485), that century when the formidable machinery of the late medieval English church attained its most elaborate and – on the whole – most harmonious stage. Despite the perennial fascination of so large a theme, and despite my own personal origins on the banks of the River Tees (where I lived within the diocese of York but looked out of the window at the diocese of Durham), nothing in fact would then have surprised me more than that I should become so frequently engaged in the history of the medieval church in the medieval north. For that unexpected circumstance I owe everything to the enthusiastic advice of the late Professor V.H. Galbraith and Mr W.A. Pantin, without whose initial stimulus many years ago this book would certainly not exist. In retrospect Mr Pantin's suggestion that I might care to study the community of St Cuthbert at Durham cathedral during the priorate of John Wessington (1416–46) was more fortunate than I could then know. Research among the dean and chapter of Durham's muniments not only led to the publication of my book on *Durham Priory, 1400–1450* in 1974 but also introduced me to one of the greatest monastic archives in medieval Europe. So voluminous and intriguing are those archives, first seriously explored by James Raine the elder in the early nineteenth century, that they are always likely to dominate our perceptions of the social as well as the religious life of northern England in the middle ages.

The records of the prior and chapter of Durham cathedral accordingly leave a heavy imprint on this volume, and particularly on Chapters 3–6. The incomparable prestige and highly dispersed landed wealth of the community of St Cuthbert in the later middle ages inevitably involved the latter in many of the most significant 'northern' problems of the age, ranging from the often contested primacy of the see of York within the diocese of Durham to the defence of the English border against the Scots. Two of the essays in this collection (4 and 5) make it only too clear how a large monastic corporation with vested interests to the north as well as the south of the Tweed usually tried, but often failed, to maintain the *status quo* between the kingdoms of England and Scotland. Nor can there be much doubt that Richard Bell, the only late medieval Durham monk ever to join the English episcopal bench, was promoted to the bishopric of Carlisle in 1478 because the future Richard III expected him to help in the protection of the north-western frontier (no. 6). However, a much more interesting feature of the Durham cathedral archives is what they can reveal about the careers conducted within the priory and its nine daughter houses by the Durham monks themselves. As Chapter 3 below may serve to indicate, we are better informed as to the education, responsibilities, devotions and aspirations of the community of St Cuthbert at Durham than those of any comparable body of men in the fifteenth-century north of England. A comprehensive prosopographical analysis of the late medieval community of St Cuthbert is yet to be achieved; but it already seems sufficiently obvious, if somewhat ironical, that in any attempt to actually understand the mentality of the inhabitants of the late medieval north, the best prospects lie neither in peasant village nor aristocratic affinity but rather within the great monastic precinct of Durham.

In many ways the records of St Cuthbert's community may seem even more remarkable and unrivalled to those historians who, like myself in 1964, find themselves migrating from Durham and points even further north to that 'second chamber of the realm', the archiepiscopal city of York. Most of the many recent attempts to identify the common characteristics of northern England have understandably failed to grapple with the interesting question of why the three cathedral cities in the region should have been -- as they still are – so utterly unlike each other. Nothing, one might suppose, would have startled a monk of Durham more than to enter the walls of medieval York for the first time at the beginning of the fifteenth century. Here he would have found a large city (perhaps 12,000 souls) as opposed to his own small one (perhaps 2,000 inhabitants); and here too he would have been immediately impressed by the difference between the largest Gothic cathedral in England, under the nominal care of thirty-six secular canons, and his own almost entirely Romanesque cathedral under the custody of approximately forty resident Benedictine monks. In a quite different way he could hardly have failed to notice the contrast between the four parish churches in the city of Durham and at least forty urban parishes in York, the largest concentration of parish churches in the north of England. And if, which is hardly conceivable, this hypothetical visiting monk had been interested in the records produced by the ecclesiastical institutions of fifteenth-century York, he would have been equally surprised at the differences between those and the muniments preserved at his own Durham cathedral. So great were and are these differences that the monks of St Cuthbert and the canons of St Peter's metropolitan church at York can now seem to us not only dissimilar, which indeed they were, but members of a completely different religious world, which of course they were not.

In other words, and not entirely inappropriately, in the case of the late medieval church of York itself it is the formal records of the archbishop and the ecclesiastical hierarchy which tend to dominate the archival scene. Fewer such official archives survive at Durham and even fewer at Carlisle, where the labours of both the bishops and the twenty or so Augustinian canons who comprised the cathedral chapter will always tend to evade the attention of the modern historian (no. 1). Nor by the fifteenth century is it at all easy to recapture the rhythms of the religious life conducted within the great monasteries of Yorkshire, deservedly celebrated though Rievaulx and Fountains, Whitby and Selby certainly were: even the great Benedictine abbey of St Mary's, located just outside the northern walls of York and wealthier than Durham cathedral priory itself, has left only two of its obedientiary account rolls to posterity. Accordingly, and above all, it is the magnificent and uninterrupted sequences of archiepiscopal registers (now preserved in the Borthwick Institute of Historical Research at York) which are always likely to dictate the course of research into the ecclesiastical history of the northern archdiocese from the thirteenth century onwards. However, and by a paradox only too familiar to medieval historians, even the most voluminous episcopal register can be singularly uninformative about the personal initiatives of a bishop himself. Only from other and at times ambiguous sources is it sometimes possible to gain an impression of the archbishop of York's own priorities and problems. Perhaps the chief conclusion to emerge from the essays devoted to this theme below (nos 7 and 8) is that the supreme spiritual lord of the northern church was under such constant pressure from his king, his pope and his subjects that he was rarely his own master. By contrast, the political as well as religious power of the small group of residentiary canons established in his cathedral (nos 9 and 10) has been much neglected but was often very considerable indeed. In many ways, it was residentiary canons like Masters William Poteman and William Sheffeld who actually ruled the church of York – to the extent that it was ruled as opposed to being administered – towards the close of the middle ages.

However, as this collection of essays suggests and as the vicars-general of the archbishops of York would certainly have agreed, far from being monolithic the medieval church in the north was pluralist to a degree. As a striking manifestation of such pluralism and for several other excellent reasons too, in recent years the perpetual chantries founded throughout England in such profusion during the fourteenth and fifteenth centuries have received much more attention from historians than ever before. The two essays on aspects of perpetual chantry foundation in the city of York printed below (nos 11 and 12) undoubtedly raise more questions than they solve; but they seem to lend much support to the current view that many of these chantries provided the laity of England's largest towns with an increasing opportunity to influence the conduct of religion at the parish level. Does the stringent control exercised by the fifteenth-century York civic council over its *équipe* of chantry priests worshipping at altars in St William's Chapel on Ouse Bridge point to a wider moral still? It would certainly not be hard to suggest that such control, like many other features of northern religious life discussed in this volume, seem to testify to the increased prominence of *l'esprit laique* within and without the late medieval church.

Nor would it be particularly difficult to make the essays in this book, highly heterogeneous though they are, conform to the conventional framework of religious rise, triumph and subsequent decline within which the story of medieval Christendom between the eleventh and fifteenth centuries is so often told. Most obviously of all perhaps, the highly-charged if somewhat wayward spiritual energy with which Benedict of Auxerre reintroduced Benedictine monasticism to the north of England in the years immediately after the Norman Conquest (no. 2) is very notable by its absence within the fragments of banal historical writing produced at York and Durham at the very end of the middle ages (no. 13). But then not even the most secluded monastery (which no religious house in the late medieval north actually was) could resist social and intellectual change for ever, above all because it was frequently an initiator of such change itself. As so often in the history of Christianity, few of the difficulties confronting the institutional church in late medieval Europe could be solved by an act of will or even a change of heart. Within that context, perhaps most of the essays in this collection reveal that the clergy of northern England towards the end of the middle ages were neither idle nor corrupt but rather practitioners of a comparatively successful conservatism – successful because they were flexible as well as tenacious in their struggles with the problems of their age.

This book is primarily about some of those problems, no doubt usually unimportant to us but undoubtedly fundamental to an understanding of what the relationship between church and society in the medieval north of England actually was. How far that relationship was significantly different from its counterpart in the province of Canterbury, how far there was a genuinely distinctive northern English church, is an issue on which opinion will perhaps always be divided. In the last few years several perceptive scholars, Professor A.J. Pollard, Professor F. Musgrove and Dr H.M. Jewell among them, have tried to strengthen the case for at least some form of northern historical identity over the medieval centuries; and it would be hard to deny that the late medieval church north of the Trent enjoyed or endured some highly characteristic features, notably perhaps the lack of a university. On the other hand, the regional, social and ecclesiastical divisions within the province of York were often greater than those which separated it from the southern province. All in all indeed, it is probably the diversity rather than unity of the supposed 'northern church' which emerges most obviously from the following pages. But even if northern England, like Italy for Prince Metternich, is only a geographical expression, that expression is notoriously capable of engendering intense human loyalty – not least among historians themselves. Among the indispensable aids to the study of the church in the north of England are the publications of those most self-consciously northern of all learned bodies, the Surtees Society and the Yorkshire Archaeological Society, not to mention the periodical *Northern History* itself. My debt over many years to the staff of the Borthwick Institute of Historical Research at York and to the late (alas) Department of Palaeography and Diplomatic at the University of Durham is more considerable still. If, as is sometimes said, the concept of regionality – like that of nationality – has to be not only invented but also constantly reinvented, the archive offices of northern England will be even more essential to the future of the north than they were to me during the writing of these essays. This volume owes a very great deal to the generous help and encouragement of Mr Martin Sheppard.

Abbreviations

BL	British Library, London
BRUC	A. B. Emden. *A Biographical Dictionary of the University of Cambridge to 1500* (Cambridge, 1963)
BRUO	A. B. Emden, *A Biographical Register of the University of Oxford to AD 1500*. 3 vols (Oxford, 1957–9)
CCR	*Calendar of Close Rolls*
Cold. Corr.	*Coldingham Correspondence*, Surtees Society, 12 (1841)
CPL	*Calendar of Papal Letters*
CPR	*Calendar of Patent Rolls*
CRO	Carlisle Record Office
CW 2	*Transactions of the Cumberland and Westmorland Antiquarian and Archaeological Society, new series*
DCD	Dean and Chapter of Durham: Muniments
DNB	*Dictionary of National Biography*
EETS	Early English Text Society, London
HCY	*Historians of the Church of York*, 3 vols, RS (1879–94)
HMC	Historic Manuscripts Commission
PRO	Public Record Office, London
RCHM	Royal Commission on Historical Monuments
RO	Record Office
Rot. Parl.	*Rotuli Parliamentorum*
RS	Rolls Series
VCH	Victoria History of the Counties of England
YCA	York City Archives

YCS   *York Chantry Surveys*, ed. W. Page, Surtees Society, 91–2 (1892–3)

YML   York Minster Library

1

Cathedral Chapters and Cathedral Cities: York, Durham and Carlisle in the Fifteenth Century

'Is Northern History a Subject?' To that particular question, raised unambiguously by the late Professor John Le Patourel of Leeds towards the end of his life, there can never be anything but an ambiguous answer. For Le Patourel himself indeed, 'northern history' finally emerged as 'no subject at all' but something much grander, 'an unattainable infinity like any other historical problem worth considering'.[1] So deliberately vague a definition, with its invaluable merit of leaving a very great deal to the eye of the beholder, must clearly apply to any attempt to compare and contrast the role of northern England's three cathedrals in the fifteenth century. No historian who has enjoyed the good fortune of spending many hours in the posthumous company of the late medieval Benedictine monks of Durham, the secular canons of York Minster or even the much less well documented Augustinian canons of Carlisle can justifiably complain of the monotony of his lot. But each of those great religious institutions, for contemporaries perhaps the most powerful corporations of any kind in the medieval north, was created to express its own 'unattainable infinity' in a highly individual and very different way. Although this essay is an attempt to discover whether the three cathedrals of northern England in the later middle ages possessed any identifiably common 'northern' characteristics at all, it must be said at once that they tend to be most intelligible when placed in the context of the *ecclesia Anglicana* as a whole. No doubt for that reason, as Le Patourel himself pointed out, the most perceptive studies of the medieval northern cathedrals of England have usually emerged from historians thoroughly familiar with the conduct of monastic and diocesan administration south of the Humber too. To take only the most striking case, Alexander Hamilton Thompson was already the most impressive national authority on English cathedrals before he joined the University of Leeds in 1922 to become in his later years the still unrivalled master of the history of the late medieval Province of York.

What Professor Hamilton Thompson would have thought of the validity of 'northern history' as such we can accordingly only guess. Perhaps, after all and like so many of us, he might have come to believe that the most important date in the history of the north of England is not 1066 or 1485

[1] J. Le Patourel, 'Is Northern History a Subject?', *Northern History*, 12 (1976), p. 15.

but 1966, the year in which his successors at Leeds University founded a periodical entitled *Northern History*. Certainly one assumes that Hamilton Thompson can only have welcomed the way in which that journal has so benevolently fostered the insidiously attractive myth of northern England. Such myths, as historians are so frequently and properly reminded these days, often prove to be more persuasive and potent than 'facts'; and even geographical expressions – like Italy itself not too many years after Metternich's death – can have the disconcerting habit of rapidly becoming something much more than that. Nevertheless, and as Professor John Le Patourel was himself well aware, the concept of northern English history as 'unattainable infinity' does raise its own difficulties – most obviously that one can't explain what such an entity is, and most seriously that one can't be certain it exists at all. All would-be northern historians are confronted with the familiar dilemma that the more they come to know about their remarkably diversified region the more conscious they become of its internal dissimilarities rather than of its common, if any, characteristics. The days have long since passed since Gaillard Lapsley and Rachel Reid could generalise with attractive-seeming simplicity about a unitary 'problem of the North' and a Tudor northern England allegedly 'almost untouched by the economic, social and intellectual changes which were breaking up mediaeval society in the South'.[2] From 1154 at least, it could well be argued that the most remarkable feature of the political history of the north of England was how little rather than how much of a 'problem' it presented to kings and governments of England increasingly located in the Thames valley. Accordingly for recent historians of the English later middle ages the importance of the history of the north has increasingly become 'not so much what is peculiar about it in isolation' as 'the influence it exercised in the affairs of the kingdom as a whole'.[3] More generally, Professor Dickens taught us all to beware not only the partly self-promoted myth of northern primitivism but also of ascribing to the north of England a completely non-existent homogeneity: long before the Tudor period the differences between the borders and south Yorkshire are indeed likely to have been 'far greater than those between south Yorkshire and Essex'.[4] As someone who spent much of his childhood in a farmhouse looking over upper Teesdale from the late and lamented North Riding of Yorkshire to County Durham, perhaps I can be forgiven for believing, with the late medieval monks of St Cuthbert, that the River Tees may form a

[2] R.R. Reid, *The King's Council in the North* (London, 1921), p. 6; cf. G.T. Lapsley, 'The Problem of the North', in *Crown, Community and Parliament in the Later Middle Ages* (Oxford, 1952), pp. 375–405.

[3] R.L. Storey, 'The North of England', in *Fifteenth-Century England, 1399–1509*, ed. S.B. Chrimes, C.D. Ross and R.A. Griffiths (Manchester, 1972), p. 129.

[4] A.G. Dickens, *Lollards and Protestants in the Diocese of York, 1509–1558* (Oxford, 1959), pp. 1–4.

much more important internal English frontier than either the Humber
or the Trent.

To such generalisations the ecclesiastical history of the north of England
is certainly no exception; and the following brief comparative essay on
the three cathedral chapters of northern England in the fifteenth century
is ipso facto a commentary on the theme of regional diversity rather
than uniformity. Not only were the secular canons of York Minster,
the Augustinian canons of Carlisle Cathedral, and the Black Monks of
Durham Cathedral unlike each other in most ways: they were positively
and at times aggressively at pains to preserve those differences and
their own autonomy. On the other hand, for anyone unwise enough to
embark upon the elusive quest for the quintessential north of England,
the history of those three cathedrals has its own peculiar fascination. In
any search through the corridors of the past for the most continuous,
most sustained and most influential institutional expression of 'northern
separatism', there can surely be no rival to the now 1200 year-old Province
of York which yoked the prelates and chapters of its three medieval sees
into indissoluble if often uneasy association. No doubt any attempt· to
define the north of England in terms of the Province of York, like all
attempts to define the north, creates serious anomalies – most obviously
that it leaves much of medieval Lancashire, let alone Cheshire, out in the
cold and brings Nottinghamshire into the warm. However, it is perhaps
not late medieval historians alone who might concede that the northern
province has, after all, proved a more enduring reflection of northern
identity than such equally anomalous and much more transient political
constructs as, say, the Anglian kingdom of Northumbria, the Viking
kingdom of York or (to compare great things with small) the Council of
the North. Nearly 500 years have passed since the author of an anonymous
Italian *relatione* was the first of many overseas visitors to this country who
expressed surprise that 'in tanta richezza della Chiesa Anglicana non sono
più di due Arcivescovi, Cantuarensis, et Eboracensis'.[5] Then as now, so
striking a peculiarity of the English scene must be attributed primarily to
an understandable organisational inertia on the part of the church itself;
but at least this inertia implied an assumption, as it still does, that northern
England is at least in one important way absolutely *sui generis*.

More intriguingly still, it might be possible to interpret the creation of
the long-lived Province of York as the first example in English history
of the unexpected and perhaps dangerous consequences of historical
research. When, in a famous letter of 22 June 601, Pope Gregory I
instructed St Augustine to consecrate 'ad Eburacam vero civitatem' a
bishop whose successors should be 'in no way subject to the authority
of the bishop of London', he may well (as the late Dr Bertram Colgrave

---

[5] *A Relation, or Rather a True Account, of the Island of England*, ed. C.A. Sneyd, Camden
Society, old series, 37 (1847), p. 40.

suggested) have actually seen documents which recorded the appearance of British bishops from York and London at church councils in the past: at the least he was presumably aware of how historically appropriate it would be to locate one of England's two new metropolitan sees in the city which had long ago been the capital of the Roman province of *Britannia Inferiora*.[6] With the optimism of someone who clearly knew very little about the north of England indeed, Pope Gregory envisaged in the not too distant future a full complement of twelve suffragan bishops subjected to the metropolitan of York. In the event of course, after many vicissitudes and against what we would now take to be the historical probabilities, the bishop of York only achieved metropolitan status in 735 and had to wait another 400 years, for the foundation of Carlisle in 1133, before his province encompassed as many as three permanently established sees. On the whole, and as Professor Robert Brentano had no difficulty in demonstrating thirty years ago, the result proved to be as bizarrely disparate an ecclesiastical triumvirate as could be found on the highly idiosyncratic map of medieval Christendom.[7] Nor were modern historians the first to appreciate the historical and geographical peculiarities that lay behind the formation and composition of the northern province. Readers of the chronicles and legal memoranda of the monks of St Cuthbert are made rapidly aware that in the privacy of their cloister the latter never altogether accepted the justice of their very occasional jurisdictional subordination to the metropolitan of York. In the fifteenth century, as earlier, few issues aroused more consternation and more research among their own archives than the possibility that the prior and convent of Durham might be required to insert the word *obediencia* in

[6] *An Inventory of the Historical Monuments in the City of York*, i, *Eburacum*, Royal Commission on Historical Monuments (1962), p. xxxvi; *Bede's Ecclesiastical History of the English People*, ed. B. Colgrave and R.A.B. Mynors (Oxford, 1969), pp. 104–7. Rather less persuasive perhaps is Sir Frank Stenton's view that this projected division of Britain into the two provinces of London and York is most easily intelligible as an attempt to reproduce in the ecclesiastical sphere the distinction between the kingdoms subject to the overlord of the southern English and independent Northumbria. In any case this famous letter of Pope Gregory was to prove fundamental not only in ensuring, most obviously against Lichfield at the end of the eighth century, that there would be only two English provinces but also in providing later archbishops of York with their most important documentary grounds for their independence from Canterbury: see *Venerabilis Baedae opera historica*, ed. C. Plummer (Oxford, 1896), ii, pp. 52–7; F.M. Stenton, *Anglo-Saxon England* (Oxford, 1943), pp. 108–9, 216, 223–7.

[7] For the 'incoherence' of the province of York as compared to Canterbury, see R. Brentano, *York Metropolitan Jurisdiction and Papal Judges Delegate, 1279–1296*, University of California, Berkeley, Publications in History, 58 (1959), pp. 23–5. The most detailed account of the complicated series of competitive claims to lordship over the new bishopric of Carlisle by the churches of York, Durham and Glasgow is still provided by G. Hill, *English Dioceses: A History of their Limits from the Earliest Times to the Present Day* (1900), pp. 279–308.

their letters of presentation to the archbishop of York.[8] On the other side of the Pennines a host of problems had inevitably followed in the wake of Henry I's and Archbishop Thurstan's apparently ad hoc and certainly politically crude anti-Scottish political manoeuvre of elevating an obscure and struggling house of canons into the *cathedra* of a new bishop of Carlisle. For at least two generations after its foundation in 1133 the future of this odd creation was highly uncertain; and in the years immediately after Magna Carta, the Augustinian chapter of Carlisle was still capable of electing a Scotsman to the vacant bishopric.[9] Not surprisingly, the always impoverished church of Carlisle was less likely than that of Durham to defy the jurisdictional wrath of its metropolitan. However, relations between Carlisle and York were by no means always amicable; and in 1411, for example, Archbishop Bowet thought it necessary to rebuke Bishop William Strickland for the *dissimulaciones multas* whereby the latter tried to evade submitting his conflict with the abbey of Holmcultram to archiepiscopal judgement.[10] For their part the monks of St Cuthbert as late as 1447–48 were still expressing indignation at Henry I and Archbishop Thurstan for 'their violent seizure' of the liberty of Hexham physically located within the boundaries of the diocese of Durham.[11]

The memories of ecclesiastical corporations are, however, notoriously long; and by the fifteenth century it would seem that most troublesome jurisdictional disputes between the three cathedral churches could nevertheless be readily contained and defused by the province's own ecclesiastical administrators, themselves commonly canon lawyers attached to the *curia Eboracensis* itself. Usually quiescent, and indeed often positively harmonious, were also the once stormy relationships between the three northern cathedral chapters and their respective diocesans. After 1400 the surviving records suggest a comparative absence of those dramatic confrontations between prelates and their chapters which had once disfigured religious life in the three cathedrals. Thus Alexander Neville (1374–88) is the last medieval archbishop of York known to have been on notoriously bad terms with his residentiary canons; and no later bishop of Carlisle seems to have encountered such outright and at times violent opposition to his authority from his own chapter as did Bishop Thomas Appleby in the years after

---

[8] Dean and Chapter of Durham Muniments (hereafter cited as DCD), Reg. III, fo. 127v; Reg. Parv. II, fo. 36; Reg. Parv. III, fos 125v–126, 128–34 passim, 173–5. Cf. R.B. Dobson, *Durham Priory, 1400–1450* (Cambridge, 1973), pp. 217–18.

[9] *Chronicon de Lanercost, 1201–1346*, ed. J. Stevenson, Maitland Club (Edinburgh, 1839), p. 27; J.C. Dickinson, 'The Origins of the Cathedral of Carlisle', *Transactions of the Cumberland and Westmorland Antiquarian and Archaeological Society* (hereafter *CW* 2), new series 45 (1945), pp. 134–43; Victoria County History, *Cumberland*, ed. J. Wilson, ii (1905), pp. 8–23.

[10] Borthwick Institute of Historical Research, Reg. 18 (Henry Bowet, 1407–23), fos 284v–285.

[11] DCD, Miscellaneous Charters, 7234 (formerly Additional Roll no. 11).

1385.[12] Nor, despite the fact that Bishop Lawrence Booth of Durham (1457–76) was accused by his successor of dilapidating the possessions of the church of St Cuthbert, did the fifteenth century witness any recrudescence on the Durham peninsula of the titanic conflicts of the age of Antony Bek.[13] To some extent this tranquillity was undoubtedly the result of absence making the heart grow fonder. As the late Professor Hamilton Thompson was always at pains to point out, prudent bishops of the fifteenth century, heavily preoccupied with royal or diocesan administration, were not only very infrequent visitors to their cathedral cities but were also wise enough not 'to compete with the canons on their own ground'.[14]

The choice of the seven archbishops of York, seven bishops of Durham and eleven bishops of Carlisle who ruled their respective sees between 1400 and 1500 was of course primarily determined by the highly uneven wealth of the three dioceses, as considered in the context of the political exigencies facing the English royal government at the moment of selection. It can accordingly go without saying that few, if any, generalisations can be safely made about the extremely different twenty-four northern prelates of the fifteenth century;[15] but what is clear is that during the course of the century the ability of the three cathedral chapters to influence that choice virtually reached vanishing-point. The last residentiary canon of York to become archbishop of York had been Thomas de Corbridge (1299–1304); the last monk of St Cuthbert ever to be bishop of Durham

---

[12] For the 'scandal of great magnitude' which 'convulsed the diocese' of Carlisle in 1385 and led to Bishop Appleby's excommunication of Prior William de Dalston as well as a threat to place the entire city under an interdict, see Carlisle Record Office (hereafter CRO), DRC 1/2 (Reg. Thomas Appleby), fos 348–54, 357; VCH, *Cumberland*, ii, p. 134. Five years later (in March 1390), Bishop Appleby had to enlist the support of both Archbishop Arundel and royal government against three rebellious Carlisle canons who had assembled an armed mob in defiance of both their bishop and their prior: *CPR, 1388–92*, pp. 218–19; M. Aston, *Thomas Arundel* (Oxford, 1967), p. 288. Some of these internecine feuds within the Carlisle chapter must date back to at least 1381 and the bitterly contested election of William de Dalston as prior that year: BL, MS Harley 669, fos 175–9.

[13] Dobson, *Durham Priory*, pp. 222–38. For the strained relationships between the Durham chapter and Bishop Lawrence Booth, perhaps 'a polished courtier who could hide hostility under a fair mask', see DCD, Reg. Parv. III, fos 92v, 128, 131–4, 300; *Historiae Dunelmensis scriptores tres*, ed. J. Raine, Surtees Society, 9 (1839), pp. cccxliv, ccclv–ccclvii; Storey, 'North of England', pp. 140–42.

[14] A.H. Thompson, *The Cathedral Churches of England* (London, 1925), pp. 23, 165. According to their surviving episcopal accounts, the fifteenth-century bishops of Carlisle were more likely than the archbishops of York or bishops of Durham to be occasional visitors to their cathedral church: see, for example, a reference to Bishop Richard Bell's residence at Carlisle Cathedral Priory when he was conferring holy orders there in 1487–88 in CRO, DRC/2/17.

[15] Lawrence Booth, bishop of Durham (1457–76) before he was translated to York (1476–80), was the only member of the English episcopal bench to hold two northern bishoprics during the course of the fifteenth century.

was Richard de Kellawe (1311–16); and the last canon of Carlisle to become bishop of Carlisle was Bishop Thomas Appleby (1363–95). Occasionally indeed the cathedral chapters of the fifteenth-century north had to face the prospect, so repugnant to the Lanercost chronicler when commenting on John Ross's provision to Carlisle in 1325, of having men from the south ('homines australes') thrust upon them as their bishops.[16] Although the majority of the twenty-four prelates were in fact natives of England north of the Humber, ranging from the youngest brother of the Kingmaker (George Neville of York, 1465–76) to the son of the common clerk of York (John Shirwood of Durham, 1484–94),[17] this was primarily because it was in the interests of the royal government itself to promote (when other things were equal) northern men to northern sees. These archbishops and bishops inevitably continued to be their cathedral chapters' single most important masters; but they were masters who had by now been transformed from jealous judges and castigators of their errors to usually benevolent and only occasionally irritable 'good lords'.[18] In a century when both chapter and bishop found it most politic to allow old jurisdictional dogs to go on sleeping, the relationship between the father and his flock had come intriguingly and perhaps perilously close, in practice rather than in theory, to one of secularised rather than spiritual authority.

It follows that the three cathedral chapters of fifteenth-century York, Durham and Carlisle, even more than in the past or indeed the future, should have been capable of exercising a very considerable autonomous influence in their respective dioceses – in comparative independence from the activities of their bishops resident at Bishopthorpe, Bishop Auckland,

[16] *Chronicon de Lanercost*, ed. Stevenson, p. 253. The geographical origins of the twenty-four northern prelates of the fifteenth century (not always precisely ascertainable in the see of Carlisle) indicate that at least nineteen were descended from families domiciled in the six northern counties. Seven of these twenty-four prelates were of noble stock and at least another eight can be shown to have been members of knightly families. Perhaps more significantly, every northern prelate of the fifteenth century has been proved to be a university graduate except for Thomas Langley of Durham (1406–37) and William Booth of York (1452–64).

[17] George Neville must have been born at Middleham, where he was christened by Prior John Wessington of Durham in 1432 (DCD, Bursar's Account, 1432–33, Expense Necessarie). Master John Shirwood, then archdeacon of Richmond, occurs as the son of John Shirwood, common clerk of the city of York, in the latter's will of 20 March 1473 (Borthwick Institute, Probate Register IV, fo. 118).

[18] Particularly illuminating for their constant invocations of the theme of 'good and tendre lordshipp' are the more informal letters, by this date written in the vernacular, sent by the prior to Durham to their bishops in the 1470s and 1480s: see DCD, Reg. Parv. III, passim; and *Scriptores tres*, ed. Raine, pp. ccclv–ccclxxi. Similarly, in April 1500, the highest commendation the mayor and aldermen of York could give to William Senhouse, then bishop of Carlisle, was that he 'hase hertofore be good and tender lord to this citie': *York Civic Records*, ii, ed. A. Raine, Yorkshire Archaeological Society, Record Series, 103 (1941), p. 148.

Rose Castle or episcopal palaces much further afield. Did they do so? To pose the fundamental and perennial questions presented by the late medieval cathedrals of Christendom as a whole: are the three northern cathedrals to be interpreted as the major religious power-houses of their dioceses or as expensive parasites on the body of the church? Were York, Durham and Carlisle the primary sources of spiritual energy and pastoral instruction in the north, as Dr Nicholas Orme has suggested might be the role played by Exeter cathedral in the southwest?[19] Or were they largely an irrelevance or perhaps even an obstacle to the much vaunted new lay spirituality of the later middle ages? More prosaically, but perhaps not less significantly, in a fifteenth-century England singularly devoid by our own standards of business corporations of any sort, is it possible to generalise about the role of the then largest business corporations in the north – above all in those three urban settings they had themselves raised to city status? To such questions there can never be either satisfactory or universally acceptable answers; but it is on the assumption that these questions are nevertheless perennially worth raising that this slender exercise in comparative history is based. Needless to say, the structural and other differences between the three northern cathedrals in the fifteenth century were positively immense; but most historians would now agree that the dissimilarities between the administrative mechanisms, material needs and even behavioural patterns of the Augustinian canons of Carlisle, the Benedictine monks of Durham and the secular clergy of York Minister were at least somewhat less pronounced in 1400 than they had been in 1200. All three cathedrals were by that latter date thoroughly enmeshed in the organisational routines of English state and church, all faced not too divergent financial problems and all were utterly entangled in complex networks of political patronage and economic forces largely outside their own control. To what extent did the canons of York, Durham and Carlisle react to these pressures in the same or different ways?

Not the least important feature of any ecclesiastical corporation is its size; and in the case of Durham Cathedral Priory, the fifteenth-century historian is in the unusually fortunate position of being able to estimate the total strength of the monastic community more or less exactly and continuously. Although they never produced an explicit admissions policy statement to that effect, it seems abundantly clear from the copious surviving evidence that, between the late fourteenth century and the eve of their dissolution, the Durham prior and chapter quite deliberately aimed at producing a complement of approximately seventy monks of St Cuthbert; of these, rather more than forty were expected to serve the cathedral church, and the remainder to staff Durham's nine (until the final loss of Coldingham in Berwickshire during the 1470s) daughter-houses.

[19] N. Orme, *The Minor Clergy of Exeter Cathedral, 1300–1548* (Exeter, 1980), p. xix.

Thus, to take a few examples at random, there were sixty-nine members of the Durham community alive at the time of Bishop Thomas Langley's election in 1406, seventy-three at Bishop Robert Neville's election in 1438, seventy at Bishop Lawrence Booth's election in 1457, and sixty-six at the elections as prior of both Richard Bell (1464) and Thomas Castell (1494). Seventy-four monks of St Cuthbert were recorded at the time of Prior Hugh Whitehead's election in 1520; and there were still sixty-six members of the chapter when it surrendered to Henry VIII on 31 December 1539.[20] Such figures necessarily imply that the Benedictine monks professed at Durham formed the single largest community of religious in the late medieval north, its closest rivals being the abbeys of St Mary's, York (fifty-one monks at its dissolution) and the Cistercian monasteries of Fountains and Furness. Although the latter were, according to the *Valor Ecclesiasticus*, the two wealthiest Cistercian houses in the whole of England, it seems doubtful whether they often supported a community of as many as forty monks during the course of the fifteenth century.[21]

By the standards of that formidable northern monastic quartet, the size of the community of Augustinian canons who served Carlisle Cathedral was obviously in a quite different and lesser order of magnitude – and indeed in a quite different order of obscurity too. At no date in the fifteenth century, to the best of my knowledge, does record survive of the complete number or names of the Carlisle canons. There could be no more obvious reminder, if such were needed, of the truth of Bishop Nicolson's plaintive early eighteenth-century lament that 'Of this remote and small diocese not many of its ancient records are now anywhere to be had'.[22] The loss not only of the chapter's own internal records but of all the fifteenth-century episcopal registers of Carlisle is of course a disaster from which the ecclesiastical history of the north-western English see can never properly recover. Nevertheless, even at Carlisle, not all hope should be completely abandoned; and thanks to a few extant sources, notably the brief but invaluable 'de suffraganeis' sections of the archiepiscopal registers at York, a little light can be shed on dark waters. Carlisle Cathedral, perhaps never intended to house a complement of more than twenty-six Augustinian canons, may have suffered especially severely in the generation after the first outbreak of the Black Death: as few as thirteen canons are recorded there in 1366, and only twelve at the time of the

---

[20] See below, p. 54; S.L. Greenslade, 'The Last Monks of Durham Cathedral Priory', *Durham University Journal*, 41 (1948–49), pp. 107–13.

[21] D. Knowles and R.N. Hadcock, *Medieval Religious Houses: England and Wales* (1971), pp. 82, 112–15, 119. The abbot and thirty-four monks of Fountains are recorded at the expulsion of an unruly colleague in 1449; *Letters from English Abbots to the Chapter at Cîteaux, 1442–1521*, ed. C.H. Talbot, Camden Society, 4th series, 4 (1967), p. 22.

[22] W. Nicolson, *The English Historical Library* (1777 edn), p. 106.

clerical poll-tax return of 1379.[23] During the following decade, however, the ordinations lists of Bishop Thomas Appleby's register suggest that an average of two canons a year were being recruited into the chapter. On 18 January 1396 Prior Robert de Edenhall returned the names of sixteen canons, not including himself, to the commissioners of the archbishop of York during a vacancy in the Carlisle see.[24] In a petition of July 1438 the Carlisle chapter presented themselves as a convent of twenty 'chaplains continually praying for the king and his progenitors'; and in the early sixteenth century the position seems to have been little altered. Accordingly, in June 1521, nineteen canons of Carlisle (of whom five were novices) responded to an archiepiscopal citation to their visitation *sede vacante*; and there were as many as twenty-three members of the cathedral chapter when it was formally surrendered on 9 January 1540.[25] Fragmentary although they are, these figures lend some support, if such were any longer needed, to the view that one of the most impressive features of the late medieval English monastic orders was their ability to maintain stable recruitment until (almost) the very end. Equally obvious, these are figures which place the community at Carlisle quite firmly within the middle rank of late medieval English religious houses, comparable to, say, Selby in the West Riding or its own sister Augustinian convent – with which the Carlisle canons enjoyed especially close relations – of Hexham. Carlisle and Rochester were much the least adequately endowed as well as the most diminutive monastic cathedrals in late medieval England; and it was one of the many ironies resulting from their serious lack of resources that the canons of Carlisle were probably less numerous and certainly less wealthy than the Cistercian monks of Holmcultram only 15 miles to the west.[26]

The secular clergy who maintained communal worship within late medieval England's largest cathedral at York were naturally a much more numerous as well as diversified group. Indeed, on the late Professor Ernest Jacob's persuasive suggestion that a medieval cathedral should be likened to an ocean liner, 'with many decks or departments',[27] the metropolitan church of St Peter of York can be plausibly said to have had more staterooms and cabins than any church in the country. Admittedly by the fifteenth century only three or four of the Minster's full complement of four main dignitaries and thirty-six secular canons were likely to be

[23] CRO, DRC/1/2, fo. 165; J.L. Kirby, 'Two Tax Accounts of the Diocese of Carlisle, 1379–80', *CW* 2, 52 (1952), pp. 70–84; VCH, *Cumberland*, ii, p. 146.

[24] CRO, DRC/1/2, fos 271–83; Borthwick Institute, Reg. 14 (Thomas Arundel, 1388–96), fo. 78.

[25] *CPR, 1436–41*, p. 185; Borthwick Inst., Reg. 27 (Thomas Wolsey, 1514–30), fo. 136v; Knowles and Hadcock, *Medieval Religious Houses*, p. 152.

[26] *Valor Ecclesiasticus*, Record Commission (1810–34), v, pp. 274–83; VCH, *Cumberland*, ii, p. 170.

[27] E.F. Jacob, *The Fifteenth Century* (Oxford, 1961), p. 289.

on board the ship at any given moment in time; and it was this small
handful of residentiaries who in practice constituted the York chapter,
regularly but somewhat incongruously assembling in the most magnificent
chapter-house in northern England, most of whose seats were however
permanently empty.[28] By a paradox certainly not anticipated in the Rule
of St Benedict it was in the secular cathedrals of England that power was
becoming increasingly concentrated in fewer and fewer hands, at exactly
the time when their monastic counterparts were displaying evident signs
of considerable delegation of authority and even a certain enhanced
individualism within the cloister.[29] Apart from the small residentiary
element within the York chapter, however, the fifteenth-century cathedral
was also served by a large number of *ministri inferiores*, including thirty-six
vicars-choral (declining somewhat in numbers as the century progressed),
over twenty chantry priests or *persones* (a number steadily increasing) as
well as six deacons, five thurifers, seven choristers, three sacrists and
two vestry clerks. A fifteenth-century archbishop, like Henry Bowet in
1423, could accordingly die comfortably in the knowledge that his obit
in York Minster would be annually attended by up to eighty members of
his cathedral's clergy.[30] Although the monks of Durham and, to a lesser
extent, the canons of Carlisle also employed the services of lay choristers
and lesser clergy, such a figure could certainly not be surpassed in the two
most northerly English cathedrals. However, in any attempt to compare
the impact of the three cathedrals on their local communities, it is necessary
to add to the inner core of cathedral clergy proper at least three concentric
rings of individuals attached to, if not constitutionally part of, these three
foundations. All three groups, elusive though they usually are, perhaps
deserve more attention from both the ecclesiastical and the social historian
than they have hitherto received.

First in status, although not in numbers, were the highly miscellaneous
groups of clerks who, although not beneficed or appointed to a specific
post within the late medieval cathedral, did in practice spend much of
their working lives in and around its precincts. No one can read the
names of those who witnessed the more formal documents produced by
the fifteenth-century churches of York and Durham without becoming

---

[28] R.B. Dobson, 'The Later Middle Ages', in *A History of York Minster*, ed. G.E. Aylmer
and R. Cant (Oxford, 1977), pp. 105–6.

[29] See also, idem, 'The Residentiary Canons of York in the Fifteenth Century', below,
pp. 195–224; and cf., idem, *Durham Priory*, pp. 51–80. Quite apart from their commitment to
at least some parochial work in the cathedral's appropriated churches, the late medieval
canons of Carlisle also practised a thoroughly devolved 'obedientiary system'. Excluding the
novices, all but one of the nineteen members of the chapter in 1521 held important offices:
as prior, subprior, sacrist, bursar, precentor, almoner, keeper of the infirmary, master of
the fabric, succentor, pittancer, subcellarer, keeper of the relics and master of the local
hospital of St Nicholas: see Borthwick Institute, Reg. 27, fo. 136v.

[30] *Testamenta Eboracensia*, ed. J. Raine, iii, Surtees Society, 40 (1865), p. 85.

rapidly aware of the number of absentee rectors and vicars as well as unbeneficed clergy who must have haunted the cathedral closes of late medieval England. The most influential of these men, and certainly the easiest to detect, were the university-trained canon lawyers who staffed the upper echelons of the episcopal administration itself and of the church courts within their respective dioceses. As Mr David Dasef's unpublished study of the thirty-one advocates and proctors who were members of the York consistory court between 1400 and 1435 reveals, these church lawyers would be especially well worth rescuing from obscurity.[31] Much more numerous, however, as well as much more difficult to identify with any certainty over a period of time, were the comparative swarms of household chaplains, notaries, unattached and would-be chantry priests, scribes, school- and choirmasters as well as other clerks and *litterati* who formed the clerical underworld of the late medieval cathedral. Sometimes in residence and sometimes not, he would be a brave man who would estimate their number, even in the exceptionally well-documented case of fifteenth-century Durham. However, during his thirty years as prior (1416–46) there, John Wessington could regularly assemble a dozen or more Durham secular clerks to witness his convent's official *acta* and judicial appeals;[32] and at York, with its multiplicity of courts and canons' households, the number of attendant clerks and chaplains must have been very much larger still. At Carlisle, by contrast, the supply of suitable secular clerks, and especially highly educated clerks, was obviously more restricted. Given the extreme scarcity of attractive ecclesiastical patronage at the disposal of either the bishop or the chapter of Carlisle, ecclesiastical administration in the diocese had to be conducted on extremely economical lines – often, to take only one example, without the services of a regularly appointed suffragan bishop.[33] The suggestion that the late medieval see of Carlisle was at times dangerously destitute of trained clerical administrators seems to be partly confirmed by the evidence of the fifteenth-century episcopal accounts of the diocese; and in 1410 Bishop William Strickland actually wrote from Carlisle to Archbishop Bowet of York to inform him that he was 'ad presens destitutus de consilio in partibus istis'.[34]

A second and more numerous group of individuals attached to the service of the churches of York, Durham and Carlisle in the fifteenth

---

[31] D. Dasef, 'The Lawyers of the York Curia, 1400–1435' (unpublished M.A. thesis, University of York, 1977).

[32] Dobson, *Durham Priory*, pp. 122–3.

[33] CRO, DRC/1/2, fos 266–83; DRC 2/7–21; VCH, *Cumberland*, ii, pp. 39–40.

[34] Borthwick Institute, Reg. 18 (Henry Bowet, 1407–23), fos 284–5. Similarly, in October 1329 the abbot of Holmcultram, then archdeacon of Carlisle, had complained of the scarcity of *juris periti* in his diocese: *Historical Papers and Letters from the Northern Registers*, ed. J. Raine, RS, 61 (1873), pp. 359–60.

century were the laymen employed on a more or less regular basis as servants or retainers of the three northern cathedrals. Although the majority probably lived and slept outside the precincts, they were all usually alike in receiving provisions as well as fees, salaries or wages from their respective chapters. A highly varied, but nevertheless apparently a very rigidly stratified group, they ranged through the entire social spectrum, from the *generosi* boarded within the household of a Durham prior or a York residentiary canon to the ubiquitous, and often casually employed, washerwoman or *lotrix*. Here again, to count is certainly to err; but on the evidence of their bursars' and other obedientiary accounts, the prior and convent of Durham may well have employed a hundred or so laymen who regularly worked within their precinct. According to the details provided by a *Liberatura Specialis* of clothing made at Durham in 1510, there were then at least nine *generosi*, forty-seven *valecti* and thirty-eight *gromi* entitled to this livery, confirming that the community of St Cuthbert normally employed a labour-force well over twice its own size.[35] Within the cathedral close of York, the number of lay servants is hardly likely to have been less, even if extreme administrative devolution and the loss of all household accounts, except for those of the vicars choral, makes it impossible to be at all exact. However the fact that, in his will of 21 April 1479, John Gysburgh (not an outstandingly wealthy York residentiary canon by the standards of many of his colleagues) left handsome monetary bequests to his five *generosi famuli* as well as to fifteen other named servants, is only one of many indications of the size of the households of the York prebendaries.[36] At the other extreme, and once again inevitably, lay the cathedral of Carlisle. According to the 1377 lay poll tax return there were then a total of only thirteen *servientes* attached to Carlisle Cathedral.[37] Although almost certainly an underestimate it is in fact not at all inconceivable that the wealthiest residentiary canons of York kept more lay servants in permanent employment than did the entire community of Augustinian canons at Carlisle.

The third and outermost circle of men who owed their livelihood to the economic needs of the northern cathedrals must comprise those who enjoyed not so much a service as a market relationship with the three chapters: those who derived a substantial part of their own incomes from supplying the clergy of York, Durham and Carlisle with everything from food to drink, from shoes to salt and from parchment to paper. The larger and more integrated the religious community (i.e. Durham Cathedral Priory in the late medieval north) the more likely it was to practise as

---

[35] *Rites of Durham*, ed. J.T. Fowler, Surtees Society, 107 (1903), pp. 144–7; cf. *The Durham Household Book*, ed. J. Raine, Surtees Society, 18 (1844), passim.

[36] Minster Library, York, Dean and Chapter Probate Register I, fos 350–1.

[37] J.L. Kirby and A.D. Kirby, 'The Poll-Tax of 1377 for Carlisle', *CW* 2, 58 (1959), pp. 110–17.

self-sufficient a household economy as possible; but even in the case of the fifteenth-century monks of St Cuthbert, their absolute reliance upon an elaborate network of local and not so local provisioning facilities is manifest in every surviving obedientiary account roll.[38] Needless to say, and despite the copious references to tradesmen, building craftsmen, carters, mercers, bailiffs, rent-collectors and other agents amidst the archives of the cathedrals of York and Durham (as well as within the more slender collection of fifteenth-century episcopal accounts of Carlisle), this is a field within which quantification is barely possible at all. Of all the aspects of the much studied 'monastic economy' of late medieval England, the demands of religious houses on the local labour market notoriously tend to be the most neglected because the most imponderable. That such demands must have been very considerable indeed in all three northern cathedral towns can go without saying, even if one must beware of assuming that they were ever the largest single determinant on the occupational structure of either Durham or Carlisle, let alone York. From time out of mind the latter had been the most important economic as well as political and ecclesiastical metropolis of its region. York was the only one of the northern cathedral cities to be sited on a navigable river; and it was to its role as a commercial entrepôt, as the 'hypermarket' of the late medieval north, rather than to the vitality of its manufacturing industries as such, that it owed its continued economic predominance throughout the fifteenth century. Large as York Minster was, it provided only one among many alternative sources of employment to the citizens who lived under its shadow.

The same can probably be safely said of Durham and Carlisle, even though both these two cities belong to that category of English towns of whose economic significance at the end of the middle ages Professor Hoskins once wrote that 'we can form almost no idea'.[39] Most recent historians have persuaded themselves, with a reasonable degree of plausibility, that the total population of York was considerably more than 10,000 at the beginning of the fifteenth century although rather below that figure by its close.[40] At Durham and Carlisle, by contrast, perhaps the most one can do is to guess that the number of their residents during the same century may have oscillated (very wildly for all we know) at a level of about 2000: the two most northerly English cathedral towns, in other words, are

---

[38] See the (highly selective) *Extracts from the Account Rolls of the Abbey of Durham*, ed. J.T. Fowler, Surtees Society, 99–103 (1898–1901).

[39] W.G. Hoskins, *Provincial England* (London, 1963), pp. 70–1.

[40] J.N. Bartlett, 'The Expansion and Decline of York in the Later Middle Ages', *Economic History Review*, second series, 12 (1959), p. 33; D.M. Palliser, *Tudor York* (Oxford, 1979), pp. 111–13.

then likely to have been considerably smaller than not only York but also Newcastle upon Tyne, Hull, Beverley and perhaps even Scarborough.[41]

No doubt Durham and Carlisle were the most active, if very inadequately documented, market and fair towns in their respective counties; but it was at York and Newcastle that the monks of St Cuthbert themselves would normally have to send to buy such comparative luxuries as spices and paper; and it was also in York that the bishop and his subjects of Carlisle can occasionally be detected buying items as diverse as religious images and supplies of sulphur and saltpetre for their civic ordnance.[42] This last purchase may remind us that for many years in the fifteenth century the city of Carlisle, although never a Calais, was the English kingdom's single closest approximation to a garrison town. Located 'en la frountore del Marche vers les Enemys d'Escoce', the city and castle of Carlisle were indeed, as the commons of Cumberland once informed one of Richard II's parliaments, 'le souverein resuit et governaille de tout le Countee'.[43] This can hardly be the place to explore the economic and other effects upon the canons and citizens of Carlisle of their extreme exposure to Scottish attack: no doubt, as in the sixteenth century, this vulnerability could at times intensify loyalty to their mayor and bailiffs as well as promote 'much trade in cattle and other stolen goods'.[44] What is clear is that by fifteenth-century standards the amount of capital invested by the royal government in the fortifications and the artillery of the castle and city walls of Carlisle could be quite considerable: in 1418 for instance part of the proceeds of the clerical subsidy collected by the prior of Durham was diverted towards Lord John Neville's repairs to the walls and three gates of Carlisle.[45] Under the regime of the Wardens of the West March, highly unstable though that often was, it can have been by no means uncommon

[41] The 1377 and 1381 enrolled poll-tax returns (which do not of course include Durham) are now most conveniently tabulated in C. Oman, *The Great Revolt of 1381* (2nd edn, Oxford, 1969), pp. 164–6. For the speculation, based on the 1548 chantry returns, that the population of Durham may have been between 2000 and 3000 at that date, see Dobson, *Durham Priory*, p. 37; and cf. C. Phythian-Adams, *Desolation of a City: Coventry and the Urban Crisis of the Late Middle Ages* (Cambridge, 1979), pp. 8–12, where the number of families recorded at Carlisle is 450 as compared to 752 at Durham.

[42] DCD, Bursars' Accounts, passim; CRO, DRC/2/17; *Calendar of Documents Relating to Scotland*, ed. J. Bain (Scottish Record Publications, 1881–88), iv, pp. 71–6.

[43] *Rot. Parl*, Record Commission (1783), iii, p. 42; iv, p. 92.

[44] D.L.W. Tough, *The Last Years of a Frontier: A History of the Borders during the Reign of Elizabeth* (Oxford, 1928), p. 15. Carlisle may have locked its gates at night and mounted a guard upon its walls until as late as 1626: with Berwick upon Tweed, it was the only place in England exempted from a parliamentary statute of 1489 which prohibited butchers from killing livestock within the walls of the town. *The Reign of Henry VII from Contemporary Sources*, ed. A.F. Pollard (1913), ii, p. 220; C.M.L. Bouch and G.P. Jones, *A Short Economic and Social History of the Lake Countries, 1500–1830* (Manchester, 1961), p. 171.

[45] PRO, E 401/683, m. 6; cf. *The History of the King's Works*, ed. H.M. Colvin, ii (London 1963), pp. 599–600.

for there to have been (as in 1382) an armed force of fifty men-at-arms, a hundred mounted archers and other auxiliaries stationed in the city.[46]

Despite Sir Walter Scott's famous line to the contrary, it was accordingly Carlisle rather than Durham which most deserved the title of 'half church of God, half castle 'gainst the Scot'. On the Wear peninsula the staffing and servicing of the bishop's diocesan administration, of his castle and the miscellaneous collection of palatinate departments (chancery, exchequer, mint and courts of law) clustered around Palace Green must have provided employment for a large number of the town's inhabitants. Nevertheless there can be no doubt that of all the three northern cities, it was late medieval Durham which was most dependent upon its cathedral for its economic welfare. Had the prior and monastic chapter of St Cuthbert not been so rapidly transformed into a dean and secular chapter on 12 May 1541 it would presumably have been hard for Durham to avoid the fate of becoming something of a ghost town, a fate which indeed befell large parts of post-Reformation St Andrews, medieval Scotland's greatest monastic cathedral city. It can hardly be a coincidence, after all, that it was Elizabethan Durham which produced the most elegiac lamentation anywhere in England for a vanished age of allegedly zealous monks 'never Idle, but either writing of good and goddly wourkes or studying the holie scriptures to the setting furthe of the honour and glorie of god, and for the edifieinge of the people'.[47] It was at late medieval Durham too that the presence of a massive cathedral corporation in its midst produced the most demonstrable, if largely inhibitory, effect on the religious and political development of a northern town. The Benedictine monks of Durham had long been notoriously reluctant to brook any rival to St Cuthbert's great influence in their own immediate vicinity; and such reluctance no doubt provides the best explanation for Durham's conspicuous absence from the list of the twenty-one places in northern England which housed at least one convent of mendicant friars by the beginning of the fifteenth century.[48] Nor, to say the least, did the prior and convent of Durham do much to promote the constitutional evolution of their burgesses' liberties. Less indeed a coherent city than a bizarre and crab-like geographical *conjuncture* of five separate burghal jurisdictions, late medieval Durham would be not too inaccurately described as an artificial compound of only semi-urbanised villages. On the copious evidence available it would seem that neither bishop nor monks encountered any serious opposition

---

[46] VCH, *Cumberland*, ii, p. 264; cf. *Proceedings and Ordinances of Privy Council*, ed. H. Nicolas (Record Commission, 1834–7), ii, p. 133; BL, MS Harley 433, fo. 188v.

[47] *Rites of Durham*, ed. Fowler, p. 88.

[48] Knowles and Hadcock, *Medieval Religious Houses*, pp. 213–46. By contrast there were four friaries at York and two at Carlisle, the only other northern towns with more than one mendicant convent in the fifteenth century being Newcastle upon Tyne (four), Scarborough (three), Hull, Beverley and Doncaster.

to an authority over the townsmen of Durham which was based, whether consciously or not, on a principle of divide and rule. Indeed of all the substantial medieval towns of northern England, Durham was perhaps the most constitutionally retarded: only in 1565 did Bishop James Pilkington at last provide the community with a charter which incorporated it as 'the aldermen and burgesses within the city of Durham and Framwellgate'.[49]

Moreover, to the extent that the townsmen of fifteenth-century Durham generated either a social elite or a common leadership at all, these seem to have been provided by a quasi-hereditary group of professional clerical and lay administrative families which owed their own fortunes very largely to the services they rendered to the cathedral church of St Cuthbert. At Durham the evolution of sophisticated craft organisation was evidently both very late and somewhat stunted by the standards of many medieval English towns; and recent intensive research upon the voluminous property deeds and rentals surviving for the city of Durham suggests that industrial activity there was also small in its scale and largely confined to providing the clerical element in the town's population with its material needs. On the evidence of fifteenth-century Durham charters, accounts and leases, it was resident families like the Berehalghs, Tangs and Racketts of Elvet, several of whose members became monks of St Cuthbert themselves, which dominated urban life on and around the Wear peninsula.[50] The ascendancy of a class of *ministeriales*, admittedly of a very different type, also seems detectable amidst the obscurity of town life in fifteenth-century Carlisle. Here of course the survival of royal charters and letters patent, although not alas of the town's internal administrative records, witnesses to a much more elaborate and vigorous degree of urban self-government than in Durham: the citizens of Carlisle enjoyed such familiar accoutrements of late medieval borough status as a mayor, bailiffs and chamberlains as well as councils of Twelve and Twenty-Four.[51] However, this civic governing elite found it necessary to co-exist with bodies of even more influential men who owed their status neither to their commercial prominence in Carlisle nor to their services on behalf of the bishop and chapter of the cathedral but to their association with the royal government in the extreme north west. When, as so often in the fifteenth century, a resident of York in 1478 needed to prove that he was not a Scot but 'ane Inglishman borne', those who attested to his Englishry at Carlisle included not only seven citizens of the town but also Humphrey, Lord Dacre, then lieutenant of the city,

[49] VCH, *Durham*, ii, p. 256.

[50] For these conclusions I am indebted to work by Dr Margaret Bonney; but cf. Dobson, *Durham Priory*, pp. 42–7.

[51] *Royal Charters of the City of Carlisle*, ed. R.S. Ferguson, Cumberland and Westmorland Antiquarian and Archaeological Society (1894), passim; idem, *A History of Cumberland* (London, 1890), pp. 204–19.

and Richard Salkeld and Richard Denton, two local esquires.[52] Thanks to the royal government's special need for reliable serjeants-at-arms, keepers of the gates and other officials in Carlisle, members of the gentry were often closely associated with the city. Sometimes common lawyers and usually (but by no means always) natives of Cumberland, men like Thomas Derwent, Thomas Colt, Richard Alanson and Avery Mauleverer are now perhaps best remembered for the way in which they came to monopolise Carlisle's parliamentary representation and make it 'a completely rotten borough' by the third quarter of the fifteenth century.[53] Much more dependent on the goodwill of their local gentry than either York or Durham, the citizens of Carlisle were also, and for similar military reasons, highly sensitive to the dramatic national political vicissitudes of that century. After suffering the miseries of the Lancastrian siege of their city in 1461, their enjoyment of the pleasures of royal beneficence was to reach its apogee in the two short years which followed the creation, in January 1483, of Richard of Gloucester's unique and short-lived great palatinate lordship in the north west.[54]

It was, however, certainly not at Carlisle but very possibly at York that Richard III planned to be buried;[55] and during the 1470s and 1480s the citizens there were well aware of the importance of cultivating the patronage of the most influential 'good lord' they ever had. Even so, and despite the fact that their confidence in their ability to manage their own affairs in their own way showed signs of considerable erosion during the last years of the century, the citizens of York could justifiably feel that they were masters of their own destinies in a way that was self-evidently not the case at Durham or Carlisle. Only the third city in England to be raised to county status (on 18 May 1396), York was in many ways entitled to its own claim to be considered 'la secounde citee du Roialme'.[56] With its eighty or more different crafts and its dominant elite of wealthy overseas merchants, this was a city which had no need to treat Yorkshire gentry or even Yorkshire magnates with excessive awe. On the evidence available, pitifully scarce for Carlisle though it is, neither of the two most northerly English cathedral cities had proved capable of generating a very substantial body of prosperous craftsmen, let alone a genuine 'merchant class' as

---

[52] *York Memorandum Book*, ii, ed. M. Sellers, Surtees Society, 125 (1915), p. 217.

[53] P. Jalland, 'The Revolution in Northern Borough Representation in Mid Fifteenth-Century England', *Northern History*, 11 (1976 for 1975), pp. 43–5.

[54] *Rot. Parl.*, v, 478; vi, 204–5. For Richard III's generosity to the canons of Carlisle, see BL, MS Harley 433, fos 48v, 120; *CPR, 1476–85*, pp. 35, 377.

[55] This at least seems a much more plausible explanation than that offered by Polydore Vergil ('to appease the envy of man and to win himself good will') for Richard III's quite 'exceptionally grandiose' plan to establish a college of a hundred priests at York: see *History of York Minster*, ed. Aylmer and Cant, p. 98; C. Ross, *Richard III* (London 1981), pp. 130, 132.

[56] York City Archives, D1, fo. 348; the already classic historical account of York at this period is provided by Professor E. Miller in VCH, *City of York*, pp. 54–113.

opposed to the occasional resident mercer. Here, it need hardly be said, the contrast with the city of York could hardly be more striking; and the somewhat obvious moral to be drawn must be that the presence of a large cathedral in its vicinity did less than an agriculturally fertile hinterland and a flourishing retail trade to accelerate occupational specialisation and mercantile efflorescence in the town itself. Indeed, as bulk purchasers of food, drink and clothing, the three cathedral chapters were better placed than most urban consumers to buy commodities from other than local suppliers and to enjoy economic horizons much wider than their own city walls. Thus, on the probable assumption that the Augustinian canons of Carlisle bought their wine from the same sources as their bishop at Rose Castle not far away, it was to the wine merchants of Hull and Newcastle upon Tyne that they usually turned.[57] Similarly, the monks of Durham Cathedral Priory, perhaps the largest single purchasers of woollen cloth in the north of England, regularly bought their textiles from the drapers of York until the 1460s. Thereafter, as is now well known, they began to provide a market for the nascent cloth industry of the West Riding by buying cloths from Halifax, Huddersfield, Wakefield and other towns with an even more famous future: in the last decade of the fifteenth century one of the most regular suppliers of both furs and woollens to the bursar of Durham cathedral priory was a certain Thomas Richardson, 'pannarius de Ledes'.[58] The material appetites of a late medieval cathedral corporation could indeed have significant economic effects far away from its own city.

What of the other and even more indecipherable side of the coin – the effect on the economic life of the inhabitants of York, Durham and Carlisle of the capital extracted by their respective cathedral chapters in the form of various types of property rent? Here lies so uncharted and mine-strewn a *terra incognita* that perhaps the only sensible course is to scamper over it as quickly as possible. However, it is certainly worth remembering that to many fifteenth-century inhabitants of the three cities their cathedral chapters would have been seen first and foremost as their landlords. It also seems comparatively safe to make the point that in the context of the total annual revenues of the three northern cathedrals, the proportion they derived from urban properties probably seemed comparatively unimportant to the chapters themselves. By the end of the fifteenth century, and on the evidence of the *Valor Ecclesiasticus* and other sources, the church of York is likely to have received an annual revenue of well over £2000, much of that admittedly siphoned away to absentee canons; the income of the monks of Durham was probably not so very much less than that figure, while the canons of Carlisle

[57] CRO, DRC/2/14/17; cf. *CPR, 1476–85*, p. 377.

[58] DCD, Bursars' Accounts, 1492–1500, Garderoba; *Durham Account Rolls*, iii, pp. 652, 656.

could probably hope for at least £400 per annum.[59] In not one of these three estimates, highly approximate as they are, is it likely that as much as 10 per cent derived from either temporalities or spiritualities physically located in the three cities. Absolutely dependent as they all were on the profits of arable agriculture in the countryside, the three cathedral chapters of the north might indeed have all agreed that urban rents were among the least cost-effective constituents of their respective annual revenues. Usually comparatively small, often encumbered with land-gable and similar charges, probably hard to farm, urban rents are likely to have caused acute problems of management and collection, even without benefit of the serious wastes and decays to which so many Durham and York account rolls bear witness from – and sometimes before – the mid fifteenth century. Certainly for the modern economic historian the accurate assessment of the real value of urban rent income to the corporate landlord is an exceptionally difficult undertaking, only possible if the costs of repairing and maintaining the properties in question can be taken into account. However, it is hardly likely to be a coincidence that the one constituent department of York Minster which relied most heavily on urban rents, the college of vicars choral (at least 90 per cent of whose income derived from York city properties), was also the one to show the most manifest symptoms of economic malaise in the second half of the fifteenth century: the vicars themselves could have no doubt that 'the occasion whereof is by reason of decaye of landes and revenues of the city of York'.[60]

On the whole too, although this may be a suggestion which will need much modification in the light of future research, it seems difficult to discover a particularly positive or even coherent policy towards the exploitation of their urban estates on the part of the three cathedral chapters. To this generalisation there are no doubt several exceptions, like the fifteenth-century Durham almoner's extension and consolidation of his unusually concentrated urban estate in the Old Borough of Crossgate; but even at Durham it is notable that the single most striking instance of managerial success yet analysed at the close of the middle ages was the hostillar's quite exceptional demesne farm (not at all dependent on urban rents) of the manor of Elvethall.[61] In general, however, the northern

---

[59] *Valor Ecclesiasticus*, v, pp. 274–7; *History of York Minster*, ed. Aylmer and Cant, pp. 54–61; Dobson, *Durham Priory*, pp. 250–9.

[60] *Yorkshire Chantry Surveys*, ed. W. Page, Surtees Society, 91–2 (1894–95), i, pp. 25–30; ii, p. 438. Cf. Bartlett, 'Expansion and Decline of York', pp. 28–32. I am indebted to Miss Sarah Croney for her advice, based on a detailed analysis of the extant York vicars choral bursars', chamberlains' and rent rolls, on these and other issues.

[61] R.A. Lomas, 'A Northern Farm at the End of the Middle Ages: Elvethall Manor, Durham, 1443/44–1513/14', *Northern History*, 18 (1982), pp. 26–53. For the exceptionally well-preserved records of the urban properties administered by the Durham almoner, see DCD, Rentale et Cartuarium Elemosinarie (1424 – *c.* 1500).

cathedral clergy of the fifteenth century seem to have been content enough to preserve their title to urban tenements while leasing them, when and if they could, at fixed and increasingly long-term annual rents to free sub-tenants: it may have been the latter rather than the cathedral corporations themselves who undertook what effective development and exploitation of urban property there was in late fifteenth-century York and Durham. On the other hand, the number of urban properties in the lordship of the three local cathedral chapters probably continued to rise rather than fall during the course of the century. The point should not be overemphasised, for it seems true of York as well as Carlisle that in the later middle ages 'no one owner of property was dominant'.[62] Nevertheless the urban history of the fifteenth-century north may present the paradox that an increasing number of inhabitants of Durham and of York became tenants of the cathedral chapters at exactly the period when the latters' landlordship tended to become most relaxed and at times even inert.[63]

However, as the late medieval tenants of the great 'monastic boroughs' of St Albans and Bury St Edmunds would have been at pains to stress, there are worse fates for inhabitants of towns than comparatively relaxed landlords. On the whole, and unless the evidence deceives, fifteenth-century York, Durham and Carlisle seem to have been reasonably free from the more savage confrontations and conflicts of economic interest between church and town which had once characterised some southern English urban communities. Yet again the very generality of this over-rapid survey runs the acute danger of being self-defeating; but it would probably be safe to suppose that the chapters of the three northern cathedral cities usually had less to fear from the hostility of their local townsmen than from the acquisitive instincts and occasional depredations of local gentry and magnates. When serious friction between the cathedrals and the citizens did show signs of escalating into a major conflict, the *casus belli* was most likely to be a dispute over the right to common pasture, as on Beaurepaire Moor near Durham in the late 1430s or on the Vicars' Leas near York in the 1490s.[64] None of these disagreements, however, permanently impaired the prospects of comparatively tranquil and at times

---

[62] B.C. Jones, 'The Topography of Medieval Carlisle', *CW* 2, 76 (1976), pp. 77–8; but it should be noted that in 1477 the canons of the cathedral absorbed the endowments of Carlisle's hospital of St Nicholas, the only substantial medieval hospital in the county of Cumberland: see *CPR, 1476–85*, p. 35; VCH, *Cumberland*, ii, p. 202. At Durham, the bishop as well as the convent held a large urban estate; and at York at least thirty-eight religious houses are known to have held properties in the city (VCH, *City of York*, p. 49).

[63] For the most detailed single study of 'remarkable insensitivity to market forces' on the part of a large fifteenth-century ecclesiastical corporation, see B. Harvey, *Westminster Abbey and its Estates in the Middle Ages* (Oxford, 1977), p. 331.

[64] DCD, Misc. Charters, nos 2608, 7147; Locellus ii, nos 5, 14; *York Civic Records*, ii, ed. A. Raine, Yorkshire Archaeological Society, Record Series, 103 (1941), pp. 107–17.

positively harmonious co-existence between the rival parties. At the least, the surviving wills of the citizens of fifteenth-century York, Durham and Carlisle show a common, if no doubt usually conventional, propensity to make a bequest – most commonly of a half a mark – to the fabric of their local cathedral.[65] Such uniformity of testamentary bequests may of course conceal very divergent attitudes within the three towns, not least because the precise nature of the citizens' loyalty to their three cathedrals must have been affected by their ability to be buried or personally commemorated there. Here there were self-evident differences between Durham Cathedral, whose monks were notoriously reluctant to admit the bodies of any laymen within their precincts, and York Minster, where very few of even the richest mayors and merchants of the fifteenth century ever contemplated burial. At Carlisle, in even greater contrast, the vanished nave of the cathedral served as one of the only two parish churches in the city, and it and the adjacent cemetery must have been positively crammed with the tombs of its townspeople.[66]

Similar enormous disparities emerge at every level of comparison between the religious roles of the three cathedrals. In Carlisle Cathedral, for example, where many of the canons continued to be committed to the cure of souls in their appropriated churches, there were apparently only four perpetual chantries; but at York Minster, where none of the cathedral clergy were involved in parochial duties, the late medieval visitor could have found the largest assembly of perpetual chantries (well over sixty) in northern England.[67] Equally dramatic is the sharp contrast between the educational attainments of the Benedictine monks of St Cuthbert, constituting a community more dominated by *les moines universitaires* than any religious house in England, and the canons of Carlisle, whose failure to send even one of their number to study at Oxford or Cambridge was regularly noted with regret at national meetings of the Augustinian general chapters.[68] The time has certainly not yet come to give a balanced impression of the educational services of the three northern cathedrals to

[65] For reasons discussed in *Testamenta Karleolensia, 1353–1386*, ed. R.S. Ferguson, Cumberland and Westmorland Antiquarian and Archaeological Society (1893), pp. vii–xiii, the survival of fifteenth-century Carlisle wills is comparatively infrequent; but see, e.g., Borthwick Institute, Reg. 14, fo. 77, for a testamentary bequest of 6s. 8d. to the fabric of his cathedral from Richard de Cardewe, a Carlisle mercer.

[66] E.g. *Testament Karleolensia*, ed. Ferguson, pp. 114–15, 118, 123, 126–7. R.H. Skaife's list of burial places appended to his three-volume manuscript 'Civic Officials and Parliamentary Representatives of York' (York City Library) reveals how very few York citizens were buried elsewhere than in their parish churches.

[67] *Cal Papal Registers, 1455–64*, pp. 195, 567, 650–1; *Valor Ecclesiasticus*, v, pp. 276–7; R.B. Dobson, 'The Foundation of Perpetual Chantries by the Citizens of Medieval York', below, pp. 255–6.

[68] *Chapters of the Augustinian Canons*, ed. H.E. Salter, Oxford Historical Society, 74 (1922), pp. 99, 130, 140, 187.

their local communities and dioceses; but here, despite the local variations and the frustratingly obscure history of the formal cathedral schools themselves, evidence is perhaps at last emerging that the cathedral close as well as the episcopal household may have been among the most assiduous promoters of 'higher education' in the north. Richard Russell, mayor of the Calais Staple as well as of the city of York (1421–22; 1430–31), bequeathed ten marks to the prior and convent of Durham 'in recompense for the support which I had there in the time of my youth'; and much better documented is the manner in which the residentiary canons of York directed the most academically able young clerks of their kinship or acquaintance towards Oxford and Cambridge.[69] On the other hand, it can hardly be denied that then as later the educational monopolies exercised by those two southern universities deprived the northern cathedral chapters of the prospect of playing an absolutely outstanding role in the history of learning.

It is therefore for somewhat different reasons that the attitude of medieval townsmen to their local cathedral can perhaps be likened to that of their modern successors to a twentieth-century university; in both cases perhaps an ambiguous mixture of slight suspicion and considerable incomprehension was alleviated by a natural pleasure that this corporate giant might contribute to their own prestige and economic welfare. Modern analogies are, however, only too likely to become more out-dated than their medieval equivalents: and no academic teacher now needs to be reminded that the life expectancy of a cathedral chapter once again looks considerably more secure than that of a contemporary university. The fact is that the cathedral clergy of fifteenth-century York, Durham and Carlisle enjoyed one fundamental asset which most modern British universities seem conspicuously to lack – an intense and deeply ingrained local pride at that 'visible display of continuous religious and family history' once so eloquently evoked by Sir Richard Southern.[70] Nor is this tolerant affection surprising at the personal level, for the cathedral clergy of the late medieval north were very much local men and often local townsmen. With a few exceptions, most obviously the largely absentee secular canons of York who so often owed their association with the Minster to a prior attachment to an archbishop translated from a southern English see, most of the clerks who served the cathedrals of York, Durham and Carlisle must have lived within a day's ride from their family homes. Any analysis of the geographical origins of the late medieval English clergy is condemned to be somewhat impressionistic; but there can be no reasonable doubt that in the best-documented case of the community of St Cuthbert, many monks

---

[69] Borthwick Institute, Probate Register III, fo. 439; Dobson, 'Residentiary Canons', below, pp. 210–11.

[70] R.W. Southern, *Western Society and the Church in the Middle Ages* (Harmondsworth, 1970), pp. 237–40.

were drawn from Durham burgess stock and most of the others originated from within thirty or so miles of the convent. The York city origins of the vicars choral of York Minster are much more difficult to prove but seem equally probable; and their local family ties may help to explain the vicars' propensity not only 'to wander through the city like esquires with knives and daggers hanging between their legs to the scandal of their order and their status' but also their tendency to form long-lasting liaisons with local York women.[71] Propinquity of course brings its own notorious dangers; and it is hardly surprising that for those occasional monks of Durham and canons of Carlisle who also found their vows of celibacy difficult to maintain, it was to the wives and daughters of the local townsmen that they looked for companionship.[72] Moreover, on the evidence of their surname toponymics, dangerously imprecise but all there is on which to hazard an assumption, the Carlisle canons too must have almost all been of Cumbrian birth. Enthusiasts for the Lake District may be intrigued to discover that the very last novice known to have been admitted to the Augustinian cathedral chapter of Carlisle was a certain 'Frater Thomas Borodale'.[73]

However, the great local *réclame* of the three northern cathedrals, easy to demonstrate in many spheres, is perhaps most strikingly apparent in the continued prestige and popularity of their patron saints. St Cuthbert's unrivalled reputation in 'the hartes and prayers of alle the Northe' was later brought to the attention of Thomas Cromwell himself on the eve of the Pilgrimage of Grace;[74] the saint's earlier role in ensuring that the fifteenth-century Benedictine community of Durham would be respected by the local population as well as visited by countless pilgrims from further afield needs no urging at all. By contrast, the late medieval cult of St William of York, admittedly not a St Cuthbert nor even a St John of Beverley, may have been unduly discounted by modern church historians: his relics were visited by no less a pilgrim than Margery Kemp in the early fifteenth century; and the major reconstruction of his principal shrine in 1472 resulted in 'the largest and latest of surviving medieval shrine bases' in England.[75] Even better known is the fact that intense popular devotion towards the memory of the first fifteenth-century archbishop of York might well have led to his official as well as informal canonisation had

[71] *The Fabric Rolls of York Minster*, ed. J. Raine, Surtees Society, 35 (1859), pp. 242–3; J.S. Purvis, *A Mediaeval Act Book* (York, 1943), pp. 14–40.

[72] BL, MS Harley 669, fos 176–7; Dobson, *Durham Priory*, pp. 77–8.

[73] Borthwick Institute, Reg. 27, fo. 136v; to be distinguished of course from his namesake, Gawen Borudale, the last abbot of Holmcultram and suspected of having poisoned one of his predecessors (VCH, *Cumberland*, ii, pp. 170–3).

[74] Dickens, *Lollards and Protestants*, p. 89.

[75] *The Book of Margery Kempe*, ed. S.B. Meech and H.E. Allen, EETS, original series, 212 (1940), p. 122; C. Wilson, *The Shrines of St William of York* (York, 1977), p. 19.

not this development been thwarted by national political considerations.[76] Less familiar perhaps is the strength of a more orthodox religious cult within the cathedral of Carlisle. In some ways the citizens of Carlisle, like the inhabitants of many Italian cities of the Quattrocento, needed a saintly guardian more than other towns in England, precisely because they were faced with the ever-latent threat of attack and destruction at the hands of an external enemy. Fortunately in the Blessed Virgin Mary herself, to whom their cathedral was dedicated, they could be assured of the most benevolent, if not the most exclusive, divine protectress in Christendom. The sparse records of late medieval Carlisle are quite liberally adorned with allusions to Our Lady of the cathedral there. In 1451, for example, the canons of Carlisle acquired a particularly sumptuous 'image of the Blessed Virgin covered with plates of silver and overlaid with gold, gems and precious stones' specifically in order to satisfy 'the devotion of Christ's faithful people daily flocking there on pilgrimage'.[77] That this was no special pleading on their own part is suggested by the will (made in July 1518) of John Cowper, an obscure butcher of the city of York: he requested that after his death 'Margaret my wyff, or anoder, ride or goo pilgramege for me, to oure Lady of Burgh, oure Lady of Kerlell, to kyng Henry of Wyndesour, and the roode of Dancastre at the brigge ende'.[78] More suggestive still is Henry Knighton's anecdotal account of the fate which befell a Scottish army which had tried to destroy Carlisle in 1385: 'for they met a woman who told them that the king of England was coming with his army; and she showed them the royal banner to such effect that the Scots were so stricken by terror that they left their ladders and siege engines at the foot of the walls of Carlisle and fled'. 'Now that woman', continued Knighton, 'is thought to have been the glorious Virgin Mary, *patrona de Carleyl*, who often appears to the inhabitants of that city.'[79] Some at least of the citizens of fifteenth-century Carlisle are likely to have attributed their comparative immunity from devastation at the hands of the Scots less to the intermittent military endeavours of successive kings of England and wardens of the West March than to the benevolence of their cathedral's patron saint.

This incident is, however, only one of many possible testimonies to the truism that the relationships between the three cathedrals of the late medieval north and their respective cities can never be properly

---

[76] J.W. McKenna, 'Popular Canonization as Political Propaganda: The Cult of Archbishop Scrope', *Speculum*, 45 (1970), pp. 608–23; *A Calendar of the Register of Richard Scrope, Archbishop of York, 1398–1405*, pt 1, ed. R.N. Swanson, Borthwick Text and Calendars, 8 (York, 1981), p. ii.

[77] *The Priory of Hexham*, i, ed. J. Raine, Surtees Society, 44 (1864), pp. xcvii–xcviii; VCH, *Cumberland*, ii, p. 139.

[78] *Testamenta Eboracensia*, iv, p. 202.

[79] *Chronicon Henrici Knighton*, ed. J.R. Lumby, RS, 92 (1889–95), ii. p. 205.

assessed in strictly material terms. Similarly, and although this paper has been exploring, in excessively general terms, some of the ways in which the welfare of cathedral and city were inextricably intertwined to their mutual advantage, it is equally important to stress that their respective fortunes were not absolutely interdependent. Obviously enough, for this is its purpose after all, the significance of a cathedral church transcends the city within which it happens to be sited: both the aims and the achievements of late medieval town council and cathedral chapter often moved in very different directions. Indeed if one were to hazard a last general comment on the three cathedral cities of northern England at the end of the fifteenth century, it might even be that it was the cathedrals rather than the cities which were then demonstrating the more interesting capacity to display new initiatives. One recent local study of the so-called late medieval 'urban crisis' has emerged with the conclusion that long before its final suppression the abbey of Bury St Edmunds was being reduced to the status of 'a jaded dowager' at exactly the time that its own local townsmen had achieved 'the apex of success'.[80] Whether or not it is safe to generalise at all about the economic welfare of northern towns at the end of the fifteenth century, this is not a verdict which can safely be applied to the cathedral cities of York, Durham and Carlisle in the generations immediately before their *bouleversement* at the hands of Henry VIII and Thomas Cromwell. In the light of the revolution that was about to come, the successful creation of a large new St William's College for the chantry priests of York Minster, the extensive rebuilding in and around Carlisle cathedral and the high reputation of the monks of St Cuthbert may indeed seem comparatively unimportant features of the northern scene. Nevertheless, at York and Durham as well as at Carlisle, it is too soon to be certain that Canon Wilson was completely mistaken when he detected 'an astonishing revival of ecclesiastical activity' in the years around 1500.[81]

One of the more intriguing manifestations of such activity is an increased emphasis on monasticism itself as an instrument of religious reform during the early Tudor period;[82] and if there could be any one ecclesiastical career which typifies some of the themes of this lecture it would have to be that of a Benedictine monk. In the summer of 1502 William Senus or Senhouse became the first monastic bishop of Durham for almost 200 years. Almost certainly a member of the Senus family of Seascale in Cumberland, he was already a monk of St Mary's abbey, York, when he progressed through

[80] R.S. Gottfried, *Bury St Edmunds and the Urban Crisis, 1290–1539* (Princeton, 1982), pp. 246–53.

[81] VCH, *Cumberland*, ii, p. 44.

[82] See, e.g., M. Bowker, *The Henrician Reformation: The Diocese of Lincoln under John Longland* (Cambridge, 1981), pp. 17–28.

holy orders in 1467–68.[83] As monk and then abbot (from April 1485) of St Mary's he was well acquainted with both the cathedral clergy and the leading townsmen of the city of York; and during his seven years as bishop of Carlisle (1495–1502) he was given the unusual and possibly dangerous privilege of continuing to hold the abbacy of St Mary's *in commendam*.[84] Few men can ever have wielded more power and influence in the three cathedral cities of the north than had William Senhouse at the end of his long career in 1505. In many ways no doubt it was also a career which would have aroused the righteous contempt of the leaders of the post-Reformation northern church. But if it would be a mistake to idealise the role played by the northern cathedral clergy of the fifteenth century, it would be equally erroneous not to appreciate that their dramatic transformation at the end of the fifteen-thirties entailed some losses as well as some gains for others as well as themselves. As the citizens of York, Durham and Carlisle all vainly but assiduously petitioned the royal government for their own universities in the early seventeenth century, they were sometimes not unconscious that they might have lost a very great deal indeed.[85]

[83] Borthwick Institute, Reg. 22, fos 185, 190v, 196v. (I am especially grateful to Dr David Smith for his help on this and other issues). It is hardly likely to be coincidental that a Thomas Senowes 'gentilman' requested burial at St Olave's Church, adjacent to St Mary's abbey, in a will of 9 December 1466, more or less exactly when William Senus became a monk there (Borthwick Institute, Probate Register IV, fo. 39v). For some observations on the bishop's career, which would repay more attention, see C.N.L. Bouch, *Prelates and People of the Lake Counties* (Kendal, 1948), pp. 133–4.

[84] *CPR, 1476–85*, pp. 522, 532–3; *1485–94*, pp. 283, 320, 366, 463, 506; *1494–1509*, pp. 58, 299, 302.

[85] For the York petition of 1648 that a new university might properly occupy the Bedern and St William's College, see G.C.F. Forster, 'Early Schemes for a Northern University', *University of Leeds Review*, 9 (1962), pp. 235–6. As early as 1617 the merchants of Carlisle petitioned James I 'to create one universitie in this poore citty of Carliell' (Bouch and Jones, *Lake Counties*, p. 166); and for the various early attempts to apply the wealth of the cathedral chapter of Durham to a new college or university, see C.E. Whiting, *The University of Durham, 1832–1932* (London, 1932), pp. 16–29.'

2

The First Norman Abbey in Northern England:
The Origins of Selby

Officina vero, ubi haec omnia diligenter operemur,
claustra sunt monasterii et stabilitas in congregatione.

Regula Benedicti, IV.

The inauguration of regular monastic life at Selby a few years after the Norman Conquest certainly deserves considerably wider fame than it has usually received. By any standards the century which followed William I's invasion of England was the most vigorous and expansionist age in the history of English monasticism; and the foundation of Selby Abbey marked the opening of the golden era of monastic history in northern England. Although almost every aspect of its foundation is mysterious and controversial, there is no serious doubt that Selby was the very first monastery founded north of the Trent since the legendary and very different age of Northumbrian monasticism. The significance of this event has tended to be overshadowed by the slightly later but more spectacular plantations of Benedictine monasticism at Durham, Whitby and St Mary's York, three abbeys which went on to enjoy a wealth and reputation that Selby failed to rival. It must be admitted that Selby's later history never quite lived up to the remarkable circumstances of its beginnings.[1]

Selby was not, of course, the first of all Benedictine houses in northern England. That distinction must go to seventh-century Ripon and Hexham where, according to his biographer, Eddius Stephanus, St Wilfrid 'brought about great improvements by introducing the rule of St Benedict'.[2] How far St Wilfrid's communities and those of his friend and associate, Benedict Biscop, at Jarrow and Wearmouth fully replaced local Celtic custom by the Benedictine Rule remains a somewhat open question. But in any case not one of the famous monsteries within the kingdom of Northumbria

---

[1] Nevertheless, Selby Abbey enjoyed a continuous and relatively prosperous existence until its surrender on 6 December 1539. During the last 150 years of its existence it maintained an average population of between twenty-five and thirty monks. See R.B. Dobson, 'The Election of John Ousthorp as Abbot of Selby in 1436', *Yorkshire Archaeological Journal*, 42 (1968), pp. 38–40.

[2] *The Life of Bishop Wilfrid by Eddius Stephanus*, ed. B. Colgrave (Cambridge, 1927), ch. 14.

survived the devastating impact of the Viking raids that began with the sacking of Lindisfarne and Jarrow in 793–94. The most formidable of all Danish invasions of northern England, that of the so-called 'Great Army' which captured York in 866, apparently led to the rapid as well as total obliteration of monasticism in the north. All attempts to prove the survival or revival of some form of monastic life in the area during the last two centuries of Anglo-Saxon history have proved unsuccessful; and between the Danish invasions and the Norman Conquest the traditional monastic life of Northumbria had been replaced everywhere by a much more chaotic organisation of groups of secular clergy living semi-communal lives at a few fixed centres.[3] Although St Oswald, a leading figure in the monastic revival of tenth-century southern England, became archbishop of York in 972 he apparently made no permanent impact upon the religious life of the northern province and at the date of the Conquest Peterborough was still the most northerly monastery in England. Later generations of Benedictine monks within the dioceses of York and Durham, particularly the community of St Cuthbert at Durham itself, had a natural vested interest in attempting to trace their origins backwards to the golden age of the seventh century. But the fact remains that in 1066 monasticism in the north had not so much to be revived as to be recreated. It was at Selby that this process began.

In 1066 Selby was neither an important urban or ecclesiastical centre nor a site hallowed by past experience of Christian sanctity. Few places would seem less likely to have become the scene for the inauguration of regular monastic life in northern England. Appropriately enough this remarkable event has a remarkable explanation. The origins of Selby Abbey have admittedly to be traced amidst a jungle of intriguing legend, absolute fiction and inadequately substantiated fact: none of the problems surrounding the circumstances of its foundation are simple and many seem likely to be for ever insoluble. Nevertheless the survival, in one solitary manuscript, of a narrative account of the monastery's early history written by a Selby monk more than a century later provides an invaluable, because unique, guide to what probably happened at Selby 900 years ago. This so-called *Historia Selebiensis monasterii* takes the form of a long letter, of over 20,000 words, written to an anonymous recipient by an unnamed Selby monk in 1174. It has itself a curious history. The *Historia* was first printed by the prolific Jesuit historian, Philippe Labbe, in 1657 as part of a collection of hagiographical material relating to the life and miracles of

---

[3] *Bede: His Life, Times and Writings*, ed. A.H. Thompson (Oxford, 1935), pp. 90–101; J. Cooper, 'Some Aspects of Eleventh-Century Northern History with Special Reference to the Last Four Anglo-Saxon Archbishops of York' (unpublished Ph.D. thesis, University of Cambridge, 1968), pp. 246–9. I am grateful to Dr Cooper for allowing me to read this thesis.

St Germanus of Auxerre.[4] The original manuscript used by Labbe then disappeared and was thought by subsequent historians of Selby to have been lost forever: in 1820 a Selby banker, Barnard Clarkson, is said to have visited Paris in search of the original text of the *Historia*, but met with no success.[5] Consequently for the last 300 years all investigations of the origins of Selby Abbey have been compelled to rely upon Labbe's inadequate and sometimes inaccurate edition.[6] Only in the late 1960s was the original manuscript of the *Historia Selebiensis Monasterii* rediscovered at the Bibliothèque Nationale in Paris by M. Pierre Janin, a research student of the Ecole Nationale des Chartes. However, the *Historia* still awaits the full and scholarly new edition it undoubtedly deserves as one of the most interesting of all twelfth-century Yorkshire chronicles to survive.

Although this is not the place to anticipate the conclusions which may emerge from a detailed assessment of the manuscript at Paris, it is already clear that the study of its original text makes the *Historia* seem more rather than less authentic. It belongs to that very popular twelfth-century genre of semi-legendary accounts of the foundation of distinguished monasteries, evidently designed – as is explicitly stated in the case of the Selby *Historia*[7] – to resolve the doubts and uncertainties on the part of monastic communities and their patrons as to the precise circumstances by which they had come into existence. Inevitably such 'histories' were intended to edify as well as to instruct their readers and contain a good deal of supernatural material as well as outright hagiology. The second half of the Selby *Historia* dwells at inordinate length on the many somewhat conventionalised miracles wrought by the agency of St Germanus in a manner which is often reminiscent of Reginald's life of St Godric, the twelfth-century hermit and founder of Finchale Priory 3 miles north of Durham.[8] On the other hand there is no doubt that these narratives incorporate accurate factual information. In this respect, the Selby *Historia* often seems considerably more reliable than such analogous chronicles as the account of the early years of Battle Abbey (also composed *c.* 1170) and the controversial *Narratio fundationis* of Fountains Abbey.[9] The Selby monk who composed his account of

---

[4] P. Labbe, *Novae bibliothecae manuscriptorum librorum* (Paris, 1657), i, pp. 594–626: reprinted in the Bollandist *Acta sanctorum* (1868), 7 July, pp. 301–15.

[5] W.W. Morrell, *History and Antiquities of Selby* (Selby, 1867), p. vi.

[6] Most accessibly reprinted as pp. 1–54 of vol. I of *The Coucher Book of Selby*, ed. J.T. Fowler, Yorkshire Archaeological and Topographical Association, Record Series, 10, 13 (1891, 1893).

[7] Ibid., i, pp. 1–2.

[8] *Libellus de vita et miraculis S. Godrici*, ed. J. Stevenson, Surtees Society, 20 (1847).

[9] R. Graham, 'The Monastery of Battle', *English Ecclesiastical Studies* (London, 1929), pp. 188–208; *Memorials of Fountains*, i, Surtees Society (1863), pp. 1–128; cf. Mr L.G.D. Baker's unpublished thesis, 'Studies in the *Narratio de Fundatione Fontanis Monasterii*' (Bodleian Library, MS B.Litt., d. 883, 1967).

the beginnings of his abbey's history did so at the command of his prior and was at obvious pains to check the authenticity of his sources of information. Whenever possible, for he had few documentary records before him except for some early abbey charters, 'he spoke by the mouths of those who saw' (illorum ore locutus sum qui viderunt).[10] Although only twenty-two years old, this anonymous monk possessed considerable literary skill and his work is liberally sprinkled with allusions to the classics and, more especially, to the Bible. He combined intense devotion to Selby itself, which he described as a 'terrestrial Paradise', with a somewhat critical approach to the careers of the early superiors of the Benedictine monastery there: not even its founder and first abbot, Benedict of Auxerre himself, escaped condemnation for tyrannical actions which resulted in the moral decline of his community. The Selby *Historia* therefore certainly conveys the impression of having been written in reasonably good faith. No exaggerated claims are made, as was the case with Symeon of Durham's 'History of the Church of Durham' written at the beginning of the twelfth century, for the privileges and immunities of the abbey. More surprisingly still, this Selby monk had no vested interest in stressing the antiquity of his abbey's foundation. He was under the mistaken impression that at the time of Benedict of Auxerre's arrival in Yorkshire the great community of St Cuthbert at Durham, where monastic life was introduced by Bishop William of St Calais as late as 1083, was already a regular monastery.[11] There are, therefore, few *a priori* grounds for believing that the author of the Selby *Historia* was deliberately fraudulent: his account of the first phase of the abbey's history honestly reflects the traditions and beliefs current within the convent two and three generations after its foundation.

According to the *Historia*, the story of the foundation of Selby Abbey began – more or less exactly in the year of the Norman Conquest of England – within the walls of the great French Benedictine monastery of Saint-Germain d'Auxerre situated 100 miles south east of Paris. Here there lived a talented but apparently restless monk named Benedict who had previously rejected the possibility of a knight's career for the regular life and was then subsacrist of the convent and hence directly responsible for the safe-keeping of its most precious relics. One night Benedict was confronted with an unexpected vision of St Germanus, the famous sixth bishop of Auxerre (418–48), who commanded him – like another Abraham – to depart

> out of thy country, and from thy kindred, and from thy father's house, unto a land that I will shew thee. This is a place in England called Selby [*Selebia*], prepared for my honour, ordained for my worship and destined for future fame and glory in my name. It is situated on the bank of the River Ouse, not

---

[10] *Selby Coucher Book*, i, p. 29.
[11] Ibid., p. 14.

far from the city of York. I have chosen and selected you as the founder of
this place in my name: and you are to establish there a cell to be held from
the King.[12]

At first Benedict hesitated to obey such a summons and only after two
further and more threatening visitations by St Germanus did he ask his
chapter at St Germain d'Auxerre for licence to leave the monastery. As
Benedict suppressed all mention of his visions, such licence was not
unnaturally denied him and he had no alternative but to steal away
from Auxerre in the middle of the night. He carried away with him
one of Auxerre's most prized relics – the middle finger of St Germanus's
right hand, which the saint had ordered him to secrete within the flesh of
his upper arm. On the following morning the absence of both Benedict
and the relic were discovered, to the consternation of the community at
Auxerre. But Benedict evaded his pursuers and reached England after a
safe and uneventful journey across the Channel.

Immediately after landing on English soil, Benedict of Auxerre made his
way to Salisbury under the mistaken impression that this was the place to
which he had been directed by St Germanus. Here he was befriended by a
local magnate, Edward of Salisbury, who not only comforted the expatriate
monk but bestowed several lavish gifts on him. The most valuable of these
was a gold reliquary still used to contain St Germanus's finger at Selby
Abbey almost a century later. Although Benedict was soon aware that
Salisbury was not his predestined objective, he remained at a loss for
some time because 'Selby was a place virtually unknown at that period'.
The monk was only rescued from his anxiety by yet another appearance
from St Germanus, who on this occasion not only re-emphasised the name
Selby but showed Benedict the site of his future settlement in a vision. On
the following morning Benedict informed his host of the need to leave
Salisbury. In the company of a clerk named Theobald, who acted as his
interpreter, Benedict travelled to a port where he boarded a cargo-boat
bound for York.[13] According to the *Historia*, the prior of Selby Abbey in
1174 had once met an old woman who remembered seeing Benedict at
this stage of his travels. After a fortnight's delay due to adverse weather
conditions, the ship took passage for York. As it approached the final
stage of its journey, Benedict at last recognised the site divinely selected
for him and went ashore with his companions. After raising a cross on
the river bank, 'he constructed a small dwelling from leaves and branches
under an enormous oak tree called *Strihac* by the natives and a place in

---

[12] Ibid., p. 7. The biblical quotation is from Genesis, 12:7.

[13] The printed text of the *Historia* is corrupt at this point; but it seems that Benedict
sailed from either Lyme Regis on the south coast or King's Lynn in Norfolk, from which
there was probably regular water-traffic to York.

royal possession'. According to the *Historia*, Benedict's arrival at Selby took place circa 1069 'qui est annus quartus Willermi primi Regis'.[14]

Once established at Selby Benedict devoted himself to the worship of God and St Germanus, gradually attracting the favourable attention of the inhabitants of the area. As his little cell was situated in full sight of the many ships which navigated the Ouse to and from York, there was little danger of his settlement languishing in obscurity. Soon after Benedict's arrival, Hugh fitz Baldric, the sheriff of Yorkshire, noticed the new cross as he was sailing along the river on a military expedition directed against the then violent Anglo-Saxon resistance to the new Norman regime in northern England. Hugh landed at Selby and proceeded to interview Benedict, who showed him St Germanus's finger and asked for the sheriff's protection and assistance. The latter willingly agreed and had his own tent erected at Selby to provide temporary shelter for Benedict. The sheriff then sent carpenters, presumably from York, to build a wooden oratory on the site – one later occupied by the *capella* or *parva ecclesia* of medieval Selby. But as Benedict's first church had been built on royal demesne land without the king's own permission, Hugh thought it advisable to arrange an interview between William I and Benedict. The results of this confrontation were decisive: not only did William order the foundation of a monastery at Selby under his own patronage but he endowed Benedict with some of his own local estates: Flaxley Wood, the vill of Rawcliffe, half a carucate of land in Brayton, a fishery at Whitgift and the indispensable carucate of land at Selby itself.[15]

On his return to Selby after his meeting with the Conqueror, Benedict could at last plan the establishment of a monastery to replace his previous anchorite's cell. Rudimentary communal accommodation was constructed around the wooden chapel and there soon gathered around the person of the Auxerre monk a group of recruits to the Benedictine Rule. Monastic life at the early abbey was still extremely insecure and, according to the *Historia*, only a series of miraculous inventions by St Germanus ensured its survival and prosperity. One night the monastery was attacked by a certain 'prince of thieves', Swain, son of Sigge, presumably the chieftain of a gang of dispossessed Anglo-Saxon outlaws and robbers who roamed the forests south of York. While trying to lift the door of Benedict's church from its hinges Swain's hand stuck to the wall: only after confessing his sacrilege to the Selby monks on the following morning did he secure his freedom. On another occasion the finger of St Germanus worked

---

[14] The fourth regnal year of William the Conqueror is, of course, the year *following* Christmas Day, 1069; and it should be stressed, however unsettling the fact, that the *Historia* makes no attempt to date Benedict's arrival more precisely.

[15] All these properties were confirmed to Benedict in William I's later foundation charter (see below, p. 39). But the *Historia* provides the only evidence that they formed, *c.* 1070, the initial endowments of Selby Abbey.

a more conventional miracle: the son of Erneis de Burun, Hugh fitz Baldric's successor as sheriff of Yorkshire, was cured of epileptic fits, and his father accordingly endowed the abbey church with two lights in perpetuity. Of the other lay patrons of the monastery in its earliest phase the most generous were two prominent Norman barons, Geoffrey de la Guerche and Guy de Rainelcourt, who alienated to Benedict their vills of Crowle in Lincolnshire and Stanford in Northamptonshire respectively. An even more significant bequest was that made at about the same time by Thomas of Bayeux, the first Norman archbishop of York, who gave the abbey the two vills of Fryston as well as that of lesser Selby. Archbishop Thomas was the prelate ordered by William the Conqueror to consecrate Benedict as first abbot of the monastery of Selby. Benedict himself made a special journey to London in order to obtain a royal charter confirming himself and his successors in possession of their new endowments. At the same time William I dispatched a writ informing the archbishop and his sheriffs that the church of St Germanus at Selby should enjoy the same protection and immunities as those already held by the cathedral church of York.[16] At this point the story of the foundation of Selby Abbey can be said to have been brought to its formal close.

Such is the account of the origins of the monastery at Selby provided by the late twelfth-century *Historia*. How reliable is it? It seems perfectly possible to reject the most dubious elements within the narrative – St Germanus's miracles and his successive nocturnal appearances to Benedict – and yet accept the main outlines of the story. Admittedly, legendary accounts of the erratic journeys of divinely inspired individuals who transported the relics of famous saints to new centres of worship are among the commonplaces of early medieval monastic tradition. It is easy to understand that twelfth-century Selby monks, like the contemporary Augustinian canons of St Andrews in Scotland who believed that the bones of their patron saint had been brought to them from Patras in the Mediterranean by St Regulus, should have found in such a journey a convincing solution to the problem of their origins. But for the modern historian as well as the medieval monk, the great attraction of the story of Benedict's wanderings is that it explains the otherwise almost inexplicable – the dedication of the abbey to St Germanus of Auxerre.

Thanks to the popularity of the *Vita* written by Constantius of Lyons about thirty years after his death in 448, St Germanus was, of course, one of the most celebrated of all medieval saints: at the end of the twelfth century the bishop of Auxerre actually claimed feudal independence from

---

[16] Both of William I's 'foundation charters' were copied into the text of the *Historia* as well as the abbey's early fourteenth-century general cartulary: *Selby Coucher Book*, ed. Fowler, pp. 18, 19, 11–12.

King Philip II of France on the grounds that he was the successor of St Germanus.[17] But the fact remains that merely a handful of English medieval churches were ever dedicated to St Germanus and only in Cornwall does there seem to have survived a distorted memory of his two visits to combat Pelagianism and the Picts in early fifth-century Britain.[18] Much the most plausible explanation of Selby's association with St Germanus is that his *cultus* was brought directly to Yorkshire by a member of the Benedictine community at Saint-Germain d'Auxerre, the centre of his legend. Originally founded in the Merovingian age on the site of the oratory where St Germanus had been buried, this monastery achieved its greatest fame under the Carolingians when it not only produced two of the greatest figures in the history of Dark Age learning (Heiric of Auxerre, *c.* 840–*c.* 876; and Remigius of Auxerre, *c.* 841–*c.* 908) but is said to have contained no less than 600 monks.[19] At the time of the Norman Conquest, Saint-Germain d'Auxerre was still one of the largest and most prestigious religious houses in France. Set against the background of a monastery recently reformed under Cluniac influence but situated in a turbulent and chaotic area of the French kingdom (the abbey itself suffered from armed attack during the war of the Auxerrois in 1057), Benedict's flight to England seems more rather than less intelligible.[20] Auxerre had long been a well-known halting-place for travellers from England and north-western France along the pilgrims' route to Rome; and the news of the Norman conquest of England and the welcome which might lie in wait there from a king and magnates eager to promote the cause of reformed monasticism conceivably had a more decisive effect on the restless Benedict than the supposed apparitions of St Germanus.[21]

[17] Constance de Lyons, *Vie de Saint Germain d'Auxerre*, ed. R. Borius, Sources Chrétiennes, 112 (Paris, 1965); *Cambridge Medieval History of Europe*, vi (1936), p. 290.

[18] F. Arnold-Foster, *Studies in Church Dedications* (London, 1899), i, pp. 453–64. Canon J. Solloway's hypothesis in his *Selby Abbey: Past and Present* (Leeds, 1925), pp. 18–20, that the monastery owed its origins to the memory of a supposed visit to Selby by St Germanus himself in the 440s is even more fanciful than the *Historia*. This theory rests only on Solloway's unconvincing interpretation of the place-name 'Garmon Carr' two miles north west of Selby.

[19] René Louis, *Autessiodurum Christianum: les églises d'Auxerre des origines au IXe siècle* (Paris, 1952); idem, *Saint Germain d'Auxerre et son temps* (Auxerre, 1950).

[20] J. Richard, *Les ducs de Bourgogne et la formation du duché du XIe au XIVe siècle* (Paris, 1954), pp. 4, 12, 30, 65–9.

[21] William I unsuccessfully applied to Abbot Hugh of Cluny for a dozen of his best monks immediately after the Conquest; and the first members of his own new foundation of Battle Abbey were transplanted from Marmoutier on the Loire. At no time in English history was it easier or more common for French monks to migrate to England than during the generation that followed the battle of Hastings: see D.J.A. Mathew, *The Norman Monasteries and their English Possessions* (Oxford, 1962), pp. 27–65; D. Knowles, *The Monastic Order in England* (2nd edn, Cambridge, 1963), pp. 100–29.

Once across the Channel the details of Benedict's adventures are also readily reconcilable with what little is known of English political and social conditions in the late 1060s, a period just before Lanfranc's elevation to the archbishopric of Canterbury in 1070 inaugurated a more disciplined and ordered organisation of the church. At exactly what stage Benedict first heard the name of Selby and decided to settle on that site must inevitably remain an open question. But there seems every reason to treat as authentic the Selby tradition that this expatriate monk spent some time at Salisbury: Edward of Salisbury, Benedict's host there and an otherwise mysterious figure, was one of the witnesses of William I's later foundation charter to the abbey.[22] Domesday Book and later evidence also makes it abundantly clear that the river-route along the Ouse to York was one regularly taken by Anglo-Norman clerks, soldiers and merchants. Given the large areas of intractable forest and marsh surrounding Selby in the late eleventh century, it would indeed have been most unlikely for Benedict to have approached the site of his future monastery by land rather than water.[23]

Much more significant is the *Historia's* identification of Benedict's first powerful Yorkshire sponsor with Hugh fitz Baldric, a Norman magnate who later patronised several other monasteries, including the nascent St Mary's, York.[24] Hugh replaced William Malet as sheriff of Yorkshire during the course of 1069; but as he continued to hold this office until at least 1078, the year in which he discovered Benedict's cell by the Ouse cannot be fixed at all precisely. As we have seen, the *Historia* itself dates Benedict's arrival at Selby to about 1069 but leaves the story of later events in a state of chronological vagueness. It is just conceivable that Benedict's initial settlement escaped the attention of Hugh fitz Baldric for several months or even years after his landing at Selby. On the other hand, the later months of 1069 marked a period of large-scale revolt in northern England, a time when the sheriff was eminently likely to have been patrolling the Ouse with a force of armed men. If it was at this time (and it cannot have been earlier) that Hugh first met Benedict, nothing would have been more natural than his rapid arrangement of an interview between the expatriate monk and the Conqueror while William was himself in the north suppressing the native rebellion. It is tempting to suppose that Benedict held his first and decisive meeting with William at York while the

[22] *Selby Coucher Book*, ed. Fowler, i, pp. [19], 12. Cf. *Early Yorkshire Charters*, ed. W. Farrer (Edinburgh, 1914), i, p. 359.

[23] D. Nicholl, *Thurstan, Archbishop of York (1114–1140)* (York, 1964), p. 16, stresses the barbarity of conditions in Yorkshire a generation after Benedict's arrival.

[24] W. Farrer, 'The Domesday Survey', VCH, *Yorkshire*, ii (1912), pp. 176–9. As Hugh also guided Aldwin, Reinfrid and Aelfwig on their fateful mission from Evesham in 1074 (Knowles, *Monastic Order*, p. 167), he deserves notice as the most influential lay patron in the history of the northern monastic revival of the late eleventh century.

latter was celebrating Christmas there during a pause in his 'harrying of the north' in the winter of 1069–70.[25] During the course of 1070 Thomas of Bayeux became archbishop of York and would thereafter have been in a position – as the *Historia* suggests – to formalise the foundation of the monastery at Selby by consecrating Benedict as its first abbot. All in all, the marginally most likely hypothesis is that Benedict disembarked at Selby in 1069 and that his monastery began its official existence, thanks to the support of the sheriff and king, during the next year. These at least seem to have been the foundation dates upheld by later Selby tradition. Against the year 1070 in a fragmentary late twelfth-century Easter table compiled at Selby Abbey, there survives the annotation 'fundata est ecclesia Sancti Germani in Seleby'.[26] More interesting still is a medieval interpolation added to the solitary surviving manuscript (in Corpus Christi College Library, Cambridge) of the late twelfth-century continuation of Symeon's 'History of the Kings of England', 'Anno MLXIX coenobium Sancti Germani de Selebi sumpsit exordium'.[27]

Selby Abbey was therefore probably founded towards the beginning of the Conqueror's reign. By the time of William I's death in 1087 there is no doubt that Abbot Benedict was a substantial landlord in southern Yorkshire and northern Lincolnshire. Here the evidence of the Domesday Survey and of the early Selby charters at last begins to insert some fixed points into the previously confused scene. The Yorkshire Domesday, notoriously unreliable as a comprehensive guide to the tenurial structure of the post-conquest county, includes no detailed description of the Selby estates in 1086. But it does record the fact that the abbot of Selby (*Selebi*) held seven carucates of land which originally pertained to the archbishop of York's great soke of Sherburn in the West Riding. These seven carucates can be identified with the land at Monk Fryston (four carucates) and Little Selby (three carucates) alienated to Benedict by Archbishop Thomas of Bayeux.[28] Elsewhere in the Domesday Survey may be found confirmation of the fact that by 1086 the abbot of Selby had entered into possession of Stanford-upon-Avon and Crowle, estates mentioned in the *Historia* as having been acquired from Guy de Rainelcourt and Geoffrey de la Guerche.[29] These Domesday references, however cryptic, are of particular value in that they confirm the authenticity of the Conqueror's own 'foundation charter', much the most important document in the history

[25] E.A. Freeman, *The Norman Conquest of England*, iv (Oxford, 1871), pp. 295, 796.

[26] BL, MS Add. 36652, fo. 5. The relevant section of this Easter Table is illustrated on p. 14 of R.B. Dobson, *Selby Abbey and Town* (Leeds, 1969).

[27] *Symeonis monachi opera omnia* (RS, 1882–85), ii, p. 186; *Symeonis Dunelmensis opera*, ii, Surtees Society (1868), p. 83.

[28] VCH, *Yorkshire*, ii, p. 210; *Selby Coucher Book*, i, p. 291.

[29] Domesday Book I, fo. 369b; VCH, *Northants*, ed. J.H. Round, i, 287, 342b; *Selby Coucher Book*, ii, pp. 258–9, 279–80.

of the foundation of the abbey.[30] Rejected as spurious by Freeman, a conclusion too readily adopted by H.W.C. Davis, William I's charter was shown to be almost certainly genuine by Farrer almost sixty years ago.[31] The list of witnesses, nearly all substantial Domesday Book tenants-in-chief, suggests that Benedict made his visit to London to obtain this royal charter towards the end rather than the beginning of the 1070s. But this dating too is readily consonant with the narrative of the *Historia*.

More generally the impressively critical analysis of early Yorkshire charters conducted by William Farrer and Sir Charles Clay during the course of the present century (too detailed to include here) has confirmed rather than impugned the evidence of the *Historia*. Occasionally an eleventh-century Selby charter has been shown to be a forgery, most notably the purported gift of property at Gunby by Gilbert Tison, who is made to describe himself as 'chief standard-bearer' of the Conqueror and to include the Anglo-Saxon Archbishop Ealdred among his witnesses.[32] But most of the stories preserved in the *Historia*, for example Erneis de Burun's veneration towards St Germanus in the 1080s, can, in fact, be confirmed from charter evidence.[33] More significant still is the discovery that Selby (the Scandinavian '-by' suffix itself suggests a Danish settlement) was already the site of an agricultural community before Benedict's arrival. 'Uper Seleby eal' ('all upper Selby') was one of the places listed as dependent on the soke of Sherburn-in-Elmet in a pre-conquest survey of the estates of the archbishop of York.[34] Benedict's isolation when he landed at Selby can therefore only have been relative. Moreover, the vill itself was then already divided, probably in equal portions of three carucates, between the king and the archbishop of York. The establishment of a monastery at Selby was absolutely conditional on the close co-operation between William I and Thomas of Bayeux revealed by both the *Historia* and the early charters.

Finally, the evidence of William's charter leaves no doubt that the king regarded himself as the founder of the abbey. On the other hand it does nothing to suggest that Benedict's arrival in Yorkshire was itself due to royal initiative. According to the traditions current at Selby in the late twelfth century, the Conqueror merely seized the unexpected chance of Benedict's settlement by the Ouse to create a regular monastery there.

---

[30] See above, p. 35.

[31] Freeman, *Norman Conquest*, iv, pp. 796–7; *Regesta regum Anglo-Normanorum*, ed. H.W.C. Davis, i (1913), pp. 48–9; *Early Yorkshire Charters*, i, p. 360.

[32] *Early Yorkshire Charters*, 12, 'The Tison Fee' (1965), pp. 47–50; cf. *Selby Coucher Book*, ii, pp. 18–19.

[33] *Early Yorkshire Charters*, 10, 'The Trussebut Fee' (1955), p. 1.

[34] W.H. Stevenson, 'Yorkshire Surveys and Other Eleventh-Century Documents in the York Gospels', *English Historical Review*, 27 (1912), p. 15; cf. *Early Yorkshire Charters*, i, p. 363.

For this reason alone, it seems advisable to reject the most famous of all Selby legends – that William's youngest son, the future King Henry I, was born at Selby, an event which his father later commemorated by the establishment of a religious house on the site. Not unnaturally the glamour of this legend has tended to mesmerise later historians. Even Farrer went to ingenious lengths to prove that it was physically possible for Queen Matilda to have given birth to Henry at Selby while travelling to York in March 1069; and for Freeman 'it is the very unlikeliness of the tale which suggests that it must have some groundwork of truth'.[35] But if this story had been at all authentic, it is almost inconceivable that it would not have been mentioned either in the *Historia* or the preambles to William I's and Henry I's own charters to Selby Abbey. In fact, the belief that Henry I was born at Selby cannot be traced back to before the dissolution of the monastery. Unknown to both Leland and Holinshed, it only achieved wide popularity with its appearance in Camden's *Britannia* of the late sixteenth century.[36] The pride of later Selby citizens in the painted chamber 'wherein they pretend that this king was born' was as unfounded as the other intriguing legend which derives Selby's coat of arms (*sable, three swans argent*) from three swans which met Benedict on his first arrival there.[37]

According to yet another tradition, preserved by the St Albans' chronicler, Matthew Paris, William I deliberately created an abbey at Selby as a complement to his other post-conquest foundation of Battle. Both monasteries were designed to expiate the Conqueror's guilt 'in killing one of his close kinsmen while hunting', an allusion to the scandal caused by William's part in the slaying of Conan of Brittany.[38] As there is no evidence whatsoever of any connection between Anglo-Norman Selby and Battle, this story, too, may be dismissed as a piece of ingenious rationalisation by a much later writer. More convincing is the general argument that William I had strong political interests in the establishment of a small colony of dependent and loyalist monks within a region of violent native opposition to his new regime. The Conqueror's well-founded fear of 'Northumbrian separatism' during the years after Hastings presumably induced him to favour the introduction of Benedictine monasticism to the north just as it led him to enforce the primacy of the see of Canterbury

[35] Ibid., pp. 362–3; Freeman, *Norman Conquest*, iv, pp. 230–1, 790–1. The exact date of Henry's birth still remains controversial.

[36] Leland's *Collectanea*, ed. Hearne (London, 1774), ii, p. 355; Holinshed's *Chronicles* (London, 1807), ii, pp. 9–10; Camden's *Britannia*, ed. E. Gibson (London, 1722), ii, p. 886.

[37] J. Burton, *Monasticon Eboracense* (York, 1758), p. 387; *Monasticon Anglicanum* (1817–30 edn), iii, p. 498.

[38] Matthew Paris, *Historia Anglorum*, RS (1866–9), i, pp. 30–4: cf. Freeman, *Norman Conquest*, iv, p. 798.

over the authority of the archbishop of York.[39] On the other hand it is extremely unlikely that William did more than exploit the opportunity provided for him by Benedict of Auxerre's arrival at Selby. The *Historia* is at its most convincing when it demonstrates that religious life there owed its origins to the free enterprise of an expatriate monk rather than to royal will and governmental policy. Benedict, like Aldwin and Reinfrid, the first superiors of Durham and Whitby, was a restless pioneer, better suited to found a new monastery than to control its later development. Selby Abbey, like so many northern religious houses – Bridlington, Whitby, Kirkstall, Kirkstead, Nostell and others – evolved on a site first made sacred by the presence of an anchorite's cell. The story of Benedict is consequently representative of a common and paradoxical theme within the history of early medieval monasticism. Although dedicated to the ideal of *stabilitas* and communal worship, the new monasteries (Citeaux is the most famous example of all) were often the creations of dissatisfied, nomadic and 'solitary' figures, monks who found it not altogether easy to practise what they preached. Benedict's own last years at Selby were marred by a collapse of discipline and morale within his cloister; and according to the *Historia* it was in a state of deep personal disillusion that he resigned his abbacy in 1096 or 1097 and retired, perhaps to Rochester where he is said to have died some time later.[40]

Benedict's disillusion with monastic life at Selby in the 1090s appears to have been thoroughly justified. Although the abbey had been formally established at an earlier date than Durham, Whitby and St Mary's, York, it apparently experienced a severe crisis of confidence at exactly the time when these three other northern Benedictine houses were passing through their most expansionist phase. Until the first decade of the twelfth century the monks of Selby still lived in a primitive settlement of wooden huts around a timber church on the river bank. In a revealing writ of between 1100 and 1108, Henry I informed the archbishop and sheriff of York that 'the abbey of St Germanus of Selby shall remain peacefully in the spot where it was founded by my father and mother, and not be moved to another place'.[41] The only obvious reason for such a command was – as Farrer noticed – that news had already reached the king of a planned migration by the Selby chapter to a new situation. Despite the close proximity of running water, Selby was undoubtedly an unattractive monastic site by medieval standards; and it is not at all unlikely that the early community contemplated removing itself to a more salubrious and

---

[39] Hugh the Chantor, *History of the Church of York*, ed. C. Johnson (London, 1961), p. 3; cf. R.A. Brown, *The Normans and the Norman Conquest* (London, 1969), pp. 76–7.

[40] *Selby Coucher Book*, i, p. [21]; cf. Henrietta Leyser's unpublished thesis, 'The New Eremitical Movement, 1000–1150' (Bodleian Library MS, B.Litt., 1967), a reference I owe to Dom Alberic Stacpoole.

[41] Ibid., pp. 23–4; *Early Yorkshire Charters*, i, p. 362.

convenient location within some other part of its estates. The migrations later in the twelfth century of Cistercian monks from Barnoldswick to Kirkstall, and from Old Byland to Byland, make it clear that a change of locale was a very real possibility during the early stages of a monastery's history. In other words, the foundation of Selby Abbey was only absolutely complete when the community there became irretrievably committed to remaining in the vill by its building of a permanent church and monastic buildings. The story of the establishment of the abbey must consequently be carried a little further.

The insecurity of the monks' position at Selby during the years immediately before and after 1100 is not in itself particularly difficult to explain. According to the evidence of its later cartulary, lay patronage towards the new monastery began to languish soon after the initial endowments provided by William I and Archbishop Thomas of Bayeux. Except for the gifts of land made by Ilbert de Lacy and Gilbert Tison,[42] the abbot and convent of Selby received remarkably little in the way of substantial lay benefaction in Yorkshire until after the end of the eleventh century. No doubt the foundation in the mid 1080s of the monastery of St Mary's just outside the walls of the city of York had a deleterious effect on Selby's fortunes by diverting the attentions of prospective patrons towards a religious house which soon became the most prosperous in northern England. It is symptomatic of the new situation created by the rapid growth of St Mary's to monastic primacy in the north that on one occasion William Rufus is alleged to have ordered its first abbot, Stephen, to arrest Abbot Benedict of Selby.[43] But the fundamental weakness of the position of the early community of St Germanus lay in the uncertainty which surrounded its exact constitutional status within the organised church. Although a royal foundation, Selby attracted the hostility rather than the favour of William Rufus. In 1093 this king formally bestowed the abbey (together with the then collegiate church of St Oswald at Gloucester) on the archbishop of York as part of his ingenious scheme to persuade the latter to renounce his claims to metropolitan authority over the bishopric of Lincoln.[44] In the words of Rufus's charter, now considered to be indisputably authentic, the archbishops of York were thereafter to hold Selby 'sicut archiepiscopus Cantuariensis habet episcopatum Roffensem'. This curious analogy with Rochester may have been intended to suggest that future prelates of York might henceforward treat Selby as their own real property, as a type of *Eigenkloster*. At first sight it seems as if Rufus had

---

[42] Ibid., iii, 123, 196–7; xii, pp. 47–50.

[43] *Selby Coucher Book*, i, pp. [20]–[21]. A valuable study of the obscure first phase in the history of St Mary's is D. Bethell, 'The Foundation of Fountains Abbey and the State of St Mary's, York in 1132', *Journal of Ecclesiastical History*, 17 (1966), pp. 17–24.

[44] *Registrum Antiquissimum of the Cathedral Church of Lincoln*, i, Lincoln Record Society (1931), pp. 11–12, provides the best published text of this famous charter.

deliberately sacrificed the independence and welfare of Benedict's abbey on the altar of political and financial profit.[45] Although this, in fact, proved not to be the case (medieval archbishops of York rarely intervened at Selby in ways unwarranted by their normal rights as ordinaries), one can hardly resist the conclusion that in Rufus's reign the abbey was under pressure from powerful external forces which threatened its autonomy and hence its future.

From this unhappy situation the new monastery of Selby was rescued by the talents and labours of its second abbot, Hugh, who ruled at Selby for the twenty-six years from 1097 to 1123. The tradition that Abbot Hugh was a member of the powerful Anglo-Norman baronial family of de Lacy cannot be traced back beyond its appearance in Burton's *Monasticon Eboracense* (1758).[46] But of the importance of Hugh's abbacy in consolidating the prestige and possessions of the convent at Selby there can be no doubt whatever. To a later generation of Selby monks he was the most distinguished of all their abbots and a personification of the ideal Christian and monastic virtues, 'a simple and God-fearing man, one who shunned evil and was of outstanding charity, humility, piety and chastity'.[47] Hugh was also able to attract substantial sources of revenue – as well as important recruits – to his monastery in a way that Abbot Benedict had failed to do.[48] More significantly still, it was Abbot Hugh who supervised the rebuilding of the abbey church and monastery in stone. Perhaps because Henry I had prohibited a migration of the community outside Selby, Hugh and his chapter decided to transfer the site of their monastery within Selby itself. The place of Benedict's original cell and the early wooden buildings was abandoned (a dependent chapel stood in this quarter of the town during the later middle ages) in favour of a new situation 150 yards farther away from the river. Abbot Hugh's personal contribution to the building of the new abbey church is recorded in the most famous passage of the *Historia*. 'Every day, clothed in a workman's smock, he carried on his shoulders stones, lime and whatever else was needed for the building of the walls: every Saturday he received his

---

[45] According to Hugh the Chantor (*History*, p. 9), 'All England knows that Bishop Robert gave King William £3,000 for this'. For descriptions of this strange episode, one of the major mysteries in the history of Selby Abbey, see E.A. Freeman, *The Reign of William Rufus* (London, 1882), i, p. 447; *Fasti Eboracenses*, ed. J. Raine (London, 1863), p. 151. Cf. Knowles, *Monastic Order*, pp. 402, 631, and the comments by A.H. Thompson in his review of the original edition, *English Historical Review*, 56 (1941), pp. 647–51.

[46] W.E. Wightman, *The Lacy Family in England and Normandy, 1066–1194* (Oxford, 1966), p. 58.

[47] *Selby Coucher Book*, i, p. [22]; cf. *Acta sanctorum*, 7 July, pp. 290–304.

[48] A convenient summary of the convent's major landed possessions by the mid twelfth century is provided by King Stephen's confirmatory charter of 1154: *Early Yorkshire Charters*, 1, pp. 368–9. Abbot Hugh's presence at the court of Henry I at Winchester is recorded in W. Farrer, *An Outline Itinerary of King Henry I* (Oxford, 1919), p. 76.

wages like any other labourer, wages which he later gave to the poor.'⁴⁹ By the time of Hugh's resignation of the abbacy in 1123 both church and monastic accommodation were sufficiently complete to have allowed him to 'lead his sheep into their new fold'. In the thirty years that followed, the prestige of Selby Abbey underwent partial eclipse once more – due to the exploitation of the convent's estates by local magnates during the turbulent 'anarchy' of Stephen's reign as well as the criticisms of reforming churchmen influenced by the coming of the Cistercians to Yorkshire in 1131–32. But despite the difficulties that lay immediately ahead, in 1123 the monastery was at last securely established and its long-term future was assured.

Fortunately the surviving abbey church at Selby still preserves – as the ruins of Yorkshire's other two great Benedictine houses of Whitby and St Mary's, York, do not – substantial remains of its original Romanesque building. Abbot Hugh's church was planned to comprise an aisled nave of eight bays, an aisleless transept with two semi-circular apses and an aisled chancel.⁵⁰ The chancel itself, presumably the first part of the church to be built, was pulled down two centuries later to make way for the present Decorated choir; and the Norman south transept was destroyed by the collapse of the central tower in 1690. Moreover, the construction of the nave was subject to long building delays, with the result that only its eastern bays and the north transept give the modern visitor an impression of the early twelfth-century original design.⁵¹ But these parts of the present church clearly reveal not only the large scale of the building but its debt to the most famous of all Norman cathedrals, the priory church of Durham. Nor is it surprising that Selby Abbey was 'probably erected by the Durham masons' yard'.⁵² Abbot Hugh visited Durham to witness the translation of St Cuthbert's relics to his new shrine in September 1104, a date by which much of Bishop Flambard's new cathedral was already standing.⁵³ Among the many architectural motifs which reveal Selby's dependence on Durham the most obvious are the alternation of massive circular with composite nave piers and the early use of abundant zig-zag or chevron decoration. One of the Selby piers, the so-called 'Abbot Hugh's

⁴⁹ *Selby Coucher Book*, i, p. [23]. The interest of this reference to an organised system of wage-labour for building purposes at a very early date in the twelfth century needs no urging.

⁵⁰ C.C. Hodges, 'The Architectural History of Selby Abbey', *Selby Coucher Book*, ii, p. iv*.

⁵¹ The western sections of the nave, together with the famous west and north doors, can be dated to the last twenty years of the twelfth century, by which time the architectural influences on building at Selby derived from York rather than Durham: see C.E. Keyser, 'The Norman Doorways of Yorkshire', *Memorials of Old Yorkshire*, ed. T.M. Fallow (London, 1909), pp. 207–9.

⁵² T.S.R. Boase, *English Art, 1100–1216* (Oxford, 1953), p. 19.

⁵³ *Symeonis monachi opera omnia*, i, pp. 248–58.

Pillar', bears the deeply incised lozenge or diamond pattern familiar at Durham, Holy Island and Dunfermline. Similarly, the precocious adoption of rib-vaulting in the eastern bays of the south aisle of Selby's nave relies heavily on the revolutionary vaulting methods first pioneered at Durham.[54] Even the detailed carvings of the capitals of the columns at Selby are recognisably the work of a school of Durham masons.[55] It is not without irony that the very first Norman Benedictine foundation in the north should owe so much of its physical appearance to the influence of a later if greater monastery. But in Yorkshire at least, Selby Abbey still provides the most impressive memorial there is to the physical impact of the Norman Conquest and to the truth of William of Malmesbury's famous comment: 'After their coming to England they revived the rule of a previously moribund religion. You might see great churches rise in every village, and in the towns and cities monasteries built after a style unknown before.'[56]

[54] As appears from the similarities between the roll-mouldings on the ribs themselves. The use on external walls of a raised billet-moulding to form the window head, most readily seen in the Norman west window of Selby's north transept, is another characteristic Durham motif.

[55] G. Zarnecki, *Later English Romanesque Sculpture, 1140–1210* (London, 1953), pp. 34–5.

[56] William of Malmesbury, *Gesta regum Anglorum*, RS (1887–9), ii, p. 306.

3

'Mynistres of Saynt Cuthbert':
The Monks of Durham in the Fifteenth Century

Perhaps no religious community of late medieval England has left to posterity more enduring visible memorials to its life and worship than have the monks of St Cuthbert. Even now, over four hundred years after their disappearance into involuntary oblivion, it still remains much more important to visit the cathedral church and precincts of the community of St Cuthbert rather than to read about them.[1] For if the stones on the Durham peninsula could speak, who can deny that they would have much more interesting stories to relate than that upon which any modern historian might care to embark? Nowhere is that truism more likely to apply than in the long-lost private prayers and conversations once held in the great common dormitory of Durham, the room within which the great majority of St Cuthbert's brethren must have spent so much more time than anywhere else within the precincts of their cathedral priory. About those prayers and conversations we now know nothing at all, except that there 'was euery nyght aboute 12 a clocke a privy searche by the supprior, who did caule at euery mounckes chambre by ther names to se good order keapt, that none should be wanting as also that there were noe disorders amongest them'.[2] By those standards the following 'privy searche' into monastic life at fifteenth-century Durham is bound to be very limited indeed. That it is possible at all depends not only on the voluminous archives preserved by the monks themselves but also on the fact that Durham has long fostered some exceptionally skilled and talented searchers. In particular, the following pages owe a great debt to the assistance and generosity of the staff of the Department of Palaeography and Diplomatic in the Prior's Kitchen.

However, the monastic dormitory – rather than the Prior's Kitchen – remains an especially appropriate room with which to begin any survey of the fifteenth-century monks of Durham. That dormitory's history symbolises, better perhaps than any other building in the precinct, the late medieval transformation of the religious life which is the major theme

---

[1] This essay was originally delivered as a Durham Cathedral Lecture on 2 March 1972. For another and less fully developed account of some of the themes discussed here see R.B. Dobson, *Durham Priory, 1400–1450* (Cambridge, 1973), pp. 51–80.

[2] *The Rites of Durham*, ed. J.T. Fowler (Surtees Society, 107 (1903), p. 86.

of this paper. Since the dissolution of the monastery of Durham on 31 December 1539 this is a room which has undergone a vicissitudinous history. For many years its southern part served as the prebendal house attached to the fifth stall while the remainder of the dormitory was used by the children of the dean and chapter as their playground. Only after substantial renovations of its fabric in the early 1820s and again between 1849 and 1853 (on the demolition of the prebendal house) was it converted into the new Dean and Chapter Library in 1854.[3] Nevertheless, with its famous timber roof and its impressive dimensions of 194 by 39 feet, it is the best preserved large monastic dormitory in England.[4] Despite the disappearance of most of its original windows and its floor of 'fyne tyled stone', it is also a room which the last generations of Benedictine monks at Durham would still find recognisable. Moreover it was with the building of this 'faire large house called the Dorter' that the architectural history of Durham Cathedral Priory in the fifteenth century began. Both the unpublished building accounts and the famous contracts with the Durham masons John de Middleton and Peter Dryng make it clear that the construction of this new dormitory began in the autumn of 1398 and was intended to be complete by All Saints' Day 1404: the monks had certainly moved into their new sleeping quarters by 1406 when Thomas Rome, the sacrist of the house, recorded an expenditure of £1 on the making of the novices' beds 'in dormitorio'.[5] Henceforward it was in this dormitory that all those Durham monks not too aged, sick or distinguished to be dispensed from doing so were to spend their broken nights.[6]

The construction of the new dormitory at the very beginning of the fifteenth century has therefore left us with an impressive memorial to three of the most fundamental features of the monastic life at late medieval

---

[3] *Rites of Durham*, pp. 159, 296; H.D. Hughes, *A History of Durham Cathedral Library* (Durham, 1925), pp. 10–11; J. Raine, *A Brief Account of Durham Cathedral* (Newcastle, 1833), p. 92; C.J. Stranks, *This Sumptuous Church: The Story of Durham Cathedral* (London, 1973), p. 93.

[4] Its only serious rival is the dormitory of Westminster Abbey, also converted into a chapter library. Extremely few medieval English monastic dorters still retain their roofs and floors: R. Gilyard-Beer, *Abbeys: An Introduction to the Religious Houses of England and Wales* (London, 1958), p. 25.

[5] DCD, Sacrist, 1406/07. The two dormitory building contracts of 21 September 1398 and 2 February 1402 respectively are printed in *Historiae Dunelmensis scriptores tres*, ed. J. Raine, Surtees Society, 9 (1839), pp. clxxx–clxxxii, clxxxvii–cxc; and L.F. Salzman, *Building in England down to 1540* (Oxford, 1952), pp. 473–7.

[6] How many Durham monks were dispensed, like the dissident William Partrike in 1446, 'to haue a godely chambre with in the fermory atte lymytacion of the prior of the monasterie' (DCD, Lytham, Miscellanea, no. 7) is impossible to know. But it was probably by no means easy to secure a dispensation to sleep outside the common dormitory: according to chapter definitions or ordinances of *c*. 1446 and 1464, even the infirm were forbidden the use of a 'cameram priuatam nisi causa gravis infirmitatis vel alia causa racionabili, et hoc tamen cum licencia prioris vel custodium ordinis' (DCD, Locellus XXVII, nos 15, 29).

Durham. In the first place, so extensive a building project would have been impossible without the active co-operation and financial subvention of the monks' all-important 'good lord', the bishop of Durham himself. Bishop Walter Skirlaw (1388–1406) was alleged to have contributed the sum of £220 to the building of the dormitory;[7] and when the prior and chapter gave him their formal permission to be buried on the north side of their cathedral choir on 6 January 1405, they singled out his assistance *ad construccionem dormitorii* as the greatest of his many benefactions to them.[8] In this sphere, as in so many others, the goodwill of their titular abbot and father – imposed upon them as he always was by the English government – continued to be the most valuable asset the fifteenth-century Durham chapter could enjoy. But Bishop Skirlaw's own financial aid to the building of the new dormitory did not relieve the prior and chapter themselves from 'serious and immense expenses' on this project. A large proportion of the total cost was met by contributions levied from the heads of Durham's daughter-houses and the obedientiaries of the mother-house.[9] The reconstruction of the Durham dormitory deserves to be interpreted, like the transformation of so many other buildings within the monastic precincts during the later middle ages, as a tribute to the monks' own economic resources. Despite the financial difficulties caused by the loss of much of the priory's landed income as a result of Border warfare, by the decline in the number of their tenants as a result of plague, and by sustained economic recession, the community of St Cuthbert retained much of its wealth throughout the fifteenth century. Except at temporary periods of exceptional economic crisis, it would be hard to maintain that

[7] By the anonymous compiler of the notes on late medieval bishops and priors of Durham added to the standard Durham history, the *Gesta episcoporum*, and printed in *Historiae Dunelmensis scriptores tres*, p. 145. As these notes, often demonstrably inaccurate in detail, were probably not composed until the early sixteenth century, they deserve to be treated with much more caution by modern historians of Durham than has usually been the case: see below, p. 295, and H.S. Offler, *Medieval Historians of Durham*, Inaugural Lecture (Durham, 1958), p. 18. Thus it seems inconceivable that Bishop Skirlaw himself should have contributed £600 to the building of the monastic cloister at Durham, a work which cannot have got seriously under way until after his death in March 1406 and which is nowhere mentioned in his will of 7 March 1404: the latter does however include a bequest of an additional 100 marks 'to the building of the dormitory of the priory of Durham if the work is not finished before my death': *Testamenta Eboracensia*, i, ed. J. Raine, Surtees Society, 4 (1836), p. 310.

[8] DCD, Reg. II, fo. 184; *Historiae Dunelmensis scriptores tres*, p. cxciii.

[9] Such contributions form a regular feature of the expenditure recorded in the surviving annual account rolls of the almoner, cellarer, chamberlain, feretrar, hostillar, master of the infirmary and sacrist as well as the heads of the most wealthy cells from 1398 to 1405. According to the unpublished accounts of the two Durham monks, Thomas Dautre and Thomas Lythe, who supervised the expenses of the building of the dormitory between 1398 and 1404, the 'subsidies' from these monastic officials and heads of cells should have totalled £40 18s. 4d. p.a. (DCD, Locellus II, no. 13).

the late medieval monks of Durham were ever prevented from taking an important initiative because they could not afford to do so.

The new monastic dormitory of the early fifteenth century tells us something of even greater interest about the late medieval prior and chapter: it was a tribute not only to the material resources of the bishop and themselves, but to their own desire for greater magnificence, for greater comfort, and above all for greater structural subdivision. In the words of the nostalgic remembrancer of the religious life at Durham on the eve of its final suppression, each monk had in the dorter 'a litle chamber of wainscott verie close seuerall by them selves'.[10] The creation within a common dormitory of a series of quasi-private individual apartments takes us close to the heart of the transformation of the monastic life in late medieval Durham. In sociological as well as religious terms, monasticism (itself paradoxically derived from the Greek word for the solitary) has always revolved around the tension between the aims of the individual and the needs of the community. All in all, the most important development at fifteenth-century Durham was the modification of the traditional medieval ideal of a large and monolithic religious community in order to meet the needs, proclivities and talents of individual monks. Individuality within a monastic community is rarely regarded as a virtue and is always difficult for the historian to detect; but no reader of the archives of the prior and chapter of Durham can be left in any doubt that it is the complex specialisation of human labour and function which stands revealed as the most distinctive characteristic of the convent's life at the end of the middle ages. Such a development was not of course confined to late medieval Durham Priory; but there is perhaps nowhere that it can be observed in such great detail. The unique *conjoncture*, within a few hundred feet of this dormitory, of surviving monastic buildings, monastic archives and monastic library gives late medieval Durham a general significance which transcends the understandable affection that residents of Durham have always felt for its own peculiar *genius loci*.

Somewhat paradoxically, it is precisely because the cathedral priory of Durham is an untypical, as well as an exceptionally well-documented, English monastery that it has so much to tell us about the nature of the religious life at the end of the middle ages. Durham's distinctiveness, in other words, often consists of the extreme forms with which it reveals the universal aspirations and preoccupations of late medieval monasticism under unusual pressures. All religious communities venerated their patron

---

[10] *Rites of Durham*, p. 85. The building contract of 1398 required John de Middelton to provide one window for every two *studia*, proof that the sub-division of the dormitory into separate sleeping cubicles was envisaged at the outset of the work (Salzman, *Building in England*, pp. 473–4). At an earlier date it seems virtually certain (although very difficult to prove) that 'the beds stood against the wall between the windows without any partitions': A.H. Thompson, *English Monasteries* (Cambridge, 1913), p. 84.

saints and founders; but the monks of Durham were often literally obsessed by their remarkable historical tradition and their position as St Cuthbert's spiritual heirs. Most large monasteries of the later middle ages set a high premium on university education for the most intellectually gifted members of their community; but 'perhaps more than any other monastery Durham came to be governed and administered by university monks'.[11] Several of the wealthiest English Benedictine monasteries possessed a number of small cells or daughter-houses; but the achievement of the monks of Durham in making the administration of nine widely dispersed dependencies an integral part of their overall monastic polity was unsurpassed anywhere. Religious houses in England held a bewildering variety of important jurisdictional immunities and spiritual franchises; but nowhere were these liberties more zealously and sometimes morbidly preserved than on the Durham peninsula. Above all it is important to remember – what is sometimes all too easy to forget – that throughout the later middle ages the community of St Cuthbert was always the single largest corporate establishment north of York. At a period in European history whose essential characteristic, despite several attempts to suggest the contrary, was a remarkably successful institutional resistance to social and intellectual change, the relevance of what took place at Durham needs no particular urging. Of all medieval Christendom's corporate institutions, the cathedral priory of Durham was one of the greatest and is one of the best recorded. Answers to the problems here are likely to be at least part of the answer to the late medieval historian's problems everywhere.

However, my subject here is not the activities of this great cathedral priory as a corporation – its administration of its landed possessions and revenues; its relations with bishop of Durham, archbishop of York and papal curia; its place within the general social context of north-eastern England – but rather the men who formed the corporation, the monks of Durham themselves.[12] Needless to say, they are not an easy subject for investigation. As nearly always in the middle ages, the men are much more inscrutable than their measures. Moreover it could well be argued that the twentieth-century historian is singularly ill-equipped, and increasingly less well-equipped, to appreciate and comprehend the passions and predilections of the late medieval monk. It may be that to the historian of the English Reformation the pre-Dissolution monasteries appear as 'the least mysterious and best-documented section of the church'.[13] But such optimism must be qualified by the realisation that the more one

[11] M.D. Knowles, *The Religious Orders in England* (Cambridge, 1948–59), ii, p. 20.

[12] The corporate activities of the monks of St Cuthbert are the primary subject of my *Durham Priory, 1400–1450* (Cambridge, 1973), a work which also discusses in a wider context some of the issues raised in this lecture.

[13] A.G. Dickens, *The English Reformation* (London, 1964), p. 52.

knows of the monks themselves the more enigmatic they often remain. Who were these men and what brought them here to live and worship? What did they do with their time? How isolated from the rest of society were they in fact as opposed to theory? did they find the practice of the religious life at Durham both psychologically and spiritually rewarding? As so often, it is the simplest questions that often prove the most difficult to answer.

Nevertheless there can be no doubt that they deserve to be asked, and asked perhaps more insistently as well as sensitively than ever before. For we seem to have entered a period when the monks of medieval England face an even greater danger than their traditional fate of being the innocent posthumous victims of passionate sectarian controversy – the danger of being quietly ignored. Within the many recent surveys of late medieval English and European society, the monastic life is becoming increasingly conspicuous by its absence.[14] No doubt this comparative indifference towards one of medieval Christendom's greatest and most characteristic ideals is itself a comment on the increasingly secular interests of the modern historian and his inability to sympathise with groups of men who received 'so much wealth just in order to pray'. In the case of English monasticism, one also suspects that David Knowles's four great volumes on the history of the English religious orders, that monumental achievement to which we all owe so much, has had a temporarily tranquillising effect.[15] But Professor Knowles's remarkable work of synthesis must not be allowed to conceal the fact that late medieval monasticism is still often discussed in terms of a highly antiquated series of unwarranted preconceptions – above all, of course, the assumption that the fourteenth and fifteenth centuries were an age of general moral decline. Nothing has been more remarkable than the manner in which successive generations of English historians and antiquaries have rushed into an arena where angels would quite properly have declined to tread, and made moral judgements about a way of life which deserves to be approached with extreme caution. To understand all may not be to forgive all; but there is little doubt that the monks of Durham and elsewhere deserve a good deal more understanding before we can begin to see what there is to forgive.

Admittedly little will ever be known for certain about the individual

[14] Of the many possible examples, one might cite the case of an accomplished French one-volume history of the late medieval church, Francis Rapp, *L'église et la vie religieuse en occident à la fin du moyen âge* (Paris, 1971).

[15] To this generalisation some detailed excellent studies of monastic estate-management provide the only important exception: see especially S.F. Hockey, *Quarr Abbey and its Lands, 1132–1631* (Leicester, 1970); I. Kershaw, *Bolton Priory: The Economy of a Northern Monastery, 1286–1325* (Oxford, 1973); E. King, *Peterborough Abbey, 1086–1310: A Study in the Land Market* (Cambridge, 1973); C. Platt, *The Monastic Grange in Medieval England* (London, 1969); J.A. Raftis, *The Estates of Ramsey Abbey* (Toronto, 1957). These words were of course written before the publication of B. Harvey, *Living and Dying in England, 1100–1540: The Monastic Experience* (Oxford, 1993).

personalities of the great majority of the Durham monks of the fifteenth century, or about their attitudes to each other, to their prior, to their order and to their religion. The few monks who have left much impression of their temperamental characteristics to posterity tend, in the nature of things, to be those who were unusually restive, troublesome and dissident members of the community. Such a man, for example, was Henry Helay, who led a turbulent as well as lengthy career as a Durham monk for more than half a century after his entry into the community at the beginning of the fifteenth century. The holder of a variety of important monastic offices at Durham, as well as successively prior of the cells of Stamford (1422–26), Holy Island (1437–42) and Lytham (1446), his behaviour was frequently the cause of *murmur et obloquicio* among his brethren at the mother house.[16] At Bishop Robert Neville's visitation of the convent in July 1442, he was accused of holding animals, money and other goods to his own use, an offence which persuaded Prior John Wessington (1416–46) to recall him to Durham.[17] A few years later he acknowledged that he had seriously slandered one of his fellow monks 'of malice, and nott of goode hert nor goode will'.[18] Helay's apparently congenital quarrelsomeness persisted into his old age when he tried to dispossess the recently retired Prior Wessington from a particularly desirable chamber in the monastic infirmary.[19]

Much more alarming was the rebelliousness displayed by William Partrike, the monk sent to serve as the head of Durham's dependency at Lytham in 1431: his subsequent attempt to emancipate both himself and his Lancashire cell from the authority of the prior and convent drew from Robert Westmorland, then monastic chancellor, the justifiable rebuke that 'sen the first fundation of the kirke of Durham was ther neuer sich a thing so preiudiciall attempt agayns the priuileges and the libertes thereof'.[20] A handful of surviving letters written by Partrike in the late 1440s, after his enforced return to Durham, present an extreme and unhappy picture of complete personal alienation from his fellows and the monastic life. In an inevitably isolated situation ('we have [a new] prior, and he luffyd me neuer, and Robert Westmorland and John Gatished and Richard Bell ar cheff wit hym, and none of them luffis me'), Partrike lamented that 'now I hafe no place nor no recreacon bot bydys stil in the abbay wit a sorry hert tyl god of is grac wyl se that better may be'.[21] A third example of a fifteenth-century Durham monk who has left some

---

[16] *Liber vitae ecclesiae Dunelmensis*, i, ed. A.H. Thompson, Surtees Society, 136 (1923), fo. 70; DCD, Reg. III, fos 111, 115v; Reg. Parv. II, fos 96, 131–2.

[17] See Appendix, p. 73, below; DCD, Misc. Charters, no. 1072.

[18] DCD, Misc. Charters, nos 1055, 1056; *Historiae Dunelmensis scriptores tres*, p. cclxxxiii.

[19] DCD, Locellus XXVII, no. 15.

[20] DCD, Locellus IX, no. 8. For a discussion of the 'Lytham case' of 1443–6, see Dobson, *Durham Priory*, pp. 327–41.

[21] DCD, Locellus IX, nos 11, 30.

record of his personal sensibility in his surviving letters is provided by Richard Billingham, the convent's representative at the papal curia on three separate occasions between 1465 and 1472. But neither the lively truculence which Billingham displayed towards the legal adversaries of his convent nor his apparently sincere devotion to St Cuthbert inhibited him from disappearing without trace on his third mission to Rome, 'quamvis ingratum et a regule sue professionis enormiter deviantem'.[22] In their very different ways, Henry Helay, William Partrike and Richard Billingham revolted, most untypically, against the routines of religious observance at Durham; but, even in the case of these three exceptionally articulate monks, it is impossible to discover the roots of their personal discontents. The private desires and aspirations of the great majority of Durham monks, fully committed as they were to their religious vows of *stabilitas*, are a priori even more of a matter for speculation.

Little as can be known about the monks of Durham as individuals, we are however better informed as to their origins, recruitment, education, employment and interests than those of any comparable group of religious in fifteenth-century England. One of the first conclusions about the community of St Cuthbert to emerge from its surviving records, itself a highly significant one, is that its size remained remarkably stable throughout the last 150 years and more of its existence. Although considerable confusion has been caused in the past by a failure to distinguish between lists of all professed members of the community and those confined to the names of monks actually resident in the mother-house at a particular date, it is not too difficult to calculate the numerical size of the convent. At almost any period in the later middle ages the total population of Durham monks stood at the average figure of seventy, a number which of course varied somewhat from year to year as old monks died and as new recruits were admitted into the monastery. Thus, to take a few examples at random, there were seventy-three members of the Durham community alive at the time of Bishop Hatfield's election in 1345, sixty-nine at Bishop Langley's election in 1406, seventy-three at Bishop Robert Neville's election in 1438, sixty-nine at Prior John Burnby's election in 1456, seventy at Bishop Lawrence Booth's election in 1457, sixty-six monks at the elections of both Prior Richard Bell (1464) and Thomas Castell (1494), seventy-four at Prior Hugh Whitehead's election in 1520, and still as many as sixty-six when the house was surrendered to Henry VIII on the last day of 1539.[23]

---

[22] DCD, Reg. Parv. III, fo. 162. Some account of Richard Billingham's misadventures (in 1468 he had to be ransomed by his fellow monks after being captured and imprisoned by the archbishop of Cologne) can be found in R.B. Dobson, 'The Last English Monks on Scottish Soil', below, pp. 120–30.

[23] The sources for these numbers are provided by Dobson, *Durham Priory*, pp. 52–5; S.L. Greenslade, 'The Last Monks of Durham Cathedral Priory', *Durham University Journal* 41 (1948–9), pp. 107–13.

Of these seventy or so monks, incidentally, slightly fewer than thirty were likely at any one time to be serving the Durham dependencies, and rather more than forty (of whom perhaps half-a-dozen would be novices) were actually resident at the mother-house.[24]

Such statistics satisfactorily dispose of the myth that the outbreak of the Black Death brought about a permanent reduction in the complement of the medieval monastery. Indeed the really significant decline in the numbers of Durham monks evidently took place in the years around 1300 rather than either 1400 or 1500, and was largely the result of the loss of many of the convent's most valuable lands on and near the Border during the first stages of the Scottish 'wars of independence'. More generally, the stability of the monastic population at Durham from the late fourteenth century onwards obviously provides some index to the material welfare of the community throughout that long period. As in any society or corporation, numerical stability within a monastery is a good deal more difficult to achieve than it may seem: at fifteenth-century Durham it seems to reflect the success of the prior and chapter in managing their financial affairs against all the apparent economic odds. The available evidence certainly fails to support the familiar criticism that 'the numbers are kept down in order that a few may live in comfort, or even in riot, where of old many lived in self-denial'.[25] Indeed during the course of a late fourteenth-century Black Monk visitation of the convent, it was Durham monks themselves who made the point that their community should be as large 'as its resources could support if they were well administered'.[26] There can be little doubt that the admissions policy of the Durham chapter was directed at replacing one dead monk by one new recruit to the monastic life. The convent's ability to achieve this end should therefore be seen as a tribute to its success in maintaining its income at a comparatively stable level throughout a period during which it received no significant new sources of revenue for years, decades, and even centuries.

The rate of recruitment into the Durham community was accordingly directly related to the incidence of mortality within the cloister, for at no time in the fifteenth century is there any evidence of a scarcity of individuals who wished to become monks of St Cuthbert. Thanks to the survival of the famous Durham *Liber vitae*, the book on the high altar of the cathedral church in which the names of all Durham monks

[24] To the examples cited in Dobson, *Durham Priory*, pp. 54, 300 n. 1, might be added the total of forty-one monks at Durham recorded in the 1381 poll-tax return: D. Knowles and R.N. Hadcock, *Medieval Religious Houses: England and Wales* (2nd edn, London, 1971), p. 64.

[25] G.G. Coulton, *Five Centuries of Religion*, ii (Cambridge, 1927), p. 412.

[26] *Documents Illustrating the Activities of the General and Provincial Chapters of the English Black Monks, 1215–1540*, ed. W.A. Pantin, Camden Third Series (1931–7), iii, p. 83.

were entered soon after their monastic profession, the chronological
pattern of recruitment can be studied in some detail. Between 1383 and
1466, a period of eighty-three years, 168 novices were received into the
Durham fraternity, an average of slightly more than 20 every decade.[27]
The evidence of both the *Liber vitae* and of the payments for clothing
to the new monks recorded in surviving chamberlains' rolls reveals that
aspirants to the regular life at Durham were usually admitted not in ones
and twos, but in groups of six or eight – an arrangement which had
the practical advantage of providing a convenient unit for instructional
purposes in the cloister. An analysis of the names recorded in the *Liber
vitae* proves even more rewarding than a study of their numbers, for
it is the former that throw some light on the important issue of the
geographical origins of the Durham monks. As all but seven of the 139
monks who made their professions at Durham between 1383 and 1446
shared the six commonest male Christian names in late medieval England
(John, William, Thomas, Robert, Richard and Henry), a second name was
an essential aid to identification.[28] Twenty per cent of the monks in this
period retained an obvious family surname after entering the religious life,
but the others all bore toponymics. Due allowance made for the possibility
that several of the latter denoted the place of origin of the monk's male
ancestors rather than of himself, they can hardly fail to provide some
impression of the provenance of the members of the community. Almost
two-thirds of the monastic toponymics of fifteenth-century monks derived
from the place-names of villages in the more densely populated central
and eastern parts of Durham county, while a further 10 per cent of the
total names related to places immediately south of the Tees (Barton,
Easby, Guisborough, Masham, Wycliffe) or north of the Tyne (Corbridge,
Hexham, Newburn, Tynemouth). Most of the remaining names seem to
point to a Yorkshire origin, sometimes within the Durham liberties in that
county (Crayk, Howden, Feriby) but quite as often in towns and villages
(Ripon, Jervaulx, Pocklington, Pontefract, Wheldrake) which enjoyed no
particularly close links with Durham. A few other names (Brougham,
Westmorland, Appleby) suggest that the Pennines were no insuperable
obstacle to the would-be Durham monk; but the only genuinely surprising
surname held by a fifteenth-century member of the convent was that
of Thomas Rome, warden of Durham College, Oxford, from 1409 to
1418.[29]

[27] *Liber vitae*, fos 70, 75.

[28] Cf. Knowles, *Religious Orders*, ii, p. 231; Kershaw, *Bolton Priory*, p. 12.

[29] That Thomas Rome was of genuinely Italian origin would seem inherently unlikely
were it not that shortly before he became warden at Oxford he received contributions
towards a journey '*versus Romam*' (almoner, 1408/9, hostillar, 1408/9); cf. *Extracts from
the Account Rolls of the Abbey of Durham*, ed. J.T. Fowler, Surtees Society (1898–1901), i,
pp. 138, 223.

The names of Durham monks of the later middle ages therefore point to a natural if not excessive provincialism. The prior and chapter obviously did draw on a somewhat more extensive recruiting ground than smaller religious houses like Selby Abbey and Bolton Priory in the West Riding.[30] On the other hand it seems equally apparent that the great majority of the Durham brethren were drawn from a region within a radius of approximately thirty-five miles from the city of Durham. Local recruitment must therefore have reinforced the particularism and patriotic *pietas* which was such a dominant feature of the communal attitudes of the late medieval chapter. Two other aspects of this recruitment seem to deserve emphasis. The comparative infrequency of monastic toponymics derivative from place-names around Durham's outlying cells is probably symptomatic of the way in which these small communities often failed to integrate themselves into their local societies. The monks of St Albans and Westminster encouraged local recruitment to their dependencies of Tynemouth and Great Malvern respectively in a way which cannot be paralleled at Durham.[31] To take the extreme if understandable case, the prior and chapter's determination not to receive Scots into their community always made their possession of a cell at Coldingham north of Berwick extremely insecure, long before they lost it for ever in the 1470s. Nor is there any very obvious correlation between the toponymics held by so many Durham monks and the villages where the convent held the bulk of its estates. Canon Pearce's suggestion that the abbots and treasurers of Westminster Abbey 'came to learn of youths with an apparent vocation for claustral life' as they perambulated that monastery's estates cannot be applied to Durham with any certainty or even confidence.[32] On balance it seems unlikely that more than a small minority of Durham monks were themselves the sons of the convent's tenants.

The voluminous evidence of the Durham muniments does however throw some light, admittedly very occasional, on one of the great unresolved problems of late medieval monasticism in general – the social origins of the monk himself. Despite the extreme scarcity of direct references to the paternity of individual members of the Durham community, there can be no reasonable doubt that the great majority of the brethren came from the middle ranks of rural and urban society in the north. On the one hand, the prior and chapter appear to have been careful to ensure

[30] R.B. Dobson, 'The Election of John Ousthorp as Abbot of Selby in 1436', *Yorkshire Archaeological Journal*, 42 (1968), pp. 38–9; Kershaw, *Bolton Priory*, pp. 12–13.

[31] *Annales Monasterii S. Albani a Johanne Amundesham*, RS (London, 1870–1), i, pp. 205–21; B.S. Smith, *A History of Malvern* (Leicester, 1964), pp. 60–1.

[32] E.H. Pearce, *The Monks of Westminster*, Notes and Documents relating to Westminster Abbey, 5 (Cambridge, 1916), p. 38. Similar reservations on this issue are expressed by Kershaw, *Bolton Priory*, p. 12.

that all their members met the canonical requirements of being 'of free condition and born of a legitimate marriage'.[33] Two monks, John Oll and Thomas Ayre, were both defamed as men 'servilis subjectionis' in 1446: both felt it necessary and desirable to go to great and expensive pains to clear themselves from the charge of being 'a bondman and nott of fre condicion'.[34] On the other hand, the argument *ex silentio* makes it equally clear that the fifteenth-century monks of Durham did not include a member of an important northern aristocratic or knightly family in their midst. The younger sons of the noble dynasties of *generosi* which dominated the political and social life of the late medieval palatinate, the Nevilles, Lumleys, Hiltons, Eures and Elmedens, did not find their way into the community of St Cuthbert. Prior John Wessington himself was indeed a member of an armigerous Durham county family, that of the Washingtons of Washington; but he was an exception which seems to prove the rule. Prior Wessington's blood connection with the main line of that family was very remote; and within a few years of his reception into the monastery in 1390 it was to become extinct on the death of Sir William de Wessington.[35] At Durham, as elsewhere in England, the lack of interest displayed in a monastic career by male members of the late medieval nobility or gentry is remarkable enough to demand more attention than it has usually received.[36]

[33] See, e.g., *The Obituary Roll of William Ebchester and John Burnby*, ed. J. Raine, Surtees Society, 21 (1856), pp. xi, 99.

[34] DCD, Reg. Parv. III, fo. 8; *The Correspondence, etc., of Coldingham Priory*, ed. J. Raine, Surtees Society, 12 (1841), pp. 155–6; DCD, Misc. Charters, nos 1055, 1056.

[35] John Wessington's relationship with the Washington family of County Durham is testified by the record of a plea of novel disseisin brought by the prior against a group of substantial local landlords in 1443. In an attempt to empanel an impartial jury of recognition, Wessington's proctor thought it advisable to argue consanguinity between the prior and a certain Robert Preston, coroner of Easington Ward, on the grounds that one of Preston's wife's ancestors had been the son 'Walteri de Wessyngton militis, fratris Johannis Wessyngton patris Walteri patris ipsius nunc prioris' (PRO, Palatinate of Durham, Chancery Enrolments, 3/43, mm. 9–10; Locellus V, no. 24). As early as 1375 one branch of the Washington family had settled at Warton in Westmorland, from which village their descendants were to leave for Sulgrave in Northamptonshire and eventually Virginia. References to the activities of the last representative of the main branch of the Durham family, Sir William de Wessington who died in 1399, may be found in 'Calendar of the Chancery Enrolments of the Bishops of Durham', Appendices of *Reports of the Deputy Keeper of the Public Records*, 32 (1871), pp. 299, 306, 315–19, 323; 33 (1872), pp. 45, 70, 81–4. See also *A Calendar of the Greenwell Deeds*, ed. J. Walton, *Archaeologia Aeliana*, fourth series, 3 (1927), pp. 108–10, 114, 190.

[36] Knowles, *Religious Orders*, ii, pp. 229–30; and for the very different situation across the channel see D. Hay, *Europe in the Fourteenth and Fifteenth Centuries* (London, 1966), pp. 56–7. Perhaps the best general impression of aristocratic membership and exploitation of large European religious houses in the fifteenth century – of which the extreme examples were the German *Reichskloster* – is to be derived from vol. iii of P. Schmitz, *Histoire de l'ordre de Saint Benoit* (Maredsous, 1942–56).

It therefore seems safe to conclude that the great majority of fifteenth-century monks of Durham were men whose family status – to use the convent's own terminology – was that of *valecti* or varlets rather than of the superior *generosi* or inferior *gromi*.[37] In more familiar if less precise language, most late medieval Durham monks were socially akin to what was beginning to be known as the English yeomanry and to its urban equivalent – the respectable lesser merchants or masters of crafts in the late medieval English town. During the course of the fifteenth century there is a little evidence at Durham, as indeed at other English religious houses, that an increasing number of monastic recruits were being drawn from burgess families, of which they were probably often the younger sons. The occasional Durham monk can actually be proved to have belonged to a merchant family: thus Thomas Nesbitt seems to have been the nephew of the Robert Nesbitt of Hull who sold wine to the monastic bursar in the early 1430s; and William Gervase was probably related to a Durham merchant of the same surname.[38] Many other Durham monks bore names which associate them with the city's own clerical and notarial dynasties (the Racketts, Ryhalls, Bonours, Bells, Dautres, Fords, Forsters and Hatfields), families which tended to serve both bishop and monks on the Durham peninsula over several generations. Nor did the taking of monastic vows necessarily emancipate the Durham monk from an obligation to provide for the material welfare of his earthly family; and the fact that so many members of the community were eager to find places in the hospitals administered by the monastic almoner for their near kinsmen or kinswomen is itself an indication that they were not of substantial wealth or high social status.[39] The kindred of the already mentioned John Oll were allegedly 'among the best *valecti* of the barony of Brancepeth', belonging to a family apparently remembered because of its

[37] The rigidity of this tripartite division in terms of social status appears most clearly in the wages and fees recorded in fifteenth-century Durham account rolls and was clearly strictly observed throughout the county: see e.g. the bequests to different members of their household staff made by Bishops Skirlaw and Langley in 1404 and 1436 respectively (*Testamenta Eboracensia*, i, p. 309; *Historiae Dunelmensis scriptores tres*, p. ccxliii). The emergence of the term 'yeoman' as an equivalent for '*valettus*' seems to have occurred later in northern than southern England: for an early example at Durham (of 1440), see DCD, Misc. Charters, no. 6056.

[38] Bursar, 1429/30, 1432/33, Empcio Vini; Bursar, 1438/39, Expense Prioris; Bursar, 1440/41, Expense Necessarie.

[39] Among several possible examples may be mentioned Alice, the sister of Thomas Dautre, subprior, who was promised a place in the *Domus Dei* in 1403 (BL, MS Cotton Faustina A.VI, fo. 108); the sister of another subprior, Robert Rypon, who was attached to the hospital of St Mary Magdalen (almoner, 1395–1401); and Alice Bell, probably the sister rather than the mother of Prior Richard Bell (1464–78), who became a pluralist in this field with places at or pensions from the convent's hospitals of Witton Gilbert and St Mary Magdalen as well as the *Domus Dei* (DCD, Reg. Parv. III, fos 130, 136–7, 141, 143–4, 156, 160). See below, p. 137.

enthusiasm for football (*ad pilam pedalem*); but on the death of her husband 'the mother of the said lord John moved to Durham with all her goods', no doubt so that she could take advantage of the patronage as well as the propinquity of her son.[40]

Whatever the *esprit de corps* displayed by the Durham monks as a corporate community, one must therefore conclude that as individuals they could not be expected to hold their own in personal confrontation with members of the thirty or so gentry families which dominated the society of County Durham in the fifteenth century.[41] These families always posed a greater threat to the liberties and possessions of the cathedral priory than any other social group; and the Durham monks were well aware of the need to avoid antagonising the magnates and lords 'whom we cannot afford to offend'.[42] The crude realities of power in the north east of England are most vividly brought home by the unfortunate experience that befell the two Durham monks serving the cell of Monk Wearmouth in 1439. In the course of a particularly violent episode of the long feud between the prior and chapter and the lords of Hilton castle, 'William of Hilton, son and hayr to the Baron of Hilton, in his comyng to the kirke for to be shryuyn, mysinfourmyd of the said dede and theroppon hely movid, with hy and stoor countenance entreed the qweer of the said kirke of Wermouth withoutyn ony prayer or reuerence theer made or shewid to the blessid sacrament, and said to the said Kepper and his felowe on this wyse, "What, maistres, make yhe heer?"; and theroppon swar a gret hooth that ther was nott so pryue a chambre ne holl within that place then he suld pull oote John Booth monke and bynde his feete undre a horse baly and so sennd hym to Dorham; and also chalangid the said Kepper and askid hym in stoor maner, "Whoo was thy sire?"'.[43] Who indeed? As in the case of nearly all fifteenth-century monks of Durham, the question cannot be answered at all precisely; but it is clear enough that he is unlikely to have been a person with whom members of the Hilton family would ever have spent the time of day. The social inferiority of the English monk to the English gentleman has many implications: not least of course it helps to account for the ease with which all the religious houses were to be destroyed in the following century.

How did so many members of the middle ranks of north-eastern society

[40] Misc. Charters, nos 1055, 1056; *Historiae Dunelmensis scriptores tres*, p. cclxxx.

[41] For an unusually comprehensive list of the Durham county gentry at a particular point of time, the twelve *milites* and twenty-one *armigeri* who were assembled together on the bridge over the Tyne at Newcastle in January 1417, see *Historiae Dunelmensis scriptores tres*, pp. ccvii–ccviii.

[42] DCD, Locellus, xxvii, no. 15; and for litigation with members of the Durham gentry, see Appendix, below, p. 80.

[43] *Inventories and Account Rolls of Jarrow and Monk-Wearmouth*, ed. J. Raine, Surtees Society, 29 (1854), p. 241.

come to commit themselves to a life of religious observance as Durham monks? A complete lack of evidence makes it impossible to answer this fundamental question in terms of the individual novice's sense of religious vocation; and it would in any case seem to be more helpful to approach this problem as one would in the case of a modern equivalent, say the reasons which induce large numbers of twentieth-century adolescents to enter a university. In other words, the decision to enter the community was no doubt the result of personal choice, but a choice which took place within the context of an extremely powerful series of family and social pressures. In the case of the fifteenth-century recruit to the monastic life it seems highly probable that the most important pressures emanated from an existing Durham monk: what little evidence survives suggests that he was the agent through whom most boys were encouraged and persuaded to join the community of St Cuthbert. It is therefore hardly surprising that several members of the Durham chapter are known to have been related to one another by blood, a fact which is likely to have been true of many others. Robert Blacklaw, William Kyblesworth and John Fishburn, all at Durham College, Oxford, in the 1390s, were blood relatives; and in a letter of April 1441 Prior Wessington referred to one of his junior monks, William Birden, as a kinsman of Richard Barton, then prior of the cell at Stamford.[44] It seems that monks of Durham regularly recommended candidates for the religious habit to their prior; only because such recommendations would usually be made by word of mouth does so little written evidence of this practice survive.[45] As it is, we may be reasonably confident that the community of St Cuthbert, like most other religious houses in late medieval England, was a genuinely self-perpetuating corporation, an institution which derived many of its strengths as well as its weaknesses from a strong tradition of family cohesiveness.

Nor can there be any doubt that entrants into the religious life at Durham usually had considerable experience of conditions within the priory's precincts before they made their professions: there can be little question of the novice being ignorant of the obligations incumbent on a monk of Durham. A mental picture of the cathedral priory in the fifteenth century must indeed find place within it for a multitude of boys of all ages wandering through the precincts, the *pueri* of the almonry mingling with the *garciones* of the obedientiaries while a third and not always distinct group of *pueri nudipedes et inhonesti* plundered for food to the intense

[44] DCD, Locellus XXV, no. 37; Reg. Parv. II, fo. 136.

[45] For an exception see the letter of Robert Blacklaw, warden of Durham College, to Prior Hemingburgh in which he recommended John Fishburn, then a clerk at Oxford, as a talented recruit to the Durham cloister (DCD, Locellus XXV, no. 37).

annoyance of the monks.[46] Of these boys much the most significant for
our purposes were the 'certaine poor children onely maynteyned and
releyved with the almesse and Benevolence of the whole house, which
weare cauled the childrine of the aumery going daily to the fermery schole
being all together maynteled by the whole Covent with meate drynke and
lerninge'.[47] Just because the boys of the Durham almonry were sustained
informally and on a charitable basis, their exact numbers and role within
the monastery are erratically and imperfectly documented: but it is clear
enough that they formed the nucleus of the convent's grammar school, a
school which served the educational needs of many boys who were not
themselves dependent on the convent's alms.[48] All the evidence we have
suggests that attendance at this school was the normal gateway into the
monastic life at Durham. A chapter ordinance of 1417 makes it clear that
the almoner only admitted boys to the almonry after their examination
by a committee consisting of prior, subprior and three other monks, and
on the 'nomination of some monk resident within the monastery'.[49] A
diffinition laid before the Durham chapter thirty years later is even more
precise: 'it is petitioned that henceforward the boys of the almonry shall
be admitted primarily and principally from kinsmen and acquaintances of
monks living within the house, and those most suited for the monastic life
[*et hoc habiliores ad monachatum*]'.[50] There could hardly be a more explicit
confirmation of the existence of blood ties within the community and of
the validity of Professor Knowles's suggestion that 'these clerks [of the
almonry] probably themselves became monks far more often than the
records suggest'.[51]

The probability that most members of the Durham community in the
fifteenth century entered the religious life from the convent's own almonry
school itself implies that they must have been in their late teens or early
twenties when they made their professions. Such an assumption seems
to be confirmed by the few cases of Durham monks whose approximate
date of birth can be ascertained from surviving records. Thus Prior John

[46] This is without doubt the most common obsession to be reflected in fifteenth-century
visitation records and chapter ordinances (DCD, Locellus XXVII, nos 15, 16, 29); cf.
Appendix, below, pp. 77, 82.

[47] *Rites of Durham*, p. 91. Cf. Reg. IV, fo. 134v.

[48] Despite A.F. Leach's account in VCH, *County of Durham*, i, pp. 365–73, the history of
medieval schools on the Durham peninsula remains to be written. Particularly instructive
is the record (DCD, Locellus II, no. 4) of the dispute in the 1450s between the priory's
almonry or grammar school and that founded by Bishop Langley in 1414.

[49] Jesus College, Cambridge, MS 41, fo. 169v.

[50] DCD, Loc. XXVII, no. 15. Several boys were also admitted to the convent's almonry
school at the request of local lords: in such cases the prior and chapter always seem to
have found it advisable to 'with good hertt tendre your entennt in resauyng of that childe
to our almose and scoole for whilke yhe have writen' (a letter of February 1448 from Prior
William Ebchester to Sir Robert Ogle: Reg. Parv. III, fo. 28v).

[51] Knowles, *Religious Orders*, ii, p. 296.

Hemingburgh (1391–1416) is alleged to have lived sixty-six of his total life of eighty-nine years as a monk of Durham: he must have been aged approximately twenty-three when he entered the community.[52] Similarly, his two successors as prior, John Wessington and William Ebchester (1446–56), both of whom were certainly educated *in scolis Dunelm.*', must have been in their very early twenties when they began to live *in monachatu.*[53] Nor would the prior and chapter have been so eager to secure a bull from John XXIII[54] (in 1414) allowing them to dispense members of their community to priest's orders in their twenty-second year had they not anticipated the need to use it. Surviving letters of dispensation of this kind were copied into the prior's registers at Durham and allow us to estimate the age of a handful of Durham monks more or less exactly. A comparison of the dates of dispensation with those of profession as recorded in the Durham *Liber vitae* reveals the presence in the cloister of several monks who had taken their monastic vows a year or two before the canonical minimum age of nineteen.[55] On the other hand, there is no evidence whatsoever among the fifteenth-century muniments of laymen and secular clerks who took the habit in the middle or towards the close of their careers. The days when Durham monks might contemplate, if only as a theoretical possibility, the reception into a monastery of two senior chancery clerks seem to have passed for ever by the fifteenth century.[56] As at Westminster Abbey, so at Durham Cathedral Priory, 'Young men were accepted in their boyhood and became, in most cases, members of the House for life.'[57]

The assumption that the great majority of Durham monks entered the community of St Cuthbert in their late teens is obviously based on slighter evidence than one would ideally wish. It is nevertheless worth bearing in mind when turning from the beginning of a monk's career to its end with his death and burial in the monastic cemetery to the east of the chapter house. At that time a standardised payment, nearly always of ten shillings,

---

[52] DCD, Locellus I, no. 27; *Durham Obituary Rolls*, p. 64.

[53] DCD, Locellus I, nos 8, 9; Locellus II, no. 4; Locellus XXI, no. 23; *Durham Obituary Rolls*, pp. vii, 72.

[54] See p. 82, n. 98, below.

[55] DCD, Reg. III, fo. 62; Reg. Parv. II, fos 65–6, 72, 75; *Liber vitae*, fo. 70. Prior Richard Bell can have been only sixteen when he made his profession at Durham in 1426–7; see R.B. Dobson, 'Richard Bell, Prior of Durham (1464–78) and Bishop of Carlisle (1478–95)', below, pp. 135–6.

[56] W.A. Pantin, 'Letters from Durham Registers, *c.* 1360–1390', *Formularies which Bear on the History of Oxford*, Oxford Historical Society, new series, 3–4 (Oxford, 1942), p. 235. For a rather different impression of elderly recruitment to the monastery of Great Malvern in the late fourteenth century, see Smith, *History of Malvern*, p. 61.

[57] Pearce, *Monks of Westminster*, p. 38. It ought to be added that the number of monks who left Durham either as apostates or to enter a more rigorous religious order seems to have been considerably less than in the case of many large fifteenth-century Benedictine monasteries: see Dobson, *Durham Priory*, pp. 74–8.

was made to the poor as alms for the deceased's soul by the Durham bursar. Record of such payments on the many surviving bursar's rolls makes it possible to establish the date of death of most Durham monks with a considerable degree of accuracy. It seems immediately apparent that by fifteenth-century standards, and despite many outbreaks of plague in the county, the mortality rate within the Durham cloister was by no means severe: quite exceptional was the case of Nicholas Bolton who died within six years of making his profession in November 1431.[58] If anything, some monks of early fifteenth-century Durham deserve to be remembered for their longevity. At least 10 per cent of the documented cases wore the habit for more than fifty years; and the seven priors of the monastery between 1341 and 1478 (John Fossor, Robert Walworth, John Hemingburgh, John Wessington, William Ebchester, John Burnby and Richard Bell) attained the venerable ages of ninety, seventy-six, eighty-nine, seventy-nine, seventy-six, sixty-four and eighty-five respectively.[59] The senescent rather than the tyrannical superior was presumably the greatest danger to the welfare of the community; and it is hard to resist the speculation that the burdens of administrative office may have lengthened rather than curtailed the lives of Durham monks. As it was, the average period of time between a monk's profession and his death at fifteenth-century Durham seems to have been only a little less than forty years. It would seem to follow that most members of the community had every prospect of living on until their late fifties, thus enjoying an average expectation of life (by the time they reached the age of twenty) at least ten years greater than most sections of the late medieval English population for whom statistics survive.[60]

It is hardly surprising that the monks of Durham lived better nourished and less physically debilitating lives than most of their contemporaries. Much more controversial is the state of their psychological and spiritual well-being. It is to some consideration of that exceptionally difficult problem that this essay must now inevitably turn. In the first place it is abundantly clear that the surviving Durham records lend no support to the outmoded views of those who would see late medieval religious houses as dens of corruption and iniquity. It is easy to forget that the large medieval monastery was subject to much more public scrutiny and critical attention

---

[58] Bursar, 1437/38, Elemonsina Consueta; cf. *Liber vitae*, fo. 70v.

[59] *Historiae Dunelmensis scriptores tres*, p. 136; *Durham Obituary Rolls*, pp. vii, xi, 64, 72; Dobson, 'Richard Bell', below, p. 160; idem, *Durham Priory*, p. 89.

[60] J.C. Russell, *British Medieval Population* (Albuquerque, NM, 1948), pp. 173–93. It seems that the monastic mortality rate at Westminster Abbey (Pearce, *Monks of Westminster*, pp. 129–78) was much more severe than at Durham. At Christ Church, Canterbury, however, the average length of the religious life led by mid fifteenth-century monks was apparently almost thirty-five years, not far short of that at Durham: *Chronicle of John Stone*, ed. W.G. Searle, Cambridge Antiquarian Society Publications, 34 (1902), pp. 5–186; Russell, *British Medieval Population*, p. 191. But now see J. Hatcher, 'Mortality in the Fifteenth Century: Some New Evidence', *Economic History Review*, second series, 39 (1986), pp. 19–38.

than its modern equivalent: in the 1420s the news that 'oon of the monkes of youre convent was not longe ago proued and founden gylty of the horrible synne of sodomye' was sufficient to persuade no less a personage than the duke of Bedford to write to Prior Wessington warning him of the ensuing 'disclaundre and dishonur of your said convent'.[61] It is precisely because the moral tone of the monastic life at Durham was a matter of public interest that the impression of respectability conveyed to the world at large by the monks of St Cuthbert deserves to be taken at its face value. Needless to say, there is evidence of the occasional sexual scandal and act of violence within the fifteenth-century community. At least three monks, Thomas Nesbitt, Richard Blackburn and John Birtley, were suspected of incontinence with the wives and widows of Durham burgesses between 1434 and 1450.[62] Nor, as we have seen, was the monastery without its inevitable quota of the idle, the trouble-makers and the alienated. It is rather more remarkable that the prior and chapter of Durham were generally successful in convincing the outside world of their moral rectitude throughout so long a period. 'There was never woman in the abbey further than the church, nor did the monks come within the town':[63] few English Benedictine monasteries on the eve of the Dissolution received so handsome if prosaic a tribute.

A more valuable assessment of the quality of the religious life in fifteenth-century Durham is bound to be that provided by the chapter for its own rather than external consumption. By their very nature the ideal monastic virtues of *stabilitas, obedientia* and *humilitas* were unlikely to leave much written record to posterity. Nevertheless a collection of interesting chapter ordinances and diffinitions among the existing archives throws considerable light on the way in which the convent saw its own activities. At regular intervals throughout the fifteenth century, committees of Durham monks were asked to review the state of the priory's administration and welfare: their proposals or diffinitions were then presented to the whole community, normally including the heads of the dependent cells, at the annual or general chapter held on the first Monday after Ascension Day.[64] For obvious reasons such diffinitions, often the basis of later chapter ordinances, usually reflect the minor irritations and annoyances of life in the cloister. Like the members of most corporate bodies at most times, the

---

[61] DCD, Locellus XXV, no. 115.

[62] Each of these monks established his innocence by the oaths of twelve compurgators chosen from among his senior colleagues. It is therefore conceivable that they were the victims of slander and false witness, even in the case of Richard Blackburn where a certain Robert White alleged 'quod sepius vidi oculis meis ipsos aduicem in uno lecto pernoctantes et, vt michi visum erat, carnaliter et incontinenter agentes' (DCD, Reg. III, fo. 250; cf. Reg. III, fo. 173; Reg. Parv. III, fos. 40–1).

[63] *Letters and Papers, Henry VIII* (1862–1932), x, pp. 64–5.

[64] For the important role of this *capitulum generale* at late medieval Durham, see below, p. 78, and Dobson, *Durham Priory*, pp. 306–7.

monks of Durham produced a stream of adverse comment on the quality of their food and clothing, the lack of hot water for washing purposes and the dilapidation of their buildings. To judge by these diffinitions, the three features of the monastic life which perturbed them most of all were the negligence and dishonesty of their servants, the thieving and vandalism of young boys within the priory precincts, and the inadequacy of the arrangements made for their own welfare in the event of sickness or old age. On the other hand, it is important to stress that the diffinitors did not neglect to criticise the conduct of the divine offices in the cathedral church. The precise forms of the liturgy, the niceties of processional arrangements within the church as well as the authority of the monastic precentor and succentor were the subject of scrupulous attention.[65] In all these cases the prior and chapter professed a determination that 'religious observance should be observed nowadays as it was in earlier times'. We can never know for certain how successful the monks were in achieving this aim; but that they were conscious of the need to achieve it there can be no doubt.

A very similar impression may be derived from the records of the visitations of Durham cathedral priory during the course of the later middle ages. As is now well known, such sources are by no means easy to interpret; to David Knowles it was matter of some 'regret that it should be necessary to make any use at all of such intimate documents'.[66] Fortunately or not, the visitation documents which survive from fifteenth-century Durham are rarely intimate. Although the prior and convent were subject to a regular triennial visitation by a prelate of the Benedictine Order, these occasions are hardly likely to have been marked by a rigorous scrutiny of monastic life on the Durham peninsula.[67] Much better documented, and much more feared by the chapter itself, was a visitation by their immediate spiritual lord, the bishop of Durham. As elsewhere in England, episcopal visitations of the community of St Cuthbert became progressively less frequent during the course of the later middle ages. There is record of only nine visitations of the convent during the century between the provision of Bishop Richard of Bury (1333) and the death of Bishop Thomas Langley (1437), an average of less than one every decade; and by the late fifteenth century few bishops of Durham can be shown to have expressed any interest in visiting their cathedral church at all.[68] All the more valuable

[65] See DCD, Locellus XXVII, nos 14, 15, 29, 34; Misc. Charters, nos 2472, 2644; Jesus College, Cambridge, MS 41, fos 169v–170 (among the most informative of the late medieval Durham chapter diffinitions and ordinances).

[66] Knowles, *Religious Orders*, i, p. 84.

[67] Dobson, *Durham Priory*, pp. 247–8. For the only important exception, of particular interest because it revealed the appalling state of the old monastic dormitory towards the end of the fourteenth century, see the *comperta* produced by two monks of St Mary's abbey, York (Misc. Charters, no. 5634; *Chapters of the Black Monks*, ed. Pantin, iii, pp. 83–4).

[68] To the references cited in Dobson, *Durham Priory*, p. 231, may be added Bishop Lawrence Booth's proposal to visit the prior and chapter on 10 December 1464 (DCD, Locellus XXVII, no. 6; 2. 7. Pont., nos 15, 16).

are the proceedings at the visitation of the convent carried out by Bishop Robert Neville in July 1442, for these provide us with the only systematic attempt to estimate the state of religious discipline at Durham Cathedral Priory during the last century of its existence. This is not the occasion to discuss the long and controversial course of Bishop Neville's primary visitation in the detail it deserves. But of the many documents produced by both bishop and prior at the time, two seem to be of sufficiently general interest to deserve publication in translation as an appendix to this essay.[69]

According to the terminology usually employed in discussions of medieval visitations of religious houses, the forty-six *articuli de et super detectis* printed below can be described as the bishop's *comperta*, his summary of the criticisms and grievances expressed by individual Durham monks under interrogation in the chapter house. It was on his instruction (of 17 September 1442) that a panel of seven monks produced their detailed replies to each of the forty-six articles: the resulting 'Deliberacio, Auisamentum et Consilium' is also printed below. Only after he had considered these replies did Bishop Neville proceed to issue his injunctions: these were addressed to Prior Wessington from Bishop Auckland on 4 November 1442.[70] Bishop Neville's injunctions closed with the familiar instruction that no monk, 'of whatsoever status or condition', should be molested by his brethren because of anything he had revealed under private interrogation. Nor does it seem likely that the results of the bishop's visitation were indeed seriously distorted by a conspiracy of silence on the part of the Durham community. Of course not every member of the chapter is likely to have told the whole truth, especially in the presence of one of their own number, William Ebchester, chosen by the bishop as his monastic assessor.[71] On the other hand it would be unduly sceptical to reject either the bishop's *comperta* or the monks' replies as seriously tainted evidence. The reader of the appendix to this essay must be left to draw his or her own conclusions as to the state of *sancta religio* at mid fifteenth-century Durham. On the evidence of this visitation, Bishop Neville himself was prepared to testify that he had found the monks of Durham to be 'men of worthy lives, chaste and sober, suffering neither the shame nor the chains of fleshly faults'.[72] In a decade when visitations by Bishop William Alnwick of Lincoln revealed that 'religio quasi perit' at

[69] See below, pp. 72–82. For a fuller discussion of these documents and the 1442 visitation, see Dobson, *Durham Priory*, pp. 232–8.

[70] A paper copy of these injunctions, slightly damaged by damp, survives as Misc. Charters, no. 2658; it is not included in the Appendix below, partly because of its length, partly because it was closely modelled on the 'Deliberacio, Auisamentum et Consilium' translated below.

[71] DCD, 2.7. Pont., no. 8.

[72] DCD, 2.7. Pont., no. 9 (Bishop Neville's letters testimonial of 18 April 1444).

several large English Benedictine monasteries, notably Bardney, Eynsham and Peterborough, this is not a compliment to be altogether discounted.[73]

Nevertheless the prevailing impression left to posterity by the Durham visitation records of 1442 is of a convent whose well-being depended absolutely on the efficiency and honesty of its monastic officials. Like the great bulk of the fifteenth-century records still extant in the Prior's Kitchen, the *comperta* compiled by Bishop Neville and his clerks reveal the so-called 'obedientiary system' in full spate: the fortunes of the house lay in the hands of the *officiarii*. To the criticism that the late medieval community of St Cuthbert lacked strong central direction, that its religious superior played a much less crucial and energising role than that of the abbot as envisaged in the Benedictine Rule, there can be no real answer. In the conduct of the monastery's external affairs, the prior's personality and influence were often all-important, but within the cloister his most important duty now consisted of the appointment of his monks to the appropriate obedience or the appropriate cell.[74] Monastic life in late medieval England was *de facto* an exercise in the effective delegation of authority within a human community; as such, it was clearly not without its dangers, but whether these were more or less than those arising from the rule of an all-powerful abbot will always remain an open question. Much closer to the heart of the monastic problem in the fifteenth century is the perennial criticism that such delegation of function and authority forced the monk himself to emulate the example of Martha rather than Mary, to abandon the word of God in order to save tables. So universal is that allegation that this brief account of the monks of late medieval Durham must inevitably conclude by a review of some of the questions it raises.

Throughout the fifteenth century there were at least twenty-five separate monastic offices at Durham, almost always held by different individuals, to be filled by the forty or so members of the community resident in the mother house. In addition to those eleven obedientiaries required to produce annual accounts and who enjoyed considerable financial independence by virtue of their offices (the almoner, bursar, cellarer,

[73] *Visitations of Religious Houses in the Diocese of Lincoln, 1420–49*, ed. A.H. Thompson, Lincoln Record Society, 7, 14, 21 (1914–29), i, pp. 1–4, 54–63; ii, pp. 9–31; iii, pp. 269–302. Cf. A.H. Thompson, *The English Clergy and their Organization in the Later Middle Ages* (Oxford, 1947), pp. 171–81.

[74] Even in this important sphere, the prior of Durham's discretion was not complete: according to conventual practice in the 1440s, 'it is to be noted that among the other liberties conferred on the prior is the one that he may appoint and remove monastic officials freely; however, by the ancient practice of the monastery, priors of Coldingham and Stamford are to be presented to the ordinary; and the sacrist, hostillar, almoner and chamberlain are to be appointed and removed by the prior and chapter in chapter; and the commoner is to be appointed and removed by the subprior and chapter without the consent of the prior' (DCD, Locellus XXI, no. 20, ii).

chamberlain, commoner, feretrar, granator, hostillar, master of the infirmary, sacrist and terrar), there were eight monastic officials with responsibility for discipline in church and cloister, namely the subprior, third prior, two deans of the order, master of the Galilee Chapel, precentor, succentor and refectorer. To this list must be added the offices of the chancellor (a monk who acted as librarian as well as general secretary of the house), the two prior's chaplains and the official of the prior's archidiaconal jurisdiction as well as a number of deputy officials, of whom the subsacrist and subferetrar have left most trace in the surviving records.[75] It is evident that after his novitiate every Durham monk of reasonably sound health and mind could count on holding some office or other for the bulk of his religious life. As readers of Professor S.L. Greenslade's invaluable card-index of Durham monks (now deposited with the Department of Palaeography and Diplomatic at the Prior's Kitchen) are well aware, the biographies of members of St Cuthbert's community can only be written in terms of their administrative duties. But whether appointment to these offices positively precluded their holders from adequate attendance at the daily performance of the *Opus Dei* in the cathedral choir is a different and difficult matter. To the complaint made at Bishop Neville's visitation in 1442 'quod xvi officiarii excusantur a matutinis racione officiariorum', Prior Wessington and the senior monks replied that only six monks had normally been excused.[76] Once again we are confronted with evidence which can be made to point in two different directions. Whatever one's conclusions, it would be as well to remember that the patterns of religious worship within the church of Durham were themselves subject to the same centrifugal pressures as those which had transformed life in the adjoining cloister: the celebration of innumerable private masses at the many altars within the cathedral was at times as essential a part of religious routines at fifteenth-century Durham as communal worship in the choir.

The same sort of argument seems to apply to the equally controversial subject of 'learning in the cloister' towards the end of the middle ages. The uniquely interesting evidence of fifteenth-century inscriptions and annotations to Durham's unparalleled collection of library manuscripts still awaits detailed analysis. For obvious reasons it is always easier to prove that books are written than that they are read. Moreover, like all great institutional libraries, that of the late medieval Durham monks sometimes had the effect of fossilising the intellectual tastes of generations previous to their own. Nevertheless there is evidence not only that a large

---

[75] The 'obedientiary system' at fifteenth-century Durham therefore reveals an elaboration of, rather than a serious departure from, the patterns created during the course of the thirteenth century. For a list of the 'nineteen major offices in the mother house' in the 1310s, see J. Scammell, 'Some Aspects of Medieval English Monastic Government: The Case of Geoffrey Burdon, Prior of Durham (1313–21)' *Revue Bénédictine*, 68 (1958), p. 234.

[76] See Appendix, below pp. 75, 82.

group of monks did consult the contents of their library but also that several members of the community acquired their own small collections of books for their personal use.[77] All allowances made for the dangers of hazarding a generalisation in this mysterious field, there are indications that as a group the monks of fifteenth-century Durham were more widely read than either their predecessors or even than many of their immediate post-Reformation successors. In a now famous phrase, Richard Kidderminster, abbot of Winchcombe in the early sixteenth century, commented on the way in which his own monastic cloister 'had all the appearance of a young university, though on a minute scale'.[78] Without wishing to make exalted claims for learning at late medieval Durham, it is only fair to point out that this was an aim which several Durham monks, under heavy Oxford influence, may have tried to anticipate in the previous century. Nor, despite a common prejudice to the contrary, was scholarship necessarily an alternative to sanctity. The devotional literature produced at fifteenth-century Durham still awaits its historian; but it is already evident that the period between the meditations of the late fourteenth-century 'Monk of Farne' and the elaborate poetic eulogy of St Cuthbert presented to Prior Thomas Castell in 1502 was not completely devoid of monks whose intellect and talents were directed towards fulfilling the spiritual as well as the material purposes of their community.[79]

This is not to deny that in the last resort the pursuit of the monastic ideal at late medieval Durham, as in most religious houses at most times, proved a comparative failure. On balance, however, this failure was always understandable and sometimes honourable. By a final irony it seems probable that the very influences which helped to preserve an acceptable standard of monastic life at fifteenth-century Durham were exactly those for which the monks have so often been censured. The very lack of uniformity and the great variety of activities conducted within this precinct were in many ways as much a source of strength as of weakness: they provided the individual monk with the liberation that comes to most human beings when able to choose between a wide range of different sorts of employment. Even the considerable administrative obligations of the Durham monks of the later middle ages hardly deserve their

[77] A preliminary, and very provisional, survey of the evidence for the intellectual activities of early fifteenth-century Durham monks may be found in Dobson, *Durham Priory*, pp. 360–86; and now see, A.J. Piper, 'The Libraries of the Monks of Durham', in *Medieval Scribes, Manuscripts and Libraries*, ed. M.B. Parkes and A.G. Watson (London, 1978), pp. 213–49.

[78] Knowles, *Religious Orders*, iii, p. 92.

[79] For the monk of Farne's own education at Oxford, see *The Monk of Farne: The Meditations of a Fourteenth-Century Monk*, ed. H. Farmer (London, 1961), pp. 2, 134: he was nearly drowned when 'walking carelessly on a plank bridging the river Cherwell'. A brief survey of late medieval devotional manuscripts from Durham may be found in W.A. Pantin, 'English Monks and the Suppression of the Monasteries', *Dublin Review*, 201 (1937), pp. 250–70; and see C. Eyre, *The History of Saint Cuthbert* (London 1858), pp. 283–7.

usual fate of casual dismissal out of hand. Like 'administration', that still ambiguous word, in the case of the modern university teacher, such obligations filled an important and not always deplorable role in the social life of the corporation. Given the peculiar stresses inherent in the life of any closed community, the opportunity to study, to supervise others and to take on important official responsibility probably had a salutary effect on most Durham monks of the period. In one of those unexpected analogies for which he is justifiably famous, Professor Southern once compared the career of a late medieval English Benedictine (William Chart of Christ Church, Canterbury) with that of William Greenwell, one of the first graduates of Durham University and minor canon of the cathedral here from 1854 until 1907.[80] Perhaps the most illuminating feature of this comparison is one which Professor Southern himself chose not to emphasise. Canon Greenwell is now best remembered for the multiplicity of his interests, ranging from his capacity to invent a new form of trout-fly ('Greenwell's Glory') to his collection of many of the sculptured crosses now assembled in this dormitory. A similar sense of heightened individuality, although it could inevitably only take much less idiosyncratic forms, may provide the most important key to monastic life at fifteenth-century Durham. As we have seen, the magnificent buildings around us are themselves among the best of all tributes to the way in which the community's environment was deliberately transformed to create smaller social and administrative units within the great monastic complex. Not least perhaps is that true in this dormitory itself – a metaphorical house of God in which 500 years ago there were many individual mansions.

[80] R.W. Southern, *Western Society and the Church in the Middle Ages* (Harmondsworth, 1970), pp. 239–40.

Appendix

The Durham Visitation of 1442:
Select Documents in Translation

A

'Articuli de et super detectis' *at the visitation of Durham Cathedral Priory by Bishop Robert Neville, 9 July 1442 (1.9 Pont., no. 3)*[81]

The articles concerning the *detecta* on the ordinary visitation of the most reverend father and lord in Christ, Lord Robert, by the grace of God bishop of Durham, actually carried out in the chapter-house of his cathedral church aforesaid on the ninth day of the month of June, in the year of Our Lord 1441 and the fifth year of his translation[82], are extracted and written below in indentured form.

1[83] Firstly, it is detected that the office of the bursary, once united, is now divided into three, and there are three monks who occupy that office; each of these, having a substitute, receives as much for his labour as the one man who once used to occupy the office when it was whole and entire, to the great burden of the house and the reduction of divine worship. There have been frequent complaints concerning this article.[84]

2 Item, that there are many dogs in the house who often enter and befoul the choir, refectory and other places because of the negligence of those who have the custody and rule of such places.

3 Item, that once upon a time the monks used to eat broth (*potagia*) made with meat on Wednesdays; but now they do not, wherefore they are less strong to serve God.

4 Item, that Adam Ponne and Thomas Pomfret, brothers and monks of the said house, having requested no licence to leave the house, departed as apostates,

---

[81] A parchment roll of two membranes, indented at the top and written on only one side. Size: 11 by 34 inches. Bears a later endorsement, 'Indentura super articulis compertis in visitacione ordinaria domini Dunelmensis episcopi: Prima 9e. Pont. C.1'.

[82] A mistake for 9 July 1442 (see below, p. 77). The fifth year of Bishop Neville's pontificate ran from January 1442 to January 1443.

[83] The numbering of the forty-six separate paragraphs does not occur in the original document.

[84] The financial responsibilities of the bursar's office at Durham (which received well over two-thirds of the total money income of the convent) were divided approximately equally between the monastic cellarer, granator and bursar from August 1438 until November 1445. For a detailed discussion of this division's controversial implications, see especially DCD, Locellus XXI, no. 20 (a file of seven documents on the issue) and the comments in Dobson, *Durham Priory*, pp. 285–90.

the said Adam about forty years ago and the said Thomas about sixteen years ago. Brother John Marley similarly apostatised. Nor was much diligence displayed in recovering these monks. There have been frequent complaints concerning this article.

5 Item, that the church there is injured by enfeoffments granted by special letters of the lord bishop of Durham as well as by the chapter's confirmations of these, for example the fee given to Christopher Boynton and similar concessions. And as it is feared that others of the same type will take place in the future, let there be a remedy.

6 Item, less than a third of the monks eat each day in the refectory, as they ought to do according to the constitutions of the Rule.

7 Item, that no provision is made for a doctor or physician to relieve the infirm; concerning which there have been many complaints.

8 Item, that the (financial) state (*status*) of the house is not made clear or declared to the chapter each year as it ought; concerning which there have been many complaints.

9 Item, that the prior does not treat his fellow brethren gently and benignly; nor does he permit them to talk freely in the common discussions touching the state of the house which are held in chapter and other places.

10 Item, that the infirm are not adequately provided with victuals and other appropriate necessities, as was observed hitherto; concerning which there have often been complaints.

11 Item, that there are many conventicles, conversations and inordinate drinking-sessions in the dormitory and other places, and especially after compline.

12 Item, that the food and drink provided for the convent do not reach the proper standards of integrity and wholesomeness which the state of the house demands and its resources permit.

13 Item, that religious worship is not observed in these present days as in earlier times.

14 Item, that the subprior is excessively negligent, worldly and partial in the matter of corrections and all other things, wherefore discontent is generated in the convent; concerning which there have been very many complaints.

15 Item, that the goods of the monastery have lost a great deal of their value, as in the case of tenements, manors, mills, the choirs of appropriated churches and various other places, which are wasted and not repaired. Therefore let a suitable remedy be provided.

16 Item, that the priors of Holy Island and Lytham hold money, animals and other goods as their private property; and their priories are greatly in debt, especially the priory of Holy Island.[85]

---

[85] The priors of Holy Island and Lytham in July 1442 were Henry Helay and William Partrike respectively, both unruly members of the community (see above, p. 53). In an angry letter written to Prior Wessington from Lytham on 4 October 1442 (DCD, Locellus IX, no. 18; Lytham, Miscellanea, no. 5), Partrike denied these charges and attributed them to the malice of his brethren at Durham.

17 Item, that the right of having a boat (*cimbam*) and of ferrying across the water of the Wear at Sunderland is withdrawn by the servants of the lord bishop against old custom.

18 Item, that silence in the choir, cloister, dormitory and other places is observed in no way at all, the reason being that the accustomed correction on this matter is withdrawn; concerning which there have been many complaints.

19 Item, that the deans of the church are completely negligent in their offices, because they do not reveal the shortcomings of the monks to the prior and subprior as they ought to do.

20 Item, that Brother Thomas Nesebett, chamberlain, withdraws the kerchiefs (*flameolas*), drawers, woollens (*stamyns*) and other adornments as well as the oblations due to the convent; and what he gives and pays he does so in a malicious spirit and with dishonest and unseemly words; he not only makes his gifts seldom but provides disgraceful and inadequate material: concerning which article there are twenty and more complaints. And when accusations are laid before the lord prior on this matter, the latter does not take steps to correct it, but says to the monks that this chamberlain is a drunkard; and so nothing is done.

21 Item, that the foodstuffs served to the convent in the refectory are of an inadequate standard, especially because of the failings of the kitcheners and cooks; thus fish and other foods are raw and insipid while broths are thin and lacking in substance. For these reasons the monks are often very reluctant to enter the refectory.

22 Item, that the subprior is obliged by his office to provide the infirm and sick with food suitable for them, but he does not do this.

23 Item, that on account of the subprior's negligence the monks do not take care to celebrate masses every day as they are obliged to do, especially in the case of the masses of the Holy Spirit, of Saint Mary and of the Cemetery.

24 Item, that because of the subprior's failings the novices and other monks do not conduct their singing, reading and study in the cloister at suitable times, as they are obliged to do.

25 Item, it is petitioned that the construction of new buildings should be postponed until old and necessary buildings which have become ruined and derelict shall be duly repaired.

26 Item, that while the office of the bursary is divided (as mentioned above) no repairs nor any provision for grain and stock are being made, to the great prejudice and inevitable cost of the house.

27 Item, that the bakehouse as well as the brewhouse of the convent, together with six mills belonging to the monastery and many other buildings, are in decay and threatened by serious ruin.

28 Item, that lords William Bawes, William Elmeden, knights, John Hedworth and Thomas Claxton detain free farms and other goods owed to various offices; nor is diligence being displayed to recover these or gain satisfaction for them. William Elmeden himself detains 20 shillings owed to the commoner each year.

29 Item, that the lord prior gives an excessive number of gifts to minstrels (*histrionibus*), mimes and fools.

30 Item, that the resources of the house and its (financial) state are in decline but its burdens in commons, liveries and other things have increased, wherefore the house is in debt.

31 Item, that the cantors sing lay and tripartite songs in the chapter house, to the great inconvenience of those sitting in the cloister.

32 Item, that the officers are so burdened with pensions that they cannot do what pertains to their offices.

33 Item, that twenty-eight almsmen used to reside in the infirmary, of whom only four now reside where all are obliged to reside; and those four receive as much in coal and other necessities as the twenty-eight used to receive.[86]

34 Item, that from the foundation of the said infirmary there was a chaplain there, who is now withdrawn because of a payment of money made to the lord prior, a payment to which he is not entitled.

35 Item, that each monk should receive at least 40 shillings a year in money; but the monks do not receive satisfaction because of the failings of the officers.

36 Item, that Thomas Claxton detains, as mentioned above, 18 shillings which he owes in virtue of a free farm.

37 Item, that the almoner withholds the payments he should make to the poor as well as other obligations incumbent upon him by reason of his office.

38 Item, that there is not a common chest to receive the surplus of resources in a fertile year in order that the house may be relieved in a dear year by the keeping of surpluses of this sort.

39 Item, that when food and drink are sound and fresh they are served less well than they ought to the monks engaged in divine services by day and night; therefore a remedy should be provided.

40 Item, that the care of the infirm by the officers is undertaken badly except in cases where worldly affection is involved.

41 Item, that sixteen officers are excused from matins by reason of their offices, whereas only one, namely the terrar, should be excused – to the reduction of divine worship.

42 Item, that the servants (*familiares*) of the house keep dogs on the orders of the monks, which results in the pretext that those monks have no responsibility at all in this matter.

43 Item, that many are ordained priests in their twenty-second year, by means of a dispensation as it is said.

44 Item, that the fees and other necessities of the convent are not well and completely paid, because whereas they used to be paid at five terms in the year,

---

[86] The reference here is to the *infirmaria extra portam* (to be distinguished from both the monastic infirmary within the precinct and the *Domus Dei*, also in the Durham Bailey) which had twenty-eight members until the Dissolution; a large number certainly were allowed to reside outside its walls: DCD, almoner, 1412–16, 1428–29; *Valor Ecclesiasticus* (Record Commission, 1810–34), v, p. 303; DCD, Reg. Parv. II, fos 84, 97, 172, 193.

they are now paid at three or four terms; this leads to great discontent and to the withholding of a large part of the portion (? of the individual monks).

45 Item, that after compline is ended many monks pass into the garden of the abbey and other places, and there they play and occupy themselves with extravagances. And such things also happen in the infirmary and other places.

46 Item, that after compline and before prime laymen enter the dormitory and there hold drinking-sessions against the old custom.

B

Replies by the prior and a committee of monks of Durham to the 1442 *visitation* 'Articuli' *of Bishop Robert Neville* (1. 8. Pont., no. 2)[87]

The deliberation, advice and counsel of the prior, subprior and other monks deputed on the chapter's behalf, concerning the *comperta* and *detecta* arising from the visitation executed by the most reverend father and lord in Christ, Lord Robert, by the grace of God bishop of Durham, in the chapter house of the cathedral church of Durham on the ninth day of July in the year of Our Lord 1442; which *comperta* and *detecta* were transmitted to the said prior, subprior and monks by the said most reverend father in the form of indentured articles.

To the first article, that the office of the bursary, once united, is now divided into three, it seems to us – having seen and understood the reasons (*racionibus*) of the lord prior on the division of the bursary[88] – that the said office should remain divided until the next annual chapter because of the arrangements already made for next year by the officers in the said three offices. In which chapter there will be ordained by the sound counsel and advice of the lord prior and the diffinitors of the chapter what shall be most useful and expedient to the house in this matter.

To the 2nd article, that there are many dogs in the house, etc., let it be enjoined on all and everyone, under the penalties laid down in the constitutions of the Order, that they shall keep no dogs within the bounds of the monastery either on their own account or through another person; and also that the esquires, varlets and boys (*armigeri, valecti et garciones*) of the prior and all others, both servants and scholars of the abbey, shall likewise remove their dogs outside the monastery under penalty of their expulsion from their offices, because they are responsible for the reduction and destruction of the alms of the house.

To the 3rd article, that once upon a time the monks used to eat broth on Wednesdays, etc., they agree that this article should be reformed according to the ancient practice.

To the 4th article, concerning apostates, etc., they say that Adam Ponne, alias Durham, apostatised long before the time of the present prior; and that Thomas Pomfraite and John Marley were incorrigible, as is well known to the seniors of the convent who were acquainted with their behaviour. Therefore according to the Rule of St Benedict and the provincial constitutions of the order, they could and ought to have been expelled. However they did depart secretly, breaking the bonds of their custody; but the prior was advised by his senior brethren that to avoid worse evils he should not labour to secure their return.[89]

To the 5th article, that the church is injured by enfeoffments, etc., they will and agree that no manner of confirmations shall be made of the lord of Durham's grants, except of offices and other things which cannot entail damage and serious

---

[87] A parchment roll of one membrane, written on both sides. Size: 11 by 33 inches. The roll is indented by a long cut down the left-hand side.

[88] Various drafts and copies of Prior Wessington's *raciones et euidencie*, all arguing the case for a divided rather than united bursary, survive as DCD, Locellus, XXI, no. 20.

[89] For references in the Durham records to these three apostates, see Dobson, *Durham Priory*, pp. 75–6. They were never recaptured.

hardship to the church and to the successors of the said lord of Durham; and except also grants of the sort which can be found in the register of the prior and chapter of Durham to have been traditionally confirmed, and these only with the wages and fees specified in those times.

To the 6th article, that a third of the monks do not eat in the refectory etc., it is ordained that henceforward a third part of the convent actually resident in the house shall eat in the refectory on both days of fish and of meat, not including the doctors, the decrepit and others who have been legitimately pardoned the burdens of choir and cloister by the prior and chapter.

To the 7th article, that no provision is made for a doctor or physician, etc., they wish that a diligent search shall be made for an honest man before Easter, a man who is a barber and surgeon and who knows how to lance and let blood.

To the 8th article, that the (financial) state of the house is not clear or declared, they say that in accordance with apostolic, legatine and provincial constitutions a general chapter is held each year at which all officers, both internal and external, have to render their accounts to auditors deputed by the chapter. Nor has this practice been otherwise in the monastery of Durham for fifty years and more.

To the 9th article, that the prior does not treat his fellow brethren gently and benignly, etc., they say that the prior does treat his brethren sufficiently gently and requires the votes (*vota*) of all on major business and then proceeds accordingly.

To the 10th article, that the infirm are inadequately provided with food and other necessities, they all wish this article to be amended and the infirm to be provided with food and other suitable necessities in so far as the resources of the house allow; and that each day the cellarer or his deputy should visit the infirm and provide to each according to the quality of his need.

To the 11th article, that there are many conventicles and feastings in the dormitory, etc., if such should be arranged – to the complete ignorance of the custodians of the order – henceforward let them be forbidden under the threat of a great penalty on those who plan such things. As for drinking, let there be none of this at all in the dormitory unless under the urgent necessity of a serious illness; and as for wanderings after compline, on this subject there is a sufficiently strict statute of the order which they wish to be observed henceforward.[90]

To the 12th article, that food and drink are not duly served to the convent, etc., they wish that the cellarer should be enjoined on his conscience that, whenever he can, he should have good broth made for the convent and cause meat and fish to be well cooked and roasted; and he should take particular care that the foodstuffs ordained for the refectory are prepared better and more soundly in the future.

To the 13th article, that religious worship is not observed, etc., they wish that the subprior, third prior and deans of the order should be strictly enjoined to take more care and supervise the reform of this article.

To the 14th article, that the subprior is excessively negligent in his corrections and other things, etc., they wish the subprior to be enjoined to correct the excesses of the culprits discreetly according to the quality of their offences, without exception of persons; and that he should cause regular observances to be firmly maintained and those who transgress to be punished according to the nature of their guilt.

---

[90] See *Chapters of the Black Monks*, ed. Pantin, ii, pp. 33–4, 71, 86, 197.

To the 15th article, that the goods of the monastery have lost a great deal of their value, as in the case of tenements, manors, etc., they say that on account of exceptional pestilences in which tenants have died many tenements lie unoccupied. Moreover lands from which the prior and convent have the tithes of corn now lie at pasture to such an extent that the receipts of churches belonging to the monastery have lost 1,000 marks and more in value within a hundred years.[91] As regards the repairs which have not been made, they say that before its division the office of the bursary was so indebted that for the last four years there have been few repairs, because the sums of money by which such repairs should have been financed were used to pay debts and buy grain at a time of great dearth (*caristia*); but once these payments have ceased, the repairs can be more easily made, for which purpose a large quantity of timber is delivered to the officers and their tenants this year. And so that the repairs can be more easily carried out, it is ordained that excessive expenses and all superfluities on the part of any persons or officers should be prevented.

To the 16th article, that the priors of Holy Island and of Lytham hold money and animals, etc., they wish that the prior of Holy Island should render his account for the two last years so that the reason why his priory is so indebted should be known; in any case, the same prior swore to the lord prior that he did not hold any animals except those pertaining to his priory. As for the prior of Lytham, it is well known to us by means of his account and inventory (*ratiocinium*) that his priory stands in a fit state.

To the 17th article, that the right of having a boat, etc., they say that the lord prior has often laboured, before both the lord of Durham and his council, to recover the passage of the said boat, and so he proposes to labour in the future.[92]

To the 18th article, that silence in the choir, cloister and other places is observed in no way at all, etc., they wish this article to be amended; and the subprior and custodians of the order to be strictly enjoined to apply themselves assiduously to its observance in the said places without exception of persons. And as for the withdrawing of the accustomed correction, they wish that this correction should be maintained as has been the practice hitherto.

To the 19th article, that the deans of the church are completely negligent, etc., the prior enjoins them to make their denunciations of faults without exception of persons; and if they do not take care to do this, they shall then be removed by the prior before Christmas and more suitable men chosen in their places.

To the 20th article, concerning brother Thomas Nessbytt, they wish that he should be enjoined to distribute necessities to the brethren as their need requires, without murmur and without delay, in a benevolent spirit and with honest words; and he is to pay oblations to his brethren impartially at the accustomed terms, as the resources of his office allow. And let him be forbidden to have inadequate

---

[91] According to a chronological table composed in the monastery during Wessington's priorate, the total 'Recepta de Ecclesiis' declined from £1466 16s. 4d. per annum in 1293 to £616 8s. 0d. in 1348 and £353 0s. 6d. in 1436, DCD, Reg. II, fos 356v–7; *Historiae Dunelmensis scriptores tres*, pp. ccxlviii–cclii.

[92] The results of Prior Wessington's labours on this issue survive in his 'Euidencie prioris Dunelmensis pro passagio inter Wermouth Monachorum et Sunderland' of 1437: see Locellus II, no. 6 and the inferior version printed in *Inventories and Account Rolls of Jarrow and Monk-Wearmouth*, pp. 247–9.

drawers and woollens (*stamina et braccas*) made from other old ones, but let the latter be applied to alms as was hitherto the custom. And as for the last part of this article, the said prior replies that he often corrected him both publicly and privately.[93]

To the 21st article, that foodstuffs are not duly served to the convent, etc., the reply is as in the 12th article above.

To the 22nd article, that the subprior is obliged by his office to provide the sick, etc., they say that he provides recreations for the sick very often; however, let him be enjoined to visit them conscientiously and impartially to enquire how they are served by the kitchener; and if he finds any faults, he should denounce them to the prior for correction.

To the 23rd article, that the monks do not take care to celebrate every day, they wish the subprior to be enjoined to search diligently for those who celebrate and those who do not, especially in the case of the mass of the Cemetery, because according to the custom of the church it is his duty to make this sort of scrutiny. And as for the masses of the Holy Spirit and of Saint Mary, let the precentor or succentor see who celebrate at the proper hours when they are intabled, and let them notify any delinquents to the president in chapter.[94]

To the 24th article, that the novices and other monks do not conduct their singing and reading, etc., they say that the novices are occupied assiduously and regularly enough. But as for the claustral monks, let custodians of the order, and especially the subprior, be strictly enjoined to apply themselves to the reformation of this article in all its points and as is expedient.

To the 25th article, namely that it is petitioned that the construction of new buildings should be postponed, let it be done as is petitioned.

To the 26th article, that the office of the bursary is divided as above, no provision, etc., the reply is as in the 15th article above.

To the 27th article, that the bakehouse as well as the brewhouse, etc., the reply is as in the 15th article above.

To the 28th article, that lord William Bowes and William Elmeden, etc., they say that the lord prior and William Bowes have placed themselves in arbitration until a fixed date, and so the issue between them is pending under hope of concord; and as for the rent detained by William Elmeden knight, the lord prior took out a writ against him, but through the mediation of friends they have come to a concord; but in the cases of John Hedworth and Thomas Claxton, they wish them to be impleaded at a suitable time.[95]

---

[93] Thomas Nesbitt, who had held the chamberlain's office since May 1439, was replaced by Richard Blackburn in November 1442 (DCD, Misc. Charters, no. 1070; Chamberlain, 1440–43).

[94] The *tabulacio* or 'intablyng' of monks to celebrate masses at the various altars within the church was a regular feature of the late medieval religious life in any large monastery.

[95] All four of these disputes with members of the local Durham gentry have left considerable record in the monastic muniments of the 1430s and 1440s. The most serious was certainly that caused by Sir William Elmeden's intransigence on the issue of common pasture near his manor of Tursdale; litigation was still proceeding in 1444 (DCD, Misc. Charters, no. 7138; Dobson, *Durham Priory*, pp. 193–4).

To the 29th article, that the lord prior gives excessively to minstrels and fools, etc., they say that the lord prior does not give to fools nor does he admit them; but that he gives to the minstrels of the king, dukes, earls and barons and others as his predecessors have done; and from these sorts of gifts he would most cheerfully wish to be excused. They wish however that he should give moderately and not excessively.

To the 30th article, that the resources of the house, etc., the reply is as in the 15th article.

To the 31st article, that the cantors sing lay songs in the chapter house, they wish that the precentor shall henceforward be forbidden to allow such lay songs there.

To the 32nd article, that the officers are so burdened with pensions, etc., they wish that pensions should be paid, whenever necessary, as they used to be paid of old; but they do not wish those pensions imposed on officers during the last three years, in order to meet a great number of debts, to be paid in future until their offices are properly maintained in buildings and other things.[96]

To the 33rd article, that in the almonry there used to be twenty-eight almsmen resident, etc., they wish that all, both brothers and sisters, who have liveries there, without exception of persons, shall come to stay within the said infirmary before Easter on pain of the deduction of four shillings due to each of them at Christmas, with the exception of those who have letters allowing them to stay outside.

To the 34th article, that from the foundation of the infirmary there was a chaplain there who is withdrawn, etc., it is replied that there was a chaplain there until the pestilence; and that the almoner does not pay money to the lord prior or his deputies except the pension imposed upon his office. However they wish that a search shall be made for an honest priest who will be master of the schools (*magister scolarum*) and serve the chapels of the infirmary and the *Maudeleyns*, as was the practice hitherto.[97]

To the 35th article, that each monk should receive yearly, etc., they wish that the officers, according to the resources of their offices, should satisfy the brethren of their oblations at the accustomed terms and without murmur.

To the 36th article, that Thomas Claxton detains eighteen shillings, etc., the reply is as in the 28th article above.

To the 37th article, that the almoner withholds the payments to be made to the poor, the prior often enjoins him to satisfy the said poor at the accustomed and usual terms.

To the 38th article, that there is not a chest to receive the surplus of resources in a fertile year, it is replied that there is such a chest.

---

[96] The pensions mentioned here were the contributions levied on various Durham obedientiaries to meet the exceptionally heavy debts incurred by Thomas Lawson while monastic bursar between 1432 and 1438 (DCD, Locellus, XXI, no. 20).

[97] Like the *infirmaria extra portam*, the hospital of St Mary Magdalen (of which ruins still survive north of Gilesgate) was administered by the monastic almoner (almoner, 1418–19, 1428–29). The expenses sections of surviving almoners' account rolls reveal the salaries and sometimes the names of the chaplains who served as masters of the convent's almonry or grammar school in the fifteenth century.

To the 39th article, that when food and drink are sound they are served in smaller quantities than they should be, it is replied that the officers to whom these duties belong have promised amends.

To the 40th article, that the care of the infirm is undertaken badly by the officers, etc., it is replied as in articles 10 and 22 above.

To the 41st article, that sixteen officers are excused from matins, etc., it is replied that only six are excused, on every night except those of principal feasts; and it is ordained that none should be excused from matins except for those who have been accustomed to be excused by the use and custom of the monastery.

To the 42nd article, that servants keep dogs on the orders of the monks with the pretext, etc., the reply is as in article 2 above.

To the 43rd article, that many are ordained priests in their twenty-second year, etc., they say that the prior and the chapter have a bull of John XXIII to dispense monks to the priesthood in their twenty-second year.[98]

To the 44th article, that fees and other necessities of the convent are not well and completely paid, the reply is as in article 35 above.

To the 45th article, that many monks cross into the garden of the abbey, etc., they wish that henceforward there should be no such wanderings and drinkings, and that the hostillar and master of the infirmary should be enjoined to denounce culprits in this matter to the custodians of the order when they see these failings in their offices.

To the 46th article, that laymen enter the dormitory, etc., such drinking and banqueting sessions are not known to us, but if such have occurred let them be completely prohibited.

[98] (Anti-) Pope John XXIII's bull to this effect (of 28 July 1414) was indeed often used to dispense Durham monks to proceed to priest's orders in their twenty-second year: see DCD, Locellus III, no. 21; *Historiae Dunelmensis scriptores tres*, pp. ccxxv–ccxxvi; *CPL*, vi (1404–15), p. 469.

4

The Church of Durham and the Scottish Borders, 1378–88

Of all the savage battles fought on the Scottish Marches, perhaps none has been more successfully mytholgised than the confused and bloody contest at or near Otterburn 600 years ago. No wonder therefore that it elicited from the late Sir George Trevelyan, who as a boy took his first steps towards becoming the most popular historian of his age at Wallington only ten miles away, the most elegiac of all accounts of Border society and of Border warfare. 'In Northumberland alone, both heaven and earth are seen.' In many ways Trevelyan's account of 'The Middle Marches', published in 1914, still provides the most evocative introduction to the *genius loci* of Redesdale, to that Northumbrian scenery which allegedly 'throws over us, not a melancholy, but a meditative spell'.[1] In an essay generally too eloquent to be particularly informative, Trevelyan did however make the not unimportant point that the clash of arms at Otterburn must have been fought within the parish of Elsdon, 'the yet unviolated shrine of the tradition of the English Border'.[2]

It follows that Otterburn must have been a battle with especial significance for the bishop and monks of Durham Cathedral. Not only was Elsdon one of the only four medieval parishes in Northumberland known to have been dedicated to St Cuthbert; but Durham historical tradition maintained that the church of Elsdon was one of the first of the many stopping-places of St Cuthbert's body, his legendary corsaint, in the winter of 875, at the beginning of that erratic seven-year-long posthumous journey which took him from Lindisfarne to Chester-le-Street.[3] However, and as will be seen,

[1] G.M. Trevelyan, *Clio, a Muse, and Other Essays, Literary and Pedestrian* (London, 1914), pp. 153–6.

[2] Ibid., p. 180; R.N. Hadcock, 'A Map of Medieval Northumberland and Durham', *Archaeologia Aeliana*, 4th series, 16 (1939), p. 167; cf. (for nineteenth-century discoveries in Elsdon church of the skeletons of men probably killed at the battle of Otterburn), J. Hodgson, *History of Northumberland*, pt ii, vol. i (Newcastle upon Tyne, 1827), pp. 1, 82; G.N. Taylor, *The Story of Elsdon* (Newcastle upon Tyne, c. 1984), pp. 10–12.

[3] A. Hamilton Thompson, 'The MS List of Churches Dedicated to St Cuthbert, Attributed to Prior Wessyngton', *Transactions of the Architectural and Archaeological Society of Durham and Northumberland*, 7 (1935), p. 172.

St Cuthbert worked no miracles at Otterburn in 1388. Nor need we be surprised; for how could a saint so closely associated with his own pre-Norman, pre-Viking, pre-Border, undivided Northumbria be expected to choose between a Melrose and a Holy Island, a Percy and a Douglas? It has often been said that in the 300 years of more or less regulated armed violence unleashed on the Anglo-Scottish Border from the 1290s onwards there were no real victors; but it may well be argued that in 1388, as earlier and later, St Cuthbert, his bishops and his monks, with their claims to spiritual jurisdiction on both sides of the Tweed, were perhaps the greatest casualties of them all.[4]

Such at least seems to have been the church of Durham's dispiriting fate in the case of the Otterburn campaign itself. From a battle which became celebrated for its outstanding deeds of heroism on both sides, the leader of St Cuthbert's church, the bishop of Durham, managed to emerge with a reputation tarnished by being among neither the victors nor the vanquished. All allowances made for chronicle sources which can be tantalisingly cryptic or positively fanciful, it seems that the bishop's unexpectedly late arrival on the road to Otterburn cost Lord Henry Hotspur and the English troops, already engaged and indeed defeated in the battle, not only a clear-cut victory but the lives of many of their fellows. Admittedly, like nearly all the issues raised by the detailed chronology of events which followed the decision of the earls of Fife and Douglas to launch their major raid on northern England in the early summer of 1388, the precise movements of the bishop of Durham are by no means easy to ascertain.[5] Trevelyan himself, eager to think the romantic best of all his protagonists, discounts the possibility that the bishop of Durham was either negligent or otherwise culpable, and positively praises his efforts as he and his men 'marched hard over the moors and streams by the light of that moon which was glinting on the flash of swords at Otterburne' only to arrive after the English defeat and Hotspur's capture.[6]

---

[4] Particularly instructive in placing Durham's economic losses on and near the Border within a general context are E. Miller, *War in the North* (Hull, 1960); J.A. Tuck, 'War and Society in the Medieval North', *Northern History*, 21 (1985), pp. 33–52; A.J.L. Winchester, *Landscape and Society in Medieval Cumbria* (Edinburgh, 1987); A. Goodman, 'Religion and Warfare in the Anglo-Scottish Marches', in *Medieval Frontier Societies*, ed. R. Bartlett and A. MacKay (Oxford, 1989), pp. 245–66.

[5] No Durham episcopal register survives for the pontificates of either Bishop John Fordham or Bishop Walter Skirlaw: see D.M. Smith, *Guide to Bishops' Registers of England and Wales*, Royal Historical Society (London 1981), pp. 268–9. Nor do the chancery enrolments of these two bishops (PRO, Dur. 3/32, 33) throw any light on their movements in the summer of 1388.

[6] Trevelyan, *Clio*, p. 182. The role of the bishop of Durham in the Otterburn campaign is often simply omitted in standard accounts of the battle, e.g. J.H. Ramsay, *The Genesis of Lancaster, 1307–99*, (Oxford, 1913), pp. 259–61; A. Steel, *Richard II* (Cambridge, 1941), pp. 166–7; R. Nicholson, *Scotland: The Later Middle Ages* (Edinburgh, 1974), pp. 198–9.

All in all, it seems difficult to accept quite so charitable an interpretation of the non-appearance of the Durham troops at Otterburn. Admittedly the Scottish chroniclers' accounts of the campaign, perhaps understandably, make no mention of a bishop of Durham who only reached the battlefield after the Scots had begun to retreat northwards.[7] More surprisingly, neither Thomas Walsingham nor Henry Knighton, usually quite well-informed on Scottish affairs, provide a detailed description of Otterburn.[8] Much more valuable is the hostile account of the bishop of Durham's actions afforded by the *Westminster Chronicle*, all the more interesting because it seems to represent the official interpretation of the defeat accepted by Richard II and his court when the news reached Westminster in late August 1388. In the chronicle's own words,

> And so it was that 550 and more of our people perished by the edge of the sword because the bishop of Durham failed to come to their aid in the way previously concerted between himself and Sir Henry Percy. For the bishop was quite close at hand at the time, with a large armed force under his command; but owing to the darkening night, he declined to approach the battle field.

Instead he returned to Newcastle upon Tyne, where if he had waited for sunrise he would allegedly have been stoned by the bereaved wives of Tyneside husbands dead on the battlefield. In what looks like a well-informed attempt to account for the humiliating disaster, the Westminster chronicler went on to offer three different explanations for the defeat – Hotspur's *excessiva audacia*, the tactical mistakes made by the English troops who succeeded in killing each other rather than the Scots when laying about them in the darkness, and finally (yet again) the bishop of Durham's negligent and probably cowardly failure to appear at Otterburn quite soon enough.[9]

Nor does the bishop of Durham emerge any more creditably in Froissart's much longer, much more verisimilitudinous, and therefore (as ever) probably most insidiously mendacious, account of the battle. On the slightly dubious assumption, however, that Froissart aimed to produce a reasonably undistorted summary of the news about the battle he had received from his well-placed informants, the bishop was indeed supposed to be reinforcing Hotspur in early August 1388 and had a force of some 10,000 (*sic!*) men at his disposal for that very purpose. After leading his troops through Newcastle upon Tyne on the very day of the battle, he set out on the road to Otterburn after night had fallen only to find

[7] *Chron. Wyntoun*, iii, pp. 34–7; *Scotichronicon Johannis de Fordun cum supplementis et continuatione Walteri Bower*, ed. W. Goodall (Edinburgh, 1759), ii, pp. 410–11.

[8] Thomas Walsingham, *Historia Anglicana*, ed. H.T. Riley, RS (London, 1863–4), ii, pp. 175–6; *Chronicon Henrici Knighton*, ed. J.R. Lumby, RS (London, 1895), ii, pp. 297–8.

[9] *The Westminster Chronicle, 1381–1394*, ed. L.C. Hector and B. Harvey (Oxford, 1982), pp. 347–51.

English fugitives flying south from the battlefield. According to Froissart, the bishop accordingly postponed a direct attack on the Scots until the following day. However, during the next morning, and 3 miles before the Durham troops reached Otterburn, the Scots produced a sound like the proverbial devils of hell from their horns and drums with the result that the bishop, after consulting a few knights, decided 'not to launch an attack and so turned back again without taking action'. For Froissart and his informants, the bishop of Durham's men 'had more to lose than to gain' – quite possibly the correct military decision but not of course one calculated to win the bishop of Durham much popularity with the Percies, the burgesses of Newcastle upon Tyne, or indeed the other inhabitants of Northumberland during the reign of Richard II.[10]

It therefore seems sufficiently clear that the major contribution of the church of Durham to the English cause at Otterburn was a negative contribution – the failure of the bishop to actually reach the battlefield. Whether the bishop himself is to be personally blamed for that failure is perhaps a more open question. Although the two-pronged Scottish invasion of the East and West Marches in late July 1388 was in some ways an entirely predictable consequence of the escalation of Border warfare during the previous decade, there can be little doubt that it must have caught the bishop of Durham as unawares as it undoubtedly did the English government. It seems absolutely clear from the highly alarmed letter of instructions which Richard II sent to John of Gaunt from Westminster as late as 13 August that the king had only then just heard the news of these major Scots invasions, allegedly involving 'the burning and wasting of his realm, the killing of children in the cradle and even the advance of the enemy almost to the city of York'.[11] By 13 August, however, the very date of that letter, the battle of Otterburn had already been fought and lost and the Scots were home again north of the Tweed. A few days later, on or before 20 August, Richard had heard the news of this withdrawal at Northampton; and even before the Cambridge parliament assembled on 9 September the king had called off his own projected military expedition to Scotland.[12] Even by the tumultuous standards set by Richard II's reign as a whole, the summer of 1388 was an exceptionally turbulent one; and it seems absolutely clear that there can never have been enough time for the bishop of Durham to receive an official royal request to array troops from his palatinate before the battle of Otterburn actually took place. How many troops – and what kind of troops – the bishop did lead to Newcastle upon Tyne in early August must remain

[10] *Oeuvres de Jean Froissart*, ed. K. De Lettenhove, 15 vols (Brussels, 1867–71), xiii, pp. 226–31; *The Chronicles of Froissart*, ed. G.C. Macaulay (London, 1895), pp. 370–81.

[11] *CCR, 1385–89*, p. 610.

[12] Ibid., pp. 604, 610; A. Tuck, *Richard II and the English Nobility* (London, 1973), p. 133.

uncertain; but at least it seems to be to his credit that he levied them on
his own initiative, probably (if the Westminster chronicler is to be believed)
after consultation with the Percies.[13] Once the Otterburn raid was over, on
20 August 1388, the status quo ante was officially restored when the Crown
ordered the bishop of Durham not to attend the opening of parliament at
Cambridge but to stay in his diocese and co-operate with Hotspur's father,
Henry Percy, earl of Northumberland, and Lord John Neville of Raby in
case the Scots should invade England again.[14]

These letters close of 20 August 1388 were addressed to John, bishop
of Durham, thereby helping to resolve another issue of some significance
– the identity of the bishop who led his Durham contingent to Otterburn,
if only too late to be of assistance to the English cause. The unprecedented
series of changes of personnel on the English episcopal bench forced
upon Richard II in the spring of 1388 meant that there were two
bishops of Durham in that year. It has sometimes been assumed that
the prelate who might have fought (but failed to fight) at Otterburn
was the second of these, the highly experienced royal chancery clerk and
keeper of the privy seal, Walter Skirlaw, whose papal bull of translation
from the diocese of Bath and Wells had been dispatched from Urban VI,
then in Perugia, as early as 3 April 1388.[15] However, the temporalities
of the see of Durham were not released to Skirlaw until 13 September,
a fact which makes it highly unlikely that he exerted military authority
in the north before that date: only thereafter did the new bishop begin
to appoint laymen and clerks to his most important temporal offices.[16]
Conversely, his predecessor, John de Fordham (bishop of Durham since
1381) had suffered the unique fate of episcopal 'demotion' to the see of
Ely by Urban VI in early April; but Fordham too did not receive the
Ely temporalities until 27 September, the day he finally did arrive at the
Cambridge parliament and made his profession to Archbishop Courtenay
of Canterbury at Barnwell priory.[17] Despite the lack of clear-cut evidence
(neither Fordham's nor Skirlaw's activities at Durham are well recorded),
there can be no doubt that the church of Durham's highly ineffective
participation in the Otterburn campaign was the last contribution of
Bishop Fordham rather the first contribution of Bishop Skirlaw to the
problem of the Borders. It may indeed be possible to go further still.
Although John de Fordham's career is exceptionally 'evasive', even by
the standards of his colleagues on the episcopal bench, Dr Richard Davies

---

[13] *Westminster*, pp. 348–9 ('prout inter eos erat condictum').

[14] *CCR, 1385–89*, p. 604.

[15] Lambeth Palace Library, Reg. W. Courtenay, fo. 321v; Le Neve, *Fasti ecclesiae Anglicanae, 1300–1541*, vi (London, 1963), p. 108.

[16] PRO, Dur. 3/33, mm. 1–6; *CPR, 1385–89*, p. 504.

[17] Cambridge University Library, EDR: G/1/3 (Reg. J. Fordham), fos 1–3; *CPR, 1385–89*, p. 510.

has suggested the existence of a certain 'estrangement' between the bishop and the Percies in the 1380s. Might it even be that the Percies used their influence to have Fordham removed from the see of Durham by making his departure a condition for their support to the Lords Appellant in early 1388?[18] If so, before his final removal (in Tout's famous phrase) 'from the flesh-pots of Durham to the more meagre temporalities of Ely', Fordham had one last, if unfortunate, opportunity to demonstrate his inability to co-operate with the Percies.[19] If the most powerful magnates of the north were so eager to see Bishop Fordham ejected from his see of Durham in early 1388, perhaps it should occasion no great surprise that Bishop Fordham was so slow to come to Hotspur's support at Otterburn a few months later?

1388, in the history of the church of Durham as well of the Scottish Borders, was no doubt an exceptional year. Nevertheless the ambiguities surrounding Bishop Fordham's conduct immediately before and at the battle of Otterburn make clear by force of contrast the highly important military role all bishops of Durham played, and were expected to play, in Anglo-Scottish relations before, during and after the reign of Richard II. However, and by a paradox central to the history of the bishopric of Durham in the later middle ages, that role was largely played on the Crown's behalf. No prelate in the realm would seem better placed, in terms of geography, administrative autonomy, wealth and prestige, to play an independent and potentially troublesome part in English politics than the bishop of Durham; but in practice, and after the pontificates of Antony Bek and Lewis of Beaumont, it would be hard to find a series of bishops anywhere in the kingdom who gave the English crown fewer grounds for concern.[20] The main reason for such harmony is well known, namely the care with which successive kings nominated to the see of Durham only the most trusted and responsible senior clerks in their Westminster-based administrative service. Only occasionally, as in 1437, might a monarch be persuaded or tempted to do otherwise: in that year, as Professor Storey first demonstrated in his study of Bishop Thomas Langley, Henry VI pressed Robert Neville upon the prior and chapter of Durham on the grounds that 'hit is right necessary and expedient . . . to set and purvey of such a notable and myghty personne to be heed and bisshop thereof as may puissantly kepe thayme best to the honour of God and the defence of this our royaume'.[21] However,

[18] For this suggestion, see R.G. Davies, 'The Episcopate and the Political Crisis in England of 1386–88', *Speculum* 51 (1976), pp. 683–6.

[19] T.F. Tout, *Chapters in the Administrative History of Medieval England* (Manchester, 1920–33), iii, p. 436.

[20] For a *locus classicus* of episcopal loyalty at Durham to the royal government in the fifteenth century, see R.L. Storey, *Thomas Langley and the Bishopric of Durham, 1406–1437* (London, 1961), pp. 22–46, 135–63.

[21] DCD, Locellus XXV, no. 96; Storey, *Langley*, p. 144.

Robert Neville, together with Archbishops Alexander and George Neville of York in the late fourteenth and mid-fifteenth centuries respectively, were very much the exceptions to the general rule; and they were exceptions too which demonstrated the dangers of elevating members of prominent northern magnate families to northern sees.[22]

It followed that at most times in the later middle ages the crown entrusted responsibility for the defence of the north to prelates who had served him in Westminster and London and who had no previous vested interest in the north. The great majority of the thirty bishops of Durham from 1083 to the Reformation were born very far south of the Tees indeed. More pointedly still, every single bishop of Durham from 1333 to 1437 served as keeper of the royal privy seal at one time or other of his career.[23] Of the three bishops during Richard II's reign, Fordham was unusual in his apparent lack of a university education and first emerged from obscurity in the early 1370s as a king's clerk and one of the Black Prince's secretaries.[24] By contrast, Bishops Thomas Hatfield (1345–81) and Walter Skirlaw (1388–1406), although of different generations, both belonged to that great East Riding clerical affinity associated with Archbishops Melton and Thoresby of York, an affinity which controlled much of the English state's bureaucratic machine during the reign of Edward III. Both Hatfield and Skirlaw were accomplished administrators and diplomats; and both could hold their own as munificent founders and patrons of architecture, even in the age of William of Wykeham.[25] However neither Hatfield nor Skirlaw, and far less Fordham, could have contemplated using their financial and military resources as bishops of Durham except in furtherance of the policies pursued by the royal masters to whom they owed their very appointment. In practice, as opposed to juridical theory, the capacity of the bishops and church of Durham to play an autonomous role on the Anglo-Scottish Border was virtually non-existent: rarely could they ever be anything but junior partners, even to the Nevilles and the Percies. The reason for this comparative inferiority is obvious enough. Although the bishops of Durham had managed to consolidate the greatest liberty held peacefully for any length of time in late medieval English history, this 'considerable accumulation of privileges

---

[22] See., e.g. R.B. Dobson, 'Beverley in Conflict: Archbishop Alexander Neville and the Minster Clergy', in *Medieval Art and Architecture in the East Riding of Yorkshire*, ed. C. Wilson, British Archaeological Association (1989), pp. 149–64; see also, below, pp. 229–31.

[23] *Handbook of British Chronology*, ed. E.B. Fryde et al., 3rd edn, Royal Historical Society, (London, 1986), pp. 93–5; R.B. Dobson, *Durham Priory, 1400–1450* (Cambridge, 1973), pp. 203–4.

[24] Tout, *Chapters*, iii, p. 330; v, pp. 46–7.

[25] J.L. Grassi, 'Royal Clerks from the Archdiocese of York in the Fourteenth Century', *Northern History*, 5 (1970), pp. 30, 33; Tout, *Chapters*, v, 19–20, 48–9; B. Wilkinson, *The Chancery under Edward III* (Manchester, 1929), pp. 178, 207.

remained a patchwork, lacking the unattainable essential which could give them cohesion and independent growth'. Might it even be, to cite another remark of Mrs Jean Scammell, that by the reign of Richard II, the liberty of Durham was no longer anything more than 'an enormous estate situated in a remote part of England and hedged by supernatural sanctions'.[26]

It would indeed be unwise to overestimate the political strength of the late medieval bishops of Durham; but in confronting the problems posed by the Scots in the late fourteenth century the English government could not afford to ignore completely the twin assets of that 'enormous estate' and those 'supernatural sanctions'. In the first place, it is absolutely clear from royal letters, as well as from parliamentary petitions throughout the fourteenth century, that the lords and commons as well as the king of England positively expected the bishop of Durham to be resident in his diocese when there was any prospect of Scottish invasion. That the defence of the north from the Scots should be the responsibility of the *Northumbrenses* themselves is often said to be Edward III's (highly successful) solution to the English strategic problem of how to fight on two fronts during long periods throughout the Hundred Years War; and it is indeed easy enough to detect a note of impatience and irritation in parliament when the northern lords failed to hold the Scots at bay.[27] As it happened, Bishop Thomas Hatfield was accompanying Edward III on the Crécy campaign when the cathedral church of Durham itself faced its single most dangerous threat from the Scots during the later middle ages; but the letters sent to Hatfield by Prior John Fossor during the summer and autumn of 1346 make absolutely explicit his monks' determination to resist 'the iniquities and perverse machinations of the Scots'.[28] In Hatfield's absence, Archbishop William Zouche had played a prominent role during the Neville's Cross campaign, a testimony to the fact that the bishops of Durham were not the only prelates to lead armies against the Scots. In July 1377 Archbishop Alexander Neville was excused attendance at Richard II's coronation because of the likelihood that he might need to defend the north against *les gentz d'Escoce*; and in 1417 Archbishop Bowet's appearance at the head of a force of belligerent priests allegedly put to

[26] J. Scammell, 'The Origin and Limitations of the Liberty of Durham', *English Historical Review*, 81 (1966), pp. 472–3. In his *The County Palatine of Durham* (Cambridge, MA, 1900), pp. 75–6, G.T. Lapsley long ago concluded that the regality of the bishop of Durham, increasingly regarded with 'perplexed toleration' by the crown, had passed its zenith by the fourteenth century.

[27] Precisely such a charge had been made publicly against Archbishop Alexander Neville and Richard II's other favourites a few months before the battle of Otterburn (*Rot. Parl.*, iii, p. 230); cf. J. Campbell, 'England, Scotland and the Hundred Years War in the Fourteenth Century', in *Europe in the Late Middle Ages*, ed. J.R. Hale, J.R.L. Highfield and B. Smalley (London, 1965), pp. 192–5.

[28] BL, MS Cotton Faustina A.VI, fos 42–3, 47; *Historical Papers and Letters from Northern Registers*, RS (London, 1873), pp. 385–9.

flight the Scots who were then besieging Berwick upon Tweed.[29] However, and for obvious reasons, it was the bishop of Durham rather than the archbishop of York who was most often, as before the battle of Otterburn, entrusted with the levying of troops against the Scots at short notice. In September 1383, for example, Bishop Fordham had been ordered to array all his available men – men-at-arms, hobelars and archers – between the ages of sixteen and sixty in order to resist a Scottish invasion.[30] To judge from the details of the military array of the clergy of the county of Durham made on St Giles's Moor in 1400, the bishop delegated the inspection of his troops to the constable of his castle and other commissioners.[31] When faced (as in 1388) with a particularly dangerous Scottish invasion south of the Border, both the king and the northern lords still assumed that the bishop himself should personally lead his Durham levies into battle, preferably with the banner of St Cuthbert flying before him.

In practice, however, and especially after the front-line defence of northern England increasingly came to be entrusted to lay wardens of the march during the late fourteenth century, the medieval bishops of Durham were to be found much less frequently on military expeditions than on diplomatic missions in Northumberland and the Borders.[32] They were regularly appointed, almost as a matter of course indeed, to the endless series of royal commissions designated to treat with the Scots, to renew the truces on the Border and to redress the grievances of the king's English subjects which arose out of Marcher problems. In the decade before Otterburn, as indeed earlier and later, it was the common practice to include on such commissions six or seven individuals, most notably Henry Percy, first earl of Northumberland, his son Hotspur, Lord John Neville of Raby, two or three Northumbrian or Cumberland knights, one or two clerks and the bishop of Durham. On 26 March 1388, for example, when Earl Douglas must already have been plotting the raid which ended at Otterburn, Bishop Fordham found himself appointed by Richard II to treat with the Scots in the company of Henry Percy, earl of Northumberland, Lord John Neville of Raby, Sir Brian Stapleton and others. Four years earlier, on 6 July 1384, Bishop Fordham together with Lord John Neville and Master John Waltham, sub-dean of York Minster, had been instructed to discuss the extension of the prevailing truce with three representatives of the Scottish kingdom at the chapel of Ayton,

---

[29] *Letters from Northern Registers*, pp. 412–13; Storey, *Langley*, pp. 151–2. By contrast, in the summer of 1388 Archbishop Alexander Neville was already in disgrace and exile: he had been captured in June, with £30 in his possession, by two royal officials near Tynemouth: T. Rymer, *Foedera* (The Hague, 1739–45), iii, pt iv, p. 26.

[30] *Rotuli Scotiae*, ed. D. Macpherson et al., 2 vols (London, 1814–19), ii, p. 54.

[31] *Historiae Dunelmensis scriptores tres*, Surtees Society, 9 (1839), pp. clxxxv–clxxxvii; cf. Lapsley, *County Palatine*, pp. 305–6.

[32] See, e.g. *Foedera*, iii, pt i, pp. 58, 68, 72, 76, 78; pt ii, pp. 63, 139, 171; *Rot. Scot.*, ii, pp. 42–4.

six miles north of Berwick.[33] Ayton was a chapel within the church of Durham's own spiritual franchise of Coldinghamshire, north of the Tweed; and throughout the tortuous course of Anglo-Scottish relations during the later fourteenth century not the least of the contributions of the Lothian liberty of St Cuthbert was to provide a series of suitable and comparatively tranquil meeting-places (not least at Coldingham itself) for discussions between English and Scottish diplomatic missions.[34]

As in the case of English diplomatic activity as a whole, it usually proves difficult and often impossible to know which of the royal commissioners appointed to treat with the Scots actually undertook the laborious work involved. In many cases one suspects that in practice the detailed negotiations were conducted by one or more of the royal clerks nominated to the commission. For example, it seems probable that the Englishman most experienced in Anglo-Scottish relations and Border problems during the first few years of Richard II's reign was neither a Neville nor a Percy nor Bishop Fordham himself but rather Master John Waltham, residentiary canon of York Minster, whose name is never absent for long from the relevant pages of *Rotuli Scotiae*: he was still being appointed an envoy to Scotland by the English government in the year (1384) he died.[35] However, this is not to disparage the diplomatic skills undoubtedly possessed by many bishops of Durham themselves. Indeed one of the great advantages to the crown of recruiting their bishops of Durham from the senior members of the chancery or privy seal office was the knowledge that most such careerist administrators in royal service must have had some, and often much, prior experience of diplomatic work. Of the three bishops of Durham during the 1380s, Walter Skirlaw exemplifies such expertise as a negotiator to perfection. In many ways this ex-secretary of Archbishop Thoresby of York played a central role in Anglo-French diplomatic relations during the highly difficult early years of Richard II's reign. In addition to at least a dozen diplomatic missions to the French court between 1378 and 1388, he was sent on other expeditions to gain support for the English cause in Brittany, Flanders, Germany and at the Roman curia.[36] This experienced envoy had also spent several weeks on a mission to Scotland itself eight years before he became bishop of Durham.[37] It is accordingly no surprise that the new Bishop Skirlaw of Durham seems to have used his diplomatic gifts to restore a reasonable degree of tranquillity to the

---

[33] *Rot. Scot.*, ii, pp. 64–5, 72.

[34] For some examples at Coldingham Priory see R.B. Dobson, 'The Last English Monks on Scottish Soil,' below, p. 114 n. 21.

[35] *Rot. Scot.*, ii, pp. 12, 22, 28, 64–5; *BRUO*, iii, pp. 1973–4.

[36] *Foedera*, ed. cit., iii, pt iii, pp. 16, 58, 72–3, 75, 90, 119–20; *BRUO*, iii, pp. 1708–10.

[37] *BRUO*, iii, p. 1709. Bishop Skirlaw also accompanied Richard II on his ill-fated Scottish campaign of 1385, to which he brought an armed *comitiva* of thirty esquires and thirty archers (Tout, *Chapters*, v, p. 48).

Borders in the years immediately after Otterburn. In 1394 the bishop was sent north of the Tweed to attempt to secure a marriage alliance with the Scottish royal family;[38] thereafter relations between the two kingdoms were to remain, however precariously, stable until the end of the century.[39] A generation earlier, Bishop Thomas Hatfield, throughout a pontificate of thirty-six years (1345–81), had been even more committed than Walter Skirlaw to strenuous diplomatic work on the Borders. A member of almost innumerable royal commissions to deal with Scottish issues from the late 1340s onwards, Hatfield was naturally heavily involved in the complications caused by the payment of King David II's ransom after his capture at Neville's Cross; and the bishop was present as a matter of course at the treaty of Berwick in October 1357.[40] During the Anglo-Scottish crises of the 1370s Bishop Hatfield was still regularly being ordered to remain in the north, just as he was acting as a warden of the east march within a few years of his death in 1381.[41] It was for his many and various services in helping to secure his Scottish frontier that Edward III had undoubtedly valued Thomas Hatfield most. By contrast, Bishop Fordham, his successor, was considerably less conspicuous in Anglo-Scottish affairs during his seven years as bishop of Durham, partly because of the ascendancy of the Percies in the north during the 1380s and partly no doubt because of his own political unpopularity in the kingdom at large as one of the young Richard II's favourite clerks.[42] Nevertheless, John Fordham too was appointed one of the wardens of the east march on no less than five occasions between March 1382 and July 1384.[43] Although Fordham was licensed to delegate the responsibilities of this wardenship to deputies, there were several other occasions in the years immediately before Otterburn when he performed what amounted to the traditional obligation of bishops of Durham and conducted peace negotiations with the Scots.[44]

At the very least therefore the three bishops of Durham during the decades before and after the battle of Otterburn were expected to pour a

---

[38] *Foedera*, ed. cit., iii, pt iv, p. 102; *BRUO*, iii, p. 1709.

[39] Nicholson, *Scotland*, pp. 216–18; Campbell, 'England, Scotland and the Hundred Years War', pp. 212–16; A. Tuck, 'Richard II and the Border Magnates', *Northern History*, 3 (1968), pp. 44–52.

[40] *Foedera*, ed. cit., iii, pt i, p. 151; cf. *English Historical Documents, iv, 1327–1485*, ed. A.R. Myers (London, 1969), pp. 101–3.

[41] *Foedera*, ed. cit., iii, pt ii, p. 192; pt iii, pp. 6, 51; R.L. Storey, 'The Wardens of the Marches of England towards Scotland, 1377–1489', *English Historical Review*, 22 (1957), p. 609.

[42] According to the *Anonimalle Chronicle*, John Fordham (then keeper of the privy seal and bishop-elect of Durham) was in serious danger of losing his head if he had not sought refuge in the Tower of London on 13–15 June 1381; *The Anonimalle Chronicle, 1333 to 1381*, ed. V.H. Galbraith (Manchester, 1927), p. 139.

[43] Storey, 'Wardens of the Marches', pp. 610–11.

[44] *Rot. Scot.*, ii, p. 42–3, 44, 54, 64–5, 70, 92.

little oil on the invariably troubled waters of the Borders, even if sometimes they did so (especially during Fordham's short tenure of St Cuthbert's see from 1381 to 1388) with comparatively little success. Indeed it would be dangerous to suppose that these bishops seemed quite as powerful figures to contemporaries as they have often done to posterity. By the standards of the retinues available to John of Gaunt, Henry Percy, earl of Northumberland, and Lord John Neville of Raby, the military forces at the disposal of Bishops Hatfield, Fordham and Skirlaw were comparatively modest and no doubt difficult to raise. It might accordingly well be that 'the bishop of Durham's frequent appearance in royal mandates shows him not as the strongest but as the most amenable of the northern magnates'.[45] Although positively useful to the English monarch, it would indeed be hard to claim that the diplomatic or military assistance furnished to the royal cause by the church of Durham was often absolutely critical in securing success north of the Border. To that extent at least the ambiguities of the Otterburn campaign were typical rather than unrepresentative of Durham's role in the defence of England against the Scots at most times of the later middle ages.

However, it is even more important to emphasise that the bishops of Durham had their own material as well as spiritual reasons for wishing to play the roles of peace-maker and defender of the English borders south of the Tweed. Perhaps the most significant material reason was their possession – as an integral part of their palatine franchise – of Norhamshire and Islandshire. Although nearly a century and a half have passed since the publication of James Raine the elder's massive *The History and Antiquities of North Durham*, the peculiarly complex development of those two shires still awaits its historian. Whether or not one supposes, with the late Sir Edmund Craster, that Norhamshire owes its origins and subsequent special attachment to the church of Durham to that distant period when St Cuthbert's body migrated to Norham, by the end of the middle ages the two shires in question had become the fossilised and truncated rumps of what was probably part of the original patrimony of St Cuthbert.[46] Presumably detached at some unascertainable time in the Anglian past, from the twelfth century onwards Norhamshire and

[45] Scammell, 'Liberty of Durham', p. 471. By the late fourteenth century it was not unusual for the crown to order the bishop of Durham to send all the troops he had arrayed within his palatine franchise to a specified lay nobleman who would lead them on campaign; self-evidently this does not seem to have been the case in the summer of 1388. See PRO, Dur. 3/32, m. 4v; Lapsley, *County Palatine*, pp. 305–7.

[46] E. Craster, 'The Patrimony of St. Cuthbert', *English Historical Review*, 69 (1954), pp. 187–9. James Raine's *The History and Antiquities of North Durham* (London, 1852), written as a memorial to the Durham liberties immediately south of the Tweed which were finally absorbed into the county of Northumberland in 1852, makes little attempt to analyse the constitutional bases of these franchises.

Islandshire together made up not much more than an equilateral triangle, of some ten miles a side, immediately south of the Tweed. As is still highly apparent to travellers by road or train from Newcastle upon Tyne to Berwick upon Tweed, the two shires comprise reasonably good agricultural land, capable during the middle ages of supporting a cluster of parish churches and chapelries as well as of generating a respectable amount of profit for the monks of St Cuthbert, either on Holy Island or at Durham, as well as for the bishop himself.[47]

For the bishop and monks of Durham it was to be the most cruel irony of the Anglo-Scottish wars of the fourteenth and fifteenth centuries that this otherwise ideally sited outpost of their bishopric should become the most vulnerable part of Northumberland. From the 1290s onward no bishop of Durham would have thought it advisable to stay in Norhamshire for long, if at all, and it went without saying that he delegated the task of defending his lordship and controlling his affairs there to the man on the spot. The spot in question was naturally Norham Castle, twelve miles up the River Tweed from Berwick, and the effective centre of both military power and civil government in north Durham throughout the Anglo-Scottish wars of the later middle ages.[48] Not surprisingly, the senior episcopal officials based at Norham, a castle highly vulnerable to Scottish raids and even sieges (as in 1327), were usually members of prominent northern Northumbrian families; and in several instances, as in the case of the Humes north of the Tweed in the early fifteenth century, such families were to become the main beneficiaries of the Anglo-Scottish wars. The most coveted office of all was the constableship of Norham Castle itself, a position increasingly combined with those of bishop's justice, steward, sheriff and escheator of Norhamshire and Islandshire. From the mid fourteenth century onwards, the office of constable of Norham was held by such well-known Northumbrians as Robert de Maners (1345), Sir John Heron (1375) and Sir Gerard Heron (1386). In June 1395 Bishop Skirlaw replaced the latter as constable by a Thomas Gray who was almost certainly the son of the author of the *Scalacronica*. Eventually, however, it was to be the violent Sir Robert Ogle, whose father had fought at Otterburn, who acquired the constableship for life in 1403; his family continued to monopolise the office throughout the first half of

[47] Hadcock, 'Map of Medieval Northumberland and Durham', pp. 159–88; Storey, *Langley*, pp. 81–2, 135–47. Not surprisingly, Norhamshire and Islandshire were a regular source of salmon and other fish frequently sent to Durham (see, e.g., the 150 salmon dispatched from Norham in 1300–1: DCD, Proctor of Norham's Account).

[48] As Sir Robert Bowes was to observe in 1551, 'That castle standeth marvellously well for the defence and the releife of the countrye as well from incourses of enemys in tyme of warre as from thefts and spoiles in tyme of peace, for it standeth upon the utter frontier': Raine, *North Durham*, p. 296, and cf. pp. 284–99, passim; H.E.H. Jerningham, *Norham Castle* (Edinburgh, 1883).

the fifteenth century.[49] Perhaps no Northumbrian family profited more from the turbulent state of the Border in the reigns of Richard II and Henry IV than did the Ogles, who owed their steady rise to prominence and noble rank, as well as their role as the most influential lay patrons of St Cuthbert's monks on Holy Island, primarily to their power-base at Norham Castle itself.[50]

Nevertheless, and however rarely he resided on the Borders, the major financial responsibility for repairing and maintaining the fabric of Norham Castle in a defensible state pertained to the bishop of Durham and not his constables there. Here again the military strength of the late medieval bishops of Durham must not be exaggerated. Although often impressive, most obviously so in the case of his castle at Durham itself, the bishop's fortified strongholds anywhere in northern England were comparatively few in number. According to a well-known list of thirty-seven Northumbrian *castella*, quite probably prepared for Henry V's attention in 1415, the bishop of Durham then held only one castle, Norham, in the area while the king had four (Newcastle, Bamburgh, Berwick and Roxburgh) and the Percies at least another four (Alnwick, Warkworth, Langley and Mitford).[51] On the other hand, Norham itself was undeniably the largest and probably the strongest Border castle on the English side of the Tweed; and in many ways the greatest contribution of the bishops of Durham to the English cause on the Border during the later middle ages was to maintain Norham Castle as a formidable obstacle to marauding or invading Scots.[52] Preserving the fortifications of Norham in a state of preparedness was no easy or inexpensive matter; but, in the years before Otterburn at least, the bishop of Durham's repairs and renovations to the castle proved to be not only an excellent investment against assault but also stimulated a major transformation of English castle design in the north.

For it was under the initial patronage of first the monks and then the bishops of Durham that in the late fourteenth century the king and lords of Northumberland came to secure the services of the most accomplished of all late medieval English military architects. Appropriately enough,

[49] PRO, Dur. 3/31, m. 5; 3/32, m. 7; 3/33, mm. 14, 15; Raine, *North Durham*, pp. 45, 46, 286, 287; GEC, x (London, 1945), pp. 26–9.

[50] For Durham correspondence relating to the Ogle family in the fifteenth century (including the accusation of a prior of Holy Island that Richard Ogle 'wald haf the gudds of Sanct Cuthbert'), see DCD, Reg. Parv. II, fos 1, 3, 55, 112; cf. Holy Island Accounts, 1410–21; J.S. Roskell, *The Commons in the Parliament of 1422* (Manchester, 1954), p. 152.

[51] T.H. Rowland, *Medieval Castles, Towers, Peles and Bastions of Northumberland* (Morpeth, 1987), pp. 10, 14–15, 96; *The History of the King's Works*, ed. H.M. Colvin (London, 1963), i, pp. 409–22; ii, pp. 554–8, 563–71, 745–8, 749–50.

[52] For various attacks on Norham Castle (rarely successful) during the later middle ages, see *Letters from Northern Registers*, pp. 344–5; E.W.M. Balfour–Melville, *James I, King of Scots, 1406–1437* (London, 1936), p. 68; Nicholson, *Scotland*, pp. 119, 405, 552, 601, 604.

the first known reference to John Lewyn, mason, occurs in 1364 when he was sent by Prior Fossor and the monks of Durham to undertake some unspecified building works at their daughter house of Coldingham priory.[53] Three years later Lewyn was engaged on his masterpiece, the Prior's Kitchen at Durham Cathedral; and at about this period he is likely to have been responsible for rebuilding the keep of Bishop Hatfield's castle at Durham itself.[54] Already by 1368–9, however, this 'Bishop's Mason' had been appointed by the crown to repair Bamburgh castle; but it is still not fully appreciated that during the two subsequent decades (and more especially after 1378) Lewyn presided over the most intensive campaign of castle building seen in northern England since the twelfth century. In 1378 itself, and in obvious response to the revival of Scottish aggression on the Borders in that year, Lewyn contracted to build a new tower with gate and barbican at Carlisle Castle for a sum of 500 marks; and it was also in 1378 that he began an enormous protective wall, thirty feet high with three towers of fifty feet in height, to defend the crown's most strategically sited but highly isolated castle of Roxburgh.[55] At more or less the same period, during the decade immediately before the battle of Otterburn, John Lewyn was supervising the construction of an entirely new castle at Bolton in Wensleydale for Sir Richard le Scrope; and he is highly likely to have thoroughly remodelled the Yorkshire castles of Sheriff Hutton and Wressle for the Nevilles and Percies respectively at this time. Among his other commissions for the Neville family were extensive repairs and renovations to their two greatest castles in county Durham, Raby and Brancepeth.[56] Of the two most formidable castles in Northumberland to be renovated, rebuilt and strengthened in the 1380s, John Lewyn certainly had a hand in the building works at John of Gaunt's Dunstanburgh and probably too at Warkworth, the most ingeniously designed of all the Percy castles in the north; and only two years before the Otterburn campaign he was working for the crown on the defences of Berwick upon Tweed.[57] Appropriately enough for this greatest of all English-born military architects, in the years immediately before Otterburn John Lewyn (last recorded as late as 1398) served as one

[53] DCD, Misc. Charters, no. 1392; *The Correspondence, Inventories, etc. of the Priory of Coldingham*, Surtees Society, 12 (1841), p. xliv.

[54] J. Harvey, *English Mediaeval Architects* (2nd edn, Gloucester, 1984), pp. 181–4.

[55] *CPR, 1377–81*, p. 257; L.F. Salzman, *Building in England down to 1540* (Oxford, 1952), pp. 456–9; *History of the King's Works*, ii, pp. 599, 819–20; J. Harvey, *The Perpendicular Style* (London, 1978), p. 116.

[56] Salzman, *Building*, pp. 455–6; Harvey, *Mediaeval Architects*, pp. 182–3.

[57] *John of Gaunt's Register, 1379–83*, ed. E.C. Lodge and R. Somerville, Camden 3rd series, 56, 57, ii, no 9220. Harvey, *Mediaeval Architects*, pp. 182–4; *History of the King's Works*, ii, pp. 568–9.

of Bishop Fordham's commissioners of array.[58] By any standards Lewyn's association with this remarkable spate of sophisticated castle-building in the north, unparalleled since Edward I's day, raises some interesting grounds for believing that both Richard II's government and his northern magnates may have been exceptionally nervous of Scottish invasions during the 1380s; and here too may be confirmation, to adopt a discrimination once made by Anthony Goodman and Professor Ranald Nicholson, that the wars of Scottish independence were over and the wars of Anglo-Scottish chivalry had already begun.[59]

However, John Lewyn owed his initial rise to fame as a military architect to the patronage of the prior and chapter of Durham, a community which could of course afford no castle. Throughout the fourteenth and fifteenth centuries it was usually the monks of St Cuthbert who suffered more acutely than either king, bishop or magnate from the sustained Anglo-Scottish enmity of the period. From the 1290s to the dissolution of their house in 1539, the economic welfare of the Benedictine community of Durham – and especially of those of its members who served the cathedral priory's three cells at Coldingham, Holy Island and Farne – was at regular risk from Scottish raids across the border; and it might even be argued that this risk was never greater than during the ten years before Otterburn. Indeed the destabilisation of Anglo-Scottish relations and the consequent escalation of Border warfare during the first decade of Richard II's reign were considerably more alarming than has usually been appreciated. It seems absolutely clear that the allegiance of the two kingdoms to rival popes after the outbreak of the Great Schism in 1378 was as much a consequence as a cause of increasing hostility between England and Scotland; but that the Schism unsettled the situation, especially for a cathedral priory which held estates, churches and even the daughter-house of Coldingham north of the Tweed, there is no doubt at all. Much more unsettling however was a perennial problem in Scottish history: the lack of an effective monarch gave the Scottish and especially Border nobles and lairds the opportunity to take their own initiatives and exploit what they saw – on the whole quite rightly – as England's weakness under a boy king.[60] Certainly the 1380s are a decade when it seems as if the English government, quite untypically, was usually negotiating with the Scots from a position of weakness. Many of these hesitations no doubt

[58] Harvey, *Mediaeval English Architects*, p. 183; and for Durham Cathedral Priory's debts to John Lewyn and his junior colleague as master mason, Peter Dryng, see DCD, Bursars' Accounts, 1386–7.

[59] Nicholson, *Scotland*, pp. 194–9; cf. A. Goodman, 'The Anglo-Scottish Marches in the Fifteenth Century: A Frontier Society?', in *Scotland and England, 1286–1815*, ed. R. Mason (Edinburgh, 1987), pp. 18–33.

[60] *Historia Anglicana*, i, pp. 435–8; ii, pp. 105, 109, 115, 133; Campbell, 'England, Scotland and the Hundred Years War', pp. 206–14; J.S. Roskell, *The Impeachment of Michael de la Pole, Earl of Suffolk, in 1386* (Manchester, 1984), pp. 101–3.

derived from Richard II's uncertainty as to how to handle the problem of the rivalry between the Nevilles and the Percies, the issue which Anthony Tuck has taught us all to see as central rather than peripheral to the politics of the reign.[61] Even the most powerful magnate of late fourteenth-century England, John of Gaunt, enjoyed little success in his various attempts to pacify the Scots: for example, Gaunt's negotiations with the Scots at Coldingham priory in June 1381, conducted at exactly the time that Wat Tyler's rebels were burning down his Savoy Palace in London, led to no effective result.[62] The same is notoriously true of the massive expedition, the largest ever led by Richard II himself, taken north of the Border for only a couple of weeks in the late summer of 1385.[63] On the available evidence, much of it admittedly emanating from the perhaps exaggerated lamentations of the victims, it seems that during the 1380s, as at no time since the crisis years after Bannockburn, northern England was largely defenceless against a series of very uncoordinated but highly mobile Scottish *chevauchées*. Of these the earl of Douglas's expeditionary force which won the battle of Otterburn is itself the most famous but not the largest example. The dangers presented by these raids, and the exceptional vulnerability of Northumberland during the 1380s, was indeed recognised by James Campbell over twenty years ago. In the words of the canons of Hexham when petitioning Archbishop Alexander Neville in 1378 for the appropriation of the church of Ilkley in Yorkshire to relieve their misery, 'the wars with the Scots these days have become more or less continuous, *quasi continua*'.[64]

It accordingly need occasion no surprise that it was during the years before Otterburn that Scottish raids seems to have come closest to attacking and plundering the *terra sancta* of St Cuthbert himself, the island of Lindisfarne. The small colony of three to five Durham monks who served the priory church of Holy Island in the late fourteenth century were inured to the need to keep a watchful eye on the activities of the Scots on the mainland across the causeway; and during the campaign which ended in the battle of Neville's Cross, for instance, they spent 6d. on the services of a watchman on the 'Snoke' of the island especially employed to observe the movements of the *incursus Scottorum*.[65] However, the Holy Island

[61] A. Tuck, 'Richard II and the Border Magnates', pp. 36–52; idem 'War and Society in the Medieval North', pp. 48–51.

[62] S. Armitage-Smith, *John of Gaunt* (London, 1904), pp. 250–1; cf. *Rot. Scot.*, ii, pp. 38–9.

[63] N.B. Lewis, 'The Last Medieval Summons of the English Feudal Levy, 13 June 1385', *English Historical Review*, 73 (1958), pp. 1–26.

[64] *The Priory of Hexham*, Surtees Society (1864–5), ii, pp. 149–51; cf. Campbell, 'England, Scotland and the Hundred Years War', pp. 209–16.

[65] Raine, *North Durham*, p. 90. It is clear from a letter of Richard II written three years before Otterburn that the Durham monks on Holy Island would have much liked to be relieved of the responsibility of defending their buildings, 'kernellati et tamquam castrum afforciati' (ibid., pp. 121–2).

account rolls never give an impression of more hectic military activity on the island than they do between 1380 and 1388. During these years the monks and their messengers went frequently not only to Durham but also to seek consultation with the Percies and Nevilles as well as with other magnates of both Scotland and England.[66] A generous gift of over £25 to the prior of Holy Island from Henry Percy, earl of Northumberland, in 1384–5 suggests a desire to strengthen the defences of the island; and, sure enough, in the same year Holy Island was being equipped with the novelty of an artillery expert and two guns.[67] Within only a year or so after the first clear indication that the Scots too were beginning to make use of gunpowder, the English community on Lindisfarne was therefore sufficiently at risk in the mid-1380s to warrant the addition of artillery to their other weapons against marauding Scots.[68] In the event, and just possibly because of those two guns, Holy Island apparently remained unmolested during the Otterburn campaign itself, though its estates – and those of its mother house on the Borders – certainly did not escape scot-free. Throughout the 1380s the priory of Holy Island's revenues from the Northumbrian mainland (*super terram*) had already been seriously reduced by its inability to collect its now wasted lesser tithes from such outlying parts of Islandshire as Tweedmouth, Scremerston and Ord; and in the annual account which survives for the year of Otterburn (7 May 1388 to 27 May 1389) to these losses was added a new misfortune, the decline in value of yet another farm owed to the Holy Island community, now 'vastata per inimicos Scotie'.[69]

An even more melancholy commentary on the vulnerability of the patrimony of the church of St Cuthbert in north-eastern Northumberland emerges from the account rolls (unfortunately missing for the years from 1385 to 1390) of St Cuthbert's smallest cell at Farne. Admittedly, the late medieval monastic settlement on the Inner Farne had never been anything but small and inadequately endowed. During the early 1380s only one master and a monk fellow were in residence on the island; and with a total income of often less than £30 p.a. their survival there was completely dependent upon an annual subsidy of £20 from the proctor of Norham as well as a fee farm of £9 13s. 4d. recently charged upon the mayor and burgesses of Newcastle upon Tyne by Edward III.[70] Such seclusion

---

[66] DCD, Holy Island Accounts, 1380–9. In 1384–5 the Master of Farne travelled on the business of his cell once to Durham but three times to Dunbar (Farne Accounts, 1384–5).

[67] DCD, Holy Island Accounts, 1384–5; Bursars' Accounts, 1384–5; *Extracts from the Account Rolls of the Abbey of Durham*, Surtees Society (1898–1901), iii, p. 594.

[68] *Exchequer Rolls of Scotland* (1878–1908), iii, p. 672; Nicholson, *Scotland*, pp. 195–6.

[69] DCD, Holy Island Accounts, 1385–9.

[70] The Farne accounts now preserved at Durham commence in 1357–8 and survive in several long consecutive series thereafter; cf. Dobson, *Durham Priory*, pp. 314–15.

and poverty no doubt sometimes fostered the practice of the ascetic and contemplative life on the Inner Farne, notably by the celebrated Durham 'monk-solitary' who lived there in the middle of the fourteenth century.[71] Not that the Durham monks on the Farne Islands were completely isolated from events on the mainland nor protected from a number of visitors. Indeed in the 1360s the Farne monks were capable of prosecuting an extensive building campaign which led to the complete reconstruction of both St Cuthbert's Hall (probably a guest hall on the beach) and a new chapel: in 1371–2 it could be proudly stated in the annual Farne account roll that 'Capella Sancti Cuthberti bene perficitur laudes deo'.[72] Much of the cost of these new buildings was met by donations from local magnates and other notables, several of them from north rather than south of the Tweed; and there seems every likelihood that during the closing years of the reign of Edward III the Farne Islands were the object of a not insignificant number of pilgrimages on the part of the Scots as well as the English.[73] It was accordingly all the more distressing for the two Durham monks on the Inner Farne when the revival of Anglo-Scottish warfare in the late 1370s led to what seems to have been a positively disastrous decade for their little settlement. In 1376–7 the master and his monk *socius* had to take shelter from the Scots in Bamburgh; and in 1380–1 they were not only having to replenish their stock at Farne with items 'quia deprehendabantur per Scottos' but also to furnish a room in their so-called *castello* for a watchman.[74] So frequently does *causa guerre* occur as an explanation for expenditure within the surviving Farne account rolls of the early 1380s that one can well understand why the master on the island for most of that decade, Richard de Birtley, finally petitioned for release from his office not only because of his own infirmities but because of the great *exilitatem* of that place.[75]

Although Durham's little monastic community at Farne was to survive for almost as long as its mother-house at Durham, it might well be argued – on the evidence of the cell's fifteenth-century annual *compoti* – that it never altogether recovered from the economic dislocation caused by Anglo-Scottish warfare in the years before the battle of Otterburn.[76]

[71] W.A. Pantin, 'The Monk-Solitary of Farne: A Fourteenth-Century English Mystic', *English Historical Review*, 59 (1944), pp. 162–86; H. Farmer, 'The Meditations of the Monk of Farne', *Studia Anselmiana*, 4th series, 41 (1957), pp. 141–245.

[72] DCD, Farne Accounts, 1360–1, 1369–70, 1370–1, 1371–2; Raine, *North Durham*, pp. 345–6.

[73] For a reference to those for whom prayers were offered at Farne see DCD, Farne Accounts, 1362–3: the accounts abound with references to the heavy use made of the community's boat or coble.

[74] DCD, Farne Accounts, 1376–81.

[75] BL, MS Cotton Faustina A.VI, fos 12v–13.

[76] The average annual income of the Farne community had decreased to only £15 in the early fifteenth century; and it was valued at no more than £12 in the 1530s: Dobson, *Durham Priory*, pp. 309, 314–15.

Whether there occurred a similarly permanent reduction of all the other revenues, primarily tithes rather than rents, enjoyed by the later medieval monks of Durham on or near the Border, must remain a more open question. So many were these sources of income, and so complex were the administrative methods used to exploit them, that it is by no means easy to trace either short- or long-term trends in their financial value to the church of St Cuthbert. In particular, and somewhat surprisingly in view of the interesting revelations they have to offer, no serious use has yet been made by northern economic historians of the long series of accounts submitted to Durham Cathedral Priory by the proctors of Norham from the tithes of that and neighbouring parishes. Not that there is any doubt of the general melancholy message the fourteenth-century accounts of these proctors, usually monks of Durham themselves, convey; by the 1370s and 1380s there was no prospect at all of any proctor ever accounting for an income remotely as high (nearly £300) as that recorded during 1300–1, the year in which the first of these accounts survives.[77] However, the detailed effect of Anglo-Scottish hostilities upon the revenues, churches and tenants of the monks of Durham in Northumberland remains an issue about which there is still much to be discovered and explained. Suffice it here to point out that when in the late 1430s Prior John Wessington of Durham (1416–46) was preparing a detailed explanation of his community's acute financial crisis, he was able (thanks to the richness of the cathedral's archives even then) to take an unusually long view. It transpired that the two greatest fiscal calamities to have befallen the monks of St Cuthbert since 1293 were, first, the collapse of their income from their spiritualities north of the Tweed in the first half of the fourteenth century; and, secondly, the more recent 'guerra inter regna, et precipue in Northumbria, ubi diverse dictarum ecclesiarum sunt situatae'.[78] Even the most cursory examination of Prior Wessington's sources, above all the convent's bursars' account rolls still carefully preserved at Durham, confirms the essential truth of his diagnosis. For the monks of Durham the greatest financial disasters had no doubt come before the Black Death, for by that time their income from their churches in Scotland had more or less vanished for ever. The cathedral priory's revenues from the churches of Norham and Holy Island, however, had continued to hold up to as much as £110 or so a year in the 1350s, only to fall to as little as £23 in 1392, four years after Otterburn.[79] These figures were rarely to be as low again, providing yet another reminder that the first half of Richard II's reign was a calamitous low point in the community of St Cuthbert's own entanglement with the course of the fourteenth-century Anglo-Scottish wars.

---

[77] DCD, Proctor of Norham Accounts, which survive in great numbers except for a large unfortunate gap between 1367 and 1401.

[78] DCD, Reg. II, fos 356v–7; *Scriptores tres*, pp. ccxlviii–ccl.

[79] DCD, Bursars' Accounts, 1351–8, 1391–8; cf. *Scriptores tres*, pp. ccxlviii–ccl.

However, the decade before the battle of Otterburn presented the monks of Durham with a greater calamity still – unquestionably the one new initiative taken by the Scots during this period which most alarmed the monks of Durham and one which would no doubt have horrified St Cuthbert himself. For it was at Perth on 25 July 1378 that Robert II of Scotland formally granted Coldingham Priory, nine miles north of Berwick upon Tweed and for long Durham Cathedral's most wealthy and prestigious daughter-house, to Dunfermline abbey.[80] So dramatic a means of cutting the peculiarly intricate Gordian knot created by the presence of a colony of English monks well within the frontiers of the Scottish kingdom was perhaps not entirely unanticipated. The Durham chapter's ability to retain control over Coldingham priory and its estates had been intermittently at risk ever since the outbreak of the Anglo-Scottish wars in the 1290s; and had it not been for Robert Bruce's own veneration for St Cuthbert in the early years of the fourteenth century, the handful of Durham monks still performing the *Opus Dei* at Coldingham might have been ejected long ago.[81] However, the decision taken in 1378 by the Scottish king to align himself with Dunfermline Abbey's more or less non-existent claims to lordship over Coldingham was as provocative as it was sudden. At one level it inaugurated that long and tortuous series of legal disputes and acts of violence which finally ended with the complete expulsion of the last English monks from Scottish soil exactly a century later in 1478.[82] At another level it was Robert II's brutal attempt to wrest Coldingham out of Durham hands in 1378 which did more than anything to politicise not only the *causa de Coldingham* itself but also the attitude of the church of Durham to the Scottish realm. Never a very powerful force for compromise on the Borders perhaps, the bishops and monks of Durham progressively made less and less attempt to be so.

For the community of St Cuthbert therefore the most pressing issue during the decade before the battle of Otterburn was the struggle to regain control over Coldingham Priory; and conversely for many of the senior Scottish clergy during these years the major objective was the permanent ejection of Coldingham's English monks. Indeed nothing in the turbulent earlier history of the priory quite prepares one for the intense xenophobia

[80] *Chron. Bower* (Goodall), ii, pp. 161–3; A.L. Brown, 'The Priory of Coldingham in the Late Fourteenth Century', *Innes Review*, 23 (1972), pp. 91–2. The fourteenth-century account rolls of the priory printed in *Coldingham Correspondence* (hereafter *Cold. Corr.*) make it clear that after the 1290s there can rarely have been more than four or five Durham monks resident there, as compared with the thirty projected in the 1230s: *Scriptores tres*, p. xliii.

[81] DCD, Misc. Charters, nos 633–5, 1014; *Cold. Corr.* pp. 3–8, 244–5; Raine, *North Durham*, appendix, pp. 17–18; Dobson, 'Last English Monks', below, p. 111.

[82] Dobson, *Durham Priory*, pp. 316–27; and for a guide to the complexities of Coldingham priory's history after the withdrawal of the Durham monks, see M. Dilworth, 'Coldingham Priory and the Reformation', *Innes Review*, 23 (1973), pp. 115–37.

of the accusations brought against the Durham monks at Coldingham in the consistory court held before the bishop of St Andrews at Holyrood in late April 1379.[83] At the heart of the savage indictment then brought against Robert Claxton, prior of Coldingham since 1374, together with his two or three fellow monks recently resident at the cell, was the belief that they had acted as a centre of Border espionage, informing English raiding parties north of the Tweed when and where to strike. So treacherous were the Coldingham monks alleged to have been that they had refused to employ Scottish servants in their kitchen for fear that the latter would inform on their conspiracies. More seriously still, the Durham monks of Coldingham had supposedly conveyed large quantities of Scottish bullion south of the Tweed; and they had even had the effrontery to send back to Durham the bones and relics of Scotland's most celebrated female saints, Aebba and Margaret.[84] Whatever one should make of these 'nationalist scare stories', they were undoubtedly used by the Scottish church to confirm Prior Claxton's deprivation, with the result that throughout the 1380s (not least during the Otterburn campaign itself) he and the other Coldingham monks were forced into exile at their mother-house. Robert Claxton was still styled prior of Coldingham but was actually resident in Durham at the time of Bishop Fordham's visitation of the cathedral priory in May 1383.[85] Not surprisingly, the dispossessed Prior Claxton joined two military expeditions from Durham into Scotland in 1383–5, on at least one occasion to carry the banner of St Cuthbert.[86] During the summer of 1388 there were certainly no Durham monks at Coldingham and probably none present at the battle of Otterburn either: but if there had been, the ejected prior of Coldingham would have been the most obvious candidate.

However, within a very few years of the battle of Otterburn a small group of Durham monks, if not Prior Claxton himself, were to be resident at Coldingham again. It would be hard to claim that this unexpected change of fortune was a consequence of the Otterburn campaign in any way; and it was perhaps only when northern English military strength gradually reasserted itself after its temporary reverse at the battle that the Scottish government (which became party to a truce between England and France in June 1389) found it unwise to take too intransigent a stand on the Coldingham cause.[87] By that date, however, it was much more important

---

[83] DCD, Misc. Charters, no. 663; CPL, iv, p. 236.

[84] Raine, *North Durham*, no. 591; cf. Dobson, 'Last English Monks', below, p. 113.

[85] DCD, 1.8. Pont. 7; *Cold. Corr.* pp. 45–67. Not surprisingly, none of Robert de Claxton's accounts as prior of Coldingham survive.

[86] DCD, Bursars' Accounts, 1383–4, 1384–5; *Durham Account Rolls*, iii, pp. 593–4.

[87] *Rot. Scot.*, ii, pp. 142–3. The truces between England, Scotland and France were regularly renewed until the end of the century (Nicholson, *Scotland*, pp. 216–17; Campbell, 'England, Scotland and the Hundred Years War', p. 210). Arrangements for collecting the ransoms incurred by Englishmen captured at Otterburn were still being made at Ely in December 1389 (Cambridge University Library, EDR: G/1/3, fo. 10v).

that the acquisitive instincts of the Benedictine monks of Dunfermline were being challenged by a well-orchestrated counter-campaign on the part of their Durham adversaries: in June 1387, Prior Robert Walworth had excused himself from attendance at the Black Monk provincial chapter then meeting at Northampton on the grounds that he was strenuously engaged 'on the recovery of our cell of Coldingham and other possessions located in those parts, to the value of 1000 marks and more, long withdrawn and detained from us by the force of the king of the Scots'. Moreover, there seems little doubt that the single most powerful weapon in the armoury of the prior and chapter of Durham was a spiritual rather than a temporal one. It may be the case, as Anthony Goodman has suggested in another context, that the sanctity of St Cuthbert gradually lost potency, especially for the Scots, as the later middle ages progressed.[88] Nevertheless, there is every indication that it was the Durham chapter's astute appeals to St Cuthbert's great reputation which did more than anything to enable them to retain their purchase on Coldingham until at last St Cuthbert himself seemed to have lost interest in their cause nearly a century later.[89] Perhaps the single most important revelation of Professor A. L. Brown's article on the vicissitudes of Coldingham's history in the late fourteenth century is the way in which, after the battle of Otterburn, George Dunbar, earl of March, was ready to protect the monks of Durham and reinstate them at Coldingham in return for the status he thereby received as St Cuthbert's greatest patron in Scotland. Here was more or less exactly foreshadowed the position held a half-century later by those new powers on the Border, Alexander and David Hume, the two brothers who finally turned and destroyed the Durham monastery in Scotland which had helped to create their family's fortunes.[90]

All in all, therefore, and despite occasional fears in the Durham cloister that their great patron had fallen asleep, in 1388 St Cuthbert was still a name with which to conjure profitably. And not by the Durham monks alone. Few passages in the late sixteenth-century *Rites of Durham* are more eloquent than the pages devoted to

> that goodly and sumptuous banner, with pipes of silver to be put on a staff, being five yards longe . . . so sumptuouslie finished and absolutelye perfitted, was dedicated to holie St Cuthbert of intent and purpose that the same should

[88] *Scriptores tres*, pp. clvi–clvii. But see the letters of fraternity issued by the Durham prior and chapter to Scottish lords in the late fourteenth and fifteenth centuries: *The Obituary Roll of William Ebchester and John Burnby, Priors of Durham*, Surtees Society, 31 (1856), pp. 107–9.

[89] Goodman, 'Anglo-Scottish Marches in the Fifteenth Century: A Frontier Society?', p. 28.

[90] Brown, 'Priory of Coldingham in the Fourteenth Century', pp. 94–100; Dobson, *Durham Priory*, pp. 321–7.

be alwaies after presented and carried to any battell as occasion should serve; and which was never caryed or shewed at any battell but by the especiall grace of God almightie and the mediacion of holie St Cuthbert: it browghte home the victorie.[91]

As that quotation suggests, and whatever may have been true in the case of the saint's other legendary insignia, Cuthbert's celebrated banner had a highly practical purpose. As a banner intended to ensure not just military victory, but victory against the Scots, it was conspicuous near St Cuthbert's feretory in the cathedral from at least the twelfth century.[92] Edward I began requiring Durham monks to carry the banner on his expeditions against the Scots in the 1290s, a precedent followed on Edward II's first Scottish campaign in 1307, and again by Edward III in the 1330s.[93] More crucial still in providing St Cuthbert's relics with their unrivalled reputation for ensuring success in battle was their appearance in the custody of Prior Fossor of Durham at the startlingly successful English victory at Neville's Cross in 1346.[94] For understandable reasons, and long before its greatest contribution to English arms at Flodden in 1513, this was not a banner likely to endear the reputation of St Cuthbert to the Scots.[95] In a military context, and more obviously than elsewhere within his astonishing cult, Cuthbert had ceased to be an impartial saint.

However, of the banner's value, as an increasingly nationalist emblem of English superiority over the Scots, to any expeditionary force riding north of the Tyne and Tweed there could be no doubt whatsoever.[96] It need therefore occasion no surprise that during the violent years of armed conflict which preceded the battle of Otterburn, St Cuthbert's banner seems to have been in greater demand than ever before or since. Thus the surviving accounts of the Durham obedientiaries, and notably those of the convent's feretrar and bursar, mention expenses *pro vexillo portando* to the Borders in 1383–4 (when it was taken to Holy Island as well as Scotland), in 1385 and again in 1389–90.[97] But what of the year

[91] *Rites of Durham*, Surtees Society, 57 (1903), p. 26; cf. pp. 94–5.

[92] *Libellus de vita et miraculis Sancti Godrici*, Surtees Society, 20 (1847), p. 83; VCH, *Durham*, 1905–28, iii, p. 14.

[93] C.M. Fraser, *A History of Antony Bek, Bishop of Durham, 1283–1311* (Oxford, 1957), pp. 129–30, 212; *Durham Account Rolls*, ii, p. 529.

[94] *Rites of Durham*, pp. 23–9; *Letters from Northern Registers*, pp. 387–9.

[95] Although very heavy, St Cuthbert's banner could be carried by one bearer, usually a Durham monk. However, no less than three members of the community accompanied the banner to Flodden Field in 1513: see DCD, Feretrars' Accounts, 1513–14; Bursars' Accounts, 1513–14; J. Raine, *Saint Cuthbert* (Durham, 1828), p. 167.

[96] For Henry IV's use of the banners of both St Cuthbert and St John of Beverley in 1400, see A.L. Brown, 'The English Campaign in Scotland, 1400', in *British Government and Administration*, ed. H. Hearder and H.R. Loyn (Cardiff, 1974), p. 45.

[97] DCD, Bursars' Accounts, 1383–4, 1384–5; Feretrars' Accounts, 1385–6; *Durham Account Rolls*, ii, p. 441; iii, pp. 593–4.

of Otterburn itself? The Durham feretrar's account roll of June 1388 to June 1389 records, as usual, the receipt of over £30 in offerings at the pyx of St Cuthbert in the cathedral; and the bursar's roll for the same period contains a more intriguing reference to a payment made to the earl of Douglas for the ransom (*pro redempcione*) of Willington and Wallsend on the Tyne in this very year.[98] Neither of these accounts however records the dispatch of St Cuthbert's Banner to any destination whatsoever. No doubt it would be unwise to rest too much weight on arguments *ex silentio* from medieval obedientiary accounts. But could it be that one of the many mistakes made by the English forces at Otterburn in August 1388, made above all by John Fordham in his last weeks as a northern bishop, was an error of omission – not to bring the banner of St Cuthbert from Durham to help them in battle against the Scots? Here at least was a year in which an English victory was not 'browghte home'.

[98] DCD, Feretrars' Accounts, 1388–9; Bursars' Accounts, 1388–9.

5

The Last English Monks on Scottish Soil: The Severance of Coldingham Priory from the Monastery of Durham, 1461–78

The history of the Benedictine priory of Coldingham, near the Berwickshire coast and 9 miles north of the Tweed, has several claims to fame and many more to notoriety. Of the medieval monastery there now remains little but the north and east walls of the church choir, built towards the end of the twelfth century; but these inadequate memorials to Coldingham's former glories have earned the priory some distinction for an architectural ingenuity and sophistication 'without parallel in Scotland'.[1] The Durham monks who built and served this church between the twelfth and fifteenth centuries were ever conscious that they preserved if not the site at least the memory of one of the oldest and most celebrated of Celtic double monasteries.[2] Even in the almost legendary pioneering years of the late seventh century the course of monasticism at Coldingham had failed, as so often in the future, to run smooth. The monk Adamnan's violent attack on the immorality of his brothers and sisters there marks 'the first known instance of monastic degeneracy in Anglo-Saxon England.'.[3] According to later Durham historical tradition, St Cuthbert (himself a personal friend of Coldingham's greatest abbess, St Aebba, and a visitor to her monastery) based his own refusal to allow women within his church at Lindisfarne on the grounds that he wished to avoid a scandal similar to that at Coldingham.[4] The connection between Coldingham and St Cuthbert was certainly the most important legacy the Celtic monastery left to the future. Symeon of Durham included Coldingham among the possessions of the see of Lindisfarne in 854; and according to the late Sir Edmund Craster

---

[1] S. Cruden, *Scottish Abbeys* (Edinburgh, 1960), p. 57.

[2] William Drax, prior of Coldingham from 1419 to 1441, chose to be commemorated by a stained-glass window (in the vestry of Durham Cathedral) which included a 'picture of St Ebba prioresse, at her prayers', *Rites of Durham*, Surtees Society (1902), p. 118. The site of Aebba's monastery probably lay within an abandoned sub-Roman fort on St Abb's Head: O.G.S. Crawford, 'Coludes Burh', *Antiquity*, 8 (1934), pp. 202–4.

[3] J. Godfrey, *The Church in Anglo-Saxon England* (Cambridge, 1962), p. 455; *Venerabilis Baedae historia ecclesiastica*, ed. C. Plummer (Oxford, 1896), i, pp. 262–6. Adamnan's condemnation of the Coldingham nuns for weaving fine clothes appears to provide the first historical reference to woollen manufacture in Scotland.

[4] Symeon of Durham, *Historia ecclesiae Dunelmensis*, RS (1882), p. 59; B. Colgrave, *Two Lives of Saint Cuthbert* (Cambridge, 1940), pp. 81, 189.

it seems highly probable that Coldingham still recognised the primacy of Lindisfarne on the eve of their destruction by the Vikings.[5] Memories of St Cuthbert's patronage of Coldingham and of Coldingham's dependence on St Cuthbert's see survived the two centuries and more in which monastic life disappeared from the site. They were adroitly revived and exploited at the late eleventh-century Scottish court by the first generation of Benedictine monks at Durham. As a direct result (and in the words of John Wessington, a fifteenth-century prior of Durham) 'hunc locum, propter reverenciam dei et Sancti Cuthberti, Edgarus Rex Scocie dedit monasterio Dunelmensi ad sustentacionem eiusdem monasterii, set, processu temporis, placuit priori et fratribus Dunelm' ibidem ecclesiam erigere et monachos eiusdem monasterii locare'.[6]

During the first half of the twelfth century the church of Coldingham was gradually and at first tentatively transformed into a regular conventual priory. Thanks to its handsome endowment by Scottish kings, ecclesiastics and magnates, Coldingham rapidly became the wealthiest and most prominent of Durham's nine cells. It was the only one of these dependencies to achieve a genuine *esprit de corps* and its priors were often successful in winning a large measure of freedom from control by their superiors at Durham.[7] Until the very end of the thirteenth century Coldingham was also one of the richest and most prosperous of all Scottish monasteries. Its resources were able to sustain a population of thirty resident Durham monks and still provide a cash surplus for transmission to the mother-house.[8]

[5] Symeon of Durham, *Opera*, Surtees Society (1867), p. 68; H.H.E. Craster, 'The Patrimony of Saint Cuthbert', *English Historical Review*, 69 (1954), p. 179.

[6] Durham, Muniments and Manuscripts of the Dean and Chapter (DCD), MS B.III.30, fo. 38. Compare the very similar modern view that 'Coldingham priory cannot be assigned to a single founder, though it grew from Edgar's gift', G.W.S. Barrow, 'Scottish Rulers and the Religious Orders', *Transactions of the Royal Historical Society*, 5th series, 3 (1953), p. 81. Coldingham has consequently lost its nineteenth-century reputation as 'probably the oldest foundation of the Benedictine order in Scotland', G. Grub, *An Ecclesiastical History of Scotland* (Edinburgh, 1861), i, p. 205. The exact date at which Coldingham became an organised religious house remains obscure; but Professor Barrow's view ('Scottish Rulers' p. 80) that this cannot have occurred much before 1140 receives indirect confirmation from the fact that only the *ecclesia de Coldingham* is mentioned in the record of the franchise conferred on the prior and subprior of Durham by Bishop Robert of St Andrews at Roxburgh on 17 July 1127, *Liber vitae*, Surtees Society (1923), fos 44, 47.

[7] The conflicts between late thirteenth-century priors of Coldingham and Durham are fully illustrated in *Durham Annals and Documents of the Thirteenth Century*, Surtees Society (1940), p. 106–18. Professor Barlow noted (ibid., p. 218) that Coldingham was probably the only Durham daughter-house 'of which the rule was considered an honour and not a burden'.

[8] *Cold. Corr.*, p. 243; *Extracts from the Account Rolls of the Abbey of Durham*, Surtees Society (1898–1901, hereafter cited as *Durham Account Rolls*), ii, p. 489. Circa 1235 it was proposed that there should always be thirty resident monks (besides the prior) at Coldingham as opposed to seventy at Durham (*Historiae Dunelmensis scriptores tres*, Surtees Society, 1839, p. xliii). The *compoti* of Coldingham's priors and sacrists, which only begin to survive from

continued

In 1304 Bishop Antony Bek persuaded Benedict XI that the revenues of Coldingham would make a suitable provision for Hugh titular bishop of Byblos in Syria.[9] Shortly before this date the turning-point in the history of the priory had already been reached with the outbreak of the Anglo-Scottish wars in the late 1290s. During the reign of Edward II the Durham monks were compelled to abandon Coldingham for the first of many times. It was only towards the end of his life that on 16 March 1328 Robert Bruce confirmed Durham's possession of the priory by inspecting previous royal and other charters.[10] Edward III's Scottish campaigns again threatened to break the connection between Coldingham and Durham but, thanks to the exertions of Prior John Fossor, the cell retained some measure of stability in its religious life between 1340 and 1378. The Coldingham account rolls of these years leave no doubt, however, that the priory had failed to recover its previous prestige and prosperity. With an annual income of less than £200, Coldingham was now only *primus inter pares* of the Durham cells. Its prior and monks had forfeited many of their spiritual and secular franchises and suffered acutely from military campaigns and the accompanying decay of arable agriculture in the coastal strip between the Lammermuirs and the North Sea. Nevertheless Coldingham remained one of the richest of border prizes,[11] and Robert II's decision in July 1378 to expel the Durham monks from the priory and replace them by other Benedictines from Dunfermline abbey introduced a century-long period during which the church of St Cuthbert fought a costly, virtually continuous and finally unsuccessful battle to preserve its rights.[12] 'The long

continued

1310–11, show that the number of resident brethren had already dropped well below this figure by the early fourteenth century. As there were only seven resident monks in 1304 (*Cold. Corr.*, p. 5), the accusation made by the Scots that by April 1379 (Raine, *North Durham*, no. 591) the number serving the cell had fallen from twenty-four to three or four may well have been justified.

[9] DCD, Misc. Charters, no. 1014; *Cold. Corr.*, 3–7; C.M. Fraser, *A History of Antony Bek, Bishop of Durham* (Oxford, 1957), pp. 163, 194.

[10] DCD, Misc. Charters, no. 635; Raine, *North Durham*, nos 79–81; *Registrum magni sigilli regum Scotorum*, ed. J.M. Thompson et al., 12 vols (Edinburgh, 1882–1914), i, pp. 433–5; cf. 331–3.

[11] Assessments made for papal taxation give some indication of the priory's prosperity towards the end of the thirteenth century, *Cold. Corr.*, p. cxiii; 'Bagimond's Roll', ed. A.I. Dunlop, Scottish History Society, *Miscellanea*, 6 (1939), pp. 35, 65. Although this prosperity undeniably declined during the changed conditions of the later middle ages, it seems probable that historians have sometimes exaggerated (at Coldingham as elsewhere) the permanent damage caused by the Anglo-Scottish hostilities of the fourteenth century. The economic resilience of the barony of Coldingham is particularly well illustrated by the priory's court roll of 1408–26 (DCD, Misc. Charters, no. 1222), which reveals not only the wide geographical range of the convent's landed interests, but also its ability to maintain its income from rents and entry-fines at a comparatively high level.

[12] *Johannis de Fordun Scotichronicon cum supplimentis et continuacione Walteri Bower*, ed. W. Goodall (Edinburgh, 1759), ii, pp. 161–3; *CPL* iv, p. 236; Raine, *North Durham*,

continued

and tortuous struggle to dissever this priory from Durham and its varied exploitation by ecclesiastics and laymen makes its history more tangled than that of any other Scottish monastery.'[13]

With this judgement no modern student of Coldingham Priory could possibly disagree. Despite both its national importance and the survival at Durham of many of its records, no adequate history of the monastery has yet been written.[14] Even the older James Raine, properly described by Professor Barrow as an antiquary who 'perhaps knew more about Coldingham and its priory than any man before or since',[15] failed to make its complicated story intelligible to others and, one suspects, to himself. Moreover his belief that the Coldingham records at Durham go back 'to a period, in a statistical and in fact in every other point of view, perfectly unillustrated by any other contemporary record of that kingdom',[16] is one that must be qualified in the light of the work of Scottish historians since his death. After 1478 however – the year in which the prior and chapter of Durham ceased to write or preserve documents relating to their erstwhile cell – our relatively detailed knowledge of Coldingham's history does give place to a period of little record and much mystery. No attempt therefore will be made here to follow the violently erratic fortunes of Coldingham between 1478 and 1606, the date of its erection into a temporal lordship

continued

no. 591. The struggle between the monks of Durham and Dunfermline for possession of Coldingham provides the main interest of the priory's history between 1378 and June 1442, when James II admitted the English candidate, John Oll, to the cell (BL, Cotton Charters, xviii, 19). No attempt can be made here to describe the complex course of this conflict; but as it has caused historians of Coldingham much confusion, it seems worthwhile to mention that Dunfermline monks actually enjoyed possession of the cell for most, though not all, of the period between 1378 and 1424: e.g. see *Calendar of Papal Petitions*, i, pp. 573–5; *CPL*, iv, pp. 247–8; *Swintons*, pp. iii–v, ix–x; *Scriptores tres*, pp. clvi–clvii; *Cold Corr.*, 47–49, 254; DCD, Holy Island Account 1401–2; Registrum Parvum II, fo. 12. Thanks to the ending of the Great Schism and the opportunity presented by the release of James I at Durham in March 1424, English monks returned to Coldingham on a more secure basis in that year. The later phases of the contest with Dunfermline are considered briefly by A.I. Dunlop, *The Life and Times of James Kennedy* (Edinburgh, 1950), pp. 48–51, where the assumption that after 1442 'no more was heard of the claims of William de Boys and the house of St Margaret' is, however, somewhat questionable. As late as 1509 James IV deliberately revived the claim that Coldingham had been annexed to Dunfermline in order to justify its acquisition by his son, Alexander Stewart, already commendator of the latter monastery (*James IV Letters*, 163–4). See also R.B. Dobson, *Durham Priory, 1400–1450* (Cambridge, 1973), pp. 316–27.

[13] Easson, *Religious Houses*, p. 18.

[14] There seems to be no point in attempting to correct the extraordinary number of errors and misconceptions to be found in A.A. Carr, *A History of Coldingham Priory* (Edinburgh, 1836); W.K. Hunter, *History of the Priory of Coldingham* (Edinburgh, 1858); A. Thomson, *Coldingham: Parish and Priory* (Galashiels, 1908); and even G. Chalmers, *Caledonia* (new edn, Paisley, 1888), iii, pp. 323–5.

[15] Barrow, 'Scottish Rulers', p. 80.

[16] DCD, L.13 (Original Report on Muniments of the Dean and Chapter of Durham, signed by James Raine on 6 March 1829).

for Alexander first earl of Hume. This essay will consider the immediately preceding period that lies between 1461 and 1478, the seventeen years in which the Durham prior and chapter fought but failed to preserve their dependency from falling into the hands of their new Scottish adversaries, Patrick and John Hume.

It is however essential to emphasise that when Patrick Hume opened the most crucial phase of the *causa de Coldingham* in 1461, this cause had already undergone a long and chequered history. Coldingham's dependence on Durham was an anomalous survival from an age when the boundary between the kingdoms of England and Scotland was settling on the Tweed but the religious orders themselves still represented international forces needing to pay scant respect to the existence of political frontiers. By the fifteenth century there was no ready parallel to the position at Coldingham where a small colony of English monks lived among their traditional enemies. The fate of the alien priories in England was an object lesson in the usual effects of national hostility in such circumstances, and the English monks resident on the Isle of May, dependent on a mother-house at Reading, had not survived even the first decade of the Scottish wars of independence.[17] The religious habits of the Durham monks at Coldingham provided only partial protection from the often virulent hatred of their neighbours. The charges made against the English community at the St Andrews consistory court in the spring of 1379 testify to Scottish fear and detestation of the alien. The Coldingham monks were accused of large-scale espionage; of sending Scottish bullion to England; of smuggling the bones and relics of Scotland's national saints, St Margaret and St Aebba, to Durham; and of terrorising the Borders with a hired retinue.[18] Propaganda of this sort may not always have been believed but it clearly appealed to a substantial audience. Walter Bower, writing of incidents in the 1420s and 1430s, compared William Drax, prior of Coldingham, to a serpent nourished in the bosom of the kingdom, and told the story of how Drax caused a famous Scottish sailor, William Alan, to be captured and eventually hanged by the English at Berwick merely because this captain had once taken six of the priory's lambs to revictual his ship.[19] Scottish prejudice was understandable enough at a time when (or so the convent's adversaries from Dunfermline claimed before Bishop Kennedy

---

[17] A.A.M. Duncan, 'Documents Relating to the Priory of May, *c.* 1140–1313', *Proceedings of the Society of Antiquaries of Scotland*, 90 (1956–57), pp. 52–80. I am grateful to Professor Duncan and to Dr I.B. Cowan for their generous help on this and other matters.

[18] Raine, *North Durham*, no. 591. The charge that relics of Scottish saints had found their way to Durham was certainly justified: Symeon, *Historia*, pp. 168–9; *Durham Account Rolls*, ii, pp. 427, 429, 431.

[19] *Chron. Bower*, ii, pp. 163–5. The verbal correspondence with *Cold. Corr.*, p. 253, makes it evident that Bower was citing propagandist material prepared by Dunfermline monks.

of St Andrews in January 1442) the tyranny and cruelty of the English were notorious throughout the world 'ut pateat manifeste de eorum usurpatione contra Franciam, Scociam, Walliam, Hiberniam et terris illis abjacentibus'.[20] The practical advantages of an English outpost in Scotland, as a place where representatives of the two countries might meet and the prior of Coldingham receive the complaints of English subjects against the Scots,[21] were outweighed by the strength of Scottish hostility.

Nevertheless it would be dangerous to assume that the severance of Coldingham from Durham, even in the disturbed conditions of the mid fifteenth century, was inevitable. The responsibility for the decisive rupture must be laid unequivocally at the feet of one man, Master Patrick Hume, whose personal ambition, extraordinary audacity and great litigious gifts made him the most formidable opponent the Durham monks had yet encountered in the long history of the Coldingham cause. A graduate of the university of St Andrews in 1437,[22] Patrick Hume's insatiable appetite for ecclesiastical preferment had brought him the archdeaconry of Teviotdale in obscure and highly controversial circumstances.[23] His career at Rome deserves to be remembered as a *locus classicus* of the rewards to be gained and the legal complexities to be created by the activities of a Scottish clerk firmly established in the entourage of the papal curia. Patrick's influence at Rome reached its highest point in 1461 when he was the recipient of a lengthy series of papal privileges and indulgences, as well as letters of appointment as papal notary on 13 August.[24] A few days earlier he had obtained the bull which was to bring about the eventual dissolution of the connection between Durham and Coldingham. On 6 August 1461 Pius II charged the bishops of St Andrews and Argyll and the archdeacon

---

[20] *Cold. Corr.*, p. 247.

[21] *CCR, 1429–35*, pp. 292–3. There are numerous cases of Coldingham's use as an Anglo-Scottish trysting-place in the later middle ages. There, for example, John of Gaunt was negotiating a truce with Scottish magnates during the week in June 1381 when his London palace of the Savoy was being destroyed by the peasants of Kent, S. Armitage-Smith, *John of Gaunt* (London, 1904), pp. 250–1; there John Harding dated some of his audacious forgeries, Palgrave, *Docs. Hist. Scot.*, i, pp. 372, 376; and there too the English and Scottish commissioners met to make peace after Flodden, Lesley, *History*, p. 105; *Letters and Papers Henry VIII*, ii, pp. 567, 574, 777. Coldingham is one of the only two Berwickshire place-names recorded (*c.* 1360) by the cartographer of the Gough Map of Great Britain.

[22] *St Andrews University Records*, pp. 14, 19; *Acta Facultatis Artium Universitatis Sancti Andree, 1413–1588*, ed. A.I. Dunlop (Edinburgh, 1964), pp. 36, 45.

[23] The brief accounts of Patrick's struggle to oust William Croyser from the archdeaconry in Dunlop in *Kennedy*, 47, 52–53, and J.H. Burns, *Scottish Churchmen and the Council of Basle* (Glasgow, 1962), pp. 23, 78, 83–84, can be supplemented by the references in *Fasti ecclesiae Scoticanae medii aevi*, ed. D.E.R. Watt (St Andrews, 1959), pp. 59–60, and the later manuscript additions to this work.

[24] *CPL*, xi, pp. 683, 691; Vatican Archives, Registers of Supplications (Reg. Supp.), 542, fo. 88v; 544, fo. 2. All citations from this source are taken from the manuscript calendar of entries relating to Scotland compiled by Mrs A.I. Dunlop and now deposited in the Department of Scottish History and Literature, University of Glasgow.

of Glasgow to investigate the accusations made by Patrick Hume against John Pencher, then prior of Coldingham – that he had dilapidated the goods of the monastery; allowed the complement of monks there to fall from eighteen to two; and was a traitor towards King James III of Scotland. If the allegations could be substantiated, Patrick was to receive Coldingham *in commendam* for the term of his life. As so often in the history of this cause, an enemy of Durham had been able to exploit the curial officials' invincible ignorance of actual Scottish conditions. Not only would Patrick's charges against Pencher have seemed disingenuous, to say the least, to any contemporary with the slightest knowledge of the recent history of the cell; but he had been guilty of an even more serious *suppressio veritatis* in failing to reveal the legal foundations of Durham's claim to hold and serve its cell.[25]

News of Patrick Hume's 'maliciouse purpose' had reached Durham by 1 December 1461 when Prior John Burnby wrote to Sir Alexander Hume and Andrew Durrisdeer, bishop of Glasgow, asking for their help in the frustration of Patrick's designs on Coldingham.[26] Perhaps more significant was Burnby's complete failure, to judge from the contents of his letter-book, to establish contact with Bishop James Kennedy of St Andrews. There is every reason to believe that in his declining years (he died on 24 May 1465) the latter was benevolently inclined towards the Humes' plans to wrest Coldingham out of English hands, and so took his revenge on the Durham monks for their resistance to him in the late 1440s.[27] Bishop Kennedy's hostility was probably anticipated at Durham and Prior Burnby clearly placed most reliance on the support of Coldingham's bailie, Sir Alexander Hume, a patron committed by oath to protect the possessions of the convent and one who had done so triumphantly at a time of apparently greater crisis in Bishop Kennedy's own consistory court at St Andrews as long ago as January 1442.[28] In his letter to Sir Alexander of 1 December 1461, Prior Burnby was careful to stress that it had been 'for his singuler promocion' that Patrick Hume had 'purchessid at the courte

---

[25] *CPL*, xi, pp. 425–6. The convent's detailed, searching and convincing protestation against Patrick's bull is printed in *Cold. Corr.*, pp. 193–6.

[26] DCD, Registrum Parvum III, fo. 108; *Cold. Corr.*, pp. 187–8. The choice of the bishop of Glasgow to defend a monastery within the diocese of St Andrews is explained by the former's nomination as future guardian of Durham's privileges in Nicholas V's bull of 30 Jan. 1451 (*CPL*, x, pp. 215–16), a copy of which was sent by Burnby to Durrisdeer at this time.

[27] *Cold. Corr.*, pp. 160–71. By October 1450 relations between Kennedy and the prior of Durham had so degenerated that the latter was ready to countenance the rumour that the bishop intended to acquire Coldingham *in commendam* 'vel saltem pro suo suffraganeo in sedem episcopalem erigere' (DCD, Reg. Parv. III, fo. 45). Kennedy was partly successful in his attempts to deprive Durham of its advowsons of several parish churches north of the Tweed; and Mrs Dunlop (*Kennedy*, p. 123) seems too ready to come to Kennedy's defence on the grounds that 'unsubstantiated rumour can carry no great weight'.

[28] DCD, Misc. Charters, no. 7193; *Cold. Corr.*, pp. 134, 256.

of Rome certayn bulles against me and my brethir'; and his letter reveals that at this stage the prior and chapter of Durham had not the slightest suspicion that the great Scottish magnate in whom they placed their trust was shortly to desert them.[29]

In the circumstances, the monastery of Durham may have felt justified in reacting to the news of Patrick Hume's manoeuvres at the curia with comparatively little alarm. In 1461, as all later accounts confirm, Patrick Hume had been acting entirely in his own interests, and he must have seemed a much less formidable adversary to the Durham chapter than their opponents of the immediate past. Durham monks presumably continued to reside at Coldingham for some months after the date of Patrick's bull. As late as 31 March 1462 two of the brethren were sent north from the mother-house in a belated effort to increase the number of resident monks at Coldingham.[30] Whether they ever reached their destination may be doubted. By mid-May 1462 the last English monks north of the Tweed had been ejected from Scotland for ever. One of the more frustrating features of the Coldingham cause is that no record seems to survive of either the exact date or circumstances of this expulsion. But when Richard Emerson, a Durham clerk, was sent to cite Patrick Hume to appear at Newcastle upon Tyne to answer the charges made against him by the Durham monks, he halted at the parish church of Fishwick a few hundred yards north of the Tweed (on 16 May 1462), confessing that for fear of death he did not dare approach either Patrick himself or the priory of Coldingham.[31] From that time onwards the priory and barony of Coldingham was literally and securely within enemy territory; and henceforward it was one of the gravest features of the Durham monks' position that they could never re-establish contact with their old servants, tenants and friends north of the Tweed. It is certain that the expulsion of the Durham monks by Patrick Hume was marked by some show of armed force and some form of dramatic incident; but no monk was killed and one may assume (for the fact would not have been left unrecorded) that no blood was shed.

The news of the expulsion of their fellows from Coldingham naturally altered the climate of opinion in Durham itself. During the spring and summer of 1462 the prior and chapter prepared themselves for legal combat in a familiar and time-honoured fashion. The records of the convent were searched for material justifying Coldingham's subjection to Durham; accurate transcripts of the most valuable evidence were authenticated by means of notarial instruments; and several general and preliminary appeals and protestations were sent to both the curia

[29] See below, p. 121.
[30] DCD. Reg. Parv. III, fo. 112.
[31] DCD, Misc. Charters, no. 689; Reg. IV, fos 140, 142.

and to Scotland.[32] Prior Burnby appealed to Edward IV at a very early stage of the crisis and properly stressed the value of 'the kings writing to be direct unto our holy fadir the pape for to be gracious and favorable unto our maters'.[33] Edward IV spent several weeks at Durham, where he was detained by a serious attack of measles or pox, during the winter of 1462–63; and it is paradoxical that this visit, the longest ever made by a ruling English monarch to Durham, should have coincided with a political situation which rendered the English government literally incapable of using force of arms to return the Durham monks to Coldingham. Although the earl of Warwick met with some initial success in his border campaigns of 1462–63, Alnwick, Dunstanburgh and Bamburgh were still firmly in Lancastrian or Scottish hands in August 1463.[34] Only after the battle of Hexham, on 15 May 1464, and the subsequent reduction of the Northumbrian castles was Yorkist control of northern England made comparatively secure; but it can be argued that even these victories hindered rather than helped Durham's prospects of regaining Coldingham. The fifteen-years truce concluded between the English and Scots at York on 1 June 1464 showed that Edward IV had no intention of prejudicing his position in the north by directing aggressive operations on behalf of his own claim to Berwick, far less Durham's to Coldingham.[35]

Not unnaturally the prior and chapter seized the opportunity of the restoration of relative tranquillity on the Borders in the summer of 1464 to seek redress directly from the Scottish government and magnates.[36] Various grievances were raised by Prior Burnby in a letter written on 1 October 1464 to Lord Robert Ogle, a prominent Yorkist captain and constable of Bamburgh Castle. Burnby enclosed copies of two Durham petitions already delivered to the Scottish commissioners of truce, one demanding compensation for the plundering of Farne and 'on for restitucion of Coldyngham with ccccxxii li. in verrey valew of certayn goods and

---

[32] DCD, Reg. IV, fos 138v–42.

[33] DCD, Reg. Parv. III, fos 112–13; *Cold. Corr.*, p. 190.

[34] During this period Durham's old patron, Henry VI, was being sheltered by Bishop Kennedy at St Andrews and elsewhere: C.L. Scofield, *Life and Reign of Edward IV* (London, 1923), i, pp. 262–9, 301, 309.

[35] *Foedera*, ed. T. Rymer (London, 1704–35), xi, p. 525.

[36] Durham's possessions in Northumberland suffered more seriously in the turbulent years that followed Margaret of Anjou's cession of Berwick to the Scots on 25 April 1461 than at any other time in the fifteenth century. The remote cell on the island of Farne was subjected to a plunder raid by a contingent of Scottish sailors from Pittenweem, as a result of which its two resident monks transferred themselves to the neighbouring Durham priory of Holy Island, itself the scene of armed warfare, and were compelled to give weeks of hospitality to raiding parties, DCD, Holy Island Accounts, 1461–4; Raine, *North Durham*, text p. 122; Scofield, *Edward IV*, i, p. 263. According to one London chronicler, 'iii C and vi Fraynysche men were take in the chyrche of Hooly Ylond' during the skirmish at Lindisfarne in the winter of 1462–63: *Historical Collections of a London Citizen*, Camden Society, new series (1876), pp. 218–19.

catalls takyn fro the same place by Sir Patrik Home and his felyshipp'.[37] Whether Ogle did in fact, as the prior requested, 'at the next day of March labur effectuously unto the deputes for a redresse and an answer of the said billes', there is no means of knowing. What is clear is that any hope the Durham monks may have placed on political and diplomatic pressures was doomed to complete disappointment. Edward IV's own failure to endorse the Durham cause stands in marked contrast to the willingness of the Lancastrian lords earlier in the century to lend their powerful influence in the face of Scottish attacks on Coldingham.[38] It is true that Richard, earl of Warwick, in a letter he wrote to Paul II at the close of 1465, expressed himself as a firm supporter of the convent's cause, rightly blamed the present crisis on the fraudulent designs 'ambitiosorum clericorum Regni Scociae', and put forward the disguised threat that the inhabitants of northern England were as ready to take up arms to defend the liberties of St Cuthbert as to protect their country from Scottish invasion.[39] The latter belief, probably suggested to Warwick by the Durham monks themselves, was emphatically proved by the Coldingham cause itself to be no longer warranted. Not even Warwick, whom the Durham prior and chapter considered their *dominus specialissimus* during the critical decade of the 1460s, seems to have been prepared to risk compromising the Yorkists' political concordat with the Scots for the sake of Durham interests. Only at the very end of Edward IV's reign did the English government begin to contemplate the undertaking of serious military operations against Scotland, at a time too late to affect the issue of the Coldingham cause.

For the seventeen years between 1461 and 1478 this cause was therefore conducted almost exclusively in the Roman curia. The story of the intrigues, negotiations and legal proceedings which took place at Rome during this period is extraordinarily complicated and many of its most significant details have left only partial and ambiguous record. Fortunately a study of the letters and documents which passed between the prior of Durham and his representatives at the curia (although only a small minority of these survive) makes it possible to establish the broad outline of events. The prior and chapter's first formal protestation to the pope had certainly reached Rome by December 1461, when Pius II entrusted the hearing of the appeal against Patrick Hume to his chaplain and auditor of causes, Master John de Cerretanis (Giovanni Cerretani).[40] The

---

[37] DCD, Reg. Parv. III, fo. 123v; Raine, *North Durham*, text p. 355.

[38] DCD, Reg. Parv. II, fos 12, 152; Reg. III, fo. 277; *Cold. Corr.*, pp. 130, 142.

[39] DCD. Reg. Parv. III, fos 128v–9; *Cold. Corr.*, pp. 206–7.

[40] DCD. Reg. IV, fos 138v–41v; Misc. Charters, no. 1491. Cerretanis's distinction as a papal lawyer is testified by his later prominence as judicial adviser to Giuliano della Rovere, L. Pastor, *History of the Popes*, ed. F.A. Antrobus (5th edn, London, 1949), iv, p. 323, and his promotion to the bishopric of Nocera in 1476, C. Eubel, *Hierarchia Catholica medii aevi* (2nd edn, Munster, 1913–14), ii, p. 205.

fifteenth-century convent normally retained the services of a permanent and resident proctor at the curia through whom the Durham case and its supporting evidence could be transmitted to Cerretanis. Since 1449 Durham's sole regular proctor at Rome had been Master John Lax, probably a native of Chester-le-Street and a clerk apparently well qualified to play the leading role in annulling the effects of Patrick Hume's bull of August 1461.[41] Lax had been handsomely rewarded for his services to the chapter, not only by a regular annual pension of 40 shillings, but also by his presentation (on 13 August 1456) to a canonry and prebend in Durham's collegiate church of Hemingbrough in the East Riding of Yorkshire.[42] Nevertheless the convent's trust in Lax proved to have been very largely unwarranted. His career at the curia is now known to have been an unusually turbulent one and the Durham monks suffered, like his other employers, from Lax's personal litigiousness, improvidence and negligent attitude towards his duties during the last years of his life.[43]

After the cause of appeal before Cerretanis began its lengthy course in 1462, the Durham monks gradually became aware that Lax seemed unable or unwilling to put forward their case in a sufficiently decisive manner. Some allowances might be made, as in a letter of 16 September 1463 from Prior Burnby, for the notorious difficulties of communication between England and Rome: according to the latest news at Durham 'M. John Lax receyvid never our evidence of Coldyngham but now of late', while the sum of £20 from England had never reached Lax at all.[44] Despite their use of Italian banking firms with branches both in London and Rome, the Durham monks were to find that the safe and speedy transmission of money to the curia was to prove one of their worst problems during the next ten years. But it remains impossible to exonerate John Lax from the accusation of a negligence so alarming that it must be counted as one of the

[41] DCD, Reg. IV, fo. 70; *Cold. Corr.*, pp. 167–81. Lax was appointed an abbreviator of papal letters on 2 May 1449 and continued to reside at Rome, first as abbreviator and then as papal secretary, until his death in 1466: *CPL*, x, p. 49; xi, p. 99; xii, p. 254; *BRUO*, ii, pp. 1113–14. I am indebted to Dr L.J. Macfarlane for his generous assistance in providing details of Lax's career.

[42] DCD, Bursars' Accounts, 1464–6, Pensiones et Stipendia; Reg. IV, fo. 101; York, St Anthony's Hall, Reg. William Booth (xx), fo. 130.

[43] Lax's often stormy relationship with the English hospice of St Thomas at Rome is discussed by several contributors to *The English Hospice at Rome* (1962), pp. 55, 67, 89, 96, 150. The Benedictine monks of Glastonbury, like those of Durham, had cause to regret their choice of Lax as proctor at the curia: *CPL*, x, pp. 530–1; *Register of Bishop Bekynton*, Somerset Record Society (1934–5), i, pp. 109, 305, 319–20, 356–7, 367. On the other hand Lax could be capable of exerting very great influence at Rome: he was largely responsible for securing the canonisation of St Osmund in 1456 (A.R. Malden, *The Canonization of St Osmund*, Wilts. Record Soc. (1901), pp. xxviii–xxxi, pp. 41–215), and at one time rumours reached Durham that he might be made a bishop, DCD, Locellus XXV, no 5.

[44] DCD, Reg. Parv. III, fos 118v–19.

most important contributory factors in explaining the convent's inability to scotch Patrick Hume's designs on Coldingham at an early stage.

Throughout 1463 and 1464 it was gradually brought home to the Durham convent that its only hope of victory was the undertaking of much more vigorous measures at Rome. A genuine transformation of the monastery's attitude towards the Coldingham cause can be dated more precisely to the autumn of 1464, when John Burnby died and was replaced as prior of Durham by the capable and ambitious Richard Bell.[45] Within a few weeks of his election on 26 November 1464 Bell placed Durham's conduct of its case at the curia on a completely new footing by arranging to supplement Lax's inadequate efforts with the personal intervention there of a Durham monk. Prior Bell's decision marked a radical departure from the convent's customary disinclination to entrust official business at Rome to one of its own brethren.[46] Previous priors of Durham had obviously considered – and the events of the 1460s and 1470s were eventually to justify their view – that a Durham monk at the curia was extremely likely to prove an innocent abroad.

John Pencher was still alive and indeed still titular prior of Coldingham in late 1464, but there were obvious reasons why he failed to prove Bell's first choice as a personal representative at the curia. Pencher's long life as monk of Durham was drawing towards its close, and the attacks on his personal character already made by Patrick Hume made it doubtful whether he could ever hope to be *persona grata* at Rome.[47] Bell preferred to use as his emissary the more obviously well-qualified Richard Billingham, professed a monk of Durham in the autumn of 1441, one of the long line of distinguished ex-fellows of Durham College, Oxford, whose hands as chancellors of the monastery still lie so heavily on the convent's muniments.[48] As monastic *cancellarius* since 7 September 1459, Billingham

---

[45] See below, pp. 147–50.

[46] Although it was by no means unusual for a Durham monk to visit Rome, he almost always did so on his own behalf (to secure a papal indulgence or remission of some grave spiritual offence) and not that of his monastery. It is virtually certain that the expedition projected by John Pencher in Sept. 1444 to defend the convent's interests at Coldingham (DCD, Reg. Parv. II, fo. 188) never materialised.

[47] Pencher entered the community in 1420 and died shortly before 16 Jan. 1467, *Liber vitae*, fo. 70v; DCD, Bursar's Account 1466–7, Expense Necessarie; *Cold. Corr.*, p. 212.

[48] *Liber vitae*, fo. 70v; DCD, Reg. IV, fos 120, 123, 129v, 151–2; Reg. Parv. III, fo. 121. Richard Billingham, the son and heir of John Taillour of Billingham, Co. Durham, received his early education at Durham and was probably recruited into the community from its grammar and almonry school in the Bailey, DCD, 2.9. Specialia, nos 3–6; cf. *Durham Account Rolls*, iii, p. 676. He was a fellow of Durham College from 1446 until 1457, DCD, Feretrar's Account, 1446–7; Reg. Parv. III, fo. 70. As Durham chancellor between 1459 and 1464, Billingham rearranged the convent's muniments and completed in his own hand the most exhaustive and sophisticated inventory of these records ever produced at Durham, DCD, 'Repertorium Magnum', fos 19v, 80. I owe these references, and much else, to the kindness of Mr Martin Snape.

had represented his community as a general proctor on several occasions and gained familiarity with a wide range of canon law procedures, all the more impressive in that no Durham monk ever received university training in canon or civil law. On 5 December 1464 Billingham was appointed one of the four proctors of the prior and chapter at the Apostolic See.[49] The preparations for Richard Billingham's mission went forward during the following two months and only on 10 January 1465 did he receive Prior Bell's personal licence to visit the curia.[50] Billingham finally left Durham on his first journey to Rome on 13 February 1465, carrying with him a bulky collection of protestations, procurations, transcripts, copies of papal bulls and memoranda as well as the chapter's authorisation to borrow money up to the value of £20 sterling at the curia.[51]

On Billingham's arrival at Rome, probably in late March 1465, he found that the Coldingham cause had been decisively and permanently transformed by the dramatic intervention of Sir Alexander Hume in the interests of his son John. It is not difficult to explain Sir Alexander's decision to bring the priory and barony of Coldingham firmly within the orbit of his own family. The inability of the Durham chapter to resist Patrick Hume's intrusion must have made it clear that the rights of the English monks could be disregarded with a considerable degree of impunity. It seems equally clear, although the personal relationship between the two kinsmen remains the most mysterious and unrecorded feature of the story, that Patrick and Alexander Hume were themselves adversaries from an early date. Alexander may have feared that Patrick's position as commendator of Coldingham would entail his own forfeiture of the extremely valuable control of the temporal assets of the cell which he had enjoyed since 14 May 1442 as bailie of Coldingham, an office for which he had been prepared to fight his uncle David Hume of Wedderburn at great length in the early 1440s.[52] The conferment of Coldingham on one of his own sons had the obvious advantage that Alexander Hume could continue to exploit the very real wealth of the priory in the interests of his own determination to play an aggressive and ambitious role in Scottish and border politics. Moreover, and on this point the Durham case was always at its weakest, monastic life at fifteenth-century Coldingham can rarely have presented an edifying

---

[49] DCD, Reg. IV, fo. 150v.

[50] Ibid., fo. 152v.

[51] Ibid., fo. 152; *Cold. Corr.*, pp. 191–3.

[52] DCD, Reg. III, fos 129, 275; Reg. Parv. II, fos 69, 96, 101; *Cold Corr.*, pp. 108–10, 113–14, 116, 119–24, 132–6, 140–2, 145–51; HMC, series 57, *Home* 19–21; *Davidis Humii de Familia Humia Wedderburnensi Liber*, Abbotsford Club (1839), p. 8. Although he founded the economic and political fortunes of his family after the death of his father at Verneuil in 1424, Alexander Hume, first Lord Hume from 1473, still awaits a biographer: see, however, *Scots Peerage*, iv, pp. 444–51, and the important correction, ibid., ix, pp. 106–7.

spectacle of religious zeal.[53] Alexander Hume's own spiritual aspirations had recently been transferred to his own foundation, the collegiate church of Dunglass.[54] He had much experience, dating from long before the 1460s, in securing papal privileges at the curia for himself and his family;[55] and the case he put forward in late 1464 was starkly simple and extremely effective. It was tactically unwise and legally unnecessary to refer at any length to the rights of Durham monks who were not even in possession of the cell; but the grant of the priory *in commendam* to Patrick Hume was pronounced illegal because the latter had been excommunicate at the time of the papal letters of 6 August 1461. In response to a supplication to that effect, a papal mandate of 10 December 1464 asked the bishop of St Andrews, the archpriest of Dunbar and William Forman to investigate the charge against Patrick. If true, these mandatories were to collate to the priory of Coldingham Alexander Hume's son John, who would then surrender his canonry at the collegiate church of Dunbar and (a clever stroke which Patrick had no hope of emulating) take the monastic habit.[56] The contents of this bull were put rapidly into operation and, as a consequence, John Hume was to hold the priorate of Coldingham apparently continuously – despite the great pressures exerted on him – until the end of the century.[57] The exact date at which John Hume took corporal possession of the priory remains, like that on which Patrick Hume ejected the Durham monks, somewhat problematical. According to a statement in a later Durham recapitulation of their cause, Alexander Hume and his son had anticipated the papal mandate of December 1464 by forcibly expelling Patrick Hume and intruding John before appealing to Rome.[58] Such a sequence of events seems inherently probable and finds indirect support in the later statements made by Patrick Hume that his own peaceful possession of Coldingham lasted only for two years and more.[59]

---

[53] The collection of service-books recorded in an inventory of the priory's goods completed on 10 Jan 1447 is extremely small, DCD, Misc. Charters, no. 1437; *Cold. Corr.*, lxxxiii; and it is clear that after 1424 priors of Durham made little attempt to provide Coldingham with more than a skeleton staff of monks from the mother-house. There were only two Durham monks at Coldingham on 20 Jan. 1438, four in June 1446, six on 18 Feb. 1449 and two on 10 Sept. 1457, DCD, Reg. III, fo. 217; Locellus XVI, no. 6f; Locellus XXVII, no. 8; Locellus XIII, no. 14.

[54] Alexander Hume probably converted St Mary's Chapel, Dunglass into a collegiate church during the 1440s, Reg. Supp., 450, fo. 36; 609, fo. 65v; *CPL*, xi, p. 397; Easson, *Religious Houses*, p. 178.

[55] Reg. Supp., 450, fo. 36; 452, fo. 220v; *CPL*, x, pp. 217–19.

[56] Reg. Supp., 577, fo. 196; *CPL*, xii, pp. 232–4; Cameron, *Apostolic Camera*, p. 148.

[57] Numerous references to Prior John or Prior John Hume in official documents suggest that he exercised effective control over Coldingham until *c.* 1500: e.g. see Reg. Supp., 680, fo. 187v; *Acts of the Parliaments of Scotland*, ed. T. Thompson and C. Innes (Edinburgh, 1814–75), ii, p. 215; *Reg. Mag. Sig.*, ii, pp. 182, 280, 290; *Acts of Lords Auditors*, p. 143.

[58] DCD, Misc. Charters, no. 1491.

[59] *CPL*, xii, pp. 251, 267.

It seems proper to assume that Alexander and his son were enjoying the fruits and revenues of Coldingham as early as the summer or autumn of 1464.

At the beginning of 1465 the Coldingham cause had therefore taken the form of a three-cornered contest which it then retained until the intervention of James III in 1472. Of the three claimants to the priory, Patrick and John Hume appealed against each other while both Scottish clerks were opposed by the Durham candidate. John Pencher's death and the succession as titular prior of Thomas Halghton on 16 January 1467 (replaced in turn by Thomas Wren on 19 February 1470) made no difference to the general legal merits of the Durham case;[60] but as Bishop Graham of St Andrews failed to admit either Halghton or Wren to the priorate on the chapter's presentation, the Durham monks were soon deprived of the argument that one of their number had been physically dispossessed of his benefice. However, even before Pencher's death, it was always in Durham's interest to raise the fundamental issues of right to the priory; equally obviously the Humes had good reason to try to avoid a searching enquiry into the exact constitutional position of Coldingham within the Scottish church. On 30 April 1465 the prior and chapter scored their first notable success when Master John de Cerretanis delivered to the Durham proctors a series of letters compulsory, citatory and inhibitory.[61] These theoretically formidable legal weapons reached Durham during the summer, but the chapter encountered its usual difficulties in securing their effective enforcement within the Scottish kingdom. The diplomatic conference between English and Scottish magnates at Alnwick on 17 July 1465 seemed to present an opportunity; but, although the monks were represented there by the prior of Holy Island and other clerks, they were refused safe-conducts into Scotland. The Scottish lords, who included the bishop of Glasgow, justified their inability to co-operate by a reference to the dangers of violence 'propter potencias amicorum consanguineorum et affinium dominorum Patricii Home et Johannis Home'. The Durham party in Northumberland had no alternative but to content itself with reciting the terms of Cerretanis's letters in the nave of Norham parish church on 18 July. On the same day, but for only a few hours William Layburn actually dared to cross the Tweed to the parish church of

---

[60] DCD, Reg. IV, fos 192v, 202; *Cold. Corr.*, pp. 211–12, 216–17.

[61] The former were addressed to the bishop and ecclesiastics of St Andrews diocese and 'compelled' them to release to Durham any written evidence in their possession that was pertinent to the Coldingham cause, DCD, Misc. Charters, no. 1491; Reg. IV, fos 162–5; *Cold. Corr.*, pp. 197, 202, 204. A full copy of these *littere compulsoriales* comprises the second item of National Library of Scotland, MS Adv. 35.4.13. Nothing is known of the provenance of this manuscript (a collection of transcripts of eight notarial instruments relating to the Coldingham cause at Rome between 1465 and 1468), but it appears to be the work of a seventeenth-century antiquary copying documents at Durham.

Upsettlington, where he cited the Humes to appear before Cerretanis. 'Quibus gestis idem nuncius regnum Angliae celeriter est regressus.'[62]

The success of the Durham monks' appeal naturally did not founder completely on their inability to deliver a personal citation to the two Humes. Cerretanis conceded the point that, as it was impossible for Durham mandatories to secure access to the two Scottish clerks, they should be cited before him by means of a public edict. Neither of the Humes responded to their summonses, however, and the case dragged slowly and inconclusively onwards during the winter of 1465–66.[63] Two letters sent to Prior Bell from Richard Billingham revealed the current atmosphere of doubt and uncertainty at Rome. In his first letter (of 16 January 1466) Billingham allowed himself to take an optimistic view of the eventual outcome of the Coldingham cause, for this would end in 'the greatest worship that ever ye had in your days', a view which seemed to be based on little but rumours that the cardinal of Spoleto had great influence at the curia and was known to 'shaw favour to Englysshe men'.[64] Billingham's second letter (of 22 January) was almost exclusively devoted to developing the hints he had already dropped of Master John Lax's complete unreliability as proctor.[65] Lax's death shortly before 29 September 1466[66] relieved Billingham of an embarrassing ally and allowed Prior Bell to replace him by the much more suitable Master Peter de Mellinis. Although an Italian and a *civis Romanus*, Mellinis (Pietro Millini) was a curial clerk well known in English monastic circles.[67] Bell had considered him a suitable candidate for the post of the chapter's proctor at Rome as early as December 1464; but it was Billingham's warm recommendation that eventually brought Mellinis the office and Lax's old pension of 40 shillings per annum.[68] The letters written by Mellinis to Durham during subsequent years leave no doubt of his astuteness and

---

[62] DCD, Reg. IV, fos 162–5; *Cold. Corr.*, pp. 196–206.

[63] DCD, Misc. Charters, no. 1491.

[64] DCD, Misc. Charters, no. 1065, printed in part and out of sequence in *Cold. Corr.*, pp. 225–7. The place and date of this mutilated letter, as well as nearly all of its contents, can be discovered by means of ultra-violet light.

[65] When Billingham had arrived at the curia in the previous year, he had found it necessary to redeem Lax from the excommunication and imprisonment into which his improvidence had led him. Nearly all the money sent to Rome by Prior Burnby had been quietly diverted into Lax's own pocket; and as crowning proof that 'simulata sanctitas duplex est iniquitas', Billingham enclosed a copy of a curiously cheerful yet facile letter that Lax had sent him from Siena in the previous September (*Cold. Corr.*, pp. 207–10).

[66] *CPL*, xii, p. 254; York, Minister Library, Chapter Acts Book 1427–1504, fos 127v–8.

[67] The priory of Christ Church, Canterbury, conferred letters of fraternity on Mellinis in Oct. 1469 for his services in entertaining two of their monks in Rome, U. Balzani, 'Un ambasciata inglese a Roma, 1487', *Archivio della società di storia patria*, 3 (1880), pp. 187, 208.

[68] DCD, Reg. IV, fos 143, 150v; Bursars' Accounts 1468–79, Pensiones et Stipendia; *Cold. Corr.*, pp. 192, 209, 211.

ability as *causarum procurator in Romana curia*;[69] but, like Billingham and Lax, he was in the habit of reporting far too optimistically about Durham's prospects at Rome. Such optimism was an occupational disease of all professional agents at the curia, for the simple reason that their continued employment might depend upon it.

Mellinis began to act as Durham's regular proctor at the curia in 1466, a year in which negotiations at Rome reached a higher point of complexity than ever before. Both Patrick and John Hume were excommunicated for their failure to respond to papal citations; and on 17 June 1466 John de Cerretanis eventually pronounced his long-awaited definitive sentence.[70] Cerretanis found completely in favour of the prior and chapter, who were to recover Coldingham and receive financial compensation from the Humes for the alienation of their rents. Both Humes appealed separately to the pope against this sentence; and, at the same time, Patrick Hume (in residence at the curia since at least the previous autumn) attempted to undermine his namesake's position by securing the annulment of the papal mandate of 10 December 1464.[71] Very surprisingly Patrick was successful. On 2 August 1466 he secured a new papal bull, addressed to the archbishop of Arles and bishops of St Andrews and Glasgow, asking them to reinstate Patrick at Coldingham on the grounds that he had only been dispossessed by means of a malicious conspiracy between Alexander Hume, his son John and the then papal collector in Scotland, Richard Vile.[72] Although aware of Patrick's counter-attack on John Hume, the Durham agents at Rome rightly continued to place their hopes on Cerretanis. The failure of the Humes to put the latter's definitive sentence into effect left him no option but to excommunicate them once again, John Hume on 11 May 1467 and Patrick shortly afterwards on 3 June.[73] Temporarily at least, there was no more that Richard Billingham could do at the curia; and after an absence of well over two years he returned to England carrying with him the written sentences of excommunication on the Humes, to be formally received at Durham by Prior Bell on 21 August.[74] At first sight Richard

---

[69] Bell admitted Mellinis into the fraternity of the convent on 12 Sept. 1467 and later entrusted him with the highly dangerous and confidential negotiations aimed at securing a bishopric for the prior, DCD, Reg. Parv. III, fo. 134v; *Obituary Roll of William Ebchester and John Burnby*, Surtees Soc. (1856), p. 111; below, pp. 152–3.

[70] DCD, Misc. Charters, no 1491; National Library of Scotland, MS Adv. 35.4.13, no. 4.

[71] Patrick had received papal collation to the canonry and prebend of Banchory in Aberdeen Cathedral on 29 Nov. 1465, Reg. Supp., 588, fo. 136v; *CPL*, xii, pp. 470, 485.

[72] *CPL*, xii, pp. 251–3. A note across the margin of the copy of this bull in the Vatican registers suggests that it was to be temporarily kept a closed secret. But Patrick's powers of persuasion earned him yet another bull on 21 March 1467, addressed to the same three mandatories and to the same general effect (ibid., pp. 267–9).

[73] National Library of Scotland, MS Adv. 35.4.13, nos 6–7.

[74] DCD, Reg. IV, fo. 196v; *Cold Corr.*, p. 212.

Billingham's first expedition to Rome, although lengthy and expensive, may seem to have ended in real achievement; but Billingham's success fell far short of total victory. Durham held a bull excommunicating both its adversaries, and Patrick Hume another requiring his reinstatement at Coldingham; but John Hume continued to hold the priorate and was himself explicitly recognised as prior by the pope in yet two other bulls of May 1467 and December 1467.[75]

The value of Cerretanis's instruments of excommunication was soon put to a concrete test. On 23 August 1467 Patrick and John Hume were formally and publicly excommunicated from the pulpit of the nave of Durham Cathedral in the presence of Bishop Lawrence Booth as well as the complete chapter. Richard Billingham himself accompanied a Durham party which then rode northwards to repeat the ceremony at Norham church on 4 September in the presence of many Englishmen and Scots who were visiting the market there that day. On this occasion no attempt was made to cross the Tweed.[76] The expedition to Norham must have been taken with no other object than to provide Richard Billingham with a notarised certificate of the excommunication of the two Humes which he could carry back to Cerretanis at the curia. Billingham returned to Rome as early as 21 January 1468, when he reported to Bell on the difficulties of his journey, subject to delays at London and Dover, 'abidyng passage, the whiche was right perilous for the thiknes of mistes'. Billingham proceeded to report on the current state of the Coldingham cause. A sudden crisis caused by the discovery that the prior and chapter had failed to provide sufficient proof of their eviction from Coldingham was overcome by the timely appearance of a papal notary, Master John Norham, who could testify to his personal presence at the expulsion of Prior John Pencher. Billingham and Mellinis were as sanguine as ever: 'And within shorte days we trust fully, be Gods grace, to have an sentence; the which shalbe to youe and the Monastery the grettist worshippe that ever ye had in your dais'.[77]

Several judicial sentences, all in favour of Durham, were in fact pronounced during the course of 1468; but, as both Patrick and John Hume immediately appealed against Cerretanis's judgements to the pope, Paul II decided to transfer the hearing of the Coldingham cause to another of his auditors of causes and papal chaplains, Master Antonius de Grassis.[78]

[75] *CPL*, xii, pp. 321–2, 620.

[76] DCD, Bursar's Account 1467–8, Expense Necessarie; *Cold. Corr.*, pp. 213–15. There was a third public recital of excommunication on the Humes in St Nicholas Church, Newcastle upon Tyne, on 26 Sept. 1467.

[77] DCD, Locellus XXV, no. 2; *Cold. Corr.*, pp. 215–16.

[78] Grassis had been commissioned to hear an appeal made by John against Patrick Hume before 21 March 1467 (*CPL*, xxi, p. 268); but he does not seem to have received authority to supervise the entire Coldingham cause until several months later. Like Cerretanis, Grassis secured an Italian bishopric (Tivoli in 1485) as reward for his activities as a prominent papal lawyer, Eubel, *Hierarchia*, ii (Munster, 1914), p. 251.

Whatever the reasons for this decision, it did the Durham cause nothing but harm. Eventually Grassis (who already had some experience in the hearing of Scottish appeal causes[79]) confirmed and re-enacted all his predecessor's judgements, but it seems to have taken him more than three years to do so. On his return journey to Durham in the spring of 1468 Richard Billingham caused an additional complication when he allowed himself to be captured and imprisoned by the archbishop of Cologne. After receiving Edward IV's licence to do so, Prior Bell paid the archbishop a hundred marks as ransom for his unfortunate monk.[80] In a letter of 10 November 1468 Bell reported that Billingham was unable to visit Rome again as originally intended because he still lay 'sore seke, abidying the mercy of Almighty God' at Durham.[81] By this date a papal bull enabling the prior and chapter to command the sequestration of the Humes's spiritualities had reached Durham, but Bell pointed out that this was of little use as long as the Durham monks and their agents were refused safe-conducts into Scotland. It was so difficult for the Durham monks to communicate with the Scottish government that Prior Bell had taken the opportunity of entrusting letters on the subject of Coldingham to an envoy of Charles the Bold, duke of Burgundy, who passed through Durham on his way to the Scottish court. Neither this informal approach nor the appointment of Richard Billingham (on 8 December 1468) as the prior and convent's proctor to discuss the Coldingham case before James III had any results.[82] The following three years (1469–71) were ones of complete stalemate. To judge from the lack of evidence, even negotiations at the curia had begun to lose their impetus. Richard Billingham, his health recovered, remained at Durham and made several fruitless journeys to London and Northumberland in an attempt to break the deadlock.[83] There is no record of any Durham agent fortunate or foolhardy enough to have entered Scotland during this period; and the political upheavals of the time made the English government more powerless than ever to intervene.

[79] *CPL*, xi, pp. 502–3.

[80] Edward IV's letter on this subject (DCD, Misc. Charters. no. 1060, printed out of sequence in *Cold. Corr.*, pp. 228–9) was written at the monastery of Stratford on 16 June: 1468 is the only year which accords with Billingham's and Edward IV's movements, Scofield, *Edward IV*, i, p. 456. Prior Bell was infuriated at the incident and hoped to persuade Paul II to punish the archbishop 'for his dampnable ded, in ensampill of all other, and elles it will lett me and all other to pursew any mater in the said Court without that he be dewly correct after his demeritts', DCD, Reg. Parv. III, fo. 140v.

[81] DCD, Reg. Parv. III, fos 139v–40.

[82] National Library of Scotland, MS Adv. 35.3.8 (a volume of transcripts of Coldingham charters made at Durham by Walter MacFarlane in 1744), fos 154–6; Raine, *North Durham*, no. 573.

[83] Billingham's travelling expenses 'pro expedicione materie de Coldyngham' are recorded in DCD, Bursars' Accounts 1468–71, Expense Necessarie.

In 1471 the recovery of his throne by Edward IV and the election of a new pope, Sixtus IV, encouraged the prior and chapter to renew their campaign for the recovery of Coldingham. In the early summer of that year Grassis, *post magnum iuris processum*, enacted a series of sentences of excommunication and interdict against the Humes and was persuaded to direct his 'letters executorial' to the kings and magnates of England and Scotland.[84] These letters (of 1 July 1471) authorised the use of the secular arm to expel John Hume from Coldingham and were the greatest single success ever achieved by the Durham party at the curia. They were supplemented by a letter sent from Sixtus IV on 10 September 1471 to Edward IV and James III, requesting the personal support of both monarchs.[85] Accordingly Edward sent Norroy king-at-arms to the Scottish court with the message that 'it belongith every Cristen prince in the right of the Chirch to put to his hand of help and defense'.[86] As the king's envoy passed through Durham on the last day of 1471, Prior Bell entrusted him with his own letter to James III, asking him to promote the peaceful reoccupation of Coldingham by Durham monks: Bell made a specific appeal to 'your grete zele luff and favour that ye have hade and as I suppose daily have unto the gloriouse confessour saynt Cuthbert, our patron, to whome the said celle and barony was giffen of grete devocion by your most noble progenitours, continually to be praied for both her and ther'.[87]

The final and ultimate irony of the Coldingham cause was provided by James III's unexpected reaction to Bell's plea for his personal intervention. The monastery's privileged position north of the Tweed had always been founded on the respect and obligation displayed by the Scottish kings towards St Cuthbert. In 1472 this long tradition was decisively rejected by the young and ambitious James III. Bell's reminder that the Humes 'for thair gret obstinacy and rebellion don against the lawes of holy kirke stande accursid' offered James the prospect that he might be able to expel John Hume from Coldingham, not on Durham's behalf but on his own. On 6 April 1472 James III successfully petitioned Sixtus IV to instruct William, bishop of Ostia, to suppress the priory of Coldingham and unite its revenues in perpetuity to his own royal chapel of St Mary at St Andrews.[88] No reference whatsoever was made to Durham's claims in the resulting papal mandate. Henceforward the king of Scotland was added to the names of those who opposed the return of St Cuthbert's monks to their old dependency.

Nevertheless the convent's involvement with Coldingham did not end

[84] BL, MS Harley 4623, i, fo. 176v; DCD, Reg. Parv. III, fos 149–50.
[85] *Cold. Corr.*, pp. 258–9.
[86] Ibid., p. 220; DCD, Bursar's Account 1471–2, Expense Necessarie.
[87] DCD, Reg. Parv. III, fo. 150; *Cold. Corr.*, p. 222.
[88] *CPL*, xiii, p. 14; Cameron, *Apostolic Camera*, p. 172.

abruptly after James III's dramatic intervention in April 1472. Although there is every reason to believe that James never (until his death sixteen years later) abandoned the plan to exploit Coldingham priory in his own interests, the Humes proved formidable and eventually successful antagonists. Thanks to the account given by Robert Lindesay of Pitscottie, it is well known that James III's renewed attempt to seize Coldingham from the Humes in 1484–88 was largely responsible for the revolt which led to his murder after 'Sauchieburn'.[89] The lack of any reliable or well-informed Scottish chronicler of these years makes it unlikely that it will ever be possible to disentangle the complicated story of the struggle for Coldingham between 1472 and 1488 or to assess its exact significance as one of the factors contributing to the factious politics of James III's reign. For only a few years after 1472 do the Durham records continue to throw some fitful light on the nature of the contest. It seems clear, however, that when James III launched his attack in 1472, he was not only fully conscious that Alexander Hume was his main opponent but acted in co-operation with Patrick Hume himself. The king's petition of April 1472 had requested that the suppression of Coldingham should only take effect on the death or resignation of the then prior. As a further papal mandate of the following year (3 April 1473) makes clear, James regarded Patrick and not John Hume as the rightful prior of Coldingham.[90] By this second date the concordat between James III and Patrick had taken a new and more practical form in the shape of a plan to convert the priory into a collegiate church under royal patronage. In exchange for resigning his priorate, Patrick Hume was to be appointed as the first dean of this new chapel royal of Coldingham. Whatever the merits, and they are obvious and many, of so radical a solution to the Coldingham problem, there was little chance that it could be put into operation at a time when Alexander Hume (Lord Home from August 1473 and soon to be a warden of the marches) was still strengthening his already impressive control over the Scottish Borders. Not for the first time, Patrick Hume had overplayed his hand. Encumbered with debt and in serious danger of imprisonment at Rome for that reason,[91] he seems to have allowed his claims to be bought off by Alexander and John Hume. On 2 August 1473, less than four months after the papal mandate ordering the erection of a

---

[89] Pitscottie, *Histoire*, i, pp. 200–1; Manchester, John Rylands Library, MS 38, fo. 94. Pitscottie's account is slight, written at second or third hand and demonstrably inaccurate in detail; but his explicit assertion that the 1488 conspiracy against James III arose 'because the Homes ever intendit to haue ane pryour in that roume of thair awin surname quhairfoir they thocht the king greatlie to be thair eneme' is indirectly subtantiated by all the available contemporary record evidence, *CPL*, xiv, pp. 45–50; *Acts Parl. Scot.*, ii, pp. 171, 179–80, 182, 184; *Acts of Council*, i, p. 113; Raine, *North Durham*, no. 445. The problem is discussed briefly in R.L. Mackie, *King James IV of Scotland* (Edinburgh, 1958), pp. 33–9.

[90] Reg. Supp., 689, fos 147v–8v; *CPL*, xiii, p. 19; Theiner, *Monumenta*, pp. 472–3.

[91] Reg. Supp., 636, fo. 221; 639, fo. 284; 658, fo. 101; 675, fo. 41.

chapel royal at Coldingham, Patrick was alleged to have resigned his rights there to his successful rival John.[92]

The reaction of Prior Bell and his fellows to the bewildering events of 1472–73 can only be surmised. Although it is far from clear how soon they learnt of James III's negotiations at the curia, they despatched Richard Billingham on his third and final visit to Rome shortly before 1 July 1472. On that day Billingham sent Bell the extraordinary news that 'within few dayes, be Goddes grace ye shall have an end in this cause' and the even more misguided comment by a Durham advocate that the Scots 'shall obey thatt is juggett, in despytt off thaim that sais the contrary'.[93] Billingham's reports to Durham had always been unrealistically optimistic, but this is the first occasion on which he can be reasonably suspected of having written in bad faith. Only four months later (on 29 October 1472) he secured a papal dispensation allowing him to occupy a secular benefice with or without cure of souls.[94] Durham's own representative at the curia had now decided to withdraw himself from the community of St Cuthbert. Armed with the most powerful weapon a dissident monk could wield, Richard Billingham rapidly proceeded to sever his relations with the Coldingham cause and with Durham. On 26 May 1475 Prior Bell wrote that he had received no news of 'dominus Ricardus' for three years and described him as 'nuper confratrem meum quamvis ingratum et a Regule sue professionis enormiter deviantem'.[95]

Richard Billingham's desertion, with its demonstration that the convent stood to lose even more than money by continuing its campaign to recover Coldingham, had an obvious effect at Durham. Prior Bell sent no other monk to replace Billingham at the curia and henceforward made no attempt to inaugurate new appeal cases of the sort heard by Cerretanis and Grassis in the previous decade. Still anxious that Mellinis and his other agents at Rome should seize any suitable opportunity to re-state Durham's claims, Bell was gradually forced to withdraw from any very active participation in the cause. On 31 August 1474 he informed Mellinis that the Coldingham suit had already cost his monastery a round thousand pounds sterling; and the Durham monks were now too poverty-stricken to provide more funds until better fortune came their way.[96] There was, admittedly, the new prospect that the contest between James III and the Humes might allow Durham Priory to re-emerge *tertium gaudens*. Although this can never have been a very real possibility, the Coldingham cause did in fact take a curious last twist when Patrick Hume reentered the field. In the last weeks of 1474, Patrick's proctors arrived at

[92] Reg. Supp., 694, fo. 129v.
[93] *Cold. Corr.*, p. 225.
[94] *CPL*, xiii, p. 326.
[95] DCD, Reg. Parv. III, fo. 162.
[96] DCD, Reg. Parv. III, fo. 156v.

Durham bringing the unlikely news that the inspiration of the Holy Ghost and St Cuthbert had led to a change of heart on the part of the convent's old enemy. Patrick was now ready, so Bell (and later historians) believed, to surrender his title to Coldingham and even to help Durham secure a general interdict 'to be execute throwoute the realme of Scotland'.[97] It need hardly be said that such a reconciliation never took place. The true explanation for Patrick's remarkable approach to Durham was provided by Mellinis in a letter to Bell of 26 April 1475.[98] Patrick, under heavy financial pressures and excommunicate once again, had opened negotiations with Durham in the hope that recognition of his status by the prior and chapter would deliver him from ecclesiastical censure. Mellinis's comment that a man of Patrick Hume's acumen 'non offeret talem concordiam si haberet bonum fundamentum in jure' carries complete conviction. Even at this late date Mellinis attempted to revive Prior Bell's flagging interest in the Coldingham cause and told him to be of good heart 'quia omnia possunt reparari'. Prior Bell refused to respond and, although Mellinis continued to act as Durham's proctor of causes until Bell's provision to the bishopric of Carlisle in February 1478, the prior's last three years of office saw no major attempt to resume the Coldingham campaign. It seems probable that disillusion as to the prospects of ever regaining Coldingham was now general among all members of the Durham chapter. Within a few months of his election on 22 May 1478, Robert Ebchester the new prior of Durham, hastened to disembarrass himself of this most irksome and frustrating of all legacies left him by his predecessor. In two letters of 14 and 16 October 1478 he informed not only Mellinis but also Master John Shirwood, Edward IV's proctor at the curia, that the Coldingham affair should 'slepe for a tyme to such season as it may pleas God & Seynt Cuthbert that we may have better spede than we can have yit'.[99] At long last a Durham monk drew the proper conclusions from the sorry history of the last sixteen years. Negotiations at Rome were both prohibitively expensive and doubtful of ultimate success:

for if it wer so that the matter were revoked, and as we obtened a sentence therein, yit we couth not have it putt in execucion without we had the goode will & benevolence of the kynge of Scotts in this mater, or els as the towne of Berwyk wer in Ynglisshmen's hands, like as it was affore we wer spolyd & put forth be force and violence of the Scotts.

---

[97] Ibid., fo. 159; *Cold. Corr.*, pp. 231–2.

[98] This badly-mutilated letter, in which Mellinis describes Patrick as *astutus homo*, is printed in *Cold. Corr.*, pp. 232–5. I have not been able to find the original.

[99] DCD, Reg. Parv. III, fos 185v–6; *Scriptores tres*, pp. ccclxvi–ccclxviii; *Cold. Corr.*, pp. 235–6.

Four years later, but more than four years too late for the Durham cause, the Scots lost Berwick and its castle for ever – to Richard, duke of Gloucester, on 24 August 1482.[100]

Although the monks of Durham never formally renounced their rights to the priory and barony of Coldingham, Prior Ebchester's letters of October 1478 can be said to mark the effective end of the convent's own participation in the Coldingham cause. Henceforward the struggle for Coldingham was to be a matter for purely Scottish concern, a *damnosa hereditas* which dragged its long and tortuous path through the next century and more of the kingdom's history. By a curious irony the convent's own withdrawal from the contest coincided almost exactly with the elimination of its first rival for the priory. Shortly before 17 October 1478 Patrick Hume died in exile at Sutri.[101] Patrick's last years had been unhappy and litigious ones, and he lived to see his own archdeaconry of Teviotdale subjected to the same sort of ruthless barratry that he had himself practised against Coldingham. The Durham monks may have derived some vicarious and understandable consolation from the knowledge that towards the end of his life Patrick Hume had cause to regret his intrusion at Coldingham. James III had not, in the event, been able to remove the priory from the strong control of Alexander Hume and his son.[102] John Hume continued as prior and even before Patrick's death it had become evident that the struggle for Coldingham was taking place in a major political arena. The elimination of the original protagonists, the convent of Durham and Patrick Hume, brought the kings of Scotland and the Lords Hume into direct, fateful and long-lived collision.

In retrospect, both to later historians and to the Durham chapter of 1478, it may have seemed that no other outcome was possible. The convent's failure to secure the active support of either Yorkist government circles or a substantial body of magnate or ecclesiastical opinion within Scotland itself can be said to have proved its ultimate undoing. But in 1461 these difficulties had been regarded as purely temporary by the

---

[100] Lesley, *History*, pp. 49–50; J.H. Ramsay, *Lancaster and York* (Oxford, 1892), ii, p. 446. The implications of the loss of Berwick were not lost on the Humes, who were apparently involved in a scheme to recapture the town as early as the autumn of 1485, A. Conway, *Henry VII's Relations with Scotland and Ireland, 1485–1498* (Cambridge, 1932), pp. 8–9.

[101] Reg. Suppl., 774, fo. 131; *Fasti ecclesiae Scoticanae*, p. 60.

[102] The Humes' primary objective was undoubtedly the financial exploitation of Coldingham's estates by means of their monopolistic hold over the office of bailie of the priory, a position confirmed to Alexander Hume for life by royal charter as early as 25 Nov. 1472 (*Reg. Mag. Sig.*, ii, p. 225); but some form of conventual life was sponsored at the priory itself well into the sixteenth century. There were enough monks at Coldingham (probably Benedictines from Dunfermline) in Dec. 1503 to form a chapter (*Swintons*, p. lxxvi); and a subprior was recorded there as late as 1522 (*HMC*, series 57, *Home*, 32–33). Coldingham was one of the religious houses required by Archbishop Forman (1514–21) to maintain a monk at St Andrews University, J. Herkless and R.K. Hannay, *The Archbishops of St Andrews*, ii (Edinburgh, 1909), p. 207.

Durham monks who, as a direct result, only prosecuted their case more thoroughly at the Roman curia. To all intents and purposes the entire course of the Coldingham cause was fought out at Rome. It can therefore hardly fail to be of interest. This was the most complex and the most important issue brought to the curia by the Durham chapter since the distant days of its vicious if heroic fight with Bishop Antony Bek. It illustrates, much more vividly than any other episode in the history of the convent, the need for efficient monastic representation at the papal court, as well as providing an extreme example of the effects of barratry by Scottish clerks in the late fifteenth century. Above all, the complex series of appeals, petitions and judicial sentences which made up the history of the Coldingham cause in the 1460s and 1470s reveals the practical inadequacies of the curia as a supreme court of appeal. The papal chaplains and auditors specially commissioned by successive popes to preside over the case were certainly capable, given all the relevant evidence, of producing an equitable judgement; but the papal administrative machinery was so cumbersome, and the curial officials so easily swayed by fees and favours, that the Durham monks could never count on a consistency of attitude that they had every right to expect. 'Woe to the man that is snared in the Camera's net!' was a sentiment common to both prior and chapter of Durham in the late 1470s; and their unwillingness to re-enter that insidious mesh is sufficient explanation for their failure to reopen the Coldingham case during the last sixty years of their existence. Yet the memory of that small colony of English monks resident in Scotland survived, and not only in Durham itself.[103] On hearing of Surrey's great victory in 1513 and the death in battle of the then prior, Alexander Stewart, Henry VIII enthusiastically and optimistically suggested that now at last Coldingham should be restored to the priory of Durham.[104] The monks of Durham may be forgiven if, like their Bishop Thomas Ruthal,[105] they believed that at Flodden St Cuthbert had exacted his full quota of revenge.

[103] An unidentified and unsuccessful English candidate for Coldingham Priory emerged in 1509–11, between the death of Prior John Hume and his replacement by Alexander Stewart, *The Letters of James IV*, Scottish History Society (1953), pp. 163–4, 230. Cf. M. Dilworth, 'Coldingham Priory and the Reformation', *Innes Review*, 23 (1973), pp. 115–37, which appeared after this essay was first published.

[104] Henry VIII combined this with the proposal (in a letter written to Leo X from Tournai on 12 Oct. 1513) that the see of St Andrews should lose its new metropolitan status, Theiner, *Monumenta*, p. 512; *Letters and Papers Henry VIII*, 2nd edn, i, pp. 1047–8.

[105] Ibid., i, p. 1021.

6

Richard Bell, Prior of Durham (1464–78) and Bishop of Carlisle (1478–95)

The disappearance of the great majority of its records makes it impossible to hope that a fully comprehensive history of the diocese of Carlisle in the later middle ages can ever be written. By comparison with its great neighbours of the northern province, York and Durham, the bishopric of Carlisle offers relatively little information to the historian interested in its organisation, its efficiency and its general prosperity in the fifteenth century. But although our knowledge of the administrative routines and practices over which the bishops of Carlisle presided remains regrettably incomplete, it is sometimes possible to examine the lives of the bishops themselves in considerable detail. Few of the fourteen bishops of Carlisle between 1400 and the Reformation played an outstanding role in the work of English church or state; but a study of their careers has its own interest and can often lead to an estimate of their attitude to their pastoral functions. The value of such an approach was illustrated by R.L. Storey's account of Marmaduke Lumley, bishop of Carlisle from 1430 to 1450, undoubtedly the best known and probably the ablest of the fifteenth century episcopate at Carlisle.[1] Dr Storey stresses that Lumley was 'a remarkable exception to the established pattern', and it might therefore seem worthwhile to examine the life of Richard Bell, a bishop somewhat more representative of the Carlisle episcopal tradition and one whose eventful early career, thanks to his fifty years as monk and prior of Durham, is exceptionally well recorded.

Richard Bell made his profession as monk of Durham before the high altar of the cathedral church in 1426 or early 1427 at the unusually young age of sixteen.[2] At Durham, as in other large English monasteries, it was usual for monks to enter the community in groups, a practice which had the advantage of producing a convenient unit for teaching purposes during the noviciate. Bell was the junior and clearly the youngest of eight

---

[1] See *Transactions of Cumberland and Westmorland Antiquarian and Archaeological Society*, new series [CW2], 55, pp. 112–31.

[2] The approximate date of Bell's birth is established by a dispensation of 30 September 1432 allowing him to receive priest's orders in his twenty-second year: DCD, Reg. Parv. II, fos 65v–66. The date of his profession can be calculated from *Liber vitae ecclesiae Dunelmensis*, Surtees Society, 136 (1923), fo. 70v and the subsequent appearance of the monks there listed in the monastic records at Durham.

novices who made their profession in 1426–27. The prior and chapter of Durham were generally careful to observe the rule that 'Nemo ante 18 annum Monachatum sine necessitate, aut evidenti utilitate profiteatur';[3] and the fact that they made an exception in Bell's case may reflect their belief that the boy already showed unusual promise, probably demonstrated by his work as a student at the convent's grammar school, the normal source of recruitment into the fifteenth-century Durham community. It is equally possible that Bell owed his early advancement to family connections. The official correspondence of Durham monks rarely preserves references to relatives outside the monastic walls, while Bell's own surname was too common to provide any reliable guide to the names of his secular kinsmen. But it can hardly be coincidental that, when prior of Durham between 1464 and 1478, Richard Bell employed a public notary, a keeper of his park at Beaurepaire and a master mason, all with the same surname as himself.[4] In a letter of 3 March 1476 Prior Bell did name one of his close relations: he declared his intention of reserving a vacant prebend in the convent's collegiate church of Howden for Elias Bell, 'Scolar of Oxenford and my welbeloved neveu'. Elias Bell, once a fellow of Merton College, must have been the nephew to whom the prior referred in the following year when he wrote to Anne Neville, wife of Richard of Gloucester, on 11 April 1477. Prior Bell reminded the duchess that he had presented his nephew to her husband during one of the latter's visits to Durham and expressed the hope that the duke would accept this clerk into his service and as 'hys man'.[5] Like other priors of Durham Richard Bell knew how to look after his own.

Much the most intriguing illustration of Bell's care for his relatives is, however, the case of a certain Alice Bell, the recipient of an extraordinary series of favours at the hands of the prior. An important part of the patronage of the prior of Durham consisted of his control of appointments to places in the two almshouses and two hospitals administered by the monastic almoner. Although some of these places were still being conferred on the poor and deserving, the introduction of licences to enjoy their emoluments without taking up residence encouraged late medieval priors to treat these 'corrodies' as sources of income for friends, servants and relations. But in the entire history of the monastery at Durham there appears to be no parallel for the manner in which Prior Bell exploited this type of patronage in the interests of his namesake Alice. In February 1465, soon after Bell became prior, she was appointed to a position in the hospital of St Mary Magdalen on the outskirts of Durham. Less than ten years later Alice had become a pluralist with additional 'corrodies'

[3] W. Lyndwood, *Provinciale* (Oxford, 1679), p. 201.

[4] DCD, Reg. Parv. III, fo. 182; Reg. IV, fo. 168. References to John Bell, master mason at Durham, are collected by J. Harvey, *English Mediaeval Architects* (London, 1954), p. 29.

[5] DCD, Reg. Parv. III, fos 168v, 175*.

at the hospital of Witton Gilbert and the almshouse or *Domus Dei* in the Durham Bailey.[6] Even more significant was the conferment by the prior and chapter of letters of sorority on Alice Bell in March 1474.[7] The admission of a secular into the fraternity of the convent was considered an exceptional honour at late medieval Durham, generally reserved for powerful magnates or helpful knights and *armigeri*. Alice Bell's claims to the title of 'sister' of the monastery remain doubtful unless it is assumed that she was a particularly close relative of the then prior. For this reason the elder James Raine suggested that Alice Bell was 'in all probability' the mother of Richard Bell, an attractive theory although it assumes that Alice must have lived on into her eighties.[8]

On Richard Bell's entry into the Durham community the obscurity of his early life and origins is replaced by a comparatively detailed knowledge of his career. An essential feature of the Durham noviciate was the steady progress of the young monk through clerical orders, so that within five or six years from his profession he was fully priested and able to celebrate mass at one of the many altars in the convent or its cells. Because of his youth, Bell was compelled to make a somewhat slower journey through the orders than was usual at Durham. Although ordained acolyte on 20 December 1427 and subdeacon a year later (18 December 1428) he had to wait for deacon's orders until 24 February 1431.[9] He was ordained deacon by Bishop Langley of Durham in the palace of Bishop Auckland; and was then said to be *per priorem presentatus*, an unusual distinction which implies that his superior, Prior Wessington, had already begun to take an especial interest in the career of this young monk. Like other monks of obvious intellectual ability, Richard Bell was destined for an immediate appearance as a student and fellow of the convent's dependency of Durham College, Oxford. Accordingly Prior Wessington took the unorthodox though not unprecedented step of sending Bell to Oxford before he had taken priest's orders in his native diocese. When Bell joined the other fellows of Durham College in the autumn of 1432, he brought with him letters dimissory from Bishop Langley as well as Wessington's own dispensation enabling him to receive priest's orders in his twenty-second year; he was ordained priest in the diocese of London on 20 December 1432.[10]

[6] Ibid., fos 130, 136v–137, 141v, 143v–144, 156, 160.

[7] DCD, Reg. IV, fo. 214.

[8] *Obituary Roll of William Ebchester and John Burnby*, Surtees Society, 31 (1856), p. 112.

[9] *Register of Thomas Langley*, Surtees Society, 164–82 (1956–70), iii, pp. 61–2, 105–6; iv pp. 5–7.

[10] Ibid., iv, p. 70; DCD, Reg. Parv. II, fos 65v–66; *Historiae Dunelmensis scriptores tres*, Surtees Society, 9 (1839), pp. ccxxxv–ccxxxvi; DCD, Bursar's Accounts, 1432, Expense Fratrum versus Cellas. See *BRUO*, i, pp. 161–2, providing the best account of Bell's career yet published.

Richard Bell's five years as a novice at the mother-house were succeeded by an eight-year period of residence at Durham College, Oxford. Like other fellows of the college, the majority of whom were always in their twenties or early thirties, Bell had presumably received some instruction in grammar and the other liberal arts as a novice at Durham. At Oxford he would at first continue his study of the Arts and then, according to the terms of the statutes of the college as refounded by Bishop Hatfield fifty years earlier, begin more intensive work on philosophy and theology. At this early stage of his career, no Durham monk was encouraged to supplicate for a university degree in theology and it would be misleading to regard Bell's eight years at Oxford as being devoted exclusively to the pursuit of learning. As a fellow of Durham College, Bell was committed to continual participation in the services of choir and celebration of masses, as well as to administrative responsibilities of considerable importance to the welfare of the community. The statutes of Durham College called for the appointment of two *receptores* who were to collect and disburse the cell's revenues, accounting quarterly to the warden and their fellow-monks.[11] The choice of these obedientiaries was in the hands of the Durham prior and it was on 16 September 1435 that Prior Wessington first introduced Bell to administrative office when he appointed him one of the two Durham College bursars for the forthcoming financial year.[12] Record survives of Bell's reappointment as bursar of Durham College and it is clear from the extant college accounts (copies of which were sent up to the mother-house each year) that Bell held the office continuously from Michaelmas 1435 to Michaelmas 1440.[13] Bell's own *compoti* as bursar of Durham College provide detailed evidence of his labours: supplying the monks and secular students of the college with their commons, paying servants and financing small repairs to the fabric. Like other bursars he travelled fairly extensively through the country on college business, making frequent expeditions to collect pensions and rents from the community's appropriated churches in the dioceses of York and Lincoln.

The records of Bell's career at Durham College, Oxford, successful though this seems to have been, hardly prepare us for the next and perhaps the most surprising episode in his long career. On 13 February 1441, Henry VI *auctoritate parliamenti* collated Bell to the priory of Holy Trinity, York.[14] The withdrawal of any Durham monk from the community of his brethren was, in itself, an exceptional event in the history of the late medieval convent. Prior Wessington was hardly likely to have agreed to the removal of one of his ablest junior monks except under considerable pressure. On 17 February 1441 Henry Percy, second earl of

[11] D. Wilkins, *Concilia Magnae Britanniae et Hiberniae* (London, 1737), ii, pp. 614–17.
[12] DCD, Reg. Parv. II, fo. 88.
[13] Ibid., fo. 93; Durham College Accounts, 1435–40.
[14] *CPR, 1436–41*, p. 524.

Northumberland, wrote to Wessington from London asking him to 'graunt a licence to Dan Richard Bell professed in youre place that he may Receyve and occupy the Office of Priory of the Trinite in Yorke late graunted to hym be oure Soverein Lord the Kyng'.[15] On 9 March Prior Wessington, after examining the royal letters patent of the previous month, licensed Bell to accept the priorate of Holy Trinity, to which the latter was instituted two days later at York by Robert Blyth, prior of Tickford.[16] The reasons for the choice of Bell as prior of Holy Trinity, York, remain mysterious, even if the collation bears witness to the Durham monk's contacts with government circles. But it became rapidly obvious that Bell's acceptance of this promotion had been most ill-advised, as it introduced him to a sordid contest with the monks of the priory from which he was to emerge defeated and humiliated nearly three years later.

The detailed history of Holy Trinity, York, like that of other alien priories in the later middle ages, is one of considerable complexity because of the English government's disinclination to provide a radical solution to the anomalies caused by the Hundred Years War. Since its foundation in 1089, Holy Trinity had been dependent on the great French abbey of Marmoutier in Touraine but the French wars of the fourteenth century had inevitably led English monarchs to claim and exercise the right to appoint priors of the monastery.[17] Nevertheless, at Holy Trinity as elsewhere, the government was reluctant to sever all links with the continental mother-house and it was only as a result of a parliamentary petition by the monks of Holy Trinity themselves that the priory received a grant of denization on 18 March 1426.[18] At the same time the brethren at the priory were conceded the right to elect future superiors from among their own ranks without the necessity of obtaining licence to do so from the king. Unfortunately a later English government found itself unwilling to sacrifice its appointment to so wealthy a priory. The death of Prior John Castell, who had ruled the monastery for over forty years, in August 1440 precipitated the crisis in which Richard Bell became so seriously involved. After Castell's death the monks of Holy Trinity immediately elected one of themselves, John Grene, as his successor; relying on the royal letters patent of fourteen years earlier, they made no attempt to secure the king's *congé d'élire*. On 4 December 1440 Henry VI commissioned several prominent York ecclesiastics and laymen to investigate this election; it was no doubt in response to their report that he collated Bell in the following February and proceeded to order his induction into the priory.[19]

[15] DCD, Misc. Charters, no. 5193; *Priory of Finchale*, Surtees Society, 6 (1837), p. xxix.

[16] DCD, Reg. III, fos 262, 296v. The alien priory of Tickford had been made dependent on Holy Trinity, York, in 1426.

[17] J. Solloway, *The Alien Benedictines of York* (Leeds, 1910), pp. 227–8.

[18] *Rot. Parl.* (1783), iv, p. 302; *CPR, 1422–29*, p. 356.

[19] *CPR, 1436–41*, pp. 503, 538; DCD, Reg. III, fo. 311.

Bell's appointment naturally earned him the immediate and intense hostility of the brethren of Holy Trinity. Not at all abashed by being ordered to appear before the king's council in the spring of 1441, John Grene began his vigorous campaign to retain the priorate by a slanderous attack on Bell's character. In the presence of John Stafford, bishop of Bath and Wells and chancellor of England, it was alleged that Bell had been guilty of an unspecified *lapsus carnis* while at Durham and that he had also stolen various goods belonging to the monastery and carried them off with him to York. At Bell's prompting, Prior Wessington wrote to Stafford on 8 June 1441 testifying to the monk's good character ('a tempore professionis sue in monasterio Dunelmense ipsum cognovi ac cognosco fuisse et esse bone fame, integri status et opinionis illese'), denying that he had taken any goods from Durham except for a few clothes and small books which the prior had allowed him to retain for a time.[20] Although this testimonial, repeated a few days later in more general terms, can hardly be said to have been unsolicited, it seems to have served its purpose for the argument as to the rightful prior of Holy Trinity then shifted to less personal grounds. The king's legal right to collate to the priory was highly questionable, as is suggested by the choice of Robert Blyth to institute Bell on 11 March 1441. Blyth was then described as proctor of the abbot of Marmoutier but it is clear that the French monastery had not been consulted about the problem at this stage. The resistance of the monks of Holy Trinity, however, persuaded Bell and his friends at the royal court that it would be advisable to do so; on 21 May 1442 the abbot of Marmoutier, welcoming the opportunity to revive his claim to appoint to the York priory, wrote from France to ratify Blyth's institution of Bell.[21] A marginal note at the side of the Durham register's copy of this letter shows that the abbot's confirmation of Bell's appointment had no effect: the king had decided to abandon his opposition to John Grene's election in face of the continued resistance of the Holy Trinity monks.[22] Bell's position throughout the years 1442 and 1443 could hardly have been less enviable. Not only had he failed to displace John Grene as prior of Holy Trinity, he now found himself in the dangerously isolated position of a quondam monk who no longer belonged to a monastery. Fortunately for Bell, Prior Wessington remained loyal to his protégé and negotiated his return to the ranks of the brethren

[20] DCD, Reg. III, fos 267, 269v; Reg. Parv. II, fo. 140v; *Priory of Finchale*, pp. xxix–xxx.

[21] DCD, Reg. III, fo. 311. The abbot of Marmoutier was still exercising spiritual authority over the monks of Holy Trinity, York, in 1448 and 1459–60. See E. Martène, *Histoire de l'abbaye de Marmoutier*, ii, Mémoires de la société archéologique de Touraine, 25 (1875), pp. 319–21, 330–1.

[22] Prior John Grene received a general pardon from the king on 30 May 1446: *Notes on the Religious and Secular Houses of Yorkshire*, ii, Yorkshire Archaeological Society, Record Series, 81 (1931), p. 90.

at Durham. Wessington asked Master John Marchall, his most trusted representative among the canons of York cathedral, to settle the business. On 10 December 1443 John Grene and his monks officially withdrew their actions against Bell in return for his formal resignation of the priorate. On 13 December Bell appeared before his fellow monks in the chapter house, made a new profession to Prior Wessington and was readmitted to the Durham community.[23]

Richard Bell's attempt to break free from the ties of his mother-house had ended in embarrassing failure and he was to remain a Durham monk for the next thirty-five years of his life. In the long term he was no doubt fortunate in his failure, for the rule of the small and truculent York community would have given him much less opportunity to demonstrate his ability than turned out to be the case at Durham itself. But this episode is especially significant as the first illustration of Bell's remarkable and, for a Durham monk, unconventional ambition – a trait of character which is readily detectable in his later career. However, although this early and abortive attempt to leave Durham may have cost Bell some popularity among his fellows, Prior Wessington did not hold the setback against him. Immediately on his return to the monastery, Bell was appointed 'Seneschallus Hospicii Domini Prioris', a position which he held until several months after Wessington had been replaced as prior of Durham by William Ebchester in July 1446.[24] In the spring of 1447 he held his first major administrative office at Durham when he began accounting as almoner, until early 1448 as a colleague of Robert Westmorland and then for a further two and a half years by himself. Although only twentieth in order of seniority of Durham monks, Bell now occupied one of the most important of the Durham obediences and was responsible for the welfare of at least fifty brothers and sisters resident in or attached to the convent's almshouses and hospitals. He was accordingly recognised as one of the *seniores capituli* by the summer of 1450.[25]

In the autumn of 1450 Bell was promoted to the wardenship of Durham College, Oxford, where he replaced John Burnby, who resigned at Michaelmas.[26] Richard Bell's return to Oxford after an absence of almost ten years was a natural development in his career. All the priors of Durham between 1446 and the Dissolution were Oxford graduates in theology. The most obvious reason for Bell's reappearance at the university was his desire to secure a degree, a distinction which had become an essential qualification for the highest office at the mother-house. The first

[23] DCD, Reg. III, fos 296–7; Reg. Parv. II, fos 177–9.

[24] DCD, Bursar's Accounts, 1443–47, Garderoba; 1446/47, Solacium Prioris.

[25] DCD, Almoner's Accounts, 1447–50; Reg. Parv. III, fo. 40v; *Scriptores tres*, p. cccxviii.

[26] DCD, Durham College Accounts, 1449/50. H.E.D. Blakiston's suggestion that Burnby did not resign in 1450 but appointed Bell as his deputy is completely untenable: *Some Durham College Rolls*, Oxford Historical Society, 32, *Collectanea*, iii (1896), p. 16.

extant register of Oxford University proves that Bell supplicated for the baccalaureate in theology as early as 11 November 1450, was admitted to oppose on 23 January 1452 and received the degree five weeks later, on 29 February.[27] A university degree gave its recipient status not only in the eyes of his fellow monks but also in those of other English Benedictines when they met every three years at their general chapter at Northampton. The prior of Durham rarely attended in person but sent one of his more distinguished university monks, normally the warden of Durham College, as his proctor. It was in this capacity that Bell appeared at the general chapter which opened at Northampton on 2 July 1453, having called at Coventry two days earlier where he made a visitation of the cathedral priory in response to a commission by Prior Ebchester of Durham.[28] No record of the visitation proceedings at Coventry, presumably perfunctory as in the case of most Black Monk visitations, nor of the *acta* of the 1453 chapter survive; but it may be inferred that Bell's presence at the Northampton meeting that year left him with no high regard for the value and effectiveness of these assemblies for he never attended another general chapter.

Shortly after his appearance at Northampton Bell returned to Durham on the reappointment of John Burnby as warden of Durham College on 20 September 1453.[29] Bell's own tenure of the wardenship had lasted for the unusually short term of three years. His willingness to return so soon to administrative responsibilities at Durham suggests that he never regarded academic life as best suited to his talents. The disappearance of the college account rolls for the period of Bell's wardenship renders it impossible to make any detailed assessment of his conduct of the office; but between 1450 and 1453 he can be found exercising his disciplinary powers, examining and admitting secular scholars to the college, protecting its revenues against aggression by local magnates and making contacts with influential secular clerks at Oxford, including the chancellor of the university, Master Gilbert Kymer.[30] It was presumably at this period of his life that Richard Bell built up a personal library of manuscripts, a practice common among Durham university monks despite the rules forbidding *proprietas*. Bell passed on several of these manuscripts to his younger colleagues among the Durham monks. As these later found their way into the safety of the monastic common library it is possible to gain some impression, however vague, of the books he may have read. Leaving aside those books which were merely assigned to the common

[27] *Register of University of Oxford*, Oxford Historical Society, i (1885), pp. 11–12.

[28] DCD, Reg. Parv. III, fo. 58*; *Documents Illustrating the Activities of the General and Provincial Chapters of the English Black Monks*, iii, Camden Society, 3rd series, 54 (1937), pp. 214–15, 242–3, 250–1.

[29] DCD, Reg. Parv. III, fos 64v–65.

[30] Ibid., fos 44v, 46–47, 50, 58–9.

library by Bell when prior of Durham,[31] contemporary inscriptions on six surviving manuscripts show that they were once in his possession before being given to a younger Durham monk.[32] Among these works (the normal inscription is *Liber Sancti Cuthberti et Ricardi Bell*) were a fine thirteenth century copy of the Bible, treatises by Anselm, Geoffrey de Vinsauf and Peter of Blois, as well as a volume of interesting material relating to Black Monk organisation, largely written by Durham monks early in the fifteenth century.[33] Another Durham manuscript of somewhat later date contains inside the elaborate initial *E* of *Explicit tractatus lincolniens' de lingua* the name 'Ric. Bell' together with the words 'Maria' and 'Emmanuel'. Although comparison of the hand with Bell's known autograph fails to support the elder James Raine's conjecture that the prior wrote this manuscript 'when he was a young man', the initial certainly suggests that Bell may have commissioned the work, a copy of Grosseteste's *De linguae viciis et virtutibus*.[34] Bell's interest in this treatise seems typical of his conservative tastes. A study of all the extant manuscripts inscribed with his name suggests that his intellectual interests varied only within the conventional framework of the traditional classics of the late medieval English monastery. Humfrey Wanley's claim that it was Bell who made copious annotations to the twelfth-century copy of Bede's *Life of St Cuthbert* now in the British Library is very doubtful;[35] and no evidence survives of an original or characteristically individual approach to literature and learning on Bell's part.

On Bell's return to Durham in the autumn of 1453 he began to play a prominent role in the discussion and execution of monastic policy. Prior Ebchester had already complained of old age and illness in June 1453 and was prepared to give Bell the opportunity to conduct important business transactions with northern lords.[36] Between 1453 and 1456 Bell travelled widely, visiting William Booth, archbishop of York, as well as John Neville (younger brother of Richard, earl of Warwick) at Pontefract in attempts to win their support for his convent.[37] On such occasions Bell no doubt

---

[31] E.g. DCD, MS B.II.5: see fo. ii v.

[32] Three of these manuscripts are still at Durham, where Bell's name appears in MSS B.III.26, fo. 2v; B.IV.41, fo. 290v; B.IV.42, fo. ii v. The other three manuscripts are Bodleian Library, Oxford, MS Laud. Misc. 368; Sidney Sussex, Cambridge, MS 56; Nottingham University Library, MS MiLM 5. (For a transcript of the inscription on a fly-leaf of the last manuscript, I am grateful to Mr J.H. Hodson, Keeper of Manuscripts at the University of Nottingham; it is only legible under ultra-violet light.)

[33] This last manuscript (DCD, B.IV.41) is described in *Documents. . . of the English Black Monks*, ii, Camden Society, 3rd series, 47 (1933), pp. x–xii.

[34] DCD, MS B.III.18, fo. 227v (the manuscript originally commenced at what is now fo. 128); cf. *Priory of Finchale*, pp. ix (for an illustration of the initial) and xxxi.

[35] BL, MS Harley, 1924, passim; cf. B. Colgrave, *Two Lives of Saint Cuthbert* (Cambridge, 1940), p. 28.

[36] DCD, Reg. Parv. III, fo. 58*v.

[37] DCD, Bursar's Accounts, 1453–55, Expense Necessarie; Reg. Parv. III, fo. 63v.

acted in his capacity as Durham terrar, an obedience to which he had been appointed by 8 June 1455 but which it seems virtually certain he had held from at least the previous Whitsuntide when he began to account as hostillar.[38] The offices of hostillar and terrar were normally held simultaneously by one monk at the fifteenth-century convent, so that the comparative wealth of the first (the hostillar's annual receipts were assessed at £170) might compensate for the poverty of the second: the terrar with an estimated annual income of £20 was the most poorly endowed of all Durham obedientiaries.[39] As hostillar, Richard Bell was entrusted with the administration of a sumptuously furnished set of six sleeping apartments in the convent's guest hall as well as a 'somerhall' and 'wynterhalle'.[40] As terrar, he had the even greater responsibility of supervising the collection of the large monastic revenues which were later recorded on the Durham bursar's annual account. He also co-operated with the priory's lay steward in general estate-management. It is therefore all the more surprising to discover that by the autumn of 1456 Bell was holding yet another and even more important obedience, that of subprior of the convent.[41] Durham Priory, unlike many large monasteries of the later middle ages, was a community which rarely tolerated the concentration of several important obediences in the hands of one or two all-powerful monks. Bell's appointment as subprior must be regarded as strong evidence of the respect his fellows held for his ability.

This respect was to be put to a sudden and dramatic test when in 1456 Bell declared himself a candidate for election to the priorate of Durham. Prior Ebchester's resignation of his office, after only ten years as superior at Durham, opened the path to that rarest of monastic occasions, at Durham as elsewhere, an openly disputed election. Of the three alternative methods of canonical election laid down by the Fourth Lateran Council's decree, *Quia Propter*, the way of compromise was much the most common at Durham although the *via Spiritus Sancti* had been used to elect Prior Wessington as recently as 1416.[42] The chapter's decision in October 1456, taken only 'post plures communicaciones et tractatus', to choose a new prior *per viam Scrutinii* (a procedure which forced all the electors to record their votes publicly) had no obvious precedent at Durham. It suggests a situation in which the claims of the candidates were too evenly balanced to allow the adoption of a method less likely to arouse ill-feeling among the community. Bell showed himself unwilling to stand down in favour of his

---

[38] *Scriptores tres*, p. cccxxxi; DCD, Hostillar's Accounts, 1454–57. All three of Bell's accounts as hostillar survive but his *compoti* as terrar are now lost.

[39] DCD, Reg. II, fo. 357; *Scriptores tres*, p. ccli.

[40] See the 'Stuffum Officii Hostillar. Dunelm.' delivered to Bell on 8 June 1454, printed in *Durham Account Rolls*, i, Surtees Society, 99 (1898), pp. 147–150.

[41] DCD, Reg. IV, fo. 110.

[42] *Scriptores tres*, pp. 72, 73, 95, 102, clxvii; DCD, Loc. XIII, no. 11.

rival for the priorate, Master John Burnby, a Durham monk whose official qualifications were certainly superior. Burnby had taken his monastic vows seven years earlier than Bell, had been a doctor of theology ten years before Bell took his baccalaureate, had been subprior of Durham six years before Bell and had been warden of Durham College, Oxford, for eleven years as against Bell's three.[43] The only obvious weakness in Burnby's claims for election in 1456 was his absence from Durham for all but three of the preceding fourteen years, a weakness Bell was quite prepared to exploit. The official report dispatched to Bishop Neville of Durham, and described by Professor Knowles as a *locus classicus* of fifteenth-century monastic election practice, shows that the contest expressed a real division of opinion among the members of the community.[44]

Durham monks were always conscious of their vulnerability when without a prior and rarely risked the dangers of a long vacancy. Prior Ebchester made his formal resignation in the prior's chapel of St Nicholas at Durham on 5 October 1456. On the following day Richard Bell, as subprior, summoned a chapter meeting in which Monday 25 October was fixed as the date of the forthcoming election. Messengers were sent to request the presence of the convent's counsellors and experts in canon law as well as the attendance of the many Durham monks then resident in the convent's dependencies.[45] Two of the seventy-one Durham monks eligible to vote failed to respond to the chapter's citations and were declared contumaciously absent; the fourteen others who remained in the cells each commissioned one of their fellows to represent them at the election. The fifty-five monks present in chapter on 25 October therefore commanded sixty-nine votes between them, votes which were recorded by the three scrutators, sitting in a corner of the chapter house as each monk in turn made his nomination before them. After the details of how each monk had voted were publicly announced, it was seen that John Burnby had received thirty-eight votes and Richard Bell twenty-five; William Seton, the monastic chancellor, collected four votes while the prior of Finchale and the ex-prior, William Ebchester, received one each. Interestingly enough the monk who voted for Ebchester was none other than Bell himself; while it may be understandable that Bell did not want to add his vote to those in favour of Burnby (who himself voted for William Seton), this curious choice suggests Bell's determination not to help the cause of a possible rival. But his hopes of becoming prior of Durham at the early age of

[43] DCD, Durham College Accounts, 1442–56; Hostillar's Accounts, 1440/41; Reg. Parv. III, fo. 64v; Loc. XXI, no. 50.

[44] Printed in *Obituary Roll of Ebchester and Burnby*, pp. 91–102, from DCD, Reg. IV, fos 112–115. Cf. D. Knowles, *The Religious Orders in England*, ii (Cambridge, 1955), pp. 251–2.

[45] DCD, Bursar's Accounts, 1456/57, Expense Necessarie. Loc. XIII, no. 13, contains a large collection of original documents relating to the 1456 election.

forty-six were foiled by his failure to win the support of the senior Durham monks, most of whom – including the ex-prior, the chancellor, the third prior, the bursar and the prior of Finchale – supported Burnby. The result was clearly a bitter disappointment to Bell, made all the more humiliating when the chapter thought it canonically necessary to supplement Burnby's claims to the priorate with the argument that he was a monk of greater merit (*meritis prestancior*) than his defeated opponent.

The election of 1456 marks the lowest point of Bell's career. Not only had he failed to reach the highest office, he now found himself in the invidious position of having to accept a successful rival as his religious superior. Not surprisingly, it was thought impossible for Bell to continue as subprior under the new regime and his future presence in the Durham chapter could hardly have failed to prove embarrassing for both himself and his fellows. Fortunately for themselves the Durham monks had long possessed a means by which this type of situation could be remedied.[46] At Whitsuntide (1457) Thomas Ayre, the existing prior of Finchale, was removed in favour of Richard Bell, who spent the next seven years of his life as superior of this Durham dependency situated in a bend of the River Wear 5 miles north east of the mother-house. Although a monk with Bell's ambitions must have regarded the priorate of Finchale as something of a backwater, it was a pleasant backwater nevertheless. With an average income of almost £200 per annum Finchale was the most richly endowed of all the nine Durham dependencies and Bell's annual account rolls as prior there show that he had no difficulty in maintaining the prosperity of the cell.[47] Nor should the isolation of Bell's new position be exaggerated: Finchale was treated as a recreational centre by the late medieval Durham community and the prior entertained many other Durham monks besides the seven or eight over whom he ruled and with whom he observed the *opus Dei*.[48] The most interesting feature of the history of Finchale Priory during the last century of its existence was its conversion into an establishment where the prior's lodgings became 'the centre of the life of a reduced convent'.[49] The construction of the new prior's quarters to the east of the existing claustral complex at Finchale cannot be dated precisely; but the accounts for 1457–65, which include many references to major building operations as well as the first recorded mention of the well-situated Douglas Tower, prove that Bell was a key figure in the

---

[46] Cf. J. Scammell, 'Some Aspects of Mediaeval English Monastic Government: The Case of Geoffrey Burdon, Prior of Durham (1313–1321)', *Revue Bénédictine*, 68 (1958) pp. 227, 241, 245.

[47] *Priory of Finchale*, Surtees Society, 6 (1837), pp. cclxv–ccxcix.

[48] DCD, Loc. XVI, no. 12(e); cf. *Priory of Finchale*, p. 30.

[49] R. Gilyard-Beer, *Abbeys: An Introduction to the Religious Houses of England and Wales* (1958), p. 48.

significant architectural transformation of the priory.[50] It was at Finchale that Bell gained the experience of large-scale building enterprises which he was later to apply both at Durham and at his episcopal palace of Rose Castle.

The sudden and apparently unexpected death of Prior John Burnby on 17 October 1464 was, however, to bring Bell rapidly back to the forefront of monastic politics and to give him the prize which he had missed eight years earlier. As in 1456, there was no long vacancy. Bell was himself one of the two Durham monks who rode to Bishop Lawrence Booth of Durham to obtain the latter's *congé d'élire*; when this had been secured, the date of election was fixed for 26 November and the appropriate citations dispatched to the cells. This time Bell had no possible rival. As the most distinguished and experienced Durham monk of the time and one of the only three university graduates then in the community, he was acclaimed prior by the sixty-six electors *per viam Spiritus Sancti*. Although some show of hesitation was expected of the elect, Bell did not allow his fellows to wait long. On 27 November 1464 in St Andrew's chapel in the monastic infirmary he formally consented to his postulation, and his confirmation as prior by Bishop Booth followed soon afterwards.[51] Richard Bell was to be prior of Durham for over thirteen years, the most vigorous and influential period of his life and certainly the best recorded.

Bell's tenure of the priorate of Durham between 1464 and 1478 presents the student of his career with special problems. The survival of the convent's muniments and, above all, of the prior's own small register or letter-book allows an examination of Bell's conduct of monastic business at a very detailed level. On the other hand, it is clear that for thirteen years Bell's own career became merged with the general history of the great Benedictine monastery of Durham; this makes it all the more necessary to stress that it would be dangerous to assume that the will of the prior was always the source and origin of all policy. At Durham, as in most English monasteries, it is notoriously difficult to distinguish the actions taken by the superior on his own initiative from those arising out of consultation with the senior monks of chapter. For this reason alone a comprehensive study of the convent's history between 1464 and 1478 would throw only partial light on Bell's own character and personality. All that need be attempted here is a brief survey of the major problems with which the prior was confronted.

The late medieval priory of Durham presents the familiar problem of an apparently extremely wealthy religious corporation whose financial position was nevertheless always a cause for anxiety and sometimes for

[50] *Priory of Finchale*, pp. cclxxix, cccvi, cccxxvii.

[51] For Bell's election in 1464, see DCD, Reg. IV, fos 158–162; Loc. XVI, no. 12; Bursar's Accounts, 1464/65, Expense Necessarie; *Calendar of Chancery Rolls of Bishop Booth*, 35th Annual Report of Deputy Keeper of Public Records (1874), p. 81.

alarm. When Richard Bell became prior in November 1464, he inherited a situation of genuine crisis. Prior Burnby's tenure of the priorate had coincided with a period of exceptional financial strain, as Burnby himself admitted when referring in a letter of 7 March 1464 to 'the gret infortunes and hurts that hath happynd us now late in brynyng of our kirke, and lone of CCCC marcs unto the quene Margaret, lesyng of our bell metall by the see, stailyng of our catall by thefes of Tyndall, with our grete losses in plee for Coldyngham, Rodyngton, Hylton and othir, and the grete necessity that we stande in'.[52] Four years later, in a letter of 10 November 1468 written to Master William Clayton, one of his several representatives at the curia, Bell allowed himself to take an even more gloomy view of the convent's problems:

> Moreover we are so oerchargid now of dayes What with dyemes new imposicions and other prestes made unto the king and what with plaiez bath temporall and spirituell and other gret losse of goods by way of extorsion and robbery that our monastery is likly within processe of tyme to be cast so ferr in dett that withoute the more speciall grace of Almighty god, supportacion also of you and other good frends of the said Courte, it shall noyt in many yeres here aftir be broght to as goode state as it was within thies few yeres.[53]

Bell's forebodings were not, however, to be realised and it is to his credit that when he left Durham in 1478 the convent enjoyed greater prosperity than it had done on his accession to the priorate. The monastery's financial resources, although inevitably limited in the conditions of the late fifteenth century, could be maintained at a satisfactory level when supervised by a prior, like Bell, who was prepared to fight vigorously in their defence. Thus the annual account rolls of the Durham bursar, which furnish the most reliable index to the economic wellbeing of the convent, show that this officer's net receipts (excluding previous arrears but including current 'wastes and decays') rose from an average of less than £1350 per annum in the 1450s and 1460s to slightly over £1400 per annum in the 1470s.[54] The most interesting symptom of some revival in the monastery's fortunes during Bell's priorate is his inauguration of the last great building enterprise ever undertaken by the monks of Durham, the complete reconstruction of the central tower of their monastic church. When he became prior, Bell found the existing tower in an extremely dangerous state and decided to replace it with a completely new structure. The late fifteenth-century Durham sacrist's rolls (unfortunately not a complete series) show that the lower stage of the present tower must

---

[52] *Priory of Coldingham*, Surtees Society, 12 (1841), p. 191.

[53] DCD, Reg. Parv. III, fos 139–140.

[54] Ibid., Bursar's Accounts, 1464–77 (an uninterrupted series); for an 'Inventarium Prioratus Dunelmensis' made at Bell's accession, see *Feodarium prioratus Dunelmensis*, Surtees Society, 58 (1871), pp. 98–211.

have been more or less complete by the time Bell left for Carlisle; but work on the second and upper stage was still proceeding in the 1480s.[55] Two of the corbels carrying the internal arcade at the foot of the tower are carved with a representation of a bell (the prior's rebus, used also on his signet seal); and the prior's personal involvement in the building led him to keep the sacrist's office in his own hands during the mid 1470s. In at least two letters of this period Bell referred to the costs of 'the re-edificacion of our steple' and admitted that lack of funds had prevented the work from being completed as rapidly as he had hoped.[56] Nevertheless, the central tower remains, despite a free restoration by Gilbert Scott in 1859 after half a century in which the upper stage was encased in Roman cement, as the most lasting memorial of Bell's priorate at Durham.

Throughout the fifteenth century the number of Durham monks remained remarkably stable and, as prior, Bell ruled over approximately seventy members of the community, of whom forty were in residence at the mother-house while thirty were dispersed among its dependencies. There are no grounds for believing that the conduct of monastic life at Durham between 1464 and 1478 was other than harmonious and at least outwardly respectable. The Durham cloister seems to have been free from the personal scandals which had interrupted the tranquillity of the first half of the century, and it is clear that Bell exercised his office in the traditional manner. Whatever his inclinations may have been, no late medieval prior of Durham could act as autocrat. Bell found it necessary to accept the advice and guidance of the senior members of his chapter and entertained all his subjects both at his table in the prior's apartments at Durham and at his *ludi*, normally held four times a year at the neighbouring manor of Beaurepaire. Although the late medieval prior of Durham was more closely associated with the daily routine of his convent than most wealthy monastic prelates of the period, much of his disciplinary authority was delegated to the subprior. Bell was unusually fortunate in that another distinguished university monk, Thomas Caley, acted as subprior throughout the entire period of his own priorate.[57]

Prior Bell's supervision of those monks he sent to serve the Durham cells is naturally more fully revealed by his register. In this sphere he showed himself a stern and vigilant superior. One unnamed fellow of Durham College guilty of frequenting the house of a common prostitute in Oxford was threatened with the severest penalties unless he amended his way of life. Thomas Knowte, one of the two Durham monks on Farne Island, was

[55] *Durham Account Rolls*, ii, pp. 412–17, prints most of the details of the *reparacio campanilis*. J. Harvey's dating of the two stages of the tower to 1465–75 and 1483–90 respectively (*English Medieval Architects*, p. 340) is more precise than the evidence allows.

[56] DCD, Reg. Parv. III, fos 158, 160. Cf. J.R. Boyle, *Comprehensive Guide to the County of Durham* (London, n.d.), pp. 204, 328–30.

[57] DCD, Reg. IV, fos 151, 158, 159v, 184; cf. *BRUO*, i, p. 342.

rebuked for rowing to the mainland and keeping suspect company there as well as because 'you layse a part thy stamyns and daily weres sarks of lynyn cloth'.[58] This last was a subject about which Bell apparently felt particularly strongly for in March 1472 he sent letters to superiors of Durham cells reminding them not to allow the use of linen shirts except in cases of severe illness or skin infection.[59] With the obvious exceptions of Durham College, Oxford and Finchale (the only two cells over which Bell had himself presided), the history of Durham dependencies in the later middle ages presents a general picture of economic decline and spiritual malaise. Nevertheless, Bell was perhaps even more devoted to the preservation of their traditional connection with Durham than any fifteenth century prior. In 1474 he went so far as to rescind his previous appointment of John Eden as prior of Lytham in Lancashire because he feared that this Durham monk might be tempted to seek papal exemption from his obedience to the mother-house 'like as dan Willyam Partrik dyd in his dayes the which god defende'.[60] Nowhere is Bell's determination to maintain the traditional liberties and possessions of St Cuthbert's church more fully obvious than in his resolute last-ditch struggle to prevent the priory of Coldingham from falling into Scottish hands. Although most of the relevant documents were published by the elder James Raine well over a century ago, a detailed account of the extraordinarily complex and tortuous process by which Coldingham was finally detached from Durham still remains to be written (but see now the survey of the course of events provided in Chapter 5 above). Yet it is clear not only that the 'causa de Coldyngham' was the foremost issue of Bell's priorate, but that the prior was fighting a battle which he could never hope to win. A regular flow of letters on the subject passed backwards and forwards between Bell and his representatives at the curia but it became gradually obvious to the Durham monks that expensive legal successes at Rome made no impression on the Scottish government. It was only after Bell's removal to Carlisle in 1478 that they were in a position to recognise the inevitable. One of the first actions of the new prior, Robert Ebchester, was to write to his proctor at the curia urging 'that the mater slepe for a tyme to such season as it may pleas God and Seynt Cuthbert that we may have better spede than we can have yit'.[61] Not surprisingly, the Coldingham case was never re-opened and Bell proved to be the last Durham prior who fought for the survival of this colony of English monks on Scottish soil.

---

[58] *Scriptores tres*, pp. cccli–ccclii; DCD, Reg. Parv. III, fos 135–6; J. Raine, *North Durham* (1852), p. 355.

[59] DCD, Reg. Parv. III, fo. 130, 151; *Scriptores tres*, pp. ccclii–cccliii.

[60] DCD, Reg. Parv. III, fos 153–4. The allusion is to a Durham *cause célèbre* of the 1440s: William Partrick, prior of Lytham 1431–46, was forced to return to Durham after a series of protracted and expensive lawsuits consequent on his attempt to hold the priorate in perpetuity. See R. B. Dobson, *Durham Priory, 1400–1450* (Cambridge, 1973), pp. 327–41.

[61] *Scriptores tres*, p. ccclxvii.

Prior Bell's defence of traditional Durham privileges involved him in several other contests, none of which was more serious than that with Lawrence Booth, bishop of Durham from 1457 to 1476 and archbishop of York from 1476 to 1480. During Bell's priorate, friction tended to centre round such issues as the prior's right to archidiaconal jurisdiction over his appropriated churches in the diocese of Durham and (after 1476) the chapter's claim not to include the word *obediencia* in their presentations to the archbishop of York.[62] Neither issue was a new one and it is difficult to avoid the conclusion that Bell irritated Lawrence Booth unnecessarily by his tactless handling of these disputes. From his very early months as prior, Bell showed himself extremely, and indeed unduly, ready to appeal for support against his ecclesiastical superior to other English magnates. It is exactly this cultivation of good relations with the English nobility, however, that forms the most characteristic and individual feature of Bell's priorate as well as providing the central explanation for his rise to the episcopate in 1478. Bell was not a political partisan by choice and, like other prominent ecclesiastics, he found the aristocratic feuds and dynastic upheavals of the period distinctly embarrassing to himself and dangerous to the country: in a letter of 29 March 1477 he advised the new bishop of Durham, William Dudley, to 'stand as one' with the Nevilles 'for mony of the gentilmen er guydit full menely, and foloweth yonge counsell'.[63] But complete political impartiality was impossible during a period when both the welfare of the monastery and Bell's own personal advancement depended on the support of the most powerful 'good lords' of the north. Bell made occasional errors of judgement and was unfortunate enough to make out letters of fraternity to George, duke of Clarence, on 29 September 1477, only a few months before the latter's execution;[64] but his major decisions in this field – to cultivate the Nevilles in the 1460s and Richard of Gloucester in the 1470s – paid him extremely handsome dividends.

Bell's ability to win the favours of the northern magnates depended directly on the skill with which he exploited the extensive patronage at his disposal on their behalf. Although his letters written in response to requests for vacant benefices show that he soon became adept at balancing the claims of one lord against those of another, the pressures imposed on him were often overwhelming; as he wrote on 3 March 1476 to a clerk interested in a forthcoming vacancy among the prebends of the convent's collegiate church at Howden:

---

[62] Ibid., pp. cccx, ccclix–ccclx; DCD, Reg. Parv. III, fos 125v–126, 128, 131, 133–4, 173v, 175.

[63] *Scriptores tres*, p. ccclix.

[64] DCD, Reg. IV, fo. 181.

I and my brether are so ofte tymes cald uppon in sich things by diverse lords of right high astate that we may noght have our liberty to dispose sich smal benefices as ar in our gifte to our frends like as our will and intent wer forto do, as God knawith and me repentith.[65]

There were other ways in which Bell was able to further the interests of the northern magnates. In his first year as prior he not only sold the marriage of Cuthbert Billingham, one of the convent's tenants by knight service, to Sir Humphrey Neville for £40 *pro utilitate et supportacione domus*, but also advanced £24 to the earl of Warwick out of the future proceeds of a clerical subsidy in the diocese of Durham, having 'putte my self in grete daunger for your sake and made shyfte of asmuch money'.[66] Bell became prior of Durham at the period when the Neville ascendancy in national and northern politics was at its height; so it is not surprising to find him sitting at the second table in hall at that most famous of all Neville gatherings, the lavish banquet which followed George Neville's enthronement as archbishop of York in September 1465.[67] Ten years later Richard, duke of Gloucester, had replaced the earl of Warwick as the convent's *dominus specialissimus*. On a visit to Durham in April 1474 he was entertained by Prior Bell and received into the fraternity of the house, an honour also conferred on Gloucester's wife, Anne Neville, two years later.[68] Throughout the mid 1470s the prior was relying on Gloucester's support in his quarrel with the archbishop of York and there is no doubt whatsoever that Richard's powerful influence secured Bell's elevation to the bishopric of Carlisle in 1478.

Bell's claims to a bishopric naturally rested on the record of his priorate at Durham and his reputation as an active administrator. But an aspiring bishop was expected to show a wider range of experience outside the monastery walls than was usual among priors of Durham. It was here that Bell's membership of several royal commissions to negotiate with the Scots added significantly to his other qualifications. He was chosen one of the English commissioners to treat *de conservatione induciarum* on

[65] DCD, Reg. Parv. III, fo. 168v. Bell's apologia is slightly disingenuous as it is clear that he expected and received substantial compensation for his use of ecclesiastical patronage on behalf of English magnates; the best example is the case of the Yorkshire vicarage of Bossall in 1477, when the original presentation of William Laxe was jettisoned in favour of one of the duchess of Gloucester's chaplains – in return for the Gloucesters' support against Archbishop Booth on the *obediencia* issue: ibid., fos 172v, 175, 175*; R. Donaldson, 'Sponsors, Patrons and Presentations to Benefices during the Later Middle Ages', *Archaeologia Aeliana*, 4th series, 38 (1960), pp. 174–6.

[66] Ibid., fo. 126; Bursar's Accounts, 1464/65, Allocaciones.

[67] Leland, *Collectanea*, ed. T. Hearne (London, 1774), vi, p. 3. Bell's expenses at this enthronement (45s. 11d) are recorded in DCD, Bursar's Accounts, 1465/66, Expense Necessarie.

[68] DCD, Reg. IV, fos 172–3, 214.

18 July 1470 and served on several similar commissions in the following years. Records of his travelling expenses to Newcastle and Alnwick '*pro trugis ibidem tenendis*', as well as of his personal expenditure of a hundred marks on a new peel tower at Shoreswood near Norham, prove his active participation in the work of maintaining peace in the marches.[69] His services on behalf of the English government naturally encouraged Bell to consider himself a prospective bishop, and his promotion to the episcopate in 1478 was the fulfilment of an ambition which dated from at least four years earlier. A letter written on 31 August 1474 to Master Peter de Mellinis, the proctor Bell employed on the Coldingham and other causes at Rome, is particularly revealing.[70] At this date Bell was hoping to become the next bishop of Chichester, although his views as to how this aim could be achieved remained extremely indefinite and naïve. Not yet certain of royal support and conscious of the dangers of infringing the statutes of Praemunire, he asked Mellinis to investigate the possibilities of a papal reservation of the see. Bell placed much confidence on the influence that the archbishop of Rouen might be able to exert on his behalf in the curia and informed Mellinis that he was prepared to send large sums of cash to Rome if the project seemed worth pursuing. On 26 April 1475 Mellinis replied with a letter in which he pointed out the dangers and difficulties of Bell's proposals: 'Sciat paternitas vestra quod tales reservationes nunquam consueverunt fieri, nec possunt aliquo modo obtineri.' It would be more sensible for the prior to wait until a suitable English bishopric became vacant and then Mellinis would do what he could to further Bell's provision.[71]

The death of John Arundel, bishop of Chichester, on 18 October 1477 gave Bell his opportunity. Although unable to obtain Chichester itself as he had once hoped, the translation there of Edward Story left vacant the diocese of Carlisle, the bishopric for which Bell was most obviously qualified. On 11 February 1478, the pope provided Bell to Carlisle and translated Story to Chichester.[72] News of Bell's promotion had reached London by 26 February when Bishop Dudley of Durham wrote to the chapter informing them of their duty to prepare for a new election.[73] In

[69] *Rotuli Scotiae*, Record Commission (1814–19), ii, pp. 422–3, 430–1, 433–4, 437–8; *Calendar of Documents relating to Scotland*, Scottish Record Office (1881–88), iv, p. 283. *Durham Account Rolls*, iii, p. 646; DCD, Bursar's Accounts, 1471/72, 1473/74, Expense Necessarie. Among Bell's fellow commissioners in the Marches were two men whose influence and favour were to bear decisively on his own future, Edward Story, his predecessor as bishop of Carlisle, and Humphrey, Lord Dacre of Gilsland. Bell received both men into the Durham fraternity, Dacre on 13 January 1477 and Story on 12 February 1478 (DCD, Reg. IV, fos 179, 181v).

[70] DCD, Reg. Parv. III, fos 156–7.

[71] *Priory of Coldingham*, pp. 232–5.

[72] C. Eubel, *Hierarchia Catholica*, ii (Munster, 1914), pp. 128, 170.

[73] DCD, Reg. IV, fo. 182.

itself, Bell's provision to Carlisle can hardly have surprised contemporaries aware of his connections with Richard of Gloucester. Much more startling was the news that Sixtus IV had accompanied his bull of provision with a licence allowing Bell to continue to hold the priory of Durham in commendam. This extraordinary attempt to deprive the Durham monks of their traditional right to be governed by a canonically elected and independent prior has no parallel in the history of the convent and few elsewhere. Monasteries in England, unlike those of France and Scotland, largely escaped the evil effects of commendam, a practice which was very rare in this country until 1472.[74] In that year Richard Redman had successfully petitioned the pope to be allowed to retain his abbacy of Shap despite his promotion to the bishopric of St Asaph, the only obvious precedent for Bell's attempt to carry out a similar manoeuvre in 1478. All allowances being made for Bell's understandable desire to supplement the slender revenues of the bishop of Carlisle with those he already enjoyed as prior of Durham, it is almost inconceivable that he can have expected to bring off such an audacious stroke. When in October 1478 the new Durham prior and chapter wrote to Master Peter de Mellinis to rebuke him for the part he had played at the curia in furthering Bell's intrigues, they expressed their genuine amazement that anyone should have attempted to introduce the practice of commendam to a monastery which had been ruled by its own prior for over 400 years.[75]

Admittedly Bell had taken the precaution of seeking Richard of Gloucester's support. On 13 April 1478, at the height of the crisis, the latter wrote from Middleham to the subprior and chapter warning them to postpone their election of a new prior, 'considering that it is said that your ffader the prior hath the prialite in a commendam'.[76] But this was an issue which even Gloucester's great influence failed to resolve in Bell's favour. Despite their consternation at the news, the Durham monks remained firm and could rely on the indispensable support of their bishop, William Dudley, who protected their interests throughout this period of 'grete daynger and heavinesse'. Rumours reached Dudley in London of Bell's attempts to put pressure on the community; and, conscious of the dangers of 'confederacions, conspiracies, or othre ungoodly demenyngs among you', he referred to the possibility that Bell had placed the convent's common seal 'under suche warde and kepyng that ye may not wele atteine ther unto'. But by late April Bell's attempt to enjoy the commendam of Durham priory had already been defeated. On the advice of Dudley and others, Edward IV had informed Bell 'ut solo Episcopatu et nullo modo

---

[74] W.E. Lunt, *Financial Relations of the Papacy with England, 1327–1534*, Mediaeval Academy of America (1962), pp. 173, 820–3.

[75] *Priory of Coldingham*, p. 235.

[76] DCD, Reg. IV, fo. 182.

prioratu gauderet'; and it was only after Bell had renounced his right to the commendam that the king agreed to accept his oath of fealty on 22 April. On the following day Bishop Dudley informed the monks of Durham that Bell's 'auctorite over you is now utterly expired and extincte'.[77]

By the time that Robert Ebchester was elected the new prior of Durham on 22 May 1478, Richard Bell had already been bishop of Carlisle for a month. The royal mandates ordering the restitution of the temporalities of the see were dated from Westminster on 24 April 1478 and in London two days later, on Rogation Sunday, Bell was consecrated by the new bishop of Chichester, Edward Story.[78] Bell's inability to adopt the normal practice and secure consecration at the hands of his metropolitan is readily understandable in view of the age and illness of Archbishop Lawrence Booth; but he was obliged to make a written profession of canonical obedience to the archbishop, an undated copy of which was entered in Booth's York register between documents of 7 May and 24 June 1478.[79] As Bell was able to exercise effective control over his diocese from the date of his consecration, he seems, like many late medieval English bishops in the same position, to have been in no particular hurry to secure installation and enthronement in his cathedral church. The mandate to enthrone Bell (a duty which pertained to the archdeacon of York) was dated as late as 24 August 1480.[80] By this time the seventy-year-old bishop had already taken up residence in his diocese and begun the last phase of his long career. Unfortunately and paradoxically the evidence for Bell's role as bishop of Carlisle between 1478 and 1495 is much less plentiful than at earlier stages of his life. However, the modern historian is in a slightly more favourable position than William Hutchinson who commented on Bell's episcopate at Carlisle that 'in the course of eighteen years we collect nothing singular in his life'.[81] The survival of a valuable collection of fifteenth-century accounts by officials of the bishop of Carlisle helps to throw some light on the obscurities of the late medieval history of the diocese. Such accounts exist for eight years of Bell's episcopate at Carlisle and several, especially the audited *compoti* of his receiver-general, make it possible to establish some conclusions about his activities as bishop.[82]

[77] DCD, Reg. Parv. III, fos 182, 186v; Reg. IV, fos 182–3; *Scriptores tres*, pp. ccclxi–ccclxv.

[78] *CPR, 1476–85*, p. 105; *Scriptores tres*, pp. 149, ccclxi; BL, MS Lansdowne. 721, fo. 56v. Story consecrated Bell in the London house of the bishops of Carlisle.

[79] Borthwick Institute of Historical Research, York: Register of Lawrence Booth, fo. 6.

[80] BL, MS Cotton Galba E.X, fos 136v–137.

[81] W. Hutchinson, *History and Antiquities of Cumberland* (Carlisle, 1794), ii, p. 627.

[82] Carlisle Record Office: DRC/2, nos 13–21 (1478–79; 1480–81; 1482; 1487–88 with duplicates; 1488–89; 1489–90; 1492–93; 1493–94). The fifteenth-century episcopal accounts of Carlisle were used by Canon James Wilson – notably in *Rose Castle* (Carlisle, 1912) and VCH, *Cumberland*, ii, pp. 37–44 – but were then mislaid and only rediscovered in 1962.

When Bell became bishop of Carlisle in 1478, he inherited an administrative and financial organisation of the diocese which was already well
established and which he himself made no attempt to change. The see
was divided into four deaneries but its one archdeacon was usually a
royal clerk absent from the diocese. The bishop's staff of officials and
servants followed the same pattern, though on an unusually small scale,
as that encountered in other English dioceses of the period. The bishop
employed the services of a vicar-general (often the prior of Carlisle), a
registrar (who can sometimes be identified with the official of the diocese)
and an apparitor, while he also found it necessary to retain a proctor at
the York curia. Bell was unable to afford the expense of a permanent
suffragan bishop, but occasionally employed the services of one of the
York suffragans to celebrate orders at Carlisle. The bishop's lay servants
included the bailiffs of his estates, of whom the most important were
those of Dalston, Penrith, Caldecote, Linstock and Aspatria, as well as
the steward of the barony of Dalston, the constable of Rose Castle and
the steward and bailiffs of Horncastle in Lincolnshire. All these officers
accounted to the bishop's receiver-general who held a central place in the
administration of the diocese and normally combined this position with
that of household steward (*seneschallus hospicii domini intrinsecus*). Bishop
Bell's household was itself probably little larger than that with which
he had been surrounded when prior of Durham; most provisions were
bought locally but the bishop's wine supplies had to be obtained from
Newcastle or even Hull and then conveyed across country to Rose at
considerable expense.

The poverty of their diocese was the greatest problem facing the
medieval bishops of Carlisle, a problem which Bell had hoped to overcome
by holding Durham in commendam. The see of Carlisle had never been
richly endowed and its revenues, like those of all northern landlords in
the fifteenth century, suffered severely as a result of Scottish raids and
falling rent values. Only their possession of the lordship and rectory of
Horncastle in Lincolnshire, which provided over a quarter of their total
income, preserved the bishops of Carlisle from complete insolvency. By the
time that Bell was provided to Carlisle in 1478 it was no longer possible
for him to expand his sources of revenue in any significant direction.
The clerical population of north-western England was neither numerous
nor wealthy enough to be able to contribute more than a few pounds to
his income in the form of fines and subsidies; another possibility, the
appropriation of churches in the bishop's patronage, had already been
exhausted earlier in the century.[83] Nevertheless, although Bell's financial
situation was always a matter for concern, there is some evidence to suggest
that he was able to achieve some stability and that, as at Durham, he left

[83] VCH, *Cumberland*, ii, p. 35; Storey, *CW 2*, 55, p. 121.

his office somewhat more prosperous than he had found it. A valor, taken in 1462, of episcopal revenues in the dioceses of Carlisle and Durham showed that there had been a fall from the previous total of £389 to a figure of £349 per annum.[84] But a comparison of the receiver-general's account for 1480–81 with that for 1487–88 suggests that the decline was being reversed during Bell's priorate. In 1480–81, the annual receipts (not including arrears) of Bell's receiver-general were £363, a figure which had risen to £427 in 1487–88. In the former year £95 was delivered into the bishop's own hands and £60 handed to the steward of his household: the comparative figures for 1487–88 are £110 and £164.[85] At the beginning of his episcopate, Bell was heavily in debt, especially to Agnes Rodes of Newcastle upon Tyne from whom he had borrowed £80 in 1478, presumably to help meet the cost of his *servitia* at Rome. But within a few years, Bell had not only repaid his creditors but was in a position to undertake extensive building operations at Rose Castle, the best-known feature of his episcopate. Although the extant accounts are somewhat less informative about the details of the rebuilding at Rose Castle than one could wish, they show that the *Novum opus* at Rose was in full progress between 1487 and 1489, resulting in the construction of a new chapel with an elaborate and probably timber-framed roof as well as a new tower which bears Bell's initials and is still known, despite extensive modifications at later periods, by his name.[86]

The rebuilding at Rose Castle suggests not only that Bell's financial resources could withstand the strain of heavy capital expenditure but that he often stayed there. His officials' accounts leave a similarly strong impression that he was normally a resident bishop and lived at Rose throughout most of his episcopate. Bell probably visited London infrequently after 1478 and allowed his predecessor, Edward Story, to remain a resident at the bishop of Carlisle's London house, Carlisle Place, on the south side of the Strand.[87] Although as a spiritual peer Bell received an individual summons to parliaments between 1478 and 1495, the rolls of parliament provide no evidence of his attendance. The most interesting of Bell's recorded excursions outside his diocese was made, appropriately enough, in the interests of the greatest of his former patrons, Richard of Gloucester. Bell was one of the five bishops who accompanied the

[84] DRC/2, no. 9.

[85] DRC/2, nos 14, 17.

[86] Wilson, *Rose Castle*, pp. 75, 86, 125–6, 212–19. The rebuilding of Rose was continued by Bell's successors, notably Bishop Kite (1521–37): Leland, *Itinerary* (1906–10), v, p. 56; *Collectanea* (1774) ii, p. 347. Another building repaired by Bell at about this time was the choir of the parish church of Crosby-on-Eden (appropriated to the bishopric of Carlisle); here, early in the eighteenth century, Bishop Nicolson noticed Bell's rebus, 'the letter R cut in stone, with a Bell hanging under it': W. Nicolson, *Miscellany Accounts of the Diocese of Carlisle*, ed. R.S. Ferguson, Cumberland and Westmorland Antiquarian and Archaeological Society, extra series (1877), p. 105.

[87] S.J. Madge, 'Worcester House in the Strand', *Archaeologia*, 91 (1945), p. 158.

newly-crowned Richard III as he rode triumphantly under Micklegate
Bar into the city of York on 29 August 1483 and was apparently still
in attendance on the king a week later when the latter invested his
son Edward as Prince of Wales.[88] There were other occasions on which
Bell left the comparative seclusion of Rose Castle: early in 1481, for
example, he spent some time at Bardney in Lincolnshire (presumably
in order to visit his neighbouring lordship of Horncastle); and five years
later he rode to Jarrow in the company of a retinue partly provided
by the prior of Lanercost.[89] Such expeditions seem, however, to have
been comparatively rare and Bell's pastoral duties within his diocese
must take the central place in any account of the last years of his life.
Whether at Rose, where he personally corrected the transgressions of
the diocesan clergy and gave his blessing to newly-elected abbots, or at
Carlisle, where he celebrated orders and presided over diocesan synods,
he showed himself a responsible ruler of his see.[90] Bell's relations with the
Austin canons of his cathedral church at Carlisle were inevitably close; he
stayed at Carlisle Priory on several occasions and like Richard III helped
to support Prior Gudybour's plans for the repair and redecoration of its
fabric. The close resemblance between one of the series of late medieval
paintings on the back of the Carlisle choir-stalls and the illuminations in
a twelfth-century Durham copy of Bede's *Life of Saint Cuthbert* has led to
the sugggestion that this manuscript was loaned to Carlisle priory at Bell's
request; and the survival of the same carved badge (a mermaid with comb
and glass) on both the tower arcade at Durham and one of the miserere
seats at Carlisle can be taken to symbolise Bell's association with both of
the northern cathedrals.[91]

At first sight Bishop Bell's withdrawal into the world of diocesan
affairs may seem difficult to reconcile with the wider role played by
most late medieval English bishops and with Bell's own reputation as an
ambitious ecclesiastic. But it is not difficult to find an explanation for Bell's
retirement from secular affairs. The theory that episcopal appointments

[88] Minster Library, York: Vicars Choral, 'Statute and Minute Book', fo. 48; Dean and
Chapter, 'Register of Terriers' (Davis, *Medieval Cartularies*, no. 1092), fo. 70; *Fabric Rolls
of York Minster*, Surtees Society 35 (1858), p. 211. See below, pp. 225–6.

[89] DRC/2, no. 14; Wilson, *Rose Castle*, p. 164.

[90] These aspects of Bell's episcopate are best recorded by his registrars' accounts, DRC/2,
nos 13, 18, 19, 20.

[91] B. Colgrave, 'The St Cuthbert Paintings on the Carlisle Cathedral Stalls', *Burlington
Magazine*, 73 (1938), pp. 17–21; idem, 'History of British Museum, Add. MS 39943', *English
Historical Review*, 54 (1939), pp. 673–7. For an earlier loan of this highly-prized manuscript
to Bishop Neville of Durham on 19 July 1438, see DCD, Misc. Charters, no. 2352. The
carving of the mermaid at Carlisle is illustrated by R.W. Billings, *Architectural Illustrations,
History and Description of Carlisle Cathedral* (London 1840), plate 35; but Billings' further
suggestion, *Geometric Tracery of Brancepeth Church in the County of Durham* (London 1845),
p. 4, that Bell influenced the design of the geometric panelling at Carlisle cathedral, is
very unconvincing.

to Carlisle were made 'not so much to give the see a bishop as Rose Castle a captain',[92] is only partly valid and fails to apply in Bell's own case. Although, as bishop, Bell headed royal commissions of peace for the counties of Cumberland and Westmorland,[93] real political power in north-western England rested throughout his episcopate in the hands of the Lords Dacre of Gilsland. Humphrey, Lord Dacre and (after 1485) his son Thomas were successively governors of Carlisle Castle and lieutenants of the west march: not only did Bell welcome visits from the Dacres but he sought their help at times of crisis, as in 1487–88 when a quarrel broke out between Lord Clifford and Sir Christopher Moresby. One lord who played a more considerable role than Bell in public affairs of the north was not only yet another supporter of Richard III but also another 'monk-bishop'. Richard Redman, although bishop of St Asaph until his translation to Exeter in 1495, was a native of Westmorland, and as abbot of Shap continued to visit Bell's diocese at frequent intervals. Relations between the two bishops seem to have been cordial, for in October 1488 Bell rode to meet Redman at Penrith.[94] Redman was much more heavily involved in diplomatic activity throughout the last quarter of the fifteenth century than Bell; the latter, although a member of the royal commission appointed on 13 February 1487 to arrange a prolongation of the Anglo-Scottish truce, took relatively little part in the official business of the marches after leaving Durham.[95]

Another reason for the apparent decline of Bell's political influence was the paradox that as bishop of Carlisle he actually had less attractive patronage at his disposal than when prior of Durham. After William Strickland's appropriation of the church of Horncastle at the beginning of the century, there remained few benefices in the bishop's gift wealthy enough to attract the serious attention of royal clerks. So impoverished were most of the churches in the diocese that the bishop often found it difficult to make suitable provision for his own ecclesiastical officials. Thus Bell instituted his registrar, Robert Fisher, to both the rectory of Cliburn and the vicarage of Torpenhow because the revenues of only one of these churches would have failed to support him.[96] Bell's control over the appointment of his lay officers was even more limited. When he arrived at Carlisle in 1478 he discovered that the important positions of constable

[92] C.M.L. Bouch, *Prelates and People of the Lake Counties* (Kendal, 1948), p. 118.

[93] *CPR, 1476–85*, pp. 556, 577; *1485–94*, pp. 484, 504; *1494–1509*, pp. 634, 664.

[94] DRC/2, no. 17. For Redman's association with Richard III, see R.J. Knecht, 'The Episcopate and the Wars of the Roses', *University of Birmingham Historical Journal*, 6 (1958), pp. 125, 127.

[95] *Materials for Reign of Henry VII*, RS (1873–77), ii, p. 120; cf. *Rotuli Scotiae*, ii, pp. 461, 464, 478, 487, 499; A. Conway, *Henry VII's Relations with Scotland and Ireland, 1485–98* (Cambridge, 1932), p. 10.

[96] DRC/2, no. 18.

of Rose Castle and bailiff of the barony of Dalston were in the hands of
John Borell and Walter Story, both of whom had received letters patent
from Bishop Story appointing them for life.[97] Many of the descendants
of Bishop Strickland 'continued at Rose and Dalston, holding the offices
of constable or bailiff to the bishop in almost hereditary succession from
1414 to 1747',[98] and there is evidence that even ecclesiastical benefices
could be partly monopolised by members of the same local family.
When Master John Whelpdale senior vacated the church of Caldbeck
in 1488 he was succeeded by John Whelpdale, *clericus*.[99] As bishop of
Carlisle, Bell ruled over a diocese largely administered by a few influential
Westmorland and Cumberland families. None of the servants employed by
Bell at Durham can be proved to have followed him to Carlisle after 1478,
and the bishop's freedom of action was more restricted by powerful local
interests than perhaps he had himself anticipated.

Any account of Bell's role as bishop of Carlisle must also take into
account the fact that he was an extremely old man throughout his
episcopate. Although Bell was the only bishop of Carlisle to resign his
office between 1246 and 1946, the decision is readily understandable
when it is remembered that he had reached his eighty-fifth year in
1495. Bell's resignation was admitted by the pope on 4 September of
that year, and William Senhouse, abbot of St Mary's, York, provided to
the see.[100] Senhouse, another Benedictine monk, received his temporalities
on 11 December and was to be more fortunate than Bell seventeen years
earlier in that as bishop he continued to hold the abbacy of St Mary's in
commendam. The traditional belief that Bell then returned to Durham
to spend the last few months of his life as a monk finds no confirmation
among the Durham records and is difficult to reconcile with his eventual
burial in Carlisle cathedral. Nor is it altogether likely that the Durham
monks ever forgave Bell for his attempt to retain the priorate in 1478,
especially as he had carried off with him to Carlisle a valuable collection of
silver plate.[101] It is probable that Bell never completely severed relations
with his old monastery; but the only extant letter he wrote to his successor
at Durham was hardly calculated to arouse affection. Bell complained that
the king's business had compelled him to find 'oon great Some of money'
and, signing himself in his own handwriting, asked the prior to loan him
'such money as ye may convenyently spare'.[102] Possibly Bell spent the

[97] Ibid., nos 14, 17.
[98] Bouch, 'Descendants of William Lowther of the Rose', *CW 2*, 39, p. 109.
[99] DRC/2, no. 18.
[100] W.M. Brady, *The Episcopal Succession in England, Scotland and Ireland* (Rome, 1876–77),
i, pp. 102–103. Cf. *CPR, 1494–1509*, p. 58.
[101] *Priory of Finchale*, pp. xxx–xxxi; DCD, Reg. Parv. III, fo. 188.
[102] DCD, I. 14. Pont. no. 16. I am grateful to Mr Martin Snape for bringing this letter
to my attention. The letter is addressed to 'my Broder the Prior of Duresme' and was sent
under the (now missing) bishop's signet seal.

very last period of his life at Carlisle rather than Durham cathedral; but speculation seems pointless in view of the complete disappearance of his name from the records after his resignation. Bell's monastic status restrained him from making a will. Even the accepted view that he died in 1496 seems to derive merely from the unsupported assertions of Nicolson and Burn in their history of Westmorland and Cumberland.[103] The inscription round the edge of his magnificent brass on the floor of the cathedral choir at Carlisle only adds to the mystery, for it includes the day but not the month and year of his death:

> 'Hic iacet Reuerendus Pater Ricardus Bell quondam Episcopus Karliolensis qui ab hac luce migrauit Videlicet Vicesima Quarto Die . . . Anno Domini . . . Et omnium ffidelium defunctorum Per misericordiam dei Requiescant in Perpetua Pace. Amen.'[104]

Richard Bell was the first of three members of the religious clergy who, between them, ruled the diocese of Carlisle for all but six of the forty-two years between 1478 and 1520. The re-emergence of the 'monk-bishop' at Carlisle towards the very end of the monastic period is a somewhat remarkable phenomenon and a commentary not only on the aspirations of the more ambitious religious prelates of the time but also on the poverty of a diocese which failed to attract the attentions of the greatest royal ministers and servants, and was consequently a prize open to the professed monk. With the possible exception of Rochester, Carlisle was the poorest of all the English dioceses. The annual income of its bishop at the end of the middle ages was only slightly higher than that of the see's richest monastery, the abbey of Holmcultram.[105] The late foundation of the diocese, the subsequent division of its already limited endowments between the bishop and the Augustinian canons of the cathedral church, together with the inability of the late medieval episcopate to augment their sources of revenue ensured that the bishop of Carlisle could never count himself among the wealthiest magnates of England. Such was certainly the case; and the familiarity of the argument that Carlisle was a relatively poor bishopric hardly lessens its importance

---

[103] Nicolson and Burn, *History and Antiquities of Westmorland and Cumberland*, ii, p. 276. Cf. Browne Willis, *Survey of Cathedrals* (1727), i, pp. 295–6.

[104] No photograph can do the original brass full justice. Bishop Bell is depicted in full mass vestments, holding the Bible in his right hand and reciting the *Credo*; he wears a high jewelled and crocketed mitre and his left hand grasps the pastoral staff. The quatrain at his feet (now barely legible and sometimes misread in the past) appears to read as follows:

> Hac Marmor Fossa Bell presulis en tenet ossa
> Duresme dudum prior hic post pontificatum
> Gessit sed renuit Christum super omnia querit
> Dispiciens mundum poscendo precamina fratrum.

[105] *Valor Ecclesiasticus*, Record Commission (1810–34), v, pp. 273–4, 282–3.

in explaining why a monk like Richard Bell secured the see. On the other hand, it is essential to emphasise, more perhaps than previous historians have done, that the financial and other responsibilities of the bishops of Carlisle were as limited as their resources. The diocese included within its boundaries only ten religious houses and less than a hundred parish churches; although its organisation may well have been as effective as those of other sees, it could clearly afford to be much less extensive and costly. Even if allowances are made for the adverse effects of the Scottish wars on the financial position of the late medieval bishops of Carlisle, there is no evidence that poverty ever prevented the adequate performance of their pastoral duties. Provided that the bishop in question was content, unlike Marmaduke Lumley, to play a role in local rather than national politics and society, it seems clear that his income allowed him the opportunity to do so. Questions of prestige and status set apart, there were at least some material advantages to be gained by Bell when he eagerly exchanged the priory of Durham for the bishopric of Carlisle in 1478. By Lumley, the see of Carlisle was clearly looked upon as a stepping-stone (on which, however, he had to wait reluctantly for twenty years of his adult life) to one of the richest bishoprics; but for Richard Bell the episcopal throne at Carlisle marked the culmination of an already long and eventful career. Despite later rumours that he aimed at the papal throne itself,[106] even Bell's ambition had its limits.

[106] Blakiston, *Some Durham College Rolls*, p. 17.

7

The Political Role of the Archbishops of York during the Reign of Edward I

It would be hard for any medievalist to deny that the episcopal bench of Henry III and Edward I was responsible for the last genuinely fundamental transformation of the administrative structures of the English church before the Reformation. On the other hand, and by a curious irony, the motives of the pontiffs who presided over the ecclesiastical changes of thirteenth-century England can be more difficult to fathom than in any other period of post-conquest history. Not that the medieval church historian can complain either of a scarcity of interesting original sources or of a lack of talented secondary historians in the case of a century adorned by scholars of the calibre of the late Maurice Powicke and Christopher Cheney. However, even the latter was compelled to acknowledge the 'cold light' often thrown by surviving records on the methods used by the hierarchy and its ecclesiastical lawyers; and accordingly the thirteenth century was for him a period in which, perhaps more than usually, the surviving documents 'represent unattained ideals'.[1] As for Professor Powicke, one hardly needs to urge the familiar point that his last and most ambitious book, *The Thirteenth Century*, illustrates to perfection what one takes to be that century's greatest problem for the historian: despite the comparative abundance of the evidence, and Powicke's own strenuous attempts to identify with its protagonists, it can be quite extraordinarily difficult to uncover the mainsprings of political or ecclesiastical action.[2] Not surprisingly, such problems of interpretation have recently re-emerged very clearly, as the author is at pains to point out, in Michael Prestwich's authoritative study of the best-documented and most influential thirteenth-century Englishman of them all.[3] May it

[1] C.R. Cheney, 'Statute-Making in the English Church in the Thirteenth Century', *Proceedings of the Second International Congress of Medieval Canon Law, Boston College, 1963*, ed. S. Kuttner and J.J. Ryan, Monumenta iuris canonici, series C, subsidia I (Vatican, 1965), repr. in C.R. Cheney, *Medieval Texts and Studies* (Oxford, 1973), pp. 155–7; cf. J.R.H. Moorman, *Church Life in England in the Thirteenth Century* (Cambridge, 1955), p. 238: 'we can only feel disappointed that so little progress was made'.
[2] See e.g. F.M. Powicke, *The Thirteenth Century, 1216–1307* (2nd edn, Oxford, 1962), pp. 227–30.
[3] M. Prestwich, *Edward I* (London, 1988), pp. 108–22, 558–67; cf. idem, 'The Piety of Edward I', in *England in the Thirteenth Century*, ed. W.M. Ormrod (Harlaxton, 1985), pp. 120–8.

be too facile to suggest that the historian of thirteenth-century England is confronted with an extreme example of a well-known paradox? There are few periods in English history during which rhetoric lies so close to public action as in the years between Magna Carta and the death of Edward I, but again and again we are left peculiarly uncertain as to whether the chief actors on the political and ecclesiastical stage actually believed their own rhetoric.

Such general and no doubt very hypothetical considerations, if valid at all, seem to apply especially forcibly to any attempts to understand the role and status of the six different ecclesiastics who sat on the metropolitan throne of St Peter of York during the thirty-five years of King Edward I's reign. Although a very great deal can be known and surmised about how these six men administered their diocese and province, on two absolutely central issues – their own order of spiritual and temporal priorities, and their conception of their role as primates within the English realm – they can only be seen through a glass very darkly indeed. Such opacity is all the more regrettable because it might well be argued that the reign of Edward I was one of the few genuinely critical epochs for the transformation of ecclesiastical authority within the 1350 years of the history of the see of York. The nature of that transformation has been emphasised by Peter Heath, who rightly stresses the significance of some alarming developments perhaps unduly neglected by Professor Powicke, Dr W.A. Pantin and even Professor Alexander Hamilton Thompson. In Mr Peter Heath's words:

> Not always through royal initiative, and certainly not by a deliberate policy, Edward I's reign witnessed some major developments to the long-term dis- advantage of the English church. Some serious steps had been taken towards that outburst of anticlericalism and, in particular, antipapalism which marked the later fourteenth century . . . resentment against the papacy – by the clergy as well as the laity – was growing . . . parliament was providing an assembly where hostility could be orchestrated, diffused and preserved. What an irony that a king renowned for his piety, who prefaced some of his legislation by alluding to his duty to defend the church, and who sought a quick end to his wars in order to pursue the crusade, should preside over these changes![4]

Ironical indeed; and, against the background of Mr Heath's not unpersuasive diagnosis, how far are we to see Edward's six archbishops of York as the accomplices or the victims, or both, of changes so important to the *ecclesia Anglicana* in the north? There is no easy answer to that question, as already

---

[4] P. Heath, *Church and Realm, 1272–1461: Conflict and Collaboration in an Age of Crises* (London, 1988), p. 63; cf. Powicke, *Thirteenth Century*, pp. 445–509; W.A. Pantin, *The English Church in the Fourteenth Century* (Cambridge, 1955), pp. 47–81; A.H. Thompson, *The English Clergy and their Organization in the Later Middle Ages* (Oxford, 1947), pp. 10–11, 30–1.

seen; but at least it is important to be reminded at the outset that to be an archbishop of York in the years around 1300 was not a responsibility to be taken lightly. Of Edward I's six northern metropolitans, one died as a frustrated expatriate at Pontigny in Burgundy; one was publicly humiliated and narrowly escaped imprisonment at the hands of his royal master; a third was so nervous of his suffragan bishop of Durham that he preferred not to take any prominent initiative against him at all; and yet a fourth was supposedly harassed by Edward I into a nervous breakdown so severe that it led to his premature death.[5]

Such difficulties and such tensions are all the more ironic, more poignant indeed, when one considers that they figure so very fleetingly in the administrative records that make these six metropolitans among the best-documented figures of the English episcopal bench in the entire middle ages. After the precocious experiment between 1225 and 1255 (during the pontificate of Walter de Gray) of preserving copies of administrative documents in roll form, the celebrated and uninterrupted series of York archiepiscopal registers proper begins to survive when Archbishop Giffard's clerks decided to adopt book form shortly after their master's translation to the north from the see of Bath and Wells in December 1266.[6] Perhaps the first scholar to appreciate fully the way in which these early registers could put the study of ecclesiastical history in the north on a new footing was James Raine the younger. By means of his enlarged edition of W.H. Dixon's *Fasti Eboracenses* as early as 1863, by his several contributions to the Rolls Series, and by his sponsorship of editions of these registers under the auspices of the Surtees Society, Raine proved himself the most effective posthumous advocate of Edward I's six archbishops of York there had ever been.[7] More significantly still, by the time that the Surtees Society had at last (as late as 1940) completed the lengthy task of publishing editions of all the York registers to 1315, Hamilton Thompson had emerged as their supreme analyst and commentator.[8]

To the extent that the most magisterial and influential of all historians of the medieval English church knew the registers of archbishops Giffard

---

[5] *Annales monastici*, RS (1864–9), iv, p. 491 (Worcester annals); *The Chronicle of Walter of Guisborough*, ed. H. Rothwell, Camden Society, 3rd series, 89 (1957), pp. 250, 351, 358–9; Prestwich, *Edward I*, p. 547.

[6] *The Register or Rolls of Walter Gray, Lord Archbishop of York*, ed. J. Raine, Surtees Society, 56 (1872), pp. vii–xiii; A.H. Thompson, 'The Registers of the Archbishops of York', *Yorkshire Archaeological Journal*, 32 (1936), pp. 245–54; D.M. Smith, *Guide to Bishops' Registers of England and Wales* (London, 1981), pp. 232–4.

[7] W.H. Dixon, *Fasti Eboracenses: 'Lives' of the Archbishops of York*, i, ed. J. Raine (London, 1863); *Historical Papers and Letters from the Northern Registers*, ed. J. Raine, RS (1873); *Historians of the Church of York and its Archbishops*, ed. J. Raine, RS (1879–94).

[8] See the introductions to *The Register of William Greenfield, Lord Archbishop of York, 1306–15*, ed. W. Brown and A.H. Thompson, Surtees Society, 145, 149, 151, 153 (1931–40); and cf. *An Address Presented to Alexander Hamilton Thompson with a Bibliography of his Writings* (privately printed, Oxford, 1948), passim.

to Greenfield more intimately than any others in the country, it is hardly an exaggeration to state that Hamilton Thompson's scrutiny of those registers lies at the centre of how the operations of the late medieval English church are still viewed today. On the whole and all the more interestingly when one remembers the severity that he could display towards many members of the fifteenth-century episcopate ('not a strong body of men'), Hamilton Thompson was very impressed.[9] In the first place, his admiration for the the system of registration at York, possibly influenced during these years by the Nassington family, officials principal at York under five successive archbishops, was itself considerable; and as the gradual improvement in the format and organisation of the York registers attained its greatest heights of sophistication under William de Greenfield and William Melton ('the finest volumes in the entire series'), Hamilton Thompson came equally to admire what he took to be the efficiency of the metropolitans for whom those volumes were compiled.[10] More specifically still, Hamilton Thompson came to be much impressed by the evidence that their registers seemed to provide of the capacity of Edward I's archbishops for very laborious administrative and judicial work indeed. The most frequently cited of Hamilton Thompson's commendations in this sphere is all the more ironical because this was praise for an archibshop (Thomas de Corbridge) who eventually had his temporalities seized by a considerably less appreciative Edward I. For Hamilton Thompson, however,

> there are few examples of consistent diligence in the episcopal office more conspicuous than that which is disclosed to us by the itinerary of Corbridge; and it is doubtful whether any other English prelate in the middle ages managed, in the short space of $4\frac{1}{2}$ years, to come within measurable distance of completing two visitations, and those exceptionally thorough, of his diocese.[11]

Such praise for such reasons exposes especially clearly its author's very influential tendency to assess the worth of a medieval bishop by the assiduity with which he made formal visitations of the churches, and especially the religious houses, of his diocese. As Hamilton Thompson saw it, and taught his readers to see it, the registers of Edward I's six archbishops of York tell a story of considerable and perhaps even remarkable success. In the first place, here is the archdiocese of York revealed, for the very first time, as a huge and complex organisation subjected nevertheless to the most detailed and vigilant bureaucratic

---

[9] Thompson, *English Clergy*, p. 45; cf. *The Church, Politics and Patronage in the Fifteenth Century*, ed. R.B. Dobson (Gloucester, 1984), pp. 16, 22.

[10] Thompson, 'Registers of the Archbishops of York', pp. 245–63; idem, *English Clergy*, 1–9; cf. VCH, *Yorkshire*, iii, pp. 28–36.

[11] *The Register of Thomas of Corbridge, Lord Archbishop of York, 1300–1304*, ed. W. Brown, Surtees Society, 138, 141 (1925–8), ii, p. xx.

control. Secondly, those registers seem equally to reveal archbishops who were personally intent on maintaining and indeed enhancing the spiritual standards of their flock, and above all of their clerical flock. From this point of view, the early registers of the church of York are the critical documents for the case that the most important achievement of the archbishops was to bring ecclesiastical order to a north which had never fully experienced such order before. To put that success in the way it was formulated over fifty years ago by Marion Gibbs and Jane Lang, these were the archbishops who pursued a deliberate programme of implementing the decrees of the Fourth Lateran Council (1215) and thereby finally 'fulfilled the promise of 1215' north of the Humber.[12]

So favourable an interpretation of the ecclesiastical objectives of Edward I's six archbishops of York – one which for obvious reasons would presumably have met with their own approval – cannot be easily discounted and could indeed be elaborated; but the purpose of this essay, as already implied, is to explore some of the factors which so often vitiated and even negated the initiatives of these would-be reforming pontiffs. How far were their failures to attain their aims the result of personal weaknesses in their own temperaments, experience and administrative skills? As ever in the case of late medieval English bishops, no confident answer to that question can be offered, regrettably.[13] However, and having made all allowances for the near impossibility of categorising the members of the late medieval episcopal bench with any precision, the most important conclusion must be that Edward I's six archbishops fell into two very different groups. Much the most experienced and most nationally influential figures of the sextet were the two archbishops of York who respectively saw Edward I onto his throne and into his grave. Archbishop Walter Giffard (1266–79) was the son of Hugh Giffard of Boyton (Wilts) and hence a member of a powerful clerical dynasty. This, together with his great administrative ability, led him to the chancellorship of England in 1265–66.[14] As the senior ecclesiastic in the country when the Lord Edward left Dover for the Holy Land in August 1270, Giffard was not only the first English prelate to swear an

---

[12] M. Gibbs and J. Lang, *Bishops and Reform, 1215–1272, with Special Reference to the Lateran Council of 1215* (Oxford, 1934), pp. 11–24, 131–79, which concludes with the observation, certainly relevant to York, that 'always the bishops were too much occupied' to carry out the Lateran decrees in full.

[13] See, e.g., R.G. Davies, 'The Episcopate', *Profession, Vocation and Culture in Later Medieval England*, ed. C.H. Clough (Liverpool, 1982), pp. 51–90; Moorman, *Church Life*, pp. 169–96; K. Edwards, 'The Social Origins and the Provenance of the English Bishops during the Reign of Edward II', *Transactions of the Royal Historical Society*, 5th series, 9 (1959), pp. 51–79; R.B. Dobson, 'The Bishops of Late Medieval England as Intermediaries between Church and State', *Etat et église dans la genèse de l'état moderne*, ed. J.-P. Genet and B. Vincent (Madrid, 1986), pp. 227–38.

[14] *The Register of Walter Giffard, Lord Archbishop of York, 1266–1279*, ed. W. Brown, Surtees Society, 109 (1904), pp. i–iv; *BRUO*, ii, pp. 762–3.

oath of allegiance to the absent Edward over Henry III's dead body in
1272 but probably did more than anyone – even more than Robert Burnell
– to ensure an untroubled accession for the new king.[15] More than a
generation later, it was similarly to be William de Greenfield, archbishop
of York (1304–15) and also an ex-chancellor (1302–4) of the king, who
acted as Edward's senior churchman at the parliament of Carlisle, only
a few months before the monarch's death at Burgh-upon-the-Sands, not
far away.[16] Immediately thereafter, like Giffard thirty-five years earlier,
Greenfield found himself serving as one of the joint regents of the realm.
In their not at all dissimilar ways – and after all, Greenfield was almost
certainly a junior kinsman of Archbishop Giffard, who had supported
him as an Oxford student as early as 1269 – these two archbishops
might well serve as classic exemplars of what an English king might
hope for from his archbishops of York, especially at times when his
archbishops of Canterbury were proving exceptionally non-cooperative
and intransigent.[17] To state the obvious, the prestige and influence of the
primates Angliae were never likely to be higher than when the *primates totius
Angliae* were suffering from the slings and arrows of royal displeasure, as
so often occurred during the reign of Edward I.

Not, in fact, that this was an asset from which Edward I's other four
archbishops of York proved capable of making as much capital as one
might have expected. The most important common denominator shared
by archbishops William Wickwane (1279–85), John le Romeyn (1285–96),
Henry de Newark (1296–99) and Thomas de Corbridge (1299–1304) was
less their remarkably poor life-expectancy as metropolitans than the fact
that, before their elevation, all four were very distinguished within the
York cathedral chapter but comparatively unknown outside it. Thus
Wickwane, whose geographical origins remain extremely uncertain, had
been chancellor of York Minster for fifteen years before his election as
archbishop;[18] Romeyn was almost certainly the bastard son (possibly by

[15] *Annales Monastici*, ed. H.R. Luard, RS (1864–9), iv, p. 462; Powicke, *Henry III*,
ii, pp. 532, 581–7, 593, 595; Prestwich, *Edward I*, pp. 73, 90. Archbishop Giffard,
Roger Mortimer and Robert Burnell were Edward I's three regents between the king's
accession (20 Nov. 1272) and his return to England (2 Aug. 1274): *Handbook of British
Chronology*, ed. E.B. Fryde et al. (3rd edn, London, 1986), p. 38.

[16] *Chronicon de Lanercost, 1201–1346*, ed. J. Stevenson (Edinburgh, 1839), p. 206; *Fasti
Eboracenses*, 367; cf. H. Johnstone, *Edward of Carnarvon, 1284–1307* (Manchester, 1946),
p. 119 n. 5.

[17] *Reg. Giffard*, pp. 121, 123; *Fasti Eboracenses*, p. 313. Cf. D.L. Douie, *Archbishop Pecham*
(Oxford, 1952); J.H. Denton, *Robert Winchelsey and the Crown, 1294–1313* (Cambridge,
1980). As Heath, *Church and Realm*, p. 31, has observed, much of the antagonism between
Edward I and these two archbishops of Canterbury centred, as in the church of York,
upon the king's need to exploit ecclesiastical patronage on behalf of his own clerks.

[18] *The Register of William Wickwane, Lord Archbishop of York, 1279–85*, ed. W. Brown,
Surtees Society, 114 (1907), pp. iii–v; R. Brentano, *York Metropolitan Jurisdiction and Papal
Judges Delegate, 1279–1296* (Berkeley, 1959), pp. 42–51; cf. C.R. Cheney, 'Letters of William
Wickwane, Chancellor of York, 1266–68', *English Historical Review*, 47 (1932), pp. 626–42.

a waiting-woman) of that Croesus of early thirteenth-century canons of York, John le Romeyn;[19] Newark had found his way to the archdeaconry of Richmond, and eventually to the deanery of York, almost twenty years before his election as archbishop in 1296;[20] while Thomas de Corbridge, chancellor of the Minster in the 1280s, holds something of a record for apparently never having held any significant benefice outside York cathedral at all.[21] Not only, therefore, was the metropolitan see of St Peter still completely immune from the slightest sign of what one might term aristocratic invasion: if anything, it tended to be the prize awarded to the long-standing canon of York most esteemed by his own fellows in the York Minster chapter. To that generalisation admittedly one needs to add the all-important qualification that the canon in question was by now required to have some genuine claims to university learning. Of these six archbishops, John le Romeyn (an outstanding scholar according to Rishanger, and *theologus magnus* according to Walter of Guisborough) was at some time a graduate and lecturer at Paris as well as Oxford; while Greenfield (a doctor in both canon and civil law) seems similarly to have taught at both those universities early in his career.[22] Thomas de Corbridge, another doctor of theology, almost certainly emerged from the Oxford schools; Wickwane and Newark definitely did so; and to Walter Giffard fell the unusual distinction of being the only Cambridge graduate, although he also studied at Oxford, to become archbishop of York before Henry Bowet inaugurated a more regular succession of Cambridge metropolitans in the north after 1407.[23]

Whatever the precise significance of their university training for the careers of Edward I's six archbishops of York – and the choice of a canon lawyer rather than the traditional theologian in 1304 did in fact prove a portent of things to come – its general import needs no particular urging. By the second half of the thirteenth century it was already more or less inconceivable to imagine an archbishop of York who was not a university graduate: within fifty years of the mysterious genesis of the University of Oxford it had become imperative that the metropolitan could be plausibly presented to the wider world as 'profunde ad plenum litteratus', to use

[19] Guisborough, *Chron.*, p. 260; *The Register of John le Romeyn, Lord Archbishop of York, 1286–1294*, ed. W. Brown, Surtees Society, 123, 128 (1913–17), pp. iii–x; *BRUO*, ii, pp. 1134–5.

[20] Guisborough, *Chron.*, p. 260; *York Minster Fasti*, ed. C.T. Clay, Yorkshire Archaeological Society Record Series 123, 124 (1958–9), i, pp. 48–9; *BRUO*, iii, p. 2200.

[21] *Reg. Corbridge*, ii, pp. xiii–xiv; *BRUO*, i, p. 485. Thomas de Corbridge did however visit the Roman curia as Archbishop Wickwane's proctor in 1281: *Reg. Wickwane*, pp. 6, 203–6, 276, 321.

[22] William Rishanger, *Chronica et annales*, ed. H.T. Riley, RS (1865), p. 111; Guisborough, *Chron.*, p. 260; *BRUO*, ii, pp. 820–1; iii, pp. 1134–5.

[23] *Historians of the Church of York*, ii, pp. 411–12; *Letters from Northern Registers*, p. 4; *Reg. Giffard*, 201; *BRUC*, pp. 83–4, 257.

William Rishanger's words about Thomas de Corbridge.[24] More surprising perhaps, and more fundamental to their future relationships with their monarch, is Edward I's apparent willingness to allow the election to the northern metropolitan see of so many clerks who had devoted their scholarly talents so exclusively to the concerns of the York cathedral chapter and to nowhere else. Can it be that the strongest of strong kings in the history of the medieval English monarchy generally allowed the canons of York more liberty in electing their own archbishop from their own number than had ever been the case before or was ever to be the case again? On the balance of the evidence available to us, the answer to that question almost certainly has to be in the affirmative. Although the formal *decreta* of English episcopal elections notoriously often conceal the personal pressures which were brought to bear on these momentous occasions, there survive what seem to be reliable accounts of the elections of Archbishops William Wickwane and John le Romeyn as they were reported to the Roman curia in 1279 and 1286 respectively. On both occasions the successful candidate won quite decisively (with eighteen votes out of twenty-one in the case of Wickwane, and fourteen votes from a larger gathering in the case of le Romeyn) at the close of what were undoubtedly genuinely competitive capitular elections, showing no traces of royal intervention.[25] Similarly, Thomas de Corbridge was to emerge as the unanimously favoured new archbishop of York in the chapter's election meeting of 12 November 1299.[26] Nor is there much reason to suppose that the York canons did anything but welcome the prospect of electing Edward I's chancellor, William de Greenfield, as their archbishop in December 1304, which they did: within a few weeks of that election indeed, their own dean, William de Hambleton, had actually replaced Greenfield as royal chancellor – a particularly instructive instance of that interchange between high office at York and high office under the king to which this essay must eventually return.[27]

Meanwhile, it might not be at all misleading to suggest that the only occasion in the second half of the thirteenth century when the canons of York failed to secure the appointment as their archbishop of the clerk they personally most favoured was in 1266, when Walter Giffard, who had never held a Minster prebend, was translated to York from Bath and Wells. Even in Giffard's case, however, it seems clear enough that

---

[24] Rishanger, *Chron.*, p. 477; cf. Gibbs and Lang, *Bishops and Reform*, pp. 25–50.

[25] *Reg. Wickwane*, pp. 305–8; *Reg. Romeyn*, ii, pp. x–xiii. The complex procedures followed in the case of both these archiepiscopal elections are described in Brentano, *York Metropolitan Jurisdiction*, pp. 46–7, 52–3.

[26] *Historians of the Church of York*, ii, p. 411; Le Neve, *Fasti ecclesiae Anglicanae, 1300–1541*, ed. B. Jones et al. (London, 1962–7), vi (*Northern Province*), p. 3.

[27] *Historians of the Church of York*, ii, p. 413; Le Neve, *Fasti*, ed. Jones, vi, pp. 3, 6; *BRUO*, ii, pp. 820–1; *Handbook of Chronology*, p. 85.

it was neither the king nor the Lord Edward who blocked the chapter's original election of their own dean, William Langton. The latter's otherwise excellent prospects of promotion were dashed by none other than Pope Clement IV himself, who intervened in the vain hope that he might persuade St Bonaventure to accept the pallium rather than remain, as he still does, the most distinguished archbishop of York there never was.[28] In any case, the main conclusion seems incontrovertible: the majority of Edward I's archbishops of York were not among the king's own most-trusted and favoured clerks. This apparently curious phenomenon has, of course, its parallels elsewhere in the thirteenth-century English church, most obviously perhaps in Edward's remarkable failure to provide his most favoured clerk of all, Robert Burnell, with a bishop's throne more impressive than that of Bath and Wells.[29] The electoral experience of the late thirteenth-century church of York, therefore, more than confirms the unduly cautious judgement that in the thirteenth century 'the best ordered [secular] chapters were more than once able to press home the claims of the worthiest of their members'.[30] Such successes were alas to become more or less completely unattainable in secular as in monastic cathedrals during the fourteenth and fifteenth centuries. Accordingly, the choice of archbishops of York during the reign of Edward I illustrates remarkably clearly not only the short-term victory for the post-1215 principle of free capitular election, but also the genuine sensitivity on this issue of a king in whom sensitivity was hardly a characteristic trait. On the other hand, a harsh price was often exacted by the king from those who attained the archbishop's throne after so comparatively 'free' an election. Edward I's readiness to accept comparatively unknown canons of the Minster as his archbishops of York made it only too likely that his rapport with those metropolitans might deteriorate and even disintegrate during the strains of a strenuous reign.

Moreover, there are good grounds for believing that the king's relationship with his northern metropolitans became progressively more and more important to Edward I as the church of York itself gradually acquired greater political significance in his own eyes. The main reason for this development was undoubtedly the extremely unsatisfactory behaviour, from Edward's point of view, of John Pecham and Robert Winchelsey, his primates of Canterbury between 1279 and the end of his reign; but then it is equally obvious that the rapid escalation of the king's

[28] *Historians of the Church of York*, ii, p. 406; Guisborough, *Chron.*, p. 203; Gibbs and Lang, *Bishops and Reform*, pp. 73–4.

[29] When in Jan. 1279 Burnell's election as archbishop of Canterbury was quashed by Nicholas III in favour of the Franciscan John Pecham, Edward I raised no objections and immediately admitted the latter to his council: Powicke, *Thirteenth Century*, pp. 469–70.

[30] Gibbs and Lang, *Bishops and Reform*, p. 93; cf. C.H. Lawrence, 'The Thirteenth Century', *The English Church and the Papacy in the Middle Ages*, ed. C.H. Lawrence (London, 1965), pp. 146–7.

involvement in Scottish affairs after Alexander III's death in 1286 was bound to give the city and church of York, as well as its archbishops, an enhanced importance for the English sovereign.[31] It had indeed been in York Minster that Alexander III had married Edward's own sister, Margaret, on the day after Christmas 1251; and even then York was already well established as the most obvious *mise en scène* for political treaties as well as marriage alliances between the kings of Scotland and England.[32] Although Edward himself seems to have only made five brief visits to York before 1290, he could never have been in any doubt of the cathedral city's role as the central agency of his authority in the north. One of the more macabre of many possible examples was the king's decision to have Rhys ap Maredudd hung, drawn and quartered at York after that unfortunate Welsh rebel was finally captured in 1292.[33] More striking still, and now well documented by Dr Simon Lloyd, is the way in which Edward I (like contemporary popes) gave to his archbishops of York, even more than to his archbishops of Canterbury perhaps, extensive responsibility for promoting the crusade. The most notable of several instances of the archbishops of York taking this responsibility very seriously indeed is the highly-organised series of mendicant sermons throughout his diocese orchestrated by John le Romeyn on 14 September 1291, presumably just after the news of the loss of Acre had reached the north of England. The most important sermon of all was to be delivered by Romeyn himself in York Minster on the same day. Preaching is unfortunately one of the more evanescent of human activities, and it may therefore be too easy to forget that oratorical gifts were among the most desirable qualities of a thirteenth-century archbishop.[34]

Not long after the débâcle at Acre, however, Edward I found it even more urgent to rely upon the prayers and sermons of his archbishops of York when in military confrontation with an enemy very much nearer York Minster than the eastern Mediterranean. He was not to be disappointed; and in June 1301, for example, the comparatively new Archbishop Corbridge,

---

[31] E. Miller, 'Medieval York', in VCH, *Yorkshire, City of York*, pp. 28–9, 54–6; cf. D.M. Broome, 'Exchequer Migrations to York in the Thirteenth and Fourteenth Centuries', *Essays in Medieval History Presented to T.F. Tout*, ed. A.G. Little and F.M. Powicke (Manchester, 1925), pp. 291–300.

[32] Guisborough, *Chron.*, pp. 183, 232; VCH, *City of York*, p. 28; and for the treaty of York negotiated between the English and Scottish kings by the papal legate Otto in 1237, see A.A.M. Duncan, *Scotland: The Making of a Kingdom* (Edinburgh, 1975), p. 533.

[33] Rishanger, *Chron.*, p. 129; Guisborough, *Chron.*, p. 224; R.A. Griffiths, 'The Revolt of Rhys ap Maredudd', *Welsh History Review*, 3 (1967), pp. 121–43; VCH, *City of York*, pp. 28–9.

[34] *Letters from Northern Registers*, pp. 93–6; *Reg. Romeyn*, i, p. 113; ii, pp. 8–9; S. Lloyd, *English Society and the Crusade, 1216–1307* (Oxford, 1988), pp. 42, 53, 55–6. For Thomas de Corbridge's sermon on the occasion of the election of an abbot of St Mary's, York in 1298, the year before Corbridge was promoted to the archiepiscopate, see *The Chronicle of St Mary's Abbey, York*, ed. H.H.E. Craster, Surtees Society, 148 (1934), p. 27.

who had recently baptised Edward's first son by his second marriage, not only led his church in its devotions and processions but also offered a forty-day indulgence to those who prayed for the king's success in his impending expedition to Scotland.[35] During the previous summer, by yet another example of what Dr Lloyd, Dr Christopher Tyerman and other historians might interpret as a potentially improper extension of a crusading practice outside the crusading arena, the same archbishop had empowered two Franciscan friars to hear the confessions of those inhabitants of the province of York who planned to follow Henry de Lacy, earl of Lincoln, into the hazards which awaited them north of the border.[36] In recent years, Dr Alison McHardy has properly drawn attention to the much-valued services of the English prelates of a slightly later period in providing prayers and propaganda for the English royal cause during the Hundred Years War.[37] It seems equally worthy of emphasis that such services were deliberately called for, and quite as highly valued if not more so, by Edward I when he was confronted by the Scots a generation earlier.

Of all the prayers to be said on the king's behalf in the province of York, no doubt the ones Edward himself thought most efficacious were those uttered in the cathedral itself. Edward I self-evidently knew York Minster well, not least because during his increasingly frequent visits to the city after 1290 he was as likely to stay in the adjacent archiepiscopal palace as in his own castle, overcrowded as the latter was between 1298 and 1304 with the personnel and paraphernalia of the exchequer, king's bench and other governmental offices.[38] During those turbulent years, moreover, Edward must have observed at first hand the early stages of the building of the new Minster nave, started as it was on 6 April 1291. Recently, Mr David O'Connor has gone so far as to suggest (not at all implausibly perhaps) that it was the king himself who 'may have found the eleventh-century nave gloomy and old-fashioned, and put pressure

---

[35] *Letters from Northern Registers*, pp. 149–50; *Chron. St Mary's*, p. 30.

[36] *Letters from Northern Registers*, p. 143. For Edward I's use of Dominicans and Franciscans to preach the crusade, see Lloyd, *English Society and the Crusade*, pp. 51–6, 63–4; and for the possibility that the king adopted a crusading banner in his Scottish campaign of 1300, see C. Tyerman, *England and the Crusades, 1095–1588* (Chicago, 1988), pp. 330–1.

[37] A. McHardy, 'The English Clergy and the Hundred Years War', *Studies in Church History*, 20 (1983), pp. 171–8; eadem, 'Religious Ritual and Political Persuasion: The Case of England in the Hundred Years War', *International Journal of Moral and Social Studies*, 3 (1988), pp. 41–57.

[38] *Select Cases in the Court of King's Bench under Edward I*, ed. G.O. Sayles, iv, Selden Society, 74 (1957), pp. xcix–cv; Broome, 'Exchequer Migrations', pp. 291–3; VCH, *City of York*, pp. 54–5, 340–1, 522. Like his son, Edward I may well have found that the most secluded accommodation available in York was within the Franciscan convent adjacent to his castle: see C. Bullock-Davies, *Register of Royal and Baronial Domestic Minstrels, 1272–1327* (Woodbridge, 1986), p. 32, 143.

on the authorities to hasten the construction of a new nave'.[39] On that possibility, however, judgement must remain suspended. Despite the characteristically strenuous efforts of Dr John Harvey, no one has yet been able to prove who exactly was the architect responsible for the revolutionary Decorated design of the new York Minster nave. Whether he was at all associated with the royal masons who worked for Edward I in and around Westminster seems likely, but it is by no means certain.[40] In fact, and quite appropriately, the only indisputable memorial to Edward still surviving in York Minster is not in stone but in stained glass. Within the so-called Heraldic Window, on the north aisle of the nave and immediately opposite what seems to be a memorial window to Archbishop Greenfield, a set of eight shields, together with an accompanying series of royal figures, proclaims the arms of England and its king's relationships with the other monarchies of Christendom. It is no surprise to discover that the window in question was given by a prominent canon of York, Dr Peter de Dene, who typifies the residentiary element within the York chapter particularly well in serving his two very different masters with apparent ease – his archbishop as a vicar general, and his king as a confidential envoy and councillor during the 1290s and 1300s.[41]

Of all Edward I's associations with York Minster, however, none was more carefully remembered by the cathedral clergy there than his presence for that auspicious occasion, on 9 January 1284, when the bones of their patron and recently-canonised saint were elevated 'ad altiorem locum' behind the high altar, transferred, that is, from their previous resting place in a tomb towards the east end of the Minster nave.[42] The Translation of St William of York, which made possible the construction of the new nave a few years later, must be seen, to adapt a phrase of Dr Anne Duggan, as one of the grand 'state occasions' of thirteenth-century England, only comparable perhaps to the translation of St Thomas Becket's relics at Christ Church, Canterbury, in 1220, and of St Edward the Confessor's remains at Westminster in 1269.[43] The York ceremony of January 1284

[39] T. French and D. O'Connor, *York Minster: A Catalogue of Medieval Stained Glass*, i, *The West Windows of the Nave* (Oxford, 1987), p. 3.

[40] J. Harvey, 'Architectural History from 1291 to 1558', *A History of York Minster*, ed. G.E. Aylmer and R. Cant (Oxford, 1977), pp. 149–60, 190; N. Coldstream, 'York Minster and the Decorated Style in Yorkshire', *Yorkshire Archaeological Journal*, 52 (1980), pp. 93–5; J. Bony, *The English Decorated Style: Gothic Architecture Transformed, 1250–1350* (Oxford 1979), pp. 7–8.

[41] F. Harrison, *The Painted Glass of York* (London, 1927), pp. 43–4; D.E. O'Connor, 'The Stained and Painted Glass', *History of York Minster*, pp. 349–50; *BRUO*, iii, pp. 2168–9.

[42] *Historians of the Church of York*, ii, pp. 544–50; C. Wilson, *The Shrines of St William of York* (York, 1977), pp. 8–9.

[43] A.J. Duggan, 'The Cult of Saint Thomas Becket in the Thirteenth Century', *St Thomas Cantilupe, Bishop of Hereford: Essays in his Honour*, ed. M. Jancey (Hereford, 1982), pp. 38–9; J.G.O. Neilly and L.E. Tanner, 'The Shrine of St Edward the Confessor', *Archaeologia*, 100 (1966), pp. 129–54.

itself was attended by both King Edward and Queen Eleanor as well
as at least ten bishops and numerous magnates. The king himself not
only helped to carry the chest containing St William's bones to its new
place of veneration, but also paid for the feeding of 200 poor: as
Dr Christopher Wilson has recently pointed out, he continued to make
gifts to the two shrines of the saint into the early years of the fourteenth
century.[44] For the archbishop and chapter it was more gratifying still that
St William managed to perform a miracle for the occasion, even if a
somewhat unusual and unexpected one. According to later York tradition,
on the very morning of St William's translation, a certain Roger de Rypon,
one of the servants of the Minster canons, was unwise enough to rest his
head, presumably because of either exhaustion or boredom, on the base of
the lectern from which the lessons for matins were actually being recited
at the time. However, when a weighty stone crashed down on his skull
from above, to everyone's astonishment, including his own, Roger shook
his head to find that it was completely intact.[45] Not perhaps a very
extraordinary nor prestigious miracle, but then it is usually agreed by
hagiographers that St William of York was a somewhat prosaic saint.
Although it is not at all surprising that the late thirteenth-century canons
of York were eager to make as much as they could of the supposed sanctity
of the most obscure of their twelfth-century archbishops, it has alas to be
conceded that the translation of his earthly remains in the 1280s failed
in its primary purpose of transforming St William into one of the more
powerful of the great galaxy of northern saints.[46]

In a quite different way the events surrounding the Translation of
St William of York on 9 January 1284 exposed some of the political
weaknesses of his archiepiscopal successors during the reign of Edward I.
In the eyes of many contemporary chroniclers, the most important event to
occur in the Minster that day was not the translation of a dead archbishop
but the consecration of a new bishop, none other than Antony Bek of
Durham, at the hands of William Wickwane.[47] For the next twenty-seven
years, until well after Edward I's own death, the archbishops of York
were to be made acutely aware that their flamboyant suffragan was
to be everything they could not be. Their sense of inferiority to that
suffragan was indeed made evident at the very outset, for it was the
new bishop-elect of Durham, and not Archbishop Wickwane, who actually

[44] *Historians of the Church of York*, ii, pp. 544–5; Wilson, *Shrines*, pp. 8–9, 24.

[45] *Historians of the Church of York*, ii, pp. 545–6, 549.

[46] However, Margery Kempe was only one of the many late medieval visitors to York
who 'come on pilgrimage to offyr her at Seynt Wiliam': *The Book of Margery Kempe*, EETS,
old series, 212 (1940), p. 122. Cf. R.B. Dobson, 'The Later Middle Ages', *History of York
Minster*, pp. 85–6.

[47] *Records of Antony Bek, Bishop and Patriarch, 1283–1311*, ed. C.M. Fraser, Surtees Society,
162 (1953), pp. 1–2; C.M. Fraser, *A History of Antony Bek, Bishop of Durham, 1283–1311*
(Oxford, 1957), pp. 37–8.

undertook the expenses of St William's translation.[48] More revealing still is the story, surely true in spirit if not necessarily to the letter, told by the Durham chronicler, Robert Graystanes, of an angry exchange between Wickwane and his new suffragan on the day after the ceremonies at York Minster. When the archbishop commanded Bek, by virtue of his new oath of canonical obedience to York, to excommunicate the prior and convent of Durham, the bishop allegedly rejoined with a forthright refusal: 'Yesterday, I was consecrated their bishop; and shall I excommunicate them today? No obedience will induce me to it.'[49] It has been correctly pointed out that the shadow of the recent humiliating conflict between Wickwane and the intransigent monks of St Cuthbert over the former's right to visit the Durham chapter must have lain heavily over the proceedings at York in January 1284; but then that shadow was never really to lift for the rest of the reign, despite the temporary relief from violent conflict afforded by Wickwane's death at Pontigny in the following year.[50] Bishop Bek was to have his own even more spectacular collisions with the community of St Cuthbert during the years ahead, but at no point did those collisions enable the archbishop of York to intervene in the diocese of Durham as *tertium gaudens*. Indeed, we are informed by the chroniclers in so many words that John le Romeyn allowed York's conflict with the Durham monks to go to sleep because he lacked the resources to do otherwise; that Henry de Newark was unwilling to reopen past issues because he was a subservient *familiarius* of Bek; and that Thomas de Corbridge similarly made no attempt to visit Durham 'eo quod timuit regem et vexacionem'.[51] Only after Bek had reached the end of his turbulent career, and Archbishop Greenfield was able to come to Durham Cathedral to preside over his suffragan's interment ceremonies on 3 May 1311, did a viable *modus operandi* – and one highly favourable to the church of Durham at that – at last return to the northern province.[52]

So bald a summary naturally pays inadequate justice to the quite extraordinary, and quite extraordinarily well-documented, conjuncture of

---

[48] *Historians of the Church of York*, ii, pp. 407–8. More remarkably still, Bek took part in the task of translating St William's body to its new shrine in York Minster, Fraser, *Antony Bek*, p. 37.

[49] *Historiae Dunelmensis scriptores tres*, ed. J. Raine, Surtees Society, 9 (1839), p. 64.

[50] Fraser, *Antony Bek*, pp. 35–9; *Ann. Mon.*, iv, p. 491. A reasonably successful compromise on the contentious issue of the archbishop of York's right to visit the church of Durham in vacancies of that see was achieved in Nov. 1286; but in effect it gave future bishops of Durham freedom from York metropolitan jurisdiction *sede plena*: Brentano, *York Metropolitan Jurisdiction*, pp. 142–7.

[51] Guisborough, *Chron.*, pp. 260, 351; cf. Brentano, *York Metropolitan Jurisdiction*, pp. 165–74. After Romeyn's attempts to enforce his spiritual lordship over Bek were crushed in the parliament of Apr. 1293, 'no future archbishop of York meddled with his suffragan of Durham unless first sure of royal support': Fraser, *Antony Bek*, p. 114.

[52] *Scriptores tres*, p. 91; Guisborough, *Chron.*, p. 391; Fraser, *Antony Bek*, pp. 226–9.

complex and insoluble disputes which makes the province of York during the reign of Edward I the *locus classicus* of jurisdictional confrontation within the late thirteenth-century English church. Needless to say, this cannot be the occasion to venture into territory so well traversed a generation ago, although perhaps not absolutely exhaustively, by Robert Brentano and Constance Fraser.[53] However, it seems undeniable that what the obsessive York versus Durham disputes of the late thirteenth century reveal most of all, and more transparently than at any other time in the middle ages, are what might be termed the inherent structural weaknesses which underlay the metropolitical authority of the archbishops of York. What those weaknesses were is obvious enough; and all ultimately stemmed from the failure of the medieval north ever to achieve that metropolitan province with twelve subordinate bishops so over-optimistically envisaged by Pope Gregory I, when he ordered St Augustine to refound the Roman see of Eboracum in 601.[54] The problem facing Edward I's archbishops was not just that their province was so small, although it was indeed one of the smallest in Christendom; it was not just that their province suffered, in Brentano's phrase, from a 'lack of coherence', although it was indeed honeycombed by what Hamilton Thompson called 'spiritual republics' to a quite exceptional extent; and it was not just that the archbishops often suffered from irresponsive or even disobedient suffragans, although it was indeed an exceptional misfortune to have Antony Bek as one's greatest subject.[55] Perhaps a more crippling weakness than any of these, as Archie Duncan suggested some years ago, was quite simply that the metropolitan of York lacked enough suffragans.[56] Despite occasional attempts to lure the bishops of Whithorn, and occasionally even those of Orkney and the Isles, into his jurisdiction, as the archbishop of York gazed sadly at his overmighty subject of Durham and undermighty subject of Carlisle, he must always have been aware that he was forever denied the essential political function of a metropolitan – to promote episcopal harmony and common intent within his province or, if that failed, at least to play one bishop against another. To this extent at least, the archbishops of York during the reign of Edward I were nearly always like generals without an army.

Some such considerations may help to explain two of the more important and, at first sight, surprising features, one positive and one negative, of York metropolitical policy during the reign of Edward I. In the first place, no one examining contemporary comments upon Edward I's six

[53] Brentano, *York Metropolitan Jurisdiction*, passim; Fraser, *Antony Bek*, pp. 100–75.

[54] *Bede's Ecclesiastical History of the English People*, ed. B. Colgrave and R.A.B. Mynors (Oxford, 1969), pp. 105–6.

[55] Brentano, *York Metropolitan Jurisdiction*, pp. 23–41; *Reg. Romeyn*, ii, pp. xxv–xxxi; Thompson, *English Clergy*, pp. 1–2.

[56] Duncan, *Scotland*, pp. 258–9, 275–80.

archbishops of York can fail to be struck by the notorious readiness of them all to risk ridicule and personal humiliation, not to say the irritation and downright hostility of the king himself, in the cause of carrying their primatial cross erect within the province of Canterbury as well as that of York. Although the full story of this more or less interminable and very well-documented *casus belli* has never been told at length, it seems clear enough that it was in Edward I's reign that, to use Hamilton Thompson's phrase, 'the perennial squabble became a public nuisance'.[57] So much was this the case that an archbishop of York's abortive attempts to process through southern England with his cross erect before him was often the only activity of a northern metropolitan that the Edwardian chroniclers actually bothered to mention at all. In an age when chroniclers like Thomas Wykes thought the archbishops' behaviour 'frivolam' and even 'pompatice', and when this issue might lead to so distinguished a prelate as Greenfield being sent packing from a meeting of parliament, why did the Edwardian archbishops of York persist for so long in doing the pointless and even dangerous?[58] No doubt one must never underestimate the alarm felt by any medieval prelate at the prospect that he might appear before his church's patron saint on Judgement Day to answer the charge that he had alienated even an iota of that church's traditional liberties, but in the case of Edward I's archbishops of York one might be tempted to go even further. The tenacity and passion with which they fought to retain the privilege of making ceremonial progresses in the southern province *cruce elevate* presumably had its roots in the belief that this was both the single most concrete and potent symbol of an otherwise excessively feeble metropolitan position, and also the most flamboyant means possible of trying to redeem an otherwise acute inferiority of status.[59]

Such status inferiority, to use an anachronistic phrase, also seems the most likely explanation for the failure of the archbishops of York to

[57] A.H. Thompson, 'The Dispute with Canterbury', *York Minster Historical Tracts*, ed. A.H. Thompson (York, 1927), p. 14. Instances of the carrying of the archiepiscopal cross in the southern province were naturally the source of particular indignation within the community of Christ Church, Canterbury: see Gervase of Canterbury, *The Historical Works of Gervase of Canterbury*, ed. W. Stubbs, RS (1879–80), ii, pp. 247–8, 313, 322–3.

[58] *Ann. Mon.*, iv, pp. 260, 281; Rishanger, *Chron.*, p. 477; Gervase of Canterbury, *Hist. Works*, pp. 322–3; *Johannis de Trokelowe et Henrici de Blaneforde, chronica et annales*, RS (1866), pp. 142–3.

[59] The archbishop's right to have his cross carried before him anywhere in England had been long established as the clearest possible expression of the traditional York view that 'there is nothing wonderful in there being two metropolitans in one kingdom, one of whom is not subject to the other': Hugh the Chantor, *History of the Church of York, 1069–1127*, ed. C. Johnson (London, 1961), p. 105, and cf. p. 129. In the event, the compromise finally reached on the issues at stake by archbishops Islip and Thoresby in 1353 allowed each primate the liberty to have his cross born upright in the other's province: A.H. Thompson, 'Dispute with Canterbury', pp. 14–15.

pursue their ambitions in a very different metropolitical sphere. On all the evidence at present available, they made no serious attempt to exploit the political and ideological conflict which arose between Edward I and the Scots in the early 1290s to revivify the traditional claim of their own metropolitan supremacy over the whole of Scotland. Such a claim one might certainly have expected, for the church of York's title to metropolitan authority throughout northern Britannia, also based on Gregory I's letter to St Augustine in 601, had of course been stridently urged by twelfth-century archbishops, at least until the nine Scottish sees were made directly subject to the papacy itself by Celestine III's *Cum Universi* in 1192.[60] Nor is there any doubt that thereafter, and indeed to the very end of the middle ages, various archbishops and even more canons of York still toyed, if not usually very seriously, with the idea of reclaiming so prestigious a northern ecclesiastical empire. Shortly before he usurped the throne in 1483, Richard of Gloucester seems to have encouraged his partisans within the York Cathedral chapter to reopen the case for English spiritual overlordship in Scotland. It is even more remarkable that one of Henry VIII's most immediate responses to the news of Lord Thomas Howard's crushing victory at Flodden was to declare his intention of restoring York's metropolitan authority north of the border.[61] By contrast, the Scottish ambitions of the northern metropolitans during the reign of Edward I seem much more muted. The Scottish clergy themselves, until and beyond the agreement of Perth in 1335, were apparently highly apprehensive that an Edwardian political overlordship might carry in its wake a York ecclesiastical overlordship of their country: here was one of the most obvious reasons why the bishops of Scotland proved to be such staunch and influential supporters of Robert Bruce and his successors.[62] However, during Scotland's twenty years of trial at the hands of Edward I, and despite his archbishops of

---

[60] Hugh the Chantor, *Hist.*, pp. 126, 129; Duncan, *Scotland*, pp. 274–8; J. Green, 'Anglo-Scottish Relations, 1066–1174', *England and her Neighbours, 1066–1453: Essays in Honour of Pierre Chaplais*, ed. M. Jones and M. Vale (London, 1989), pp. 62–3.

[61] R.B. Dobson, 'Richard III and the Church of York', below, pp. 227, 249; *British Library, Harleian Manuscript 433*, ed. R.E. Horrox and P.W. Hammond, 4 vols (Gloucester, 1979–83), iii, pp. 76–98; *Letters and Papers, Foreign and Domestic, of the Reign of Henry VIII*, ed. J.S. Brewer et al. (2nd edn, London, 1920), i, pp. 1047–8; R.B. Dobson, 'The Last English Monks on Scottish Soil', above, p. 133.

[62] The Anglo-Scottish agreement concluded at Perth on 18 Aug. 1335 specifically safeguarded the liberties of the holy church in Scotland and was therefore presumably designed to 'prevent the resurrection of metropolitan claims by Canterbury or York': R.S. Nicholson, *Edward III and the Scots* (Oxford, 1965), p. 215. Cf. A. Grant, *Independence and Nationhood: Scotland, 1306–1469* (London, 1984), p. 91; R.S. Nicholson, *Scotland: The Later Middle Ages* (Edinburgh, 1974), pp. 52–3, 70–2; and for Edward I's own remarkably savage treatment of the bishops of St Andrews and Glasgow after their capture in 1306, see M. Prestwich, 'England and Scotland during the Wars of Independence', *England and her Neighbours*, pp. 193–5.

York's close and personal involvement in Scottish diplomacy from at least 1291, when le Romeyn, Newark and Greenfield all played a role in helping to administer the Great Cause at Norham together, there seems little evidence that they ever claimed to exercise metropolitical authority north of the Tweed.[63] For whatever reason, perhaps because they were obstructed by Antony Bek or by Edward I himself, here again the archbishops of York seemed incapable of seizing one of their major opportunities.

One major reason for that incapacity, and for the weakness of the archbishops of York when confronted by their rivals, is almost certainly those archbishops' lack of material resources. By an unfortunate irony, most of the administrative activities centred around the medieval metro-politans of York are particularly well documented with the notable exception of the sources and extent of their revenues. However, and even though this is a hazardous field, there seems every reason to believe that most and perhaps all of Edward I's six archbishops of York suffered from intermittent financial emergencies and not infrequently genuine financial crises. The keepers' accounts (now preserved among the Ministers' Accounts in the Public Record Office) of the York temporalities during the period (1304–6), after Edward had confiscated the latter from Archbishop Thomas de Corbridge, are by no means easy to interpret, but they do seem to suggest the fundamental weakness that, by comparison with their fellow bishops, the archbishops of York were conspicuously under-endowed with landed estates.[64] More certain still, because Edward's archbishops complained about these burdens bitterly and incessantly, were the baneful effects of papal *servitia* and other exactions at the time they received the pallium. Perhaps the most eloquent example of these lamentations is the letter sent by Archbishop Giffard to the curia in 1270, which complains that: 'I am worn out with work, continually weary and obliged to consume the whole of my substance, both spiritual and temporal.'[65] To judge from their own surviving letters, debt was the spectre most dreaded by the York archbishops just as, according to the chroniclers, prudence, circumspection and even avarice had to be their most common characteristics.[66] As early

[63] Rishanger, *Chron.*, p. 240; *BRUO*, iii, 2200; *Edward I and the Throne of Scotland, 1290–1296*, ed. E.L.G. Stones and G.G. Simpson (Oxford, 1978), ii, pp. 22, 80.

[64] PRO, SC 6/1,144 (1). Despite the survival of the occasional cartulary, *valor* (as in 1482–3) and other documents, the sources for the history of the pre-Reformation archbishops of York's estates are 'sparse in the extreme': see *British Library Harleian Manuscript 433*, ed. R. Horrox (Gloucester, 1979–83), iii, pp. 217–32; C. Cross, 'The Economic Problems of the See of York: Decline and Recovery in the Sixteenth Century', *Agricultural History Review*, 18 (1970), pp. 64–6.

[65] *Letters from Northern Registers*, pp. 35–7, 44–5; *Historians of the Church of York*, iii, p. 205; VCH, *Yorkshire*, iii, p. 28; *Reg. Giffard*, p. 245; *Reg. Wickwane*, p. 288.

[66] For the alleged *avaricia maxima* of le Romeyn, see Guisborough, *Chron.*, p. 260; and for Corbridge's qualities of prudence and circumspection, see Rishanger, *Chron.*, p. 477.

as 1267 Archbishop Giffard had been in debt to two merchants of Lucca for no less than 1000 marks, and for the next twenty years his successors were more or less continuously involved in dealings with the Riccardi, who took the highly unusual step of opening a resident branch in the city of York at this very period. It is now well known that there existed a highly active credit network in late thirteenth-century, post-1290 Yorkshire; but all the evidence there is suggests that the archbishops of York were more likely to be the debtors than the creditors of that network.[67]

If Edward's six archbishops of York had little to offer in the way of capital, they did, however, have at their disposal something even more valuable to a needy king than money, namely ecclesiastical benefices. Whatever the deficiencies and limitations of the authority of an archbishop of York, he did control (at least in theory) perhaps the most extensive range of ecclesiastical patronage in Edward I's England. Such patronage was, moreover, all the more desirable because so many of its fruits, at Beverley, at Ripon, at Southwell and above all in his own cathedral church, could be enjoyed by clerks who had no intention of ever coming to reside in northern England at all.[68] It would therefore seem that for late thirteenth-century archbishops of York, as for fifteenth-century monks of Durham, such valuable patronage might justify Benjamin Disraeli's definition: 'Patronage is the visible and outward sign of an inward and spiritual grace, and that is Power.'[69] Alas, the archbishops of York in the years around 1300 probably saw their control over appointments in a very different light. So harried were the northern metropolitans of Edward's reign by the voracious appetites of pope, king and their own canons that in many ways this period in the history of the church of York provides the best-documented case in medieval England of what might happen when an extensive ecclesiastical patronage system could no longer be controlled by its overlord. It was precisely because York cathedral prebends like those of Masham, South Cave, Driffield, Langtoft and Wetwang were among the very wealthiest in the kingdom that 'canonries at York always led to dispute', a remark that seems even more applicable to the pontificate

[67] *Reg. Giffard*, p. 153; and cf. pp. 106, 115, 153, 254, 274; *Records of the Wardrobe and Household, 1286–1289*, ed. B.F. Byerly and C.R. Byerly (London, 1986), pp. 235, 238; R.W. Kaeuper, *Bankers to the Crown: The Riccardi of Lucca and Edward I* (Princeton, 1973), p. 30–1, 61. For the most notorious case of an archbishop of York (le Romeyn) denounced in parliament for his illegal dealings with a Jewish financier (Bonamy of York), see R.B. Dobson, 'The Decline and Expulsion of the Medieval Jews of York', *Transactions of the Jewish Historical Society of England*, 26 (1979), pp. 45–6. The credit transactions of Edward I's archbishops of York would repay much greater attention than they have received here.

[68] *History of York Minster*, pp. 52–75; K. Edwards, *The English Secular Cathedrals in the Middle Ages* (2nd edn, Manchester, 1967), pp. 83–96.

[69] W.F. Monypenny and G.E. Buckle, *The Life of Benjamin Disraeli* (London, 1910–20), iv, p. 174; cited in R.B. Dobson, *Durham Priory, 1400–1450* (Cambridge, 1973), p. 144.

of Boniface VIII (1294–1303) than to those immediately before and afterwards.[70]

Accordingly, during the reign of Edward I, the archbishops of York usually found that their nominal control over the richest ecclesiastical benefices in the north brought them more pain than profit. In the eloquent words of Archbishop Wickwane to the notorious absentee treasurer of his cathedral, Bogo de Clare, there seemed a grave danger that greed for its milk and wool might lead to the death of the ecclesiastical sheep. If anything, Edward I's archbishops of York progressively found it more and more difficult to resist external pressures to divert the wealth of York Minster's prebends to either papal or (much more often) royal administrators. Perhaps the most instructive example is provided by the 'golden prebend' of Masham itself, with revenues valued at £166 13s. 4d. in the *Taxatio Vetus* of 1291 and thus the richest single cathedral prebend in medieval England.[71] During the thirty years (1265–94) when the notorious Bogo de Clare ('multarum rector ecclesiarum vel potius incubator') held the prebend *in absentia*, he was more or less continuously resistant to any mandate issued by successive archbishops of York; and his successor as prebendary of Masham, John de Droxford (1296–1309), was not only one of Edward I's most distinguished clerical administrators, and keeper of his wardrobe, but also capable of an attempt to wrench the treasurership of York Minster from another royal clerk, Walter Bedwin.[72] In what Professor Prestwich has called the competition for rich livings among Edward I's clerks, the competition for dignities and prebends at the cathedral of York was the keenest of all.[73] No wonder that in the late 1280s and 1290s archbishops John le Romeyn and Henry de Newark believed that the only solution to such scandals might be to divide outstandingly wealthy York cathedral prebends like Masham into three or five portions.[74] However, despite such intense competition and despite the ensuing legal disputes of almost unfathomable complexity – for many years during the reign of Edward I no one could be quite sure who the rightful dean or treasurer of York Minster actually was – the voracious appetite for these York dignities and prebends on the part of royal and

[70] T.S.R. Boase, *Boniface VIII* (London, 1933), p. 310; cf. *History of York Minster*, pp. 55–6.

[71] *Reg. Wickwane*, p. 286; *Taxatio ecclesiastica Angliae et Walliae auctoritate P. Nicholai IV* (London, 1802), pp. 297–8.

[72] *Flores historiarum*, ed. H.R. Luard, RS (London, 1890), iii, p. 93; Le Neve, *Fasti*, ed. Jones, vi, p. 66; *CCR, 1296–1302*, pp. 223, 301; M. Prestwich, *War, Politics and Finance under Edward I* (London, 1972), p. 154.

[73] Prestwich, *Edward I*, pp. 546–7; A. Deeley, 'Papal Provision and Royal Rights of Patronage in the Early Fourteenth Century', *English Historical Review*, 43 (1928), pp. 497–527.

[74] *Reg. Gray*, pp. 216–17; *Reg. Romeyn*, ii, pp. 25, 306; *Calendar of Entries in the Papal Registers relating to Great Britain and Ireland: Papal Letters I (1198–1304)*, ed. W.H. Bliss (London, 1893), p. 496; Le Neve, *Fasti*, ed. Jones, vi, p. 66.

papal *curiales* had its occasional compensations for Edward's archbishops.[75] The ferocity of the competition for their patronage may have put the latter under intolerable pressure, as indeed they often complained, but at least it ensured that they were never ignored. More interestingly still, it was the large number of prebends at the archbishops' disposal which provided the economic basis for that famous connection between the royal chancery and those south Yorkshire and northern Lincolnshire clergy who operated much of the engine of the English state for at least the next two generations. According to John Grassi, it was the first of Edward I's archbishops, Walter Giffard, who originally forged this connection; and there can in any case be no doubt that this clerical affinity was the most influential legacy of the thirteenth-century church of York to the England of Edward II and III.[76]

However, as Edward I's archbishops struggled to preserve their patronage from what they saw as the predators in high places around them, they were unlikely and unable to take so sanguine and long-term a view. When, to take the most striking case of all, Archbishop Thomas de Corbridge tried to retain control over his own favourite, and extremely lucrative, benefice at York Minster (the sacristship of St Sepulchre's chapel) he illustrated to perfection the dangers of resistance to the royal will in the matter of ecclesiastical patronage. Corbridge himself had been sacrist of this chapel, alternatively known as the chapel of St Mary and the Holy Angels, for a decade before his election to the archbishopric in November 1299; and, while at the curia to receive consecration at the hands of Boniface VIII in February 1300, he had taken steps to secure for himself the future nomination to the sacristship.[77] Archbishop Corbridge's explicit refusal to confirm the appointment to the sacristship of Edward I's nominee, his notary, Master John Bush, was therefore understandable, but it led to an impasse which exposed the vulnerability of the archbishop of York more starkly than any other incident in the reign. When no lawyer could be found to speak on his behalf, the unfortunate Corbridge was sentenced to lose the York temporalities, provoking not only his own early demise

---

[75] External pressures to control the choice of dean and treasurer of York Minster were never more intense than during the last decade of Edward I's reign, not least because of the ambitions of Francis Gaetani senior and junior, Boniface VIII's kinsmen: see *Reg. Romeyn*, ii, p. 302; *Reg. Greenfield*, i, pp. 10–11, 12; *Cal. Papal Regs.*, i, pp. 580, 586, 611; ii, p. 28; *Select Cases before the King's Council, 1243–1482*, ed. I.S. Leadam and J.F. Baldwin, Selden Society, 35 (1918), pp. 18–27; Le Neve, *Fasti*, ed. Jones, vi, pp. 6, 12–13; A.H. Thompson, 'The Treasurership of York and the Prebend of Wilton', in *Reg. Greenfield*, i, pp. 299–305.

[76] J.L. Grassi, 'Royal Clerks from the Diocese of York in the Fourteenth Century', *Northern History*, 5 (1970), pp. 15–18; cf. *Reg. Corbridge*, ii, p. xxvii.

[77] A.H. Thompson, 'The Chapel of St Mary and the Holy Angels, Otherwise Known as St Sepulchre's Chapel, at York', *Yorkshire Archaeological Journal*, 36 (1945), pt 2, pp. 216–17; *Reg. Corbridge*, ii, pp. xiii–xiv; *Reg. Romeyn*, i, pp. 134, 301, 385–9.

but, according to Walter of Guisborough, Edward I's famous and mordant comment that 'our father the archbishop has a lion's heart: soon he will have a sheep's tail.'[78] Whether or not that remark provides an insight into the personality of an often enigmatic monarch, it certainly illustrates only too well the dangers in store for an archbishop of York who dared to resist the royal will on any grounds whatsoever.

Nearly thirty years ago the late Dom David Knowles ended a lecture on the medieval archbishops of York in a somewhat disenchanted manner: 'We could not have expected the northern province to have rivalled Canterbury with its galaxy of great men, but if bishops are to be marked, like Tripos candidates, with Alpha and Beta, it is probable that Durham, Winchester and Lincoln, and perhaps other sees also, would be able to show more of the First Class than York.'[79] If so, and a considered judgement of the medieval metropolitans in the north as a whole is by no means easy to make, then it is not hard to diagnose some of the external pressures and internal weaknesses which prevented the late thirteenth-century archbishops of York from attaining that much desired First Class mark.

[78] As soon as Archbishop Corbridge had died (on 22 Sept. 1304), the dean and chapter of York admitted John Bush to the sacristship of St Sepulchre's at Edward's request: see Borthwick Institute of Historical Research, York, Reg. 5A (Sede Vacante), fo. 645; *Reg. Corbridge*, i, pp. 31–2; Guisborough, *Chron.*, pp. 358–9; *Historians of the Church of York*, ii, pp. 411–12; Dixon, *Fasti Eboracenses*, p. 356; Prestwich, *Edward I*, p. 547.

[79] M.D. Knowles, *The Medieval Archbishops of York*, Oliver Sheldon Memorial Lecture, York (1961), pp. 15–16. I am most grateful to Dr David Smith for his comments upon an earlier version of this essay.

8

The Authority of the Bishop in Late Medieval England: The Case of Archbishop Alexander Neville of York, 1374–88

> Every bishop that beareth cross, by that he is holden
> Through his province to pass, and to his people to show him,
> Tellen them and teachen them on the Trinity to believe,
> And feden them with ghostly food, and nedy folk to fynden.
> As Isaiah of you speketh and Hosea both,
> That no man should be bishop but if he had both
> Bodily food and ghostly food to give where it needeth[1]

William Langland wrote those familar words (from passus XV of the B-text of *The Vision of Piers Plowman* and, in their way, the most eloquent statement of the traditional ideal of the Christian bishop to have survived to us in late medieval English literature) at exactly the time – c. 1377 – when the archbishopric of York was held by perhaps the least ideal prelate that fourteenth- and fifteenth-century England ever knew. 'There is another king in your land', ran an anonymous petition to 'the commons of England' in the mid 1380s, 'that is one Alisaundre Nero bishop of Yorkshire: he destroyeth all that land in the north: there never was sich a tyrant in Holy Church, for he oppresseth more the country and doth more extortion, destruction and disease there than the king and all the lordes of Ingelond ... he is a predo, a thief, a traitor both to his Godde and to his king'.[2] Harsh words – but not of course by any means the only harsh words written about the fourteen-year-long pontificate of Alexander Nero, alias Neville, between 1374 and 1388. Even a century or more later the compiler of the somewhat emaciated *Chronica pontificum ecclesiae Eboracensis*, a member of the York cathedral clergy, refused to let bygones be bygones: he interrupted the usual conventional sequence of conventional eulogies of previous archbishops with a remarkably ferocious attack (to quote again) on *iste Alexander archiepiscopus* who, unmindful of his oath to God and St Peter on the day of his enthronement, laid siege

[1] William Langland, *The Vision of Piers Plowman: A Complete Edition of the B-Text*, by A.V.C. Schmidt (London, 1978), p. 196: passus XV, lines 568–74.
[2] W. Illingworth, 'Copy of a Libel against Archbishop Neville, temp. Rich. II', *Archaeologia*, 16 (1812), pp. 82–3. Cf. M. Aston, *Thomas Arundel: A Study of Church Life in the Reign of Richard II* (London, 1967), p. 279 n. 2.

to the dean and chapter of the cathedral (and especially to Master John Clifford, treasurer thereof) as well as to the canons of the collegiate churches of Beverley and Ripon – trying, in whatever ways he could, to annul the ancient and laudable liberties and customs of the church of York.[3] So serious were his *plures absorbitates et iniurias graviores* that no tears could still be shed at York itself for Alexander Neville's eventual melancholy fate – judicial banishment from England in 1388, fictitious translation to the bishopric of St Andrews in Scotland thereafter and death four years later in the Low Countries.[4]

An archbishop of York who enjoyed the unique distinction of ending his days as a parish priest at Louvain in Brabant can hardly be said to be a representative English prelate of the later middle ages. But it is of course precisely because Alexander Neville's tenure of the see of York in the late fourteenth century put the exercise of the episcopal office in late medieval England to perhaps its single greatest strain that his career seems especially worth recalling. Not perhaps that there has ever been any real danger that the misjudgements and misdemeanours of so stormy an ecclesiastical petrel would be forgotten by English church historians. Alexander Neville makes a characteristic appearance on page five of the late Professor Hamilton Thompson's *The English Clergy and their Organization in the Later Middle Ages* to furnish the one major exception to the author's general rule that by the end of the fourteenth century a genuinely active conflict of rival jurisdictions within English dioceses had come to an end.[5] More recently, Dr Richard Davies of Manchester and Dr Susan Calkin of Berkeley, California, have produced admirable detailed studies of various aspects of Alexander Neville's pontificate – sometimes to come to intriguingly different explanations of the notorious cruxes in his career.[6] Dr Davies indeed concluded his own study of the archbishop with the reflection that 'an attempt at characterisation, even were such possible, would not serve any useful purpose'.[7] I rather wish I could agree; but the fact is that Alexander Neville exemplifies to perfection that most familiar and frustrating of all problems facing the historian of *le pouvoir épiscopal* in late medieval England: – that so little, so remarkably little, can be

[3] *Historians of the Church of York and its Archbishops*, ed. J. Raine, RS (London, 1879–94), ii, pp. 423–4.
[4] Ibid., p. 424; cf. *Kirkstall Abbey Chronicles*. ed. J. Taylor, Thoresby Society, 42 (1952), p. 70.
[5] A.H. Thompson, *The English Clergy and their Organization in the Later Middle Ages* (Oxford, 1947), p. 5; idem, *The Cathedral Churches of England* (London, 1925), pp. 22–3.
[6] R.G. Davies, 'Alexander Neville, Archbishop of York, 1374–1388', *Yorkshire Archaeological Journal*, 47 (1975), pp. 87–101; S.W. Calkin, *Alexander Neville, Archbishop of York (1373–1388): A Study of his Career with Emphasis on the Crisis at Beverley in 1381*, Ph.D. dissertation, University of California, Berkeley, 1976 (University Microfilms International, Ann Arbor, Michigan, 1981).
[7] R.G. Davies, 'Alexander', p. 100.

known for certain about the individual personalities of the seventeen men who exercised power in state and church.[8] Moreover, the biographer of Archbishop Alexander Neville has even more formidable, and less predictable, evidential problems lying in his wait. Despite the deservedly high reputation of the voluminous church records still in the York archives, neither Archbishop Neville's own register nor the contemporary York dean and chapter act book provide penetrating personal insights into the prelate's conduct of northern ecclesiastical affairs in the 1370s and 1380s: Neville's own register in any case comes to an abrupt halt in June 1384, exactly when the archbishop is becoming most interestingly entangled in Richard II's ill-fated political machinations.[9] To some extent it is accordingly always likely to be the case that Neville's aims and ambitions, as well as his personality, will remain obstinately inscrutable. That acknowledged, there is perhaps no need to be absolutely defeatist: although this short essay can only anticipate the results of future research, a detailed investigation of the personnel of the clerical elite in the late fourteenth-century province of York (a prosopographical study of the careers of Alexander Neville's clerical enemies and his friends) seems to shed at least some light on the mainsprings of the archbishop's remarkable acts of aggression.[10] More significantly still perhaps, they can help to reveal why those acts of aggression finally failed; for in the last resort the archiepiscopate of Alexander Neville is a commentary on the symptomatic failure of a powerful English prelate who knew his own mind to get his own way, a commentary on the *limits* of episcopal power when faced with the inner clerical establishment of the late medieval English church and state.

In the course of a famous epitaph Samuel Johnson once wrote of Oliver Goldsmith that 'nullum quod tetigit non ornavit'.[11] By contrast, it can be quite safely said that the most remarkable feature of Archbishop Alexander Neville's tenure of the metropolitan see of York was that he

---

[8] For an excellent survey of the English episcopal bench between 1375 and 1461, see idem, 'The Episcopate', in *Profession, Vocation and Culture in Later Medieval England: Essays Dedicated to the Memory of A.R. Myers*, ed. C.H. Clough (Liverpool, 1982), p. 51–89. For the exceptional 'affluence', by the standards of Christendom as a whole, of all the English bishoprics except Carlisle and Rochester, see also the comments by J.R. Lander, *Government and Community: England, 1450–1509* (London, 1980), p. 120.

[9] Borthwick Institute of Historical Research, York, Register 12 (Reg. Alexander Neville, I), fos 95–111, 140–1; cf. D.M. Smith, *Guide to Bishops' Registers of England and Wales: A Survey from the Middle Ages to the Abolition of Episcopacy in 1646*, Royal Historical Society (London, 1981), pp. 239–40.

[10] See my paper on 'Beverley in Crisis: The Urban and Ecclesiastical Conflicts of the 1380s', in *Medieval Art. Architecture and Archaeology in the East Riding of Yorkshire*, ed. C. Wilson, Proceedings of British Archaeological Association Conference (1983).

[11] Boswell's *Life of Johnson*, Oxford Standard Authors Edition (Oxford, 1969), p. 778; 22 June 1776.

touched nothing that he does not seem to have disturbed. Other members of the late medieval English episcopal bench often found themselves at odds with the vested ecclesiastical and other jurisdictional interests within their dioceses. Despite Hamilton Thompson's doubts to the contrary, what Robert Swanson has called 'jockeying for a position of jurisdictional supremacy' over the capitular bodies never lay far below the surface of the outwardly harmonious relationship between large ecclesiastical corporations and their spiritual superiors, a relationship usually semi-secularised in late medieval English conditions to one of *de facto* if not *de jure* 'good lordship'.[12] What is distinctive about Alexander Neville's attitude to these problems of authority is not just his disinclination to allow sleeping dogs to go on sleeping, but his apparent determination to kick so many of them abruptly awake at the same time. By the time the then forty-two-year-old Alexander Neville was consecrated archbishop of York at Westminster Abbey in June 1374, he already had a track record (including a bitter but abortive campaign to secure the archdeaconry of Cornwall in the 1360s) which suggested a potentially lethal combination of extreme ambition, exceptional litigiousness and a lack of detailed application to ordinary business. Within a few months, rather than years, of his return to Yorkshire, these qualities were self-evidently in abundant display. Almost immediately the archbishop's pontificate was disfigured by an ugly series of disputes and altercations, including (several years before the crisis year of 1381) widespread riots on the part of his tenants in and around Ripon, Beverley and Sherburn-in-Elmet who were protesting against the archbishop's financial exploitation of his position as their landlord.[13] On all these issues, whenever the evidence survives, it seems clear that the intransigence of the archbishop led to unnecessary personal confrontations, most startlingly perhaps on the occasion when the mayor of Kingston on Hull (allegedly struck to the quick by archbishop's arrogance) is said to have snatched the archiepiscopal crozier from Neville's hands and used it – not at all as Langland would have approved – to strike down one of the latter's attendants, drawing blood in the process.[14]

However, as all students of Archbishop Alexander Neville's career have tended to agree, without a fair measure of irascibility (that not entirely unusual episcopal quality) the vicissitudes of his pontificate would be very hard to explain. Less often emphasised, and therefore perhaps all the more important to do so now, is the element of marked calculation and premeditation in Neville's determination to make the very most of his metropolitan and diocesan authority. Nowhere is this more obvious

[12] R.N. Swanson, 'Archbishop Arundel and the Chapter of York', *Bulletin of the Institute of Historical Research*, 54 (1981), pp. 254–5; see above, pp. 5–7.

[13] *CPR, 1374–77*, p. 227; *1377–81*, p. 90.

[14] G. Oliver, *The History and Antiquities of the Town and Minster of Beverley* (Beverley, 1829), p. 144.

than in the case of the archbishop's audacious if theoretically defensible attempt to enforce his jurisdictional superiority over the see of Durham. As readers of *The Guinness Book of Records* will be aware, the relationship between the sees of York and Durham can be plausibly maintained to have resulted in the longest legal dispute (still technically unresolved) in world history. Since the conflict began in the 1280s, Alexander Neville has been the only archbishop of York altogether prepared to grasp so stinging a nettle quite so firmly. Without the knowledge of either the king or of Bishop Thomas Hatfield, who had consecrated him archbishop the previous year, in September 1375 Neville secured a papal bull authorising him to visit the diocese of his suffragan. As is well known, this peremptory and undoubtedly devious attempt to demonstrate his power in the most spectacular of possible ways rapidly called forth from Edward III (and later Richard II) letters which rebuked the archbishop for his 'unheard-of and unusual actions', reminding him that the defence of England from the Scots was bound up with the spiritual as well as temporal privileges of the *comes palatinus* of Durham.[15] Quite as indefensible in terms of English ecclesiastical custom was the archbishop's attempt, on Bishop Hatfield's death in 1381, to exert his canonical right to visit the vacant see of Durham not *iure diocesano* but *iure metropolitico*. Once again a storm of protest from the community of St Cuthbert at Durham brought all to a standstill.[16] Whatever the canonical merits of Neville's case, it is indeed horribly hard to see (as Dr Davies has shown) how the archbishop could ever have thought he might hope to prevail.

It could of course be argued that Alexander Neville was particularly unfortunate in having as one of his only two suffragans a bishop in many ways more powerful than himself. But then by the late fourteenth century many if not most of the metropolitans of northern Christendom were in a not dissimilar position of political weakness;[17] and it would certainly have been wise for Neville not to have wasted his energies on a lost and unpopular cause. However, equally abortive, and infinitely more disastrous for the church in the north and for the archbishop himself, were Neville's assaults on the great collegiate chapters of the largest (in terms of size) diocese in England. Of the four great 'minster' churches

[15] *Calendar of Papal Letters*, iv, p. 212; *Historiae Dunelmensis scriptores tres*, ed. J. Raine, Surtees Society, 9 (1839), p. cxliii. Cf. R.G. Davies, 'Alexander Neville', pp. 95–6; R.B. Dobson, *Durham Priory, 1400–1450* (Cambridge, 1973), p. 218.

[16] *Reg. Alexander Neville*, i, fo. 113v. The incident is well discussed in R.G. Davies, 'Alexander Neville', p. 96.

[17] 'Avant le début du xve siècle le métropolitain de Mayence était, en dehors de son propre diocèse, un personnage muni de plus de privilèges honorifiques que de pouvoirs réels', F. Rapp, *Réformes et reformation à Strasbourg: église et société dans le diocèse de Strasbourg (1450–1525)*, Collection de l'Institut des Hautes études Alsaciennes, 23 (Paris 1974), pp. 65–6, which also provides useful references to the scholarly literature on this topic.

of Southwell, Ripon, Beverley and York Minster itself – in Hamilton Thompson's phrase, the most highly privileged spiritual republics in the see of York – Alexander Neville is known to have quarreled bitterly with all but Southwell. The reasons for his conflict with the secular canons of Ripon have alas not yet been investigated; but, by contrast, the explosions which followed the archbishop's announcement of an impending visitation of Beverley Minster on 26 February 1381 provoked the most notorious 'clerical strike' in late medieval English history. In this case the copious records of the dispute allow us to study in very great detail indeed the bitter and often violent strife between Neville and the Beverley canons, the ensuing mass walk-out (to Lincoln and London) of the great majority of the Beverley clergy, and the archbishop's provocative and unparalleled response – the compulsory replacement of the refugees by a body of York Minster vicars choral.[18] The fascinating developments whereby Archbishop Neville's head-on clash with the canons of Beverley became entangled in the struggle between *potentiores* and *mediocres* within the town of Beverley and gradually forced the prelate into his fatal alliance with Michael de la Pole of Hull, Richard II's dominant favourite of the mid 1380s, must lie outside the scope of this essay.[19] More relevant to our purposes is the way in which the quite exceptional documentation of the Beverley disputes of 1381–88 lays bare the deliberation with which Alexander Neville attempted to recapture what he regarded as illegally lost archiepiscopal authority. When Neville came across the dossier produced by his recalcitrant Beverley canons for the papal curia, in which they pointed out that previous archbishops had never laid claims to a Beverley canonry as such, the instantaneous response of the archbishop was to have noted in the margin: '*Et male*; and badly – *this* archbishop will purge [*purgabit*] the negligence of his predecessors'.[20] Even more striking is the way in which the ferocity of the Beverley conflict finally forced Neville to challenge – as virtually no other bishop of late medieval England was ever prepared to challenge – the single most practical restraint on *pouvoir épiscopal* – royal authority itself. At the moment when the crown was doing its very best to find a not at all unachievable compromise, and in words reminiscent of the age of Becket and Langton, the archbishop solemnly declared that 'We protest that we are ready to obey our king in all *lawful* demands, saving however always the right of ourselves in the church of

[18] The most important original source for this dispute (Borthwick Institute, Reg. 13. Alexander Neville II) was edited by A.F. Leach in *The Chapter Act Book of the Collegiate Church of St John of Beverley, AD 1286–1347*, Surtees Society, 108 (1903), pp. 202–65; cf. A.F. Leach, 'A Clerical Strike at Beverley Minster in the Fourteenth Century', *Archaeologia*, 55 (1896), pp. 1–20.

[19] See S.W. Calkin, *Alexander Neville*, p. 231, for the interesting suggestion that Archbishop Neville's alliance with Michael de la Pole 'could at least incline him against the baronial opposition to Richard II'. See also above, n. 10.

[20] *The Chapter Act Book of Beverley*, p. 212.

York and our jurisdiction and visitation of the church of Beverley.'[21] So intransigent by this time had the archbishop's attitude become that it seems inconceivable that the hornet's nests he had raised about his head could ever have been pacified without his own departure from the see of York.

That Archbishop Neville had become obsessively intent upon the assertion of episcopal power on principle there seems to be no gainsaying. But, as always, the pursuit of that curious abstraction we call power can only be analysed in the context of the detailed, practical issues that give the word positive substance. The most plausible explanation for the archbishop's determination to destroy the autonomy of the Beverley chapter was his desire to break the stranglehold on the exceptionally lucrative canonries there exercised by members of the great Thoresby clerical affinity. As Hamilton Thompson taught us, in a conclusion later amplified by John Grassi, 'it is not too much to say that for a century after the reign of Edward I much of the executive work of English governmental offices was in the hands of Yorkshire clerks under the aegis of Archbishops Giffard, Melton and Thoresby'.[22] Nor can there be much doubt that it was the death of John of Thoresby, the previous archbishop's nephew and provost of Beverley, in January 1381 which tempted Neville to launch a frontal assault on the independence of the Beverley chapter as a prelude to installing as many as possible of his own most favoured and trusted clerks there. What makes such an interpretation of the conflict in terms of a struggle for clerical patronage so persuasive is that a highly similar situation can be detected amidst the obscurities of the archbishop's equally suicidal dispute with the canons of his own cathedral church of York. Here his primary antagonist was Master John Clifford, a prominent royal clerk thrust into the fabulously wealthy treasurership of York Minster apparently against the archbishop's will.[23] More interestingly still, the recent discovery by Dr Robert Swanson of copies of a section of a papal bull in a York chapter memorandum book seem to make it clear that Neville was the only late medieval archbishop of the see to try to break the tight monopoly over the affairs of the church of York exercised by a tiny handful of residentiary canons. By persuading the pope to prohibit those 'convivia sollempnia excessiva et nimis sumptuosa' required at York on the part of all canons

---

[21] Similarly outspoken remarks (e.g. 'intendimus reducere canonicos ad primam fundacionem') among the marginalia of Reg. Neville II (*Chapter Act Book of Beverley*, pp. 213–65) leave no doubt of the archbishop's personal commitment to his intransigent constitutional stand.

[22] A.H. Thompson, 'The Medieval Chapter', *York Minster Historical Tracts, 627–1927* (London, 1927), pp. 13–14; J.L. Grassi, 'Royal Clerks from the Archdiocese of York in the Fourteenth Century', *Northern History*, 5 (1970), pp. 12–33. See above, p. 183.

[23] *Historians of the Church of York*, ii, p. 423–4. Although Alexander Neville was formally enthroned archbishop of York in the Minster there on 18 December 1374, the crown conferred the treasurership of the cathedral on Master John Clifford nine months later (22 September 1375) on the grounds of the recent vacancy in the see: *CPR, 1374–77*, p. 177.

seeking primary residence, Archbishop Neville would have destroyed the exclusivity of what was in many ways the most exclusive clerical elite in late medieval England – the residentiary canons of York Minster itself.[24]

Needless to say, Archbishop Neville failed where only (150 years later) Henry VIII and Thomas Cromwell were to succeed – and then perhaps not completely. The fact is that the fourteen stormy years of Alexander Neville's tenure of the see of York can be used to produce almost too many morals to illustrate the limits of episcopal power in late medieval England. Paradoxically enough, one of the important lessons the archbishop conspicuously failed to learn was the importance of not putting too much trust in popes. Misled no doubt by his own lengthy sojourn at Avignon in the five years before 1374 (a sojourn which almost certainly did more than anything else to gain him the archiepiscopal pallium),[25] it is now much clearer than it was ten years ago that Neville wildly over-estimated the chances of implementing the many papal bulls he secured to support his authority. Even less easy to explain however is the way Alexander Neville consistently under-estimated the formidable strength of the prevailing English clerical establishment, itself of course indissolubly tied to the governmental oligarchy of his age. Obviously enough, the archbishop's career illustrates the dangers (well known to us all) of appointing the wrong man to the top job: but it is perhaps possible to go further and suggest that Neville suffered in his confrontations with the highly professionalised clerical elites of late fourteenth-century England by being every inch a *non*-professional. Ironically perhaps, it even proved to be a disadvantage (as for Archbishop Richard Scrope fifteen years later) to have been a member of one of the north's outstanding aristocratic families. Alexander Neville, the first scion of a prominent northern noble *lignage* ever to sit on the archiepiscopal throne at York, belongs of course to that highly interesting cluster of aristocratic promotions to the English episcopal bench characteristic of the closing years of the reign of Edward III.[26] Despite the well-known dangers of trying to establish over-precise social categorisation of the bishops of late medieval England – even Alexander Neville attended Oxford University, though no one has discovered precisely where – the archbishop's largely self-inflicted misfortunes must be highly relevant to the as yet not fully resolved problem of why the much canvassed 'aristocratic invasion' of the English episcopal bench was largely confined

[24] R.N. Swanson, 'Archbishop Arundel', pp. 254–5; see below, pp. 195–224.

[25] For a somewhat different view however see R.G. Davies, 'Alexander Neville', p. 92: it seems to me less than certain that the York chapter's formal election of Neville in early December 1373 'seems to rule out any possibility of an independent papal initiative'.

[26] W.A. Pantin, *The English Church in the Fourteenth Century* (Cambridge, 1955), pp. 22–5; J.R.L. Highfield, 'The English Hierarchy in the Reign of Edward III', *Transactions of the Royal Historical Society*, 5th series, 6 (1956), pp. 115–38.

to the century between the 1350s and 1450s.[27] As we have already seen
in the case of the chapters of Beverley and York, the archbishop's by
no means unfettered control of senior ecclesiastical appointments in his
diocese provided him with some of his greatest problems as well as some
of his greatest influence. Perhaps too often in late medieval England the
episcopal *familia* has been seen, even by the late Hamilton Thompson,
as the chief instrument of a prelate's power. For a Neville who became
archbishop of York, even more than for most bishops, Samuel Johnson's
famous definition of a clergyman can forcefully apply: 'the father of a
larger family than he is able to maintain'.[28]

Of course none of these many constraints on their activities should
have prevented the bishops of later medieval England from following
Langland's advice and providing their spiritual subjects with both 'bodily'
and 'ghostly' food. It is indeed a paradoxical aspect of Alexander Neville's
unhappy story that in the first ten years of his pontificate, when he resided
almost exclusively at his palace of Cawood eight miles south west of his
cathedral city, he may have proved a more attentive spiritual pastor to
his flock than most of his contemporaries and successors.[29] However the
limitations on his freedom of action, as Alexander Neville revealed only
too immediately when he tried to remove them, were real enough. Despite
their great wealth and sumptuous state, in terms of authority and of
power, the bishops of late fourteenth-century England were not at all the
free agents they might have appeared to contemporaries. Just because he
tried so strenuously to prove otherwise, Alexander Neville's career may be
the best memorial we have to the fact that long before the Reformation the
evolution of the English church had proved St Cyprian wrong: in terms of
ultimate authority and practical power the archbishop could hardly have
shown us more melodramatically that 'Ecclesia *non* est in Episcopo'.[30]

---

[27] Of the nineteen bishops selected by Edward IV and Richard III only four came from
noble (in the English sense) families; and Henry VII, too, notably 'avoided' aristocratic
promotions to the episcopal bench: J.R. Lander, *Government and Community*, pp. 120–21.
For the dominance by aristocratic families of the archbishoprics of Mainz, Trier and
Cologne, see the summary account in F.R.H. Du Boulay, *Germany in the Later Middle
Ages* (London, 1983), p. 189. For the noblemen who became bishops of Strasbourg in
the later middle ages, see F. Rapp, *Réformes et reformation*, pp. 55–7, 171–82. Nor of course
could any English cathedral chapter have been conceivably invited to elect their bishop with
the words ('Vous êtes nobles, agissez noblement') addressed to the canons of Strasbourg in
October 1506 (ibid., p. 180).

[28] Boswell's *Life of Johnson* (1969 ed), p. 956: 17 April 1778.

[29] Reg. Neville, i, fos 100–111; cf. R.G. Davies, 'Alexander Neville', p. 93 for Neville's
almost continuous residence, during the first years of his pontificate, at Cawood Castle.

[30] W.A. Phillips, 'Episcopacy', *Encyclopaedia Britannica* (11th edn, 1911), ix, p. 699. Even
the most sympathetic, as well as most learned, modern historian of the late medieval
English bishops concedes that in the great Ricardian crisis of 1386–88 'the episcopate
could not exercise any decisive influence to avert extreme conflict in political affairs',
R.G. Davies, 'The Episcopate and the Political Crisis in England of 1386–1388', *Speculum*,
51 (1976), p. 693.

9

The Residentiary Canons of York in the Fifteenth Century

No doubt the metropolitan church of St Peter of York has always been a difficult institution for the outsider to comprehend; but in the later middle ages its organisation was at its most formidably complex. The reasons for that complexity need no particular urging nor indeed explanation. Even more than other major medieval cathedrals York Minster fulfilled a wide variety of very different and at times conflicting purposes.[1] As the single largest church within the pre-Reformation *ecclesia Anglicana*, it was inevitably committed to an especially elaborate series of acts of worship in choir, in nave and at the many subsidiary altars with which the cathedral literally abounded. As a house of God deliberately rebuilt and refurnished as magnificently as possible during the later middle ages, it provided a focus of spiritual allegiance for the inhabitants of York and Yorkshire as well as courting the attention of pilgrims and visitors from other parts of England. As the largest religious corporation in the region, York Minster was especially familiar to popes and kings as the most important agency through which the surplus wealth of northern churches and their parishes could be diverted to the professional 'permanent civil service' which administered the detailed operations of the English church and state. Most important of all, and despite the personal absence of the archbishop himself, the cathedral of York was still performing its original function as the administrative and judicial headquarters of the northern province in an age when 'if we come, therefore, to a general conclusion with regard to the organisation of English dioceses in the fifteenth century, we find that it has become highly centralised'.[2]

How far the fifteenth-century cathedral of York was successful in fulfilling these and other obligations, and how far its various roles could in any case be reconciled with one another, is an issue always likely to be

---

[1] See the survey, with fuller bibliographical references than can be provided here, in chapter 2 of *A History of York Minster*, ed. G.E. Aylmer and R. Cant (Oxford, 1977), pp. 44–108 ('The Later Middle Ages, 1215–1500'). This present essay is an attempt to develop and extend some of the suggestions made towards the end of that chapter.

[2] A.H. Thompson, *The English Clergy and their Organization in the Later Middle Ages* (Oxford, 1947), p. 70; cf. R.L. Storey, *Diocesan Administration in the Fifteenth Century*, St Anthony's Hall Publications, 16 (1959), pp. 23–6.

controversial and certainly one still unresolved. To that difficult question a final historical judgement must await an intensive exploration of the voluminous and almost entirely unpublished records of the late medieval chapter and diocese of York. However, it is already apparent that the coordination of these various functions, and the arduous task of achieving harmony amidst such diversity, was the responsibility of an exiguous but all-powerful minority within the large clerical population of medieval York. This essay's limited objective is to identify the extremely small group of fifteenth-century ecclesiastics whose duty it was to supervise the often cumbersome engines of church administration in the diocese of York and to preserve stability and central direction against the pressures of highly particularist and centrifugal forces. Attention will be directed exclusively towards those thirty-four clerks who became residentiary canons of the Minster between 1400 and 1500. As will become rapidly apparent, although an extremely cohesive and in many ways homogeneous group, the residentiaries of fifteenth-century York fall into no absolutely uniform pattern; and there is certainly no doubt that several canons of York Minster who abstained from taking up residence were often to be found within its precincts as influential members of the cathedral chapter and the archiepiscopal administration. On occasion indeed, as in the case of Robert Dobbes on 7 May 1451, a non-residentiary canon of York could constitute a chapter on his own 'with the consent of the residentiary canons then absent';[3] but a close examination of the composition of the chapter meetings at late medieval York nevertheless reveals that the residentiaries were nearly always the dominant and often the only ecclesiastics present in the chapter house. More generally but also more significantly, the residentiary canons of fifteenth-century York were united by a particularly solemn act of self-commitment to the religious and administrative purposes of the Minster. Their wills, their epitaphs and the administrative records produced under their direction leave no doubt whatsoever that they and others were extremely conscious of their special status among the cathedral clergy as its *canonici residentiarii*. These sharply delimited clergy who saw themselves as members of an exclusive and distinctive circle would accordingly seem to repay some attention as a group. As individuals who were amongst the most prominent university graduates of their age, and amongst the most prominent agents too of the medieval English church and state, many of these York residentiaries are of course already comparatively familiar figures in their own right.[4] But

---

[3] York Minster Library (hereafter cited as YML), H 2/3 (Chapter Acts, 1427–1504), fo. 75.

[4] The standard guide to the careers of all the fifteenth-century York residentiary canons known to have attended a university (with the exceptions of Henry Gillow and Thomas Portyngton) is of course provided by the relevant entries in A.B. Emden, *A Biographical*

continued

in attempting to discover what sort of men took up residence at York Minster between 1400 and 1500, they can be seen not only as individuals but in the common perspective which makes them a particularly instructive microcosm of their class.

By the fifteenth century, moreover, the York residentiary canons can be identified more precisely and studied in much greater detail than their predecessors at previous periods of the Minster's long history. Within a generation or two of the fateful decision by Archbishop Thomas of Bayeux (1070–1100) 'to divide some of the waste lands of St Peter's into separate prebends', because 'above all he desired to have good and reputable clerks', the number of canons physically present within the precincts of the Minster had already become comparatively small; and by 1200 power and influence over the church of York was accordingly becoming concentrated within the hands of a small, if still ill-defined, residentiary element within the chapter.[5] As early as 1226, nearly seventy years before the total number of York canonries and prebends attained its final complement of thirty-six in 1294, Pope Honorius III had been informed that 'very few canons make residence in the church of York'.[6] But it is only from 1370–71, the date of the first extant minster chamberlain's half-yearly account roll, that record of the payments of daily commons to residentiary canons who attended the principal cathedral services makes it possible to ascertain the actual periods of canonical residence with absolute precision. Despite several large and regrettable *lacunae* in the long series of unpublished fifteenth-century chamberlains' accounts (1405–26; 1430–63; 1465–71), the latter throw a vivid light on the business activities of the York residentiaries and especially on their sources of income.[7] Similarly it was shortly before the fifteenth century that the previously very heterogeneous volumes of York chapter acts and memoranda became much more systematised, documenting the formal business of the York residentiaries in chapter with meticulous if

Register of the University of Oxford to AD 1500 (Oxford, 1957–9), and *A Biographical Register of the University of Cambridge to 1500* (Cambridge, 1963), hereafter cited as *BRUO* and *BRUC*, respectively. Additional information is often provided by Le Neve, *Fasti ecclesiae Anglicanae 1300–1541*, vi, *Northern Province*, compiled by B. Jones (London, 1963). Of the various notes on York canons to be found in numerous volumes of the Surtees Society, much the most comprehensive and scholarly are those appended to 'Documents relating to Visitations of the Diocese and Province of York', in *Miscellanea*, 2, Surtees Society, 127 (1916), ed. A.H. Thompson, pp. 291–302 (hereafter cited as *Visitations of York*).

[5] *Hugh the Chantor, The History of the Church of York, 1066–1127*, ed. C. Johnson (London, 1961), p. 11; cf. *History of York Minster*, pp. 20–43.

[6] *Register of Walter Gray*, Surtees Society, 56 (1872), p. 155; *CPL*, i, p. 115.

[7] YML, E 1/1–59, *passim*.

sometimes arid detail.[8] More illuminating still for the purpose of this essay are the registered copies of their last wills and testaments which survive for each of the thirty-four canons of York who became a residentiary during the course of the fifteenth century. Although the occasional canon's will was also subjected to the archbishop's own testamentary supervision, it was a matter of course that the probate of all these wills pertained to the peculiar jurisdiction of the dean and chapter of York. In a manner highly symptomatic of the introspective and closely related world of the York chapter, the wills of recently deceased residentiary canons were usually proved before their erstwhile colleagues sitting in the York chapter house.[9] Even their wills of course provide only a partial and hazardous guide to the personalities and individual idiosyncracies of these men; but we are nevertheless better informed about their education, their recruitment to the cathedral, their multifarious services on behalf of church and national government, and their general aspirations than in the case of their thirteenth- and fourteenth-century predecessors and indeed of most of their contemporaries in fifteenth-century England itself. Such an opportunity seems to deserve a tentative exploration, even if a full account of their careers and work must await the results of much more detailed research, research which seems certain to reveal them as even more significant figures than this essay will suggest.

The formal procedures for admission as a residentiary of York Minster, although abundantly documented in surviving chapter act books, need not in fact detain us for long. Like such procedures in other late medieval English secular cathedrals, the rules and conventions in force at fifteenth-century York had become completely stereotyped. In order to apply for residentiary status a canon of York's first obligation was to speak to the dean or senior canon already in residence and ask him for permission to make a formal protestation before the chapter of his intention to fulfil his *residentia magna* according to the customs and statutes of the church. At the subsequent meeting in the chapter house itself, the president of the chapter received the prospective residentiary's written and verbal protestation on behalf of his colleagues before requiring the cathedral chamberlain to enter the date of the commencement of this

---

[8] A short account of the somewhat complex series of York chapter act and memoranda books is available in K.M. Longley's *Ecclesiastical Cause Papers at York*, i, *Dean and Chapter's Court, 1350–1843*, Borthwick Texts and Calendars, 6 (York, 1980). It should be added that a highly abbreviated calendar compiled by James Torre in the late seventeenth century (now YML, L 1/2) helps to compensate for the loss of a chapter act book which dated from the beginning of the fifteenth century.

[9] E.g., the will of John Wodham, made on 7 March 1435, was proved nineteen days later before Dean Robert Booth, John Barnyngham, John Selowe and Thomas Morton, all residentiaries of the cathedral (YML, L 2/4, Reg. Test, i, fo. 240). Only occasionally does the York chapter seem to have delegated the probate of the wills of its own members to the *auditor causarum* (ibid., fo. 285v).

major residence in the latter's calendar. Throughout the next twenty-six weeks the canon in question was obliged to attend matins, vespers and all other requisite hours and masses within the cathedral choir, as well as to reside continuously within the Minster precinct and to appear periodically before the chapter to certify that he was so doing.[10] At the completion of his half-year's major residence the canon reappeared before the chapter, where his admission to continuous minor residence thereafter was symbolised not only by a kiss of peace but by the payment of his first day's commons, a source of income he could expect to enjoy for the rest of his life. Despite the formality of these arrangements, the details sometimes preserved in the chapter act books make it clear that the six months' period of probationary residence was a good deal more than an elaborate legal fiction. Although no canon who embarked upon the arduous conditions of major residence ever failed to secure the chapter's approbation at the end of six months, that half year was still regarded as a genuine test of a canon's determination and ability to reside and an indispensable preliminary before admission to the residentiary body on a permanent basis. When, for example, William Sheffeld and John Hert were admitted to minor residence on 16 December 1488, the president of the chapter was at considerable pains to discover by means of secret interviews with the vicars choral, sacrists and porters of the cathedral that these two canons had indeed attended the *Opus Dei* in the Minster and had slept in their prebendal houses within the close every night.[11] Self-evidently enough, the decision to become a residentiary canon at York must in all cases have been carefully considered. It was a career choice of considerably greater personal import to most clerks than the acquisition of a parochial benefice or indeed of a canonry and prebend at the cathedral itself.

On completion of his major residence, the York canon was obliged by the statutes of the cathedral to reside for twenty-four weeks in the year, a period which might be concentrated within the first half of the chamberlain's accounting year (Martinmas to Whitsuntide) but was more likely to be dispersed throughout the calendar year.[12] When in residence, canons were expected to be present at vespers, matins and various masses within the cathedral 'nisi alias fuerint praepediti', a saving clause which no doubt permitted considerable flexibility in an individual

---

[10] *The Statutes etc. of the Cathedral Church of York*, ed. J. Raine (Leeds, 1900), pp. 10–11. For a particularly well-documented instance of the various procedural forms (as fulfilled by Dean Robert Booth in 1479–80), see YML, H 2/3, fos 166–9; and for a general discussion of the methods adopted elsewhere, see K. Edwards, *The English Secular Cathedrals in the Middle Ages* (2nd edn, Manchester, 1967), pp. 50–67.

[11] YML, H 2/3, fo. 198.

[12] *York Statutes*, p. 11; see the exceptional case of William de Waltham who received no commons from the chamberlain between Whitsuntide and Martinmas 1402 'quia perfecit residenciam suam termino precedente' (YML, E 1/36).

canon's arrangements.[13] It would in fact be very difficult to estimate how much of a residentiary's time was occupied in divine service; but of the assiduity with which he attended chapter meetings while in residence the act books leave a generally highly favourable impression. Much more precise, however, are the payments of the *communia canonicorum* which form an invariable section of the chamberlains' accounts and record the number of days for which the residentiaries were entitled to commons at the rates of 3s. 0d. on double feasts, 2s. 0d. on feasts of the nine lessons and 1s. 0d. on all other days. Allowance has to be made for the possibility that commons might still be paid to a residentiary canon if he was absent from York on cathedral business: in 1412, for example, it was agreed in chapter that Thomas Haxey, then away on the affairs of the church and chapter of York, should be allowed his residence 'tanquam personaliter presens fuisset', while eighteen years later Thomas Morton was similarly given permission to be absent for thirty-one days in London on the Minster's affairs.[14] Nevertheless, such dispensations were comparatively rare and there can be no reasonable doubt that the chamberlains' rolls do provide a generally reliable guide to the terms of residence of individual canons. It accordingly appears that the great majority of the fifteenth-century residentiaries of York completed their required quota but little more, usually spending between twenty-five and thirty weeks in residence. No canon admitted to residence after 1400 is known to have rivalled Nicholas de Ferriby's remarkable feat of ensuring himself the maximum possible commons by being in residence for fifty-two weeks and one day in 1400–1; but in 1463–64 John Gysburgh was a resident for thirty-seven weeks and one day. Neither Ferriby nor Gysburgh seems to have been heavily committed to diocesan administrative responsibility however; and for most of the residentiary canons longer periods of absence from York were certainly unavoidable. During the period when he was official, vicar-general and commissary general of the archbishop of York in the 1470s and 1480s, William Poteman took advantage of the shorter terms of residence incumbent upon archdeacons (he was successively archdeacon of Cleveland and of the East Riding between 1470 and 1493) to be in residence for only three months or so a year.[15] In this, however, he was exceptional; and most of the thirty-four residentiary canons of York between 1400 and 1500 could be seen within the precincts of the Minster for approximately half the year, being much more likely to be there – as again the chamberlains' accounts reveal – in the period between Martinmas and Whitsuntide than in the summer and autumn months.

---

[13] *York Statutes*, p. 11.

[14] *The Fabric Rolls of York Minster*, ed. J. Raine, Surtees Society, 35 (1859), p. 200; *Testamenta Eboracensia*, Surtees Society (1836–1902), iii, p. 106n.

[15] YML, E 1/33, 40, 50–7; cf. *York Statutes*, p. 14; Le Neve, *Fasti*, vi, pp. 21, 23.

Such a system had the obvious advantage that it enabled these thirty-four canons to combine their residentiary status with frequent journeys throughout the north and indeed the whole of England on royal, archi-episcopal, chapter and their own business. It also allowed many of them to exercise some personal supervision over the collection of the chapter farms assigned to them as well as to hold state for at least several weeks a year in their prebendal manor houses in the countryside. The occasional surviving inventory reveals how lavishly stocked and furnished some of these country retreats could be; and it is no surprise to discover that several residentiaries of York made their wills (and died) outside York itself.[16] The ability to be absent from the Minster for half the year also provided these canons with an opportunity to visit, however briefly, some of the many parochial and other benefices they held throughout England; pluralists although they universally were, their wills usually suggest the existence of at least some attempt to maintain a personal association, however intermittent, with several of the churches from which they drew their large incomes. More unexpectedly perhaps, it enabled some of the residentiaries of fifteenth-century York to be residentiary canons elsewhere too. Between 1466 and 1476 John Pakenham was a residentiary of Ripon and appears to have transacted business in the chapter house there quite frequently, as did William Poteman (who made his protestation of residence at Ripon in March 1478) during the following decade. Most scandalous of all was John Barnyngham who at various times during his long period as a York canon in residence (1433–57) was also a residentiary of Beverley and a stagiary of St Paul's Cathedral, London.[17] Barnyngham's may be an exceptional case; but the fact remains that in practice the residentiary arrangements at late medieval York allowed, as no doubt they were partly designed to do, a handful of senior ecclesiastics to maximise their combined emoluments from the Minster and elsewhere. Naturally enough the wealth of the individual York residentiaries varied very considerably indeed, depending as it did on the income to be derived from their particular cathedral dignities and prebends as well as from their many other benefices: three years before he became a York residentiary in 1400 William de Waltham's total revenues were already reckoned at 480 marks a year.[18] But even for the richest clerks of late medieval England the rewards of residence at York, including the right to daily commons and to a yearly share of the

---

[16] Thus William de Waltham made his will at Dunnington and William Pelleson his at Copmanthorpe, in 1416 and 1434, respectively (YML, Reg. Test., i, fo. 238; *Testamenta Eboracensia*, iii, p. 55).

[17] *Acts of the Chapter of Ripon*, Surtees Society, 64 (1875), pp. 148–247; *Memorials of Ripon*, ii, Surtees Society, 81 (1888), pp. 196–7; *Memorials of Beverley Minster*, ii, Surtees Society, 108 (1903), pp. 338–9; *A History of St Paul's Cathedral*, ed. W.R. Matthews and W.M. Atkins (London, 1957), p. 91.

[18] *CPL*, v, p. 79; cf. *Visitations of York*, p. 301.

common fund as well as to supplementary income from chapter farms, were sufficiently great to be very tempting indeed.[19] There can, moreover, be no doubt whatsoever that this was a temptation deliberately placed beyond the reach of all but a very few. In this respect Henry VIII's new statutes for the cathedral church of York issued on 3 June 1541 accused the late medieval chapter of positive malpractice: clerks had been deterred from taking up residence at York because their preliminary expenses in feasting and other hospitality would have amounted to no less than a thousand marks.[20] Although the exact accuracy of this figure may well be dubious, it seems clear enough that the resident York canons did indeed deliberately exploit the obligation to largesse on the part of a prospective residentiary to restrict recruitment to their own body.[21] In the most direct of all possible senses the York residentiary chapter of the fifteenth century was a self-perpetuating corporation, only likely to admit to its own membership those canons who were already wealthy, already mature and established ecclesiastical figures and already prepared to devote the remainder of their lives to the purposes of the church of York.

Indeed the first and perhaps most important observation to be made about the thirty-four canons who protested their major residence at York between 1400 and 1500 is that thereafter they almost all stayed, lived and died in the service of the Minster. To that general rule there are only two exceptions, namely William Gray and Robert Gilbert, the successive deans of York between 1420 and 1436, both of whom left the northern cathedral to become bishops of London.[22] By force of contrast, Gray and Gilbert establish the general proposition that the decision to become a residentiary canon of York, unlike institution to nearly all other ecclesiastical benefices and offices available to the medieval secular clerk, must have been taken in the knowledge that it was a commitment for life. To put this commitment in its simplest possible terms, it was nearly always one undertaken by very senior and experienced ecclesiastical administrators who either believed they had no prospects of promotion to a bishopric or who had no desire for such elevation in any case. There is certainly little doubt that the great majority of the fifteenth-century residentiaries of York were in

---

[19] For a brief description of the rewards of residence at York, too complex a topic to be easily summarised here, see *History of York Minster*, pp. 52–62.

[20] *York Statutes*, 43; C. Cross, 'From the Reformation to the Restoration', *History of York Minster*, pp. 197–8.

[21] When Archbishop John Kempe visited the cathedral in 1440 complaint was made 'de nimiis expensis in conviviis in introitu faciencium residencias, ad quod nullum statutum artat: per quod multi impediuntur a residencia, qui alias vellent eam ad honorem Dei facere', *Visitations of York*, p. 240. It was certainly required of canons in their major residence that they should spend considerable sums on meat and drink 'tam extraneis quam de civitate Ebor' et ecclesia', YML, H 2/3, fo. 198.

[22] Le Neve, *Fasti*, vi, pp. 7–8.

advanced middle age by the time that they made such a commitment. Although, as in all types of late medieval biographical investigation, it proves frustratingly difficult to establish even approximate dates of birth, there is enough indirect evidence to establish that most canons must have been in their forties or even more when they came before the York chapter to protest their residence. Thus in the case of the many canons who had previously studied at Oxford and Cambridge, an interval of twenty years or so between their graduation with a higher university degree and their admission as residentiaries seems to have been much more common than not.[23] Clerks already well advanced in years when they took up residence at York were not of course likely to live for an inordinately long period thereafter. It need therefore occasion no surprise that the life expectancy of the York residentiary was comparatively low. The average tenure of the thirty-four canons who protested their residence between 1400 and 1500 was only 10·5 years, a figure which, however, itself conceals some marked personal and chronological variations. At one extreme were Thomas Grenewod and William Beverley who died within months of their applying for residence at York in 1421 and 1493 respectively; at the other was William Poteman whose period in residence lasted for no less than twenty-five years (1468–93). For whatever reason, several of the York residentiaries of the middle and late fifteenth century tended to enjoy the fruits of their honorific position for a considerably longer period than had most of their early fifteenth-century predecessors. Six of them indeed (Thomas Morton, 1427–49; John Barnyngham, 1433–57; Richard Andrew, 1455–77; John Pakenham, 1456–77; John Gysburgh, 1463–81; and William Poteman himself) all lived as residentiaries of York for eighteen years or more and provided the church and cathedral of York with its major source of personal stability and continuity for well over half the century.[24]

Equally noticeable and of greater general significance was the tendency for the total number of residentiaries at York to contract during the course of the later middle ages. Even in the mid thirteenth century, when a certain amount of evidence begins to survive, there had admittedly rarely been more than eight or nine canons living near the cathedral at any one time; and it was to this comparatively small group of clerks that the chapter had then owed its growing *esprit de corps* and confidence, qualities which found their most enduring expression in the decision to begin rebuilding the already massive Romanesque cathedral in the Gothic style. Soon after

[23] A quite representative example is John Marchall who was acting as a notary public at Oxford in 1424 and graduated there as a Bachelor of Canon and Civil Law by 1428 but was only admitted to minor residence at York in August 1448 (*BRUO*, ii, p. 1228).

[24] For these and similar references to the tenure of York residentiary canons see the details provided in the appendix to the original version of this essay.

1300 the number of York canons in residence fell to an average of as low as four or five, a figure which rose to seven or eight in the 1370s.[25] At the very beginning of the fifteenth century, however, there were only four residentiaries at the Minster (Nicholas de Ferriby, Thomas Walworth, John de Newton and William de Waltham); and, except for a brief period between 1412 and 1415 when the number rose to six and seven, the total complement of canons in residence remained consistently low for the next generation.[26] Whereas before 1450 the number of residentiaries was usually four or five, rising to six for a very few months at the beginning of 1451, during the second half of the century it was often lower still. Throughout the 1460s and again in the 1480s there were normally only three canons in residence, a figure which fell to as low as two in the 1490s. In that last decade indeed York Minster only avoided the fate of not having a residentiary at all by the narrowest of margins: on 7 December 1496 Hugh Trotter completed his major residence only one day before the death of his only colleague, William Sheffeld.[27] When allowances are made for absence, illness and old age, it was accordingly more common than not in the later fifteenth century for meetings of the York chapter to comprise only one or two canons: attended by the chapter clerk and a handful of the lesser minster clergy, the latter sat in splendid isolation within a magnificent chapter house, the great majority of whose seats were always empty. The reasons for this ever-increasing concentration of canonical power in fewer and fewer hands were, as has been seen, primarily financial. Precisely because so large a proportion of an individual residentiary's annual income derived from his share in the commons and the farms of St Peter, he was understandably reluctant to see these emoluments shared by too many of his fellow canons. Unlike most bureaucratic institutions at most times, the secular cathedral chapters of late medieval England fostered a kind of anti-Parkinsonian law, a vested interest in contraction rather than in growth. Moreover, in a situation where the liturgical life of the cathedral was firmly in the hands of an increasingly autonomous minor corporation of vicars choral as well as of a large group of minster chantry priests or 'parsons', this was a vested interest which few archbishops of York would have thought worth the trouble of antagonising. On the evidence of numbers alone, it would seem that the residentiary element within the York chapter was disturbingly successful in limiting recruitment into its own body to a bare and at times hardly tolerable minimum.

[25] YML, M 2(4) g, fos 12, 16, 26; *Memorials of Beverley Minster*, i, Surtees Society, 98 (1898), p. 62; YML, E 1/1–6.

[26] YML, E 1/29–39; and see below, p. 213.

[27] YML, H 2/3, fo. 213v; Torre's 'York Minster', p. 174; *Testamenta Eboracensia*, iv, p. 119n.

In doing so it rarely had to pay much attention to entrenched local interests. Although they were to identify themselves with the cathedral church of York and nearly always to be buried there, the residentiary canons of the fifteenth century almost certainly included no native of the city of York among their numbers. In so far as they can be detected, the geographical origins of these thirty-four men were extremely dispersed; and perhaps a majority rather than a minority were born and bred south of the Humber. As will shortly appear, most of York's residentiary canons had originally come to the northern city in the wake of archbishops who had themselves been translated to the archdiocese from other and usually southern sees.[28] It is, therefore, hardly surprising that the former derived from places as far away from York as Bristol (William Felter), Kent (John Pakenham), Adderbury in Oxfordshire (Richard Andrew) and Houghton-le-Spring in County Durham (Henry Gillow).[29] By the early fifteenth century the great and long-lived if somewhat amorphous clerical affinity from northern Lincolnshire and the East Riding of Yorkshire, which had done so much to staff the crown's administration between the reigns of Edward I and Edward III, was evidently drawing to a close; but it is noticeable that clerks from the county and diocese of Lincoln continued to be well represented among the York residentiaries in the persons of William de Waltham, William Duffeld, William Sheffeld and others.[30] Yorkshire itself naturally fostered more future minster residentiaries than any other area of England; but most of these, like William de Kexby, Stephen Scrope, William Cawode, Thomas Grenewod, John Selowe and William Poteman, had returned to their native county after lengthy exposure to a university education at Oxford or Cambridge.[31] Only rarely, moreover, is it possible to demonstrate a correlation between a canon's local connections and his desire and ability to become a residentiary of the Minster. While not unimportant, one may safely surmise that such regional considerations were less decisive for the careers of the York canons than for any other prominent public figures in the north. In other words, the lives of the canons who took up residence at York are usually an object-lesson in the geographical mobility likely to be the lot of the careerist ecclesiastical administrator of late medieval England.

[28] Of the seven fifteenth-century archbishops of York, only Lawrence Booth (1476–80) was translated from a diocese in the northern province: he had been bishop of Durham from 1457 to 1476.

[29] YML, Reg. Test., i, fos 267, 327, 355; *Testamenta Eboracensia*, iii, pp. 232n., 236.

[30] *BRUO*, i, p. 601; *CPR, 1476–85*, p. 207. William de Waltham was a member of a large clerical affinity associated with Waltham near Grimsby and related to Archbishop Thoresby of York (1352–73); see *Testamenta Eboracensia*, iii, pp. 55–9; *BRUC*, p. 614.

[31] YML, Reg. Test., i, fos 154, 246–7; *Testamenta Eboracensia*, iv, pp. 78–83; and the relevant entries in *BRUO* and *BRUC*. It appears from their respective wills that John Selowe's parents were buried in the parish church of Beeford in Holderness and that William Poteman had been baptised at Water or Ferry Fryston in Yorkshire.

Even more obviously the careers of the thirty-four residentiaries of fifteenth-century York illustrate the theme of social mobility and corroborate the popular view that the church provided a career more genuinely open to talent than any other in late medieval England. Of all these men, much the most distinguished by birth was Stephen Scrope, the younger son of Stephen, second Lord Scrope of Masham, and the nephew of Archbishop Scrope: he became a York residentiary in 1411, six years after his uncle's untimely death and eleven years after his own promotion to the fabulously wealthy archdeaconry of Richmond.[32] William Gray and Thomas Morton were two other York residentiaries who could justifiably be described in papal dispensations as members 'of a noble race'.[33] Similarly, Robert Booth, dean of the cathedral from 1477 to 1488, was connected – in his case as a bastard – to another of these fifteenth-century families which amassed so much of the ecclesiastical wealth of Lancastrian and Yorkist England. Thomas Portyngton, apparently the last male heir of his family, was temporal lord of Portington in the East Riding; while William Sheffeld was a member of a Lincolnshire knightly family destined to produce a famous speaker of the English Commons before its elevation to the peerage in 1547.[34] The origins of the other York residentiaries of the fifteenth century are considerably more obscure, an obscurity which admittedly derives from little but the absence of reference to exalted lineage in their wills. It would certainly be extremely dangerous to assume that many York canons, whether residentiaries or not, emerged from genuinely humble backgrounds; but it seems equally clear that the great majority of them owed their predominance at York to their personal qualities rather than to their family connections.

As is now well known, the arena in which those qualities would have most commonly been tested was that of the Oxford and Cambridge schools. The thirty-four men who became residentiaries of York between 1400 and 1500 provide indeed a *locus classicus* of the vocational purpose of university education in the later middle ages. By the close of the century it is no exaggeration to state than only an Oxford or Cambridge graduate had any serious prospect of becoming a York residentiary; with the solitary exception of John Gysburgh, a personal chaplain of Archbishop Bowet who became receiver of that archbishop's exchequer, every single canon who took up residence between 1435 and 1500 held a university degree. At the beginning of the century this had been less invariably the case. All allowances made for the possibility that in a few instances the inadequacies of the late fourteenth-century evidence conceal the fact of some university

[32] *Testamenta Eboracensia*, i, pp. 385–9; cf. *BRUC*, p. 515.

[33] *CPL*, vii, p. 283; viii, pp. 378–9.

[34] *CPR, 1476–85*, p. 207; *Testamenta Eboracensia*, iv, p. 118; *BRUC*, p. 521; cf. *DNB sub* 'Sheffield'.

experience at that earlier date, it seems clear that during the pontificates of archbishops Scrope and Bowet (1398–1423) a university education was not as essential for the senior ecclesiastical administrator as it was later to become. In particular, experience in the more specialised departments of the royal administration often served as an alternative prelude to a late career as canon in residence of York: thus the non-graduates John Nottingham, Thomas Haxey and Thomas Morton had been chancellor of the royal exchequer, chief clerk of the common bench and chancery clerk respectively, long before they settled in the northern city.[35] By the middle and later fifteenth century, however, the migration of members of the Westminster civil service to residence within York Minster was undoubtedly much less usual, perhaps because so many of the more specialised offices in crown service were by then increasingly being filled by laymen to the exclusion of clerical graduates.[36]

The role played by university experience in promoting the careers of the clerks who eventually died as York residentiaries was therefore always fundamental and became even more pronounced as the century progressed. Of York's thirty-four residentiaries between 1400 and 1500, twenty-seven are known to have studied at Oxford or Cambridge; and of these, all but three (Richard Pittes, William Duffeld and Thomas Portyngton) held a degree higher than that of master of arts. Not surprisingly the great majority were bachelors or (most frequently of all) doctors of canon law. Only four of the fifteenth-century York residentiaries held higher degrees in theology. Two of these, William de Kexby and John Castell, were precentors of the Minster and seem not to have been involved in the detailed administrative and judicial duties which were the lot of most York canons in residence. A third, Robert Gilbert, had attended the councils of Constance and Pavia and was perhaps the single most distinguished residentiary at fifteenth-century York before his promotion to the bishopric of London in 1436. Finally Hugh Trotter, a Cambridge doctor of theology, also served the cathedral of York as precentor for a few months in 1494 before becoming its treasurer until his death in 1503.[37] Among the York chapter as a whole, as opposed to its small residentiary nucleus, there is detectable towards the very end of the fifteenth century a tendency for the proportion of theologians to increase at the expense of the canon lawyers – a tendency which was to gather momentum in the generation immediately before the Reformation and had indeed its

---

[35] *Visitations of York*, 295–7; *CCR, 1413–19*, pp. 368–9, 384; *1422–29*, pp. 27, 99–100.

[36] This possibility, put forward and investigated by Professor R.L. Storey, would seem the most obvious solution to the problem of 'the pronounced decline in the success rate of Oxford's secular alumni' at this period revealed by the statistics collected in T.H. Aston, 'Oxford's Medieval Alumni', *Past and Present*, 74 (1977), pp. 27–32.

[37] *Testamenta Eboracensia*, iii, p. 43; *BRUO*, i, pp. 367–8; ii, p. 766; *BRUC*, p. 595.

own significance for the progress of the English Reformation debate.[38] But for the residentiary York chapter, dominated at it was by clerks who served successive archbishops as their vicars-general, their officials and their commissaries general, a sophisticated training in the canon law was always the most common educational qualification. How precisely and how often they could apply their academic learning of the canon and civil law to the detailed business of supervising the direction of the church of York is still a very open question; and it may well be that a university doctorate was highly valued by kings and archbishops of York quite irrespectively of its practical utility in office.[39] What the wills and occasional surviving inventories of these men leave in no doubt is the size of their law libraries: the residentiaries of York undoubtedly possessed the largest private collections of legal works in the north of England.[40]

The academic background of the York residentiary canons also illustrates one of the better known, but still largely unexplained, developments in English higher education towards the close of the fifteenth century: the increasing importance of Cambridge as a recruiting-ground for ecclesiastical administrators. After a short period during the first two decades of the century when a few of the residentiaries were Cambridge graduates (William de Waltham, Stephen Scrope, William Pelleson and Richard Pittes), not a single canon who protested his residence between 1418 and 1480 is known to have studied at Cambridge.[41] In the last two decades of the century, however, the wheel was to turn full circle and all five men admitted to residence between 1482 and 1500 were Cambridge graduates. In several of these cases, and especially those of Hugh Trotter and Martin Colyns, there can be no doubt that they owed their promotion at York to Archbishop Rotherham, himself a Cambridge graduate.[42] Conclusive proof that a particular future archbishop of York first met and first favoured members of his future administrative staff at their common university is naturally impossible to produce; but in general the biographies of archbishops and canons alike suggest that acquaintanceship at university was one of the single greatest determinants upon a clerical administrator's future career. The translation of a Cambridge or Oxford graduate to the

[38] The total number of all York canons (thirty-four) with a recorded higher degree in theology rose from one in 1400 to five in 1500 and eleven in 1540–41.

[39] Cf. R.B. Dobson, *Durham Priory, 1400–1450* (Cambridge, 1973), p. 357.

[40] See, e.g., the inventory of Thomas Grenewod's library in 1421, *Testamenta Eboracensia*, iii, pp. 76–7; and that of Martin Colyns's library in 1509, YML, L 1(17), no. 18; *Testamenta Eboracensia*, iv, pp. 279–82. Similarly, books of canon and civil law are more often mentioned as bequests in the wills of York fifteenth-century residentiaries than any other type of volume.

[41] For general confirmation of this dominance of Oxford over Cambridge in the middle years of the fifteenth century see Aston, 'Oxford's Medieval Alumni', pp. 27–8.

[42] Trotter and Colyns had both been at Cambridge in the 1470s, a decade during which Rotherham had been chancellor of the university, *BRUC*, p. 489.

see of York automatically ensured that the York chapter, and especially its residentiary members, was shortly to be recruited from one of those universities too. Indeed it is hardly possible to exaggerate the importance of the university background of the great majority of York canons. They had nearly all spent long years of their adolescence and early manhood in fairly continuous residence at the university; while for many it was at Oxford and Cambridge that they first undertook heavy administrative responsibility. Robert Gilbert, for example, had been warden of Merton College (1417–21) at a time when the younger William Duffeld was also a fellow there; while John Castell was master of University College (1411–20) and Richard Andrew the very first warden of All Souls College (1437–42).[43] Late fifteenth-century residentiaries of York also included an ex-principal of Athelstan Hall, Oxford (John Pakenham) and an ex-principal of Burden Hostel, Cambridge (Martin Colyns) among their numbers.[44]

The prolonged exposure to Oxford and Cambridge influences of so many of the York residentiaries was no doubt as important in conditioning their attitudes to their later positions as it is now difficult to evaluate at all precisely. But to judge from their wills many of the canons who lived out their later and declining years at York retained as great an affection for their *alma mater* as for the cathedral itself. As outstanding beneficiaries of the prevailing higher educational system of their day, the York residentiaries were not unnaturally predisposed to foster its continuance rather than to make major new educational initiatives within the church of York itself. For good or ill, and as so often in the history of English education, graduates of the two universities ploughed back capital into the collegiate institutions which had given them their own first opportunities at the expense of providing much in the way of local educational patronage. Throughout the fifteenth century York's own cathedral schools are most remarkable for their almost complete obscurity, an obscurity partly due to the deficiencies of the surviving documentation but also due to the comparative indifference of the residentiary chapter as well as of a long line of non-resident Minster chancellors.[45] Similarly, the establishment of a separate cathedral library building at York in the second decade of the fifteenth century, although largely due to two residentiary canons, John Newton and Thomas Haxey, did not prevent their successors from leaving many and often most of the items in their substantial book collections to their Oxford or Cambridge colleges. In so far as a common pattern emerges from the bequests mentioned in their

[43] *BRUO*, i, pp. 34, 367, 601; ii, p. 766.

[44] *BRUO*, iii, p. 1419; *BRUC*, p. 152.

[45] *History of York Minster*, pp. 69–73. Alone among the dignities of the cathedral the chancellorship was never held by a residentiary canon during the course of the fifteenth century, Le Neve, *Fasti*, vi, pp. 9–10.

wills, the residentiary canons were at considerably more pains to leave their service-books to the Minster choir than their academic books to the Minster library. Dean Richard Andrew, for example, died in 1477 hoping that 'librum meum vocatum *Sanctilogium* in duobus voluminibus' would be chained before his two stalls in the cathedral; and in August 1503 Treasurer Hugh Trotter similarly left his two-volumed breviary to the Minster 'so that it should lie before the treasurer when he is present in the church'. Six years before his death, however, Andrew had given many of his legal and other books to All Souls College, Oxford; while Trotter's theological works were to go to Queens' College, Cambridge, his copies of Ovid and Virgil to the hostel of St Bernard's and his *Pollicronicon* to the common library of the university itself.[46] In the same way most of the books which can be associated with William Duffeld and William Poteman found their way into the libraries of Merton and All Souls Colleges.[47]

Less well documented but no doubt more influential was the role played by the York residentiary canons as patrons of education at a more personal level. Northern knights and others were undoubtedly eager to secure the attachment of their younger relatives and friends to the *familia* of a canon in residence;[48] and it seems certain that this was the avenue through which many Yorkshire boys first embarked upon their own educational and clerical careers. Not uncommon were legacies of the type made by Stephen Wilton in June 1457 to his nephew John: the latter was to receive eight marks a year 'ad sustentacionem suam pro studio exercendo in universitate Oxon' sive Cantabr' durante termino quinque annorum' together with an additional bequest of £10 for his expenses if he eventually proceeded 'ad gradum doctoralem sive in legibus aut decretis'.[49] Although exceptionally specific, Stephen Wilton's bequest is thoroughly representative of the manner in which the residentiary canons of York sponsored the education of their own most academically gifted relatives and, especially, nephews. When William Poteman made his will in February 1493, he asked his executors to provide his kinsman Richard with an adequate exhibition to study grammar and then the higher sciences and faculties until he reached the age of twenty or more.[50] In the following year Poteman's colleague, William Beverley, was to show his awareness of the new educational opportunities now available outside Oxford and Cambridge: his estate was expected to support Thomas Beverley's studies 'vel in universitate vel in civitate London' ad jus temporale'.[51] Such of

---

[46] *Testamenta Eboracensia*, iii, p. 234; iv, p. 220; *BRUO*, i, p. 35.

[47] *BRUO*, i, p. 602; *Testamenta Eboracensia*, iv, p. 81.

[48] See the legacies in the will (4 September 1432) of Treasurer Robert Wolveden, not himself a graduate, to 'aliis generosis qui mihi committuntur causa eruditionis', YML, Reg. Test., i, fo. 235; *Testamenta Eboracensia*, iii, p. 92.

[49] YML, Reg. Test., i, fos 284–5.

[50] *Testamenta Eboracensia*, iv, p. 82.

[51] YML, Reg. Test., ii, fo. 4v.

course was the type of patronage, no doubt as common before the testator's death as after it, which did so much to ensure that the clerical élite of late medieval England remained a largely self-perpetuating caste: like senior ecclesiastics throughout the country, the canons resident at York were often members of clerical affinities related by blood.[52] But it would be a mistake to be too cynical; for there can be no doubt that the York residentiaries genuinely regarded the patronage of talented young scholars as a worthy and indeed pious objective in its own right. In August 1508 the exceptionally wealthy Treasurer Martin Colyns made a legacy of six marks p.a. for seven years in order to sustain at either Oxford or Cambridge a scholar to be chosen by his executors from the poorest and most deserving candidates they could find.[53]

Although academic prowess at one of the two English universities was increasingly the most important foundation for the future success of the clerks who became York residentiaries, it need hardly be said that the paths which eventually led these men to the northern cathedral city were many and diverse. In some ways that aspect of their careers which is much the most abundantly and comprehensively documented – their presentation and institution to a veritable host of English parochial and other benefices – is the least satisfactory guide to the realities of their working lives and responsibilities. With hardly an exception, these clerks were among the most indefatigable chop-churches of their century; and many of them had begun to secure their first benefices quite early in their university careers. These were men best known at the papal curia for their continuous stream of requests for dispensations to hold incompatible benefices. During the years he had been warden of All Souls College (1459–66) for example, William Poteman was at one time or another also rector of Standlake in Oxfordshire, vicar of Stowe in Buckinghamshire, rector of Limpsfield in Surrey, rector of Elmley in Kent, rector of High Roding in Essex and rector of St Mary Woolnoth in the city of London.[54] Poteman's long sequence of churches, to be augmented rather than diminished during his later career at York, is a characteristic example of the rewards an Oxford graduate in law could often expect – as well as of the value placed upon such men in a society which set a higher premium on a university degree than has ever been the case since. That said, the precise significance for the prospects of a future York residentiary canon of his promotion to and resignation from any one of his large number of benefices depends on so

---

[52] Thus (of many possible examples) the nephew of William de Kexby, precentor of the cathedral from 1379 to 1410, eventually became non-resident chancellor there from 1427 to 1452 (*Visitations of York*, p. 296); while Thomas Grenewod's younger brother Robert became an advocate of the York ecclesiastical courts in the 1430s (*Testamenta Eboracensia*, iii, p. 62).

[53] *Testamenta Eboracensia*, iv, p. 278.

[54] *BRUO*, iii, p. 1506.

many unknown financial and other considerations that it only occasionally elucidates the progress of his career. Amidst such complexities, however, it is possible to discern that the residentiaries of York tended to fall into two distinct if overlapping categories – those who owed their success primarily to intensive administrative duties on behalf of the crown, and those whose services in the government's employ seem to have been much more intermittent and who are normally to be found engaged in judicial and secretarial work within the English dioceses.

Among the York residentiary canons of the fifteenth century it was the first group, those most often styled 'clerici regis' in the royal chancery records, who were always in a minority, and a minority which tended to become smaller as the fifteenth century progressed. They nevertheless often comprised the most widely experienced, the most wealthy and the most distinguished residentiaries of their period. As already noticed, the non-graduates John Nottingham, Thomas Haxey and Thomas Morton came to York at the beginning of the century from a background of governmental service at Westminster during the reign of Richard II. Nor can it be a coincidence that the only two York residentiaries of the fifteenth century to be promoted to the episcopal bench, William Gray and Robert Gilbert, were closely associated with the English court: the first was a king's clerk before taking higher orders in 1414 while the latter was dean of the chapel royal to Henry V and the young Henry VI. John Castell, a royal clerk before he became chancellor of Oxford University in 1421–5, was apparently even less involved in detailed administrative work at the diocesan level. More interesting still are the exceptionally well-documented careers of two near contemporaries, Stephen Wilton and Richard Andrew, respectively chancellors of Cardinal Henry Beaufort and of Archbishop Henry Chichele, whose patronage led them to responsible work (and especially diplomatic work) as king's clerks when there was no active king. Wilton died in the summer of 1457 after less than seven years as a York residentiary; but Andrew, forced upon a reluctant chapter as their dean while Henry VI's secretary, continued to serve the church of York and the English government until his death in 1477.[55] His successors as residentiary canons of York were to be much less personally involved in service for the English crown, with the highly interesting exception of William Beverley. As rector of Middleham in Wensleydale when the castle there was Richard of Gloucester's principal residence, Beverley became the latter's 'fulle trusty clerk and counsellour'. Perhaps no clerk in England benefitted so handsomely from Richard's usurpation of the throne in the summer of 1483; he then became dean of St George's Chapel, Windsor, and the first dean of the newly founded collegiate church of Middleham as well as the first precentor of York Minster to whom a cathedral prebend

[55] *CPR, 1452–61*, p. 116; *BRUO*, i, pp. 34–5.

(that of Driffield) was permanently attached. Beverley survived a period of temporary disgrace after Bosworth and was admitted to residence at York in December 1493, only a few weeks before his death.[56]

Residentiary canons like Wilton, Andrew and Beverley were, however, always outnumbered by those ministers of the northern diocese who had been brought to York in the entourage of successive holders of the see. This second category of residentiaries also often had some experience of royal service; but they owed their success directly to the favour of particular archbishops and illustrate to perfection that transition from household clerk to permanent administrator which provides the essential clue to the operations of ecclesiastical administration in the fifteenth century.[57] Each archbishop in succession tended to promote his most trusted clerks to vacant canonries at York; and as the decision to take up residence was often made only after an interval of some time, the residentiary element within the chapter was largely the creation of the prelates who had held the see during the previous twenty years or more. Thus at the beginning of the century the largest single group among the York residentiaries appears to have been the erstwhile protégés, like the future Archbishops Scrope and Bowet themselves, of Thomas Arundel.[58] A generation later, both Stephen Scrope and Richard Pittes, fellow residentiaries between 1411 and 1415, asked for burial near the graves of their two great patrons, Archbishops Scrope and Bowet, respectively.[59] More instrumental still in fostering the careers of future York residentiaries was John Kempe, archbishop of York for more than a quarter of the century after his translation from the bishopric of London in 1425. Nine years before that date John Barnyngham and William Duffeld had been appointed joint custodians of the temporalities of the then vacant see of Rochester, to which Kempe was about to be consecrated.[60] Both men followed Kempe to York where they were to be joined by William Felter and John Marchall as the central figures in the permanent administration of one of England's most notorious absentee bishops: for all four men Kempe was always to be remembered, even after his translation to Canterbury, as their 'dominus singularissimus'.[61] Nearly all the late fifteenth-century York residentiaries similarly owed their promotion to the patronage of successive archbishops. John Gysburgh, in residence

[56] Borthwick Institute of Historical Research, York, Reg. Rotherham (Reg. 23), fos 100–1; *Documents relating to the Foundation and Antiquities of the Collegiate Church of Middleham*, Camden Society, 38 (1847), pp. 64–5; *CPR, 1485–94*, pp. 24, 39, 126, 141; *1494–1509*, p. 7. See below, pp. 243–6.

[57] Storey, *Diocesan Administration*, pp. 5–6, 21–2.

[58] M. Aston, *Thomas Arundel: A Study of Church Life in the Reign of Richard II* (Oxford, 1967), pp. 304–19.

[59] YML, Reg. Test., i, fos 172, 185; *Testamenta Eboracensia*, i, p. 385.

[60] *CPR, 1436–41*, p. 36; cf. *CPL*, vii, p. 544; ix, p. 10.

[61] *Testamenta Eboracensia*, iii, p. 126; and cf. YML, Reg. Test., i, fo. 267.

at York Minster from 1463 to 1481, had been William Booth's personal chaplain as early as 1451; William Poteman apparently first entered George Neville's service at Oxford; while Archbishop Lawrence Booth was responsible for sponsoring the careers at York of his kinsman Robert (dean of York, 1477–88) and of Henry Gillow who had previously served as his temporal chancellor at Durham.[62] The powerful triumvirate of clerks (William Sheffeld, Hugh Trotter and Martin Colyns) who effectively ruled the diocese of York throughout the reign of Henry VII were all brought northwards from Cambridge and from Lincoln by Archbishop Rotherham.[63]

Although they were usually men who owed their success to a highly personal association with an archbishop, it can go almost without saying that the residentiary canons of late medieval York must have spent most of their time engaged in the highly impersonal business of directing northern England's most formidable and complex administrative machine. No attempt can be made here to describe the operations of that administration, especially as its full elucidation must await the detailed study and publication of its copious surviving records. What already seems absolutely certain, however, is that the bureaucracy of the fifteenth-century diocese of York was very highly centralised indeed; and that most of its important executive and legal decisions were regularly taken within the Minster and especially its chapter house, or inside one of the prebendal mansions within the cathedral close.[64] It accordingly followed that the commitments of a residentiary canon to attendance at divine offices for a minimum of twenty-four weeks a year were comparatively easy to reconcile with the routines of diocesan administration. Far from signifying a partial withdrawal from the latter, the decision to protest one's major residence seems to have been taken by clerks who positively expected to continue and indeed extend their role as diocesan administrators. William Felter, for example, remained Archbishop Kempe's chancellor throughout the ten years (1441–51) he was a residentiary canon; while it was after he was admitted to residence in December 1468 that William Poteman became commissary general as well as official and vicar-general of the diocese.[65] As fifteenth-century archbishops of York tended to concentrate the most important administrative offices into fewer and fewer hands so

---

[62] *Testamenta Eboracensia*, iv, p. 84n.; *BRUO*, iii, pp. 1506–7; *BRUC*, pp. 79–80; *Fasti Dunelmenses*, Surtees Society (1926), p. 51.

[63] *BRUC*, pp. 152, 521–2, 595–6. For Trotter's arduous role as executor of Archbishop Rotherham's will, see *Testamenta Eboracensia*, iv, pp. 146–7.

[64] See, e.g., *The Register of Thomas Rotherham, Archbishop of York*, i, Canterbury and York Society (1976), p. 65. In the early 1480s, when Archbishop Rotherham's vicar-general, William Poteman regularly conducted archdiocesan business in his prebendal house at Strensall as well as at his mansion in the Minster close (ibid., i, pp. 21ff).

[65] *Visitations of York*, p. 295; Storey, *Diocesan Administration in the Fifteenth Century*, p. 23; *Register Rotherham*, i, pp. 1, 187; *BRUO*, iii, p. 1507.

the effective authority of the residentiary canons undoubtedly increased rather than declined. It may well be that no ecclesiastic has ever wielded more real administrative authority in the north than did William Sheffeld during the eight years (1488–96) he was a canon in residence at the Minster. As treasurer and then dean of the cathedral he dominated its multifarious affairs; as Archbishop Rotherham's vicar-general and official he was the *de facto* governor of the church of York at large.[66]

Nor of course were the duties of the fifteenth-century residentiaries of York confined to the welfare of the chapter and the see of York. Their careers illustrate to perfection the general rule that the services of successful public administrators are eagerly courted in a wide variety of fields very different from those which brought them to high office. Nowhere is such courtship more apparent than in the relationship between the York canons and the mayor and councillors of the city of York itself. To the cathedral indeed, that huge and often bizarre corporate monster within their walls, the attitude of the citizens of York was undoubtedly one of considerable ambiguity. Like a modern university, a medieval cathedral was often within a city but not quite of it, a generalisation which certainly applies to the canons of York themselves. To the latter, however, the prevailing posture of the aldermen of late medieval York was normally one of deference, a deference all the more marked because it contrasts so sharply with the usually much more truculent stance they adopted towards other religious institutions in the city and even to so wealthy and powerful a religious house as St Mary's abbey just outside their walls. There the customary civic tone was one of extreme jurisdictional and economic sensitivity, finding frequent expression in attempts to cajole, to bully, to prosecute at law and at times even to physically assault. The residentiary canons of the Minster, however, although not its vicars choral or its chantry priests, were largely immune from this sort of hectoring: these were men to flatter and to cultivate. It was after all from the dean of York and his fellows that the mayor and aldermen of the city were most likely (as in April 1483) to hear of the deaths of kings; and it was in the chapter house of the Minster (as in September 1483) that they were most likely also to meet a visiting sovereign and to lay their problems before him.[67] Not surprisingly, nearly all late fifteenth-century residentiaries of the Minster became members of York's newest and most prestigious religious fraternity, the guild of Corpus Christi, of which indeed two of their number (John Marchall and Richard Andrew) were

[66] *Register Rotherham*, i, pp. 84, 89, 210, 236; cf. A.H. Thompson, *The English Clergy*, p. 194.

[67] *York Civic Records*, Yorkshire Archaeological Society, Record Series (1939–53), i, pp. 71, 82.

among the leading sponsors at the time of its incorporation in 1458–59.[68] But it is as benevolent arbitrators that the canons resident at the Minster appear most frequently in the civic records of the century. In June 1500, like their predecessors on innumerable previous occasions, Hugh Trotter and Martin Colyns were the mediators of the 'diverse variaunses, quarels and debates' between the city and the abbey of St Mary's; and it was of course to the canons that the aldermen went for a peaceful settlement in the many cases of strife and bloodshed between the citizens of York and the lesser clergy and lay servants of the cathedral.[69] When one of Dean Robert Booth's esquires assaulted an enfranchised inhabitant of the city in 1483, the mayor and council nevertheless thought it politic to pardon him because of the importance to them of 'the great zele and luff that the Dean has had and has to thys Cite'.[70]

It is as benevolent sources of aid and comfort at times of tension and distress that the residentiary canons of York also appear in the archives of a very different corporation – those of the prior and chapter of the cathedral monastery of Durham. In view of the traditionally notorious jurisdictional enmity between the medieval churches of Durham and of York, it may at first sight seem somewhat surprising that the monks of fifteenth-century Durham should have consulted the canons of York and taken their advice on a multiplicity of issues. It was, however, from the ecclesiastical establishment of the diocese of York that the priors of Durham drew the great majority of their legal counsellors. Quite apart from the advocates and proctors whom the Durham monks regularly employed and retained at the various York ecclesiastical courts, they were in frequent and close contact with the York residentiaries themselves. Thus John Selowe, who had already served the Durham monks as a notary at their Oxford college while studying law at the university, attended the election of Prior John Wessington at Durham in 1416. For the next twenty years and more, while registrar, vicar-general and residentiary canon at York, he continued his indefatigable services to Wessington and his fellow monks, representing them at York synods and convocations, supervising their ecclesiastical franchises of Howden and Hemingbrough in the diocese of York and preparing legal briefs for a wide variety of pleas in the York courts. Prior Wessington wrote to him as a friend who regularly performed invaluable services on his behalf.[71] Nor was Selowe at all untypical in this respect: one

[68] *The Register of the Guild of Corpus Christi in the City of York*, Surtees Society, 57 (1871), pp. vii–viii, 255–8; cf. ibid., pp. 35, 40, 45, 52, 64, 74, 108, 109, 111.

[69] *York Civic Records*, ii, p. 157; cf. ibid., i, pp. 61, 92, 178–9. Treasurer William Sheffeld actually sat with the city council in the Guildhall when helping to resolve particularly violent craft disputes within the city in 1490 (ibid., ii, pp. 56–8).

[70] *York Civic Records*, i, p. 70.

[71] See especially Prior Wessington's letter of 10 March 1432 addressed to Selowe as 'reverende domine et amice singularissime' (DCD, Reg. Parv. II, fol. 58); cf. Borthwick Institute, Reg. Bowet, ii (Reg. 17), fo. 15v, and Dobson, *Durham Priory*, pp. 137–8.

of the reasons the York visitation of the vacant see of Durham in 1437–38
was conducted in an atmosphere of harmony rather than acrimony was
that Archbishop Kempe's main commissary on that occasion was John
Marchall, a York residentiary canon well known and liked at Durham.[72]
Towards the end of the century Henry Gillow, temporal chancellor of the
bishop of Durham between 1465 and 1476, went on to be subdean of York
Minster.[73] The wheel, in a sense, seemed to have turned full circle since
the turbulent and sometimes savage jurisdictional disputes of the twelfth
and thirteenth centuries; for the once most bitter adversaries of Durham's
claims to distinctive ecclesiastical franchises appear to have become the
convent's most trusted advisers and *amici singularissimi*. It may well be that
the comparative quiescence of clerical conflict in the late medieval province
of York was due less, as Professor Hamilton Thompson and others have
maintained, to institutional inertia than to the pacifying effect throughout
the north of these senior ecclesiastical administrators and managers based
at York.

The services of these administrators were equally appreciated by yet
a greater source of authority than the monks of Durham – by the
Lancastrian, Yorkist and Tudor dynasties themselves. The very fact that
the residentiary canons of York were permanently settled in and around
the northern city made them a natural and highly suitable choice for a
wide variety of secular local governmental business. In particular, Dean
Robert Booth, as well as William Poteman and Hugh Trotter at a slightly
later date, were regularly appointed to commissions of the peace for
the East Riding.[74] In June 1486 Poteman was made one of the royal
commissioners *de walliis et fossatis* in Holderness; while both he and
William Sheffeld were at various times commissioned to settle disputes
concerning the Esk fisheries in Cumberland.[75] In the 1430s and 1440s
William Felter and John Barnyngham had also been appointed to raise
loans in the city and county of Yorkshire.[76] More interesting still are
the numerous occasions, especially in the second half of the century,
when residentiary canons of York served on diplomatic missions to the
Scots. Obviously enough, Richard Andrew's extensive previous diplomatic
service on the crown's behalf when he had been royal secretary made
him an ideal representative vis-à-vis the Scots' envoys during the years
(1455–77) he was a York residentiary; similarly William Cawode, as king's

[72] DCD, Loc. I., fo. 51; Reg. Parv. II, fos 100, 103, 107, 127–8, 132; Dobson, *Durham Priory*, p. 220.

[73] *Testamenta Eboracensia*, iii, pp. 281–2.

[74] *CPR, 1476–85*, p. 579; *1485–94*, p. 506; *1494–1509*, p. 667.

[75] *CPR, 1485–94*, p. 103; *Rotuli Scotiae*, Record Commission (1814–19), ii, p. 496; T. Rymer, *Foedera* (1704–35), xi, p. 851.

[76] *CPR, 1429–36*, pp. 528–30; *1441–46*, pp. 68, 430.

clerk, had been a prominent commissioner of truce in the early 1390s.[77] But John Selowe, a canon lawyer who had apparently never been a royal emissary during the early part of his career, was also made an envoy to treat with the Scots in January 1430. Fourteen years later Dean William Felter was appointed to negotiate a seven-year truce at Durham; while in the last thirty years of the century William Poteman and William Sheffeld regularly served as commissioners appointed to meet with the Scots.[78] As in the case of most late medieval diplomatic ventures, it is by no means easy to discover which particular individuals actually took the most important initiatives in relationships between England and Scotland; but there seems to be at least a prima facie case for the argument that the residentiary element within the York chapter must have built up a remarkable amount of experience, expertise and case lore in this field, qualities perhaps not always present among most of the lay magnates intermittently sent up to Scotland and the northern border by the English government. During the late fifteenth century indeed the chapter house of York Minster seems to have increasingly replaced Durham and Newcastle upon Tyne as the scene of important negotiations between the Scots and English, most notably at the time of the so-called truce of York in the summer of 1464.[79]

However, it is to the wills of the thirty-four residentiaries of fifteenth-century York, all of which survive, that one must turn for a final appreciation of the multiplicity of their interests.[80] It is there that they are revealed, however partially, in yet other and perhaps even more important roles – as heads of large households, as distributors of largesse and as the most significant sources of personal patronage within the walls of York. No attempt can be made here to subject these thirty-four wills to the quantitative analysis they deserve, an analysis which would nevertheless be hazardous in the extreme. The capacity to make particularly lavish bequests naturally depended on the highly variable liquid assets at the disposal of the testator shortly before his death; and as a general rule it was always those residentiary canons who held the most lucrative York dignities, like the deanery, the treasurership and the archdeaconry of Richmond, who made the largest and most spectacular series of legacies. But the length of the wills varies very considerably for other reasons;

---

[77] Most of the references are collected in *BRUO*, i, p. 35; iii, p. 2160. Cf. A.I. Dunlop, *The Life and Times of James Kennedy* (Edinburgh, 1950), p. 163.

[78] *Calendar of Documents relating to Scotland*, Scottish Record Office (1881–8), iv, p. 238; Rymer, *Foedera*, xi, pp. 748, 776; xii, p. 483; *Rot. Scot.*, ii, pp. 482, 496, 507.

[79] Rymer, *Foedera*, xi, pp. 525–7; for Edward IV's personal share in these negotiations, see C. Ross, *Edward IV* (London, 1974), pp. 61–2.

[80] Of these thirty-four wills, twelve (those of John Nottingham, Thomas Haxey, Richard Pittes, William Pelleson, Thomas Parker, John Selowe, John Wodham, John Marchall, Stephen Wilton, John Gysburgh, Thomas Portyngton and William Beverley) are still unpublished; the remaining twenty-two have been printed, with very varying degrees of accuracy and comprehensiveness, in the first four volumes of *Testamenta Eboracensia*.

and there can be no doubt that before their deaths many residentiaries had made important gifts never recorded in their testaments. It was also common for canons of York to leave a very considerable degree of discretion in disposing of their goods to their executors. The absence of a particular bequest to a particular purpose may accordingly be quite misleading: perpetual chantries founded by several of the fifteenth-century York residentiaries are often not mentioned in their wills at all. A comparison of the four surviving inventories of the estates of Thomas Grenewod, Thomas Morton, William Duffeld and Martin Colyns with their respective wills reveals how very inadequate are the latter as reliable guides to the wealth of the testator. Thomas Grenewod's total estate was valued at £899 1s. 1d., Thomas Morton's at £431 14s 4½d., William Duffeld's at £1317 18s. 1¼d. and Martin Colyns's at £1437 15s. 5¾d.[81] Although these totals incorporate debts, they represent very considerable wealth indeed. Most noticeable of all are the large collections of silver and gilt plate which adorned the prebendal houses, at York and elsewhere in Yorkshire, surveyed in these inventories. Such abundance of plate seems to be fully confirmed by the evidence of the wills of all the residentiary canons, in which drinking and other vessels are the single most common legacies except for gifts of money itself.

The wills of the fifteenth-century York residentiaries have, however, many other and more specific elements in common. First and most obviously, very nearly all of them made provision for burial within the cathedral to whose service they had dedicated the latter part of their lives. The few residentiaries, like John Wodham, John Pakenham and Thomas Portyngton, who expressed their readiness to be interred where divine providence dictated were in fact buried within the Minster; and so too were Thomas Parker and William Beverley, who had envisaged the alternative resting place of the Yorkshire churches of Bolton Percy and Middleham respectively.[82] Accordingly only five of the thirty-four residentiaries were buried elsewhere than in the Minster: in addition to William Gray and Robert Gilbert, who died as bishops of Lincoln and London respectively, these included William de Waltham, Henry Gillow and Stephen Wilton, interred in Lincoln Cathedral, the parish church of Houghton-le-Spring and Beverley Minster.[83] Moreover, the great majority of the canons buried at York chose the site of their graves as well as their gravestones with great care. By the later fifteenth century it had become traditional for the dignitaries of the cathedral, and especially the deans

[81] YML, L 1 (17), nos 18, 37, 44; and cf. Borthwick Institute, D.C. Probate Records, 1410 (the inventory of William de Kexby); *Testamenta Eboracensia*, iii, pp. 64–5, 107–15, 129–52; iv, pp. 279–307.

[82] YML, Reg. Test., i, fos 215–16; ii, fo. 4v; but cf. F. Drake, *Eboracum* (York, 1736), p. 504.

[83] YML, Reg. Test., i, fos 179, 284, 355.

and treasurers, to be buried in close proximity to their predecessors. Other residentiaries elected sites near the tombs of the archbishops to whom they owed their early success; and it is certainly no surprise to discover that in 1418 Stephen Scrope desired burial in St Stephen's chapel 'near my lord the archbishop of York who laid his helping hands on me when he was alive and whose prayers I beseech now that he is in heaven'.[84] As some residentiaries (like John Selowe and John Castell) wished to be buried as far apart as the doorway of the vestibule and the font of the cathedral, there is no need to labour the point that by the end of the middle ages, the Minster floor was crowded with memorials – usually in the form of marble slabs – to men whose epitaphs unfailingly recorded that they were *canonici residentiarii*.[85]

A good deal less stereotyped, although by no means easy to interpret, are the devotional preambles with which their wills begin. Like the wills themselves, these are of very varying lengths; and despite a large element of common phraseology (*'bonis michi a deo collatis'*; *'terram terre'*) they often display individual traits which presumably stemmed from the wishes of the testator rather than his scribe. John Castell, for example, in what the younger James Raine correctly described as a 'beautiful and striking will' of 1456, made a series of direct and highly unusual appeals to the name of Jesus.[86] In this case the fact that Castell was one of the few graduate theologians among the fifteenth-century residentiaries may not be entirely coincidental; but it would certainly be dangerous to make confident deductions from this type of evidence. As it happens, several of the criteria sometimes proposed as evidence of religious unorthodoxy in late medieval wills are detectable in those drawn up by the highly orthodox and conventionally pious canons of York. Comparatively few of the latter, for example, invoke the names of Mary or other saints: quite untypical in this connection is the will of John Wodham who mentioned saints Peter, Paul, Andrew, John, Wilfred and Nicholas as well as the Virgins Etheldreda and Katherine at the beginning of his will.[87] Similarly several of the York residentiaries laid emphasis on their unworthiness (*indignus sacerdos*) and expressed contempt towards their bodies (*corpus meum vilissimum*): it may not be altogether inappropriate that the only surviving memorial of a late medieval York canon at York takes the form of Thomas Haxey's much mutilated cadaver effigy.[88] Most common of all was the request on the part of the residentiaries that their funeral expenses *'sint moderate absque pompa'*. Such alleged distaste for the

[84] *Testamenta Eboracensia*, i, p. 385.
[85] YML, Reg. Test., i, fos 246v, 281; cf. Drake, *Eboracum*, pp. 500–5.
[86] *Testamenta Eboracensia*, iii, pp. 153–4.
[87] YML, Reg. Test., i, fo. 239v.
[88] YML, Reg. Test., i, fos 239v, 281; *History of York Minster*, p. 107 (plate 11).

'empty and worthless pomp of this world' cannot of course always be taken at its face value; but the cumulative impression left by their wills certainly suggests that most residentiaries were at greater pains to be remembered by their acquaintances and servants among the Minster establishment than to impress by a dazzling display of candles and torch-bearers. The most common of all funeral bequests consisted of sums of money paid to canons, vicars, chantry-priests, choristers and others present at the exequies. Not untypically, when he died in 1462 John Marchall left a special bequest for a meal to be held on the day of his obit in his prebendal mansion, a meal to which the canons and all other ministers of the cathedral would be invited.[89]

However, there can be no doubt that the foundation or augmentation of a perpetual chantry was the way in which most of the richer York residentiaries hoped to ensure their immortality on earth. As in other English secular cathedrals, the great majority of the sixty or more Minster chantries were founded by canons of the church; and there are no signs of any marked decline in this aspiration as the fifteenth century progressed. The single most lavish chantry founded by a residentiary in this period was that which commemorated Thomas Haxey at the altar of St Thomas after his death in 1425; unusual in many respects, Haxey's chantry was supported by an annual annuity of £12 regularly paid by the city chamberlains of York from the proceeds of Haxey's original bequest of no less than 600 gold marks.[90] In 1454 Dean William Felter's executors founded a chantry at the altar of St Jerome; while his successor as dean, Richard Andrew, was remembered at a chantry whose two priests were required to pray for the souls not only of Henry VI, Edward IV and Archbishop Neville, but of the residentaries John Pakenham, William Poteman and John Gysburgh.[91] William Cawode and John Barnyngham also founded perpetual chantries within the cathedral; while many other canons, like Stephen Wilton in the case of Archbishop Bowet, associated themselves with the chantries founded to commemorate even greater ecclesiastics than themselves. Not all the York residentiaries preferred to endow chantries within the Minster itself: Dean Robert Booth gave a bequest of 100 marks to augment the chantry founded by his father in London, while Henry Gillow endowed a chantry priest at eight marks per annum within the church of Houghton-le-Spring where his mother

---

[89] YML, Reg. Test., i, fo. 299. In the widest sense of the term, funeral expenses seem always to have been a heavy charge on the executors of deceased canons: they amounted to nearly £70, for example, even in the case of the comparatively unwealthy William de Kexby when he died in March 1410 (Borthwick Institute, D.C. Probate Records, 1410; and cf. YML, Reg. Test. i, fo. 154).

[90] YCA, C. 82, 4; C. 1:3–4:4; *York Fabric Rolls*, p. 304. Cf. the comments at p. 256 below.

[91] YML, L 2(2)a ('Domesday Book'), fo. 150; *York Fabric Rolls*, pp. 287, 301.

had been buried.[92] Nevertheless there can have been few of the fifteenth-century canons in residence at York whose names were not being commemorated at some altar or other within the Minster on the eve of the Reformation. Even after their deaths these thirty-four men continued to control the liturgical activities of many of the lesser cathedral clergy.

In that respect the York residentiaries were indeed to discover that 'all is vanity'; for the perpetual chantries upon which they had placed so high a premium were all to be swept away in the 1540s, leaving scarcely a visible trace to posterity. Much more abiding memorials of their influence and wealth survive in the fabric of the Minster and its associated buildings. This 'small body of residents, into whose hands naturally fell the executive control of the church' proved itself capable of taking and responding to important initiatives until the very end of the middle ages.[93] There seems no reasonable doubt that it was the York residentiaries, and especially John Marchall and Stephen Wilton, who were instrumental in securing the foundation of St William's College in 1461, the largest college of cathedral chantry priests ever established in England. Similarly the four York canons in residence before and during the troubled reign of Richard III (Poteman, Gillow, Booth and Portyngton) were absolutely ready to approve that king's exceptionally ambitious if rapidly abortive project for a college of no less than a hundred chaplains near their cathedral.[94] But their greatest corporate memorial still stands – for that was, and is, York Minster itself. Bequests to the fabric of the cathedral figure prominently in nearly all the surviving wills; but they must certainly have been far surpassed by the sums bestowed on the building and the furnishings of the Minster while the canons in question were still alive and in residence.[95] Two surviving stained-glass windows in the northern aisle of the cathedral nave were originally presented by Thomas Parker and Robert Wolveden and allegedly may still 'reflect both the careers and the private devotion of the donors'.[96] A few years earlier, in late 1407, William de Waltham had been one of the supervisors entrusted with the selection

[92] YML, Reg. Test., i, fo. 355; *Testamenta Eboracensia*, iv, p. 31. Quite apart from his perpetual chantry at York, Richard Andrew had benefited from royal licences to found chantries at Deddington in Oxfordshire and Chipping Sodbury in Gloucestershire, *CPR*, *1441–46*, pp. 407–8; *1446–52*, p. 566.

[93] 'The Medieval Chapter', *York Minster Historical Tracts, 627–1927*, ed. A.H. Thompson (1927), p. 11.

[94] To the references collected in *History of York Minster*, pp. 97–8, add the allusion to the timber 'quod fuit de domo constructa per regem Ricardum Tertium pro cantaristis per eundem fundandis', *Testamenta Eboracensia*, iv, p. 79. See below, p. 248.

[95] The largest bequests to the fabric of York Minster recorded in the thirty-four wills of York residentiaries were those of William de Waltham (£40 in 1416) and Thomas Haxey (100 marks in 1424).

[96] G. Benson, *The Ancient Painted Glass in the Minster and Churches of the City of York* (York, 1915), pp. 92–7; *History of York Minster*, p. 373.

of workmen to rebuild the great tower of the Minster; and, even more appropriately, the south-western tower of the present cathedral (almost the last part of the present fabric to be built) still bears the carved name of John Barnyngham, during whose period of residence at York (1433–57) the largest single work of English Gothic architecture was brought almost to completion.[97]

Men whose greatest memorial was and is the cathedral church of York perhaps need no other memorial at all. Whether they need, and deserve a more general justification is of course another matter entirely. On the assumption, still to be fully investigated, that the records of the church of York are a reliable testimony to their own administrative skills, the residentiary canons of the fifteenth century no doubt deserved their high status and their wealth: it might even be possible to argue that the diocese of York was never to be administered quite so skilfully again. Nor can there be any doubt of the assiduity with which they protected their own privileges and those of the church of York against all comers.[98] Otherwise it must be admitted that all the familiar questions raised by the role of such clerical possessioners in late medieval England remain obstinately open. It is, for example, almost impossible to know how large a proportion of their very considerable wealth they devoted to the religious and charitable purposes of the Christian life. Many of the York residentiary canons no doubt conceived their own personal riches as a fitting and seemly reflection of the Minster in whose service they lived and died. Committed as they were to an endless round of hospitality and entertainment, as well as of executive and judicial business, it seems unlikely that they often found the burden of their wealth too unbearable. Similarly the failure of the most prominent private owners of books in the north of England to write books themselves is understandable without perhaps being absolutely excusable. The most fundamental problem of all is the purpose to which those residentiaries applied their talents; for it ought not to be forgotten that their successors in the early sixteenth century did more to aid than oppose the progress of the Henrician Reformation. As elsewhere in the late medieval *ecclesia Anglicana* it is sometimes hard to avoid the suspicion that one has been witnessing an unconscious *trahison des clercs*, the dangers of a situation in which the ecclesiastical administrator may become more obsessed by the administration than by the church. But the careers of the residentiary

---

[97] *CPR, 1405–8*, p. 383; *York Fabric Rolls*, p. 51n.

[98] Perhaps the most remarkable example of solidarity among the York residentiaries in the fifteenth century was the attempt of John Barnyngham, John Castell, William Duffeld, John Marchall and Stephen Wilton to prevent the intrusion of Richard Andrew as their dean in 1451–2, an opposition which led them into direct confrontation with both pope and king: *CPL*, x, pp. 112, 239–40. For important evidence relating to the possible involvement of York residentiary canons in Archbishop Scrope's rebellion of 1405, see R.L. Storey, 'Clergy and Common Law in the Reign of Henry IV', *Medieval Legal Records*, ed. R.F. Hunnisett and J.B. Post (London, 1978), pp. 394–401.

canons of fifteenth-century York present many other obvious, perhaps too obvious, morals for posterity – the dangers of over-concentration of power, the possibly corrupting effect of excessive wealth, the hazards of working for the national government, and even perhaps the deleterious effects of university graduates being too handsomely rewarded. Trevor Aston once reminded us that medieval Oxford was much more successful than is a modern university in 'meeting the requirements of the society that the University exists and solely exists to serve'.[99] Quite so; but perhaps the later careers of those university graduates who eventually died as residentiary canons of York reveal the dangers of meeting those requirements too exactly and too well.

[99] Aston, 'Oxford's Medieval Alumni', p. 35.

10

Richard III and the Church of York

Throughout the later middle ages York Minster, publicised by its own clergy as the oldest and most distinguished 'metropolitical Temple' in Britain,[1] was a much visited cathedral. Yet no visit made to the metro-politan church of St Peter by a ruling English sovereign in the fifteenth century can have been more eagerly awaited than that by the recently crowned Richard III on Friday, 29 August 1483. Of all the days in his short and troubled reign, this may well have been the one on which, as Polydore Vergil later surmised, the new king could enjoy his greatest 'publyk and open tryumph' and most confidently 'advance himself openly to all men, yea to the country people'.[2] Not that there was anything particularly rustic or plebeian about the dignitaries who welcomed Richard's return to a city and a cathedral he already knew so well as duke of Gloucester. Met by the mayor, sheriffs and aldermen of York on the road from Pontefract and Tadcaster, Richard III then passed under the bar once adorned by his own father's severed head into Micklegate, where he and his retinue were diverted by a series of the most elaborate and most carefully rehearsed 'shews' the citizens could provide.[3] However, the climax of this exceptionally 'joyful entry' came not in the streets of York themselves but at the west door of York Minster, where Richard was received by the dean and chapter, 'together with all the ministers of the church in their blue silk copes'. Only after a lengthy sequence of anthems and prayers within the cathedral, most memorably perhaps

[1] J.S. Purvis, 'The Tables of the York Vicars Choral', *Yorkshire Archaeological Journal*, 41 (1967), pp. 742–3; R.B. Dobson, 'The Later Middle Ages, 1215–1500', *A History of York Minster*, ed. G.E. Aylmer and R. Cant (Oxford, 1977), p. 108.

[2] *Three Books of Polydore Vergil's English History*, ed. H. Ellis, Camden Society, old series, 29 (1844), p. 188. Richard of Gloucester had last been seen in York Minster in mid April 1483, when he allegedly held a solemn funeral service for his brother and was the first magnate present to swear an oath of fealty to Edward V, *Ingulph's Chronicle of the Abbey of Croyland*, ed. H.T. Riley (London, 1854), pp. 485–6.

[3] For the advice given by the new king's secretary, John Kendal, as to the 'pageants' and other spectacles which would be appropriate for this royal visit to York, see *York Civic Records*, ed. Angelo Raine, Yorkshire Archaeological Society, Record Series, 8 vols (1939–52), i, pp. 78–9. Citations from these volumes (hereafter YCR) have been compared with the appropriate entries in Lorraine C. Attreed, *York House Books, 1461–1490*, 2 vols (Stroud, 1991).

Dean Robert Booth's own invocation to the Lord to deliver the new king from temptation, did Richard and his train process towards the adjacent archiepiscopal palace north of the Minster. So began what was probably one of the longest and certainly one of the most auspicious sojourns by an English monarch within the walls of York. Of the many unusual royal occasions witnessed by the inhabitants of the city during the following three weeks, the most spectacular of all occurred – once again – in the cathedral. For it was there, on Monday, 8 September, that Richard and his queen made an exceptionally elaborate ceremonial progress, and it was there too that they remained with their crowns on their heads until the sixth hour of the night. Not less remarkable was a four-hour-long banquet in the hall of the archbishop's palace immediately thereafter, during which the investiture of Richard's only son with the insignia of the principality of Wales was celebrated with so much splendour that it later gave rise to the misunderstanding that the king himself had undergone a second coronation at York Minster. 'Et ibi erant Decanus, Robertus Both; canonici, scilicet thesaurarius Portington, Poteman archdiaconus Ebor., ac subdecanus, et quatuor alii prebendarii; decem personae ecclesiae Ebor.; xij vicarii chorales cum aliis ministris ecclesie.'[4]

The reign of King Richard III is almost as notorious for its unexpected historical ironies as it is for its unresolvable problems of interpretation; but it is perhaps one of the lesser noticed but more startling consequences of Richard's usurpation of the throne in July 1483 that the archbishop of York himself was not present at the most prestigious ceremonies held in his own cathedral and his own palace during the entire course of the fifteenth century. That the senior prelate officiating at those ceremonies should have been none other than a bishop of Durham, Richard III's loyal adherent, William Dudley, would in itself have given Archbishop Thomas Rotherham's predecessors in the see of St Peter considerable food for thought.[5] More generally, the celebrated visit of Richard III

[4] York Minster Library (hereafter cited as YML), M 2(2) C (Repertorium), fo. 70; *The Fabric Rolls of York Minster*, ed. James Raine, Surtees Society, 35 (1859), pp. 210–12. As this account of the *Receptio Regis Ricardi Tercii apud Ebor.* was composed on behalf of the cathedral's vicars choral soon after the event, it is to be preferred to other surviving descriptions of Richard's visit to York in August–September 1483: for the latter, the most detailed but sometimes question-begging discussion is provided by P.M. Kendall, *Richard the Third* (London, 1955), pp. 256–9; and for the later completely erroneous belief that the king was crowned at York Minster 'the second time by Dr Rotherham, Archbishop of York', see, for example, George Buck, *The History of King Richard the Third (1619)*, ed. A.N. Kincaid (Gloucester, 1982), p. 51.

[5] YML, M 2 (2) C, fo. 70. Cf. the exceptionally prominent role of Bishop Dudley of Durham at the coronation of Richard at Westminster a few weeks earlier (6 July 1483): *The Coronation of Richard III*, ed. A.F. Sutton and P.W. Hammond (Gloucester, 1983), pp. 275–82. Some examples of the jurisdictional issues which continued to create political sensitivity between the churches of York and Durham in the fifteenth century are briefly mentioned in R.B. Dobson, *Durham Priory, 1400–1450* (Cambridge, 1973), pp. 214–22.

to York in the late summer of 1483 has for long been interpreted as the apotheosis of the duke of Gloucester's intimate if by no means unambiguous special relationship with the citizens of York; but could it be more historically significant still that this visit marked the moment at which the duke finally gained undisputed sway over an even more influential body, the church of York itself? For the spiritual father of that church, Thomas Rotherham, such a triumph can presumably never have been anything but unwelcome, later to be forgotten as an unfortunate but transient interlude in a twenty-year-long pontificate. But for Masters Robert Booth, William Poteman and Thomas Portyngton, the powerful triumvirate of wealthy residentiary canons who actually directed the cumbersome but not unimpressive machinery of the church of York in the summer of 1483, the evidence is predictably less straightforward. Aware for many years of the need to cultivate the good favour of the north of England's *dominus specialissimus* at Middleham Castle, they were now made equally aware that as king of England that lord was in a position to become the most benevolent lay patron that York Minster could ever hope to secure. As Sir Thomas More pointed out in another Ricardian connection, 'whoso diuineth vppon coniectures, maye as wel shote to farre as to short'.[6] However, in the case of Richard III's policies and attitudes towards the church of York, it is tempting to suppose that the king's posthumous partisans may for once not have shot far enough. Neither Polydore Vergil nor – more remarkably – John Rous had any doubt that what the new monarch projected at the cathedral of the northern province deserved some explanation.[7] Admittedly, no one will now ever know precisely what did transpire at that mysterious York *concilium* held by Richard at this time, 'in quo postea quam de statu illius provinciae mature

---

[6] *The History of King Richard III*, ed. R.S. Sylvester, in *Complete Works of St Thomas More*, ii (Newhaven, 1963), p. 9.

[7] For Vergil's doubts as to whether or not Richard III genuinely adopted 'a certane new forme of lyfe' at this time, see *Three Books of Polydore Vergil*, p. 192, a passage which Charles Ross discusses twice in *Richard III* (London, 1981), pp. xxvi–xxvii, 127–8. John Rous's even more startling concession that Richard deserved praise (*laudandus*) for his religious building projects, and because 'hic Ebor' in ecclesia cathedrali nobilem cantariam centum capellanorum fundavit', is most conveniently accessible in the photograph of the relevant folio of BL, MS Cotton Vespasian A. XII, which forms plate II of Alison Hanham, *Richard III and his Early Historians* (Oxford, 1975), opposite p. 121. Distorted memories of Richard's abortive chantry project at the Minster passed into the muddy waters of later Ricardian mythology, as, for example, in the reference to *centum sacrifitiis* to be found in Act III of the play of *Richard Tertius* which Dr Thomas Legge apparently composed for a production at St John's College, Cambridge, in 1579; but there seem to be no allusions to Richard III's enterprises at York in the tediously lengthy *The Ghost of Richard III: A Poem*, published in 1614 by that city's own native poet and MP, Christopher Brooke. See *The True Tragedy of Richard III, to Which is Appended the Latin Play of Richard Tertius by Dr Thomas Legge*, ed. B. Field, Shakespeare Society (London, 1844), p. 145; and cf. *The Ghost of Richard III*, ed. J.P. Collier (London, 1844), pp. xiii, 4.

constitutum est'; but is it not most probable that it was while he was residing at the archiepiscopal palace in early September 1483 that Richard III took the first and most influential steps whereby 'he fowndyd a colledge at York of an hundreth priests'? And for Masters Booth, Portyngton and Poteman, still the only three residentiary canons of York two years later, was not the single most important consequence of the battle of Bosworth that it deprived their cathedral of the entrancing prospect of becoming the site of the most ambitious chantry foundation ever contemplated by an English king?[8]

If Richard III had much to offer the cathedral church of York, it is equally obvious that the latter had much to offer Richard of Gloucester. On 3 July 1472, only nine days before the latter's marriage to Anne Neville had committed him absolutely to residence in the north and the role of Yorkshire's outstanding magnate, the dean and chapter had celebrated the final completion of the largest Gothic building in England by a service of solemn consecration and rededication.[9] It could well be argued too that it was in the 1470s that the institutional as well as architectural development of the northern metropolitan cathedral attained its most advanced and elaborate stage. Only a decade earlier (on 11 May 1461), the Neville family had remedied the most obvious deficiency in the Minster's organisational arrangements by founding the college of St William, the most substantial college of chantry priests thereafter to be found anywhere in England; and with its thirty-six canons, thirty or so vicars choral, twenty parsons or chantry priests as well as its lesser clergy and large complement of ecclesiastical lawyers and administrators, this was a cathedral which supported – altogether appropriately – much the largest concentration of ecclesiastics in the north.[10] Nor would it have been easy, anywhere in Yorkist England, to find an ecclesiastical institution which could rival York Minster in its concentration of clerical wealth. In the absence of all but a few fragments of the individual financial records of the canons of York themselves, no estimate of the total resources at the disposal of the cathedral clergy can be anything but hazardous; but in the late fifteenth century there is every reason to believe that the annual revenues enjoyed

---

[8] *Polydore Vergili Urbinatis Anglicae historiae libri XXVI* (Basle, 1546), pp. 546–7; *Three Books of Polydore Vergil*, pp. 190, 192. The most striking example of the Minster clergy's inability to remain immune from the political pressures of the fifteenth century had occurred in May 1454 when a Percy conspiracy led to the seizure of the mayor and recorder of York while they were actually in the cathedral chapter house: R.L. Storey, *The End of the House of Lancaster* (London, 1966), pp. 142–6.

[9] YML, M 2 (4) g, fo. 47; cf. K.M. Longley and J. Ingamells, *The Beautifullest Church: York Minster, 1472–1972* (York, 1972), p. 7. The interior of the recently completed central tower of the Minster was painted in the following year: see YML, E 3/26 (Fabric Account Roll, 1473); *Minster Fabric Rolls*, p. 77; cf. C. Wilson, *The Shrines of St William of York* (York, 1977), p. 19.

[10] *CPR, 1461–67*, pp. 47, 383; See above, pp. 10–11.

by the dean and chapter still amounted to well over £2,000, of which considerably more than half was regularly directed towards the hands of the vast majority of absentee canons.[11] In the north of England dominated by Richard of Gloucester, the cathedral of York accordingly continued to function as the single most important agency for the diversion of local clerical resources to maintain the wealthy possessioners who served both church and state at the highest possible levels. This was a cathedral which could offer not only the most valuable non-episcopal office in the entire *ecclesia Anglicana*, the deanery of York Minster itself, but also the exceptionally lucrative archdeaconry of Richmond as well as a wide selection of the richest canonries available to the most distinguished clergy of the day. To take only the most famous example, during the half-century between 1447 and 1494 the 'golden' prebend of Masham was held in succession by a future archbishop of York (George Neville), a chancellor of Queen Elizabeth Wydeville (Roger Radclyff), a future bishop of Durham (John Shirwood), a future bishop of Salisbury (John Blithe) and the chaplain and confessor of Henry VII at the time of that monarch's own greatest hour of need (Christopher Urswick).[12]

That the struggle to exploit such remarkable wealth should prove to be the most continuous and troublesome theme in the late medieval history of the cathedral church of York need therefore occasion no particular surprise; and it was equally predictable that the duke of Gloucester, as the leading member of the fifteenth-century English royal family regularly resident within its diocese, should become involved in such struggles. Appropriately enough, indeed, it had been on the first recorded of his many visits to the Minster that the young Richard, still less than thirteen years old, encountered the most conspicuous public display ever made of the largesse available to those who controlled the church of York. On 22 September 1465 George Neville, accompanied by a considerably larger galaxy of bishops, abbots, earls and other magnates than that which was to enter York with Richard III eighteen years later, made his long awaited ceremonial procession to the Minster for his public investiture with the pallium and subsequent enthronement as archbishop. During the gargantuan banquet that followed the enthronement, the young Richard was protected from excessively close proximity to the hordes of Nevilles, their allies and their retainers, as the latter ate their way through 1000 muttons, 400 swans, 2000 geese and 2000 'hot custardes' as well as many more exotic 'suttleties' still, to the accompaniment of 100 tuns of wine

[11] *History of York Minster*, pp. 52–62. The large income enjoyed by the York residentiary canons of the 1470s and 1480s from their commons and – more especially – their *magne firme* can, however, be documented in detail from an exceptionally full series of surviving Minster chamberlains' accounts for those two decades (YML, E 1/45–56).

[12] J. Le Neve, *Fasti ecclesiae Anglicanae, 1300–1541*, vi, *Northern Province*, compiled by Bridget Jones (London, 1963), pp. 67–8. Cf. *BRUC*, pp. 68, 469, 605–6.

and 300 tuns of ale. However, on the main table in 'the cheefe chamber' leading from the crowded hall, room was certainly made for 'the Duke of Gloucester, the kynges brother', sitting in the company of the duchess of Suffolk and the countesses of Westmorland and Northumberland as well as of 'two of the Lorde of Warwickes daughters'; to the younger of those daughters, herself still aged less than ten, Richard was to become married – after many unexpected turns of political fortune – seven years later.[13]

Whether or not it is at all significant that the archiepiscopal enthrone-ment ceremonies and feast at York in September 1465 were unattended by King Edward IV himself, no one actually present on this much remembered day is likely to have predicted that the young Richard should so rapidly prove to be the most dangerous cuckoo in the Neville nest. A few years later, at the close of the 1460s, the mayor and aldermen of York naturally found it politic to present both the duke of Gloucester and Richard Neville, earl of Warwick, with generous quantities of red wine on their respective visits to the city;[14] but by 1472, when Richard returned to more or less regular residence in the north, the need to court the good will of what remained of the decimated junior branch of the Neville family had disappeared completely. For the next decade it was either alone, or in the company of his powerful but ambivalent political partner in the north, Henry Percy, fourth earl of Northumberland, that Richard of Gloucester presented himself to the inhabitants of York as their 'ful tendre and especiall gude lord', worthy of 'a singler confidence in your high and noble lordship a fore eny other'.[15] However, for the cathedral clergy of York in the 1470s it was undoubtedly no less important that there was no longer a Neville to welcome Richard to York Minster itself. Archbishop George Neville's active participation in the abortive dynastic counter-revolution of 1470-71 thereafter presented the English crown with the not unfamiliar political problem of a potentially powerful prelate whom it was impossible to forgive or to trust but whom it would have been extremely hazardous to thrust aside before the term of his natural life. Such considerations are the most obvious explanation for the vicissitudes

[13] Cambridge University Library, MS Ff. v. 14, fos 75–80, providing minor variants on the account of the guests, provisions and protocol at Archbishop Neville's enthronement feast (printed 'out of an old paper roll'), in John Leland, *Collectanea*, ed. Thomas Hearne (1774), vi, pp. 2–14. The preceding religious ceremonies in the Minster are described at some length in YML, A 1 (2), items ii and iii.

[14] *York City Chamberlains' Account Rolls, 1396–1500*, ed. R.B. Dobson, Surtees Society, 192 (1980), p. 126 (account for 1468–69).

[15] *YCR*, i, 23; and cf. M.A. Hicks, 'Dynastic Change and Northern Society: The Career of the Fourth Earl of Northumberland, 1470–89', *Northern History*, 14 (1978), pp. 78–107. At no time perhaps was the alliance between Gloucester and Northumberland more publicly displayed than on that remarkable occasion in March 1476 when they passed under Bootham Bar into the city of York at the head of (allegedly) no less than 5000 men (*YCR*, i, 2).

and obscurities of George Neville's personal fortunes during the five years between 1471 and his death five years later. For most of that period the archbishop seems to have lived comparatively quietly – although probably not altogether voluntarily – at the Augustinian priory of Bisham on the eastern border of Berkshire, a residence that may have 'spoken to him in more than one way of the vanity of worldly ambitions' because of its close proximity to the bodies of his parents as well as of his brothers, Richard and John, who had been buried there after the battle of Barnet.[16] Certainly George Neville seems to have made little serious attempt to revisit his see after 1471, excusing himself on grounds of ill health even from attending a meeting of the convocation of York; and it was only in May 1476 that, by a curious anticipation of the melancholy last weeks of Cardinal Wolsey two generations later, he at last set out for a final visit to his cathedral church which he proved too ill to complete. George Neville's death at Blyth in Nottinghamshire on 8 June 1476 obviously closed one period in the history of Richard of Gloucester's relationship with the church of York only to open another.[17]

Like the minority of Henry VI in the case of the realm of England, so the political eclipse of George Neville between 1471 and 1476 provides an obvious commentary on the ability of the church of York to function more or less normally despite the absence of the effective personal leadership upon which its operations were usually assumed to depend. Nevertheless, the severe limitations placed upon the disgraced archbishop's powers of personal patronage, and especially his all-important prerogative of collating to York Minster's own canonries, can hardly have failed to create novel and delicate problems for both the cathedral clergy and for the magnate at Middleham, who had suddenly become the most assiduous and formidable petitioner for that patronage. Was it perhaps primarily for this reason that in November 1473, according to a famous letter written by Sir John Paston to his brother, the duke of Gloucester's influence seemed to provide the best hope that 'my Lord Archebyshop shall come hom' from his temporary imprisonment at Guisnes?[18] But the extent to which Edward IV's policies in the 1470s were ever seriously influenced by the

[16] Much the most detailed discussion of the archbishop's last years is provided by G.I. Keir, 'The Ecclesiastical Career of George Neville, 1432–1476' (unpublished B.Litt. thesis, University of Oxford 1970), pp. 145–55. See also *Chronicles of London*, ed. C.L. Kingsford (Oxford, 1905), pp. 228, 273, 331.

[17] *Historians of the Church of York*, ed. James Raine, RS, 3 vols (London, 1879–94), ii, p. 437. Although Archbishop Neville was buried in the Minster (see below, p. 234), no trace of his tomb survives there. As Mrs Keir, 'Ecclesiastical Career of George Neville', p. 150, suggests, a possible explanation for the archbishop's otherwise surprising failure to make a last will and testament is that Edward IV never returned to him the personal possessions of which he had been deprived in 1472.

[18] *The Paston Letters*, ed. James Gairdner (1904), v, p. 199; *Paston Letters and Papers of the Fifteenth Century*, ed. N. Davis, i (Oxford, 1971), p. 472.

advice of his younger brother remains, in this as in other spheres, one of the most notoriously unresolved cruxes of both their careers. Although it seems readily apparent that the effective selection of canons of York between 1471 and 1476 passed directly to the king himself, it is a good deal less than clear that Edward IV's distribution of these prizes was much affected by Gloucester's own views.[19] One of the most persuasive elements in Professor Ross's interpretation of Richard of Gloucester's political position in the 1470s is that it was his ability to become 'the heir to the Neville affinity' which laid the foundations of his future power;[20] but in the case of Richard's ecclesiastical, as opposed to lay, affinity this was a process complicated and delayed – no doubt frustratingly – by the survival in disgrace of a Neville as archbishop of York. For the cathedral clergy at the Minster, moreover, the situation in the early 1470s must have been more difficult still. No longer able to commit their trust to their rightful spiritual lord, the disgraced archbishop, they were also deprived in these years of new recruits to the senior ecclesiastical establishment of York, recruits on whom the successful future welfare of the church of York depended. It is, for example, hardly likely to be a coincidence that during the nine years between 1468 and 1477 no members of the York chapter joined the exclusive but all-important band of residentiary canons within the Minster.[21] In such circumstances, it is hardly surprising that as early as 1474, two of the existing residentiaries, canons John Gysburgh and William Poteman, should have thought it useful and advisable to ride the 40 miles to Middleham to consult Richard of Gloucester *in negociis ecclesie*.[22] For by that date, the year in which the monks of St Cuthbert are first known to have entertained Richard on a visit to Durham and then received him into their confraternity, it was already abundantly clear to all the prelates of the province of York that Gloucester had become firmly ensconced as the most formidable, if most recent, of those northern magnates 'quos offendere non possumus'.[23]

[19] Such at least is the impression to emerge from the names of new canons admitted to their stalls between 1471 and 1476 as recorded in the contemporary York chapter act book (YML, H 2 [3], fos 142–57). Edward IV's enhanced control over appointments to prebends at Beverley Minster during this period is suggested in R.T.W. McDermid, 'The Constitution and the Clergy of Beverley Minster in the Middle Ages' (unpublished M.A. thesis, University of Durham, 1981), i, p. 285.

[20] Ross, *Richard III*, pp. 44–59; and cf. A.J. Pollard, 'The Tyranny of Richard III', *Journal of Medieval History*, iii (1977), pp. 147–66; idem, *The Middleham Connection: Richard III and Richmondshire, 1471–1485* (Middleham, 1983); R.E. Horrox, *Richard III: A Study of Service* (Cambridge, 1989).

[21] See above, pp. 203–4.

[22] This expedition to Middleham lasted three and a half days and cost £2 2s. 5d.; see YML, E 3/27; *Minster Fabric Rolls*, pp. 81–2.

[23] See above, p. 152; Dobson, *Durham Priory*, p. 172.

Nor do George Neville's archiepiscopal registers and the contemporary chapter-act book at York Minster leave any doubt that John Gysburgh and, more especially, William Poteman were the two canons in effective command of the administration of the vast archdiocese of York during the years when Richard of Gloucester first began to establish his ascendancy in the north.[24] Of the only two other residentiaries alive in that period, Master Richard Andrew, previously the first warden of All Souls College, Oxford, had been dean of York for over twenty years and was already old and comparatively inactive; he resigned the deanery in June 1477 only a few months before his death at the end of that year.[25] Dean Andrew was to be immediately preceded to the grave by his equally long-serving colleague, Master John Pakenham, residentiary at York since 1456 and holder of the exceptionally opulent treasurership of the Minster since 1459.[26] Both natives of the south of England, Andrew and Pakenham had owed their promotion at York to their secretarial and administrative services on behalf of the Lancastrian church and state. By contrast, the much less considerable figure of Canon John Gysburgh (the only York residentiary of the second half of the fifteenth century not to hold a university degree) derived his membership of the cathedral chapter from his important place in the *familia* of Archbishop William Booth, first as the latter's domestic chaplain and later as the receiver of his exchequer.[27] Although an assiduous attender of chapter meetings during his eighteen years (1463-81) as a residentiary canon at York, Gysburgh's prebend of Bugthorpe was not among the most spectacular endowments offered by the cathedral; and he never held particularly high administrative office in the diocese during his later years.

Dr William Poteman, on the other hand, has claims to be considered the most powerful ecclesiastic physically present at York throughout the twenty-five years (1468-93) he was a residentiary canon of the Minster. A Yorkshireman from Fryston north of Pontefract, it was as an Oxford canon lawyer who became fellow and subsequently warden (1459-66) of All Souls College that Poteman attracted the attention of George Neville, then chancellor of that university. As James Raine the younger first noticed over a century ago, it was in the wake of Neville's translation to York in 1465 that Poteman began to secure important preferment at the northern

[24] YML, H 2 (3), fos 142–66; and for detailed evidence that 'the chief responsibility for the diocese fell on the shoulders of William Poteman' during the last five years of George Neville's pontificate, see Keir, 'The Ecclesiastical Career of George Neville', pp. 154–64.

[25] YML, H 2 (3), fo. 159; *Testamenta Eboracensia*, ed. James Raine et al., Surtees Society, 6 vols (1836–1902), iii, pp. 232–7; *BRUO*, i, pp. 34–5.

[26] YML, H 2 (3), fo. 162; *Test. Ebor.*, iii, pp. 229–31; *BRUO*, iii, pp. 1419–20.

[27] Borthwick Institute, Reg. 20 (William Booth), fo. 49; *Test. Ebor.*, iv, p. 84; see above, pp. 213–14.

cathedral; by the end of that year he was already serving as official of the archbishop's consistory court, a position to which he was regularly reappointed for the rest of his long life.[28] As he was also vicar-general of the diocese, either alone or in co-operation with one or other of his fellow cathedral canons, throughout much of this period, Poteman rapidly became the most senior and experienced ecclesiastical administrator of the church of York. Well rewarded for his incessant labours by the wealthy prebend of Strensall, the archdeaconry of Cleveland and, later, the East Riding, as well as by his generous portions of the chapter's *communia* and farms, there were many occasions in the 1470s and 1480s when Poteman directed the affairs of the diocese of York more or less single-handedly, either from the cathedral chapter house or his own substantial *mansiones* in the Minster Close and at Strensall itself.[29] Here was a York ecclesiastic to be treated with the greatest respect, even by so powerful a magnate as Henry Percy, earl of Northumberland, in whose will of 27 July 1485 occurs a request 'that my gossep, Mr William Poteman, have a tonne of wyne of Gascoigne, yerelie duryng my lyve and his'.[30] In his own will, compiled shortly before his death early in 1493, Poteman predictably requested burial not only in the Minster he had served so assiduously for so long, but more specifically near the funeral chapel of George Neville himself.[31] This was only the last of many indications of William Poteman's special position in the cathedral as the most powerful ecclesiastical heir of the archbishop whose own executor he had been seventeen years earlier. Whatever Poteman's personal attitudes towards the duke of Gloucester, both before and after the *coup d'état* of June 1483, there can be little doubt that he was always the most influential figure in the York chapter with whom Richard had to deal.

Not perhaps that William Poteman can have remained quite as formidable a figure in the church of York after George Neville's death in June 1476 as he had been in the last years of that unhappy prelate's life. The speedy decision, presumably taken personally by Edward IV himself, to replace the deceased archbishop by a prelate who had already

[28] DCD, Reg. Parv. iii, fos 131–2; Borthwick Institute, Reg. 23 (Thomas Rotherham), fos 352–3; *Registrum Thome Rotherham*, i, ed. E. Barker, Canterbury and York Society, 69 (1976), pp. 1, 34, 47, 187, 193, 197, 217, 231, 236, 250; *Test. Ebor.*, iv, pp. 78–83; A.H. Thompson, *The English Clergy and their Organization in the Later Middle Ages* (Oxford, 1947), p. 193.

[29] *BRUO*, iii, pp. 1506–7; YML, E/147–57; YML, H 2 (3), fos 141, 201, and passim; *Reg. Rotherham*, i, pp. 21, 47, 65.

[30] 'And, aftir my disceas, duryng his lyve, two tonnes of Gascoigne wyne, to be delyverd as is aforesaid' (*Test. Ebor.*, iii, p. 308; and cf. p. 306). According to a letter which the earl wrote to the mayor of York in January 1487, Northumberland's respect for 'Maister Poteman' led him to the erroneous belief that the latter was actually dean of York Minster (*YCR*, i, p. 178).

[31] *Test. Ebor.*, iv, pp. 78–79.

been bishop of Durham for nineteen years was certainly then – if not later – unconventional. Admittedly, Bishop Lawrence Booth's rapid elevation to the archiepiscopal throne earlier held by his half-brother William can be regarded as a justifiable reward for recent loyal services performed by an ex-Lancastrian clerical partisan to the house of York;[32] but perhaps the most important political consequence of Booth's translation to the metropolitan see in the summer of 1476 was to liberate both Richard of Gloucester and Prior Richard Bell and the monks of St Cuthbert from the inhibiting and 'vexatious' activities of a bishop of Durham whom they had consistently found much less obliging than was to be his successor, William Dudley.[33] At York Minster, however, the most obvious effect of having to endure a second Booth as archbishop was to enhance the influence there of 'the widely spreading family of that name which took the church of York by storm ... and held the great posts within it without any regard to decency or propriety'.[34] James Raine's understandable distaste for the methods whereby the cathedral church of York was suddenly subjected to a dramatic invasion by the most powerful clerical affinity of the Yorkist period must certainly have been shared by many clerks and laymen of the time. For although several of the numerous descendants of Thomas Booth of Barton in south Lancashire, 'the progenitor of the most illustrious clerical lineage of the epoch', were already well known at York, it was on the elderly Lawrence Booth's elevation to the archdiocese that this invasion attained its most startling successes.[35] By the time of the archbishop's death in May 1480, one Booth was archdeacon of York, one prebendary of Ampleforth and yet another was abbot of St Mary's, the richest monastery in the north of England.[36] Of much greater consequence for the cathedral clergy of York was the particular favour shown by the archbishop to his much younger

[32] *BRUC*, pp. 78–9; R.J. Knecht, 'The Episcopate and the Wars of the Roses', *University of Birmingham Historical Journal*, 6 (1958), pp. 111–12, 115–16. An account of Archbishop Lawrence Booth's enthronement at York, on a day (8 September 1477) marred by heavy rain and muddy streets, occurs in YML, H2 (3), fos 159v–61.

[33] DCD, Reg. Parv. III, fos 128, 131–2, 133–4, correspondence upon which Professor Storey based his interpretation of Lawrence Booth as 'a polished courtier who could hide hostility under a fair mask'. See R.L. Storey, 'The North of England', in *Fifteenth-Century England, 1399–1509*, ed. S.B. Chrimes et al. (Manchester, 1972), pp. 139–41.

[34] *Test Ebor.*, iv, pp. 30–2; and for strident contemporary criticism of Archbishop William Booth, see *History of York Minster*, p. 99; and cf. A.C. Reeves, *Lancastrian Englishmen* (Washington, DC, 1981), pp. 284–330.

[35] E. Axon, 'The Family of Bothe (Booth) and the Church in the Fifteenth and Sixteenth Centuries', *Transactions of the Lancashire and Cheshire Antiquarian Society*, 53 (1938), pp. 37–47; M.J. Bennett, 'Sources and Problems in the Study of Social Mobility: Cheshire in the Later Middle Ages', *Medieval Cheshire, Transactions of the Historical Society of Lancashire and Cheshire*, 128 (1979), pp. 68, 74, 80, 85–7.

[36] *BRUC*, pp. 77–80; and for Abbot Thomas Bothe, see *CPR, 1476–85*, p. 530. Cf. *Reg. Rotherham*, i, p. 192.

and inexperienced kinsman, Robert Booth, like himself a Cambridge educated canon lawyer as well as a bastard member of a sprawling cosinage. Even before Lawrence Booth visited York for his enthronement at the Minster in September 1477, Robert Booth had become in rapid succession a canon of Beverley, a canon of York and – on the resignation of Richard Andrew – dean of the cathedral chapter itself.[37] Despite his titular headship of the chapter, *Magister Robertus Bowthe, magnus decanus ecclesie cathedralis Eboracensis*, was never to undertake as much sustained administrative responsibility as Canon William Poteman. However, he served as Archbishop Thomas Rotherham's commissary-general and as one of his vicars-general at various dates in the 1480s; and he also committed himself personally to life in the cathedral close by protesting his residence as a canon during the first year of that decade.[38] Like Canon Poteman, Robert Booth accordingly came to know Richard of Gloucester well after he became dean of York in the summer of 1477: seven years later, for example, he could have been encountered in Richard III's presence at Nottingham Castle when the king welcomed ambassadors from Scotland there in September 1484.[39]

Dean Robert Booth was accordingly a very obvious choice to serve as one of Archbishop Lawrence Booth's six executors when that elderly prelate finally made his last will in the autumn of 1479. Among his colleagues in that capacity was yet another canon of York, Master Thomas Portyngton, a clerk who also owed his high status and wealth at the Minster to the patronage of the archbishop. Portyngton, a member of a prominent gentry family of that name from Howdenshire in the East Riding, had also first become a member of the cathedral chapter during the pontificate of George Neville, who had promoted him to the prebend of Apesthorpe as long ago as the summer of 1470; but it was Archbishop Booth who made him one of the wealthiest clerks in the province of York by conferring the treasurership of the Minster upon him in October 1477.[40] Like the great majority of other treasurers of York in the fifteenth century, Portyngton too spent the rest of his career at York itself; and, shortly before the death of John Gysburgh in November 1481 created a desirable vacancy, he followed the examples of canons William Poteman and Robert Booth to become the third residentiary canon of the chapter in the summer

[37] YML, H (2) 3, fos 162–6v; *Fasti ecclesiae Anglicanae*, vi, pp. 8, 28, 91; *BRUC*, pp. 79–80.

[38] *The Register of the Guild of Corpus Christi in the City of York*, ed. R. Skaife, Surtees Society, 57 (1872), p. 108; *Reg. Rotherham*, i, pp. 1, 187, 210, 217; see above, p. 214.

[39] *Letters and Papers Illustrative of the Reigns of Richard III and Henry VII*, ed. J. Gairdner, 2 vols, RS (1861–3), i, pp. 64–7.

[40] YML, Reg. Test., i, fo. 364; *CPL*, xiii, p. 821; *Fasti ecclesiae Anglicanae*, vi, pp. 14, 30. Dr Pollard informs me that Portyngton had been in the service of Lawrence Booth during the latter's last years as bishop of Durham.

of 1481.[41] So was completed the clerical triumvirate that had already dominated the affairs of the church of York during the late 1470s and provided the effective leaders, as well as the only residentiary canons, of the cathedral throughout the reign of Richard III. Nor is there any evidence to suggest that the authority and influence of Poteman, Booth and Portyngton was at all reduced when Thomas Rotherham succeeded Lawrence Booth in the metropolitan see of St Peter in July 1480. Rotherham's translation from Lincoln to York was an entirely predictable and appropriate outcome of his services as chancellor of England during the previous six years; but the very fact that the new archbishop continued to head the royal chancery until his deprivation at the hands of Richard himself in May 1483 meant that it was unlikely he would be able to devote much of his time to diocesan affairs.[42] Although the new archbishop did travel to York for his enthronement there on 8 September 1481, an occasion at which he allegedly held a *magnum et notabile convivium*, it was to the existing Minster establishment, Canons Poteman, Booth and Portyngton, that he entrusted the day-to-day administration of his church during his absences at Westminster and his southern palaces.[43]

On all the available, if limited, evidence, these three residentiary canons showed themselves responsive and amenable to the desires of Richard of Gloucester, long before the duke's accession to the throne made those desires absolutely irresistible. Given the complete absence at York of any genuinely personal correspondence between Richard and the cathedral chapter (of which at least a few examples survive within the contemporary registers of the city of York and the prior and monks of Durham), it would be pointless to speculate too closely upon the real nature of their relationship to one another. However, it is certain that the York canons were careful to consult Gloucester on a wide variety of issues; and on at least one occasion William Poteman, as official and commissary-general of Archbishop Rotherham, allowed and may even have encouraged Richard to accept the highly unorthodox position of arbiter in a purely ecclesiastical dispute about parochial responsibilities between the abbot and convent of Selby, on the one hand, and the inhabitants of Snaith in the West Riding,

[41] YML, H (2) 3, fo. 173; cf. *Test. Ebor.*, iv, p. 85.

[42] On Rotherham's political difficulties in the summer of 1483, H.L. Bennett, *Archbishop Rotherham* (Lincoln, 1901), is less informative than the account of the archbishop's career in *BRUC*, pp. 489–91.

[43] *Historians of the Church of York*, ii, p. 439; *YCR*, i, p. 47. It was only gradually during the reign of Richard III that Rotherham's own most trusted senior ecclesiastical administrator, Master William Sheffeld, began to take on major official responsibilities at York, responsibilities for which he was later to be rewarded with the treasurership (1485–94) and then the deanery (1494–96) of the Minster (Borthwick Institute, Reg. 23, fo. 96v; *BRUC*, pp. 521–2). For the prominence of Canon Poteman and Dean Booth in the archiepiscopal vacancy of 1480, see BL, MS Cotton Galba E.X, fos 133–7v.

on the other. The subsequent award produced by Richard, completed
when he was visiting York on 15 March 1481, no doubt owed much
to 'thadvise of his counsell spirituall and temporall' but seems to evince
a genuine concern to produce a viable compromise between the two
parties in the interests of harmony within the diocese.[44] More obviously
still, the canons of York were sensitive to the advantages of using their
own patronage in the duke's interests. Thus, Miles Metcalfe of Nappa in
Wensleydale, appointed recorder of the city of York in 1477 because of his
special place in Gloucester's confidence, subsequently became the cathedral
chapter's choice as their own steward or *seneschallus*; appropriately enough,
this long-standing member of Richard's affinity was buried in York Minster
on 29 February 1486 after a career which had finally brought him, like
his own servants, 'many an evyl night and daye'.[45] Even more desirable,
however, for the new and powerful potentate of the north – with an urgent
need for administrative expertise greater than anything Wensleydale could
provide – were those members of the clerical establishment of the city and
cathedral of York prepared to join his service at Middleham. No less a
person than the future king's own secretary, John Kendal, expressed a
'singuler zele and love that I bere to you and your Cite, afore all other';
and it may even be that Kendal is either to be identified with, or was more
probably related to, the man of the same name who had been serving as the
sacrist of York Minster in 1470.[46] Yet another member of Richard's ducal
and later royal counsel who must have been well known to the cathedral
chapter was Master Nicholas Lancaster, unique among the citizens of
late medieval York in leading a prominent career which crossed all the
conventional boundaries. Admitted to the freedom of the city in 1472 as
both a *clericus et mercator*, his acquisition of a doctorate of civil law may
have made him an almost over-qualified common clerk of York between
1477 and 1480; and it was probably under the influence of Richard of
Gloucester (whom he was certainly serving as a proctor by January 1479)
that he resigned that clerkship to become an alderman and twice mayor of
York, the very mayor indeed who must have summoned that now famous
meeting in the council chamber of York on 23 August 1485 to ponder 'the

[44] *Reg. Rotherham*, i, pp. 193–95; cf. Ross, *Richard III*, p. 55.

[45] YML, E 1/47–53 (Minster Chamberlains' Accounts, *Feoda Ministrorum*); F. Drake,
Eboracum (York, 1736), p. 368; *York Chamberlains' Accounts*, pp. 125, 136, 163–4, 166–8;
YCR, i, 145, 147, 151; *Test. Ebor.*, iv, pp. 9–10.

[46] YML, H (2) 3, fo. 141v; cf. *CPR, 1476–85*, p. 324; *YCR*, i, pp. 78–9, 81, 93, 103. A
useful attempt to distinguish between 'no less than four distinct John Kendalls' of the late
fifteenth century is made, appropriately enough, in Kendall, *Richard the Third*, pp. 487–8.
It is certainly not yet established 'that the secretary was of York': see Dr Rosemary Horrox's
reservations as recorded in 'The Kendales of York', *The Ricardian*, 5 (1981), pp. 368–9, and
recently confirmed in a letter to the author.

grete hevynesse of this Citie' at the news of the battle of Bosworth on the previous day.[47]

Of all the senior members of the English clergy who must have found the result of Bosworth difficult to bear, none is likely to have been more distressed than the elderly Robert Stillington, bishop of Bath and Wells for the previous twenty years. When he was brought involuntarily to York ('sore crased, by reason of his trouble and caryng') in the immediate aftermath of Richard's death, many years had of course elapsed since this most unfortunate *mauvais évesque* of Richard III's reign had himself been a canon of York; and exactly when, where and for what reasons Bishop Stillington became the usurper's most committed episcopal ally and fellow-conspirator still remain problems as obstinately mysterious as they were to Philippe de Commynes. However, the fact that Richard should have been provided with his most ingenious if implausible claim to the English throne by a bishop who had begun his life as the son of John Stillington of Nether Acaster and the godson of a precentor of York is only the extreme example of the propensity of the vale, city and church of York to spawn the clerks who were to become the king's most trusted and well rewarded supporters.[48] Yet another, and very different, example of this phenomenon occurred early in 1484, when Richard decided to replace the deceased Bishop William Dudley of Durham by that notable humanist and royal representative at the papal curia, John Shirwood. Master Shirwood had long been familiar to both the duke of Gloucester and the inhabitants of York in two other capacities, as a son of a city common clerk and as the archdeacon of Richmond within whose spiritual jurisdiction Richard had actually resided in the preceding decade.[49]

Admittedly, neither Richard nor the York Cathedral clergy can often have had the opportunity to meet Shirwood during that decade; and to discover a senior ecclesiastical figure more likely to have been directly

---

[47] YCA, House Book B. 2–4, fo. 169v; *Register of the Freemen of the City of York*, i, ed. F. Collins, Surtees Society, 96 (1897), pp. 192, 208, 217; *York Memorandum Book*, iii, ed. J.W. Percy, Surtees Society, 186, (1973), pp. 120, 207, 218, 222–3, 247; *YCR*, i, pp. 78, 80, 106, 117, 118–19, 146.

[48] Borthwick Institute, Probate Reg. ii, fo. 149v; *Rot. Parl.*, vi, pp. 256–7; *YCR*, i, pp. 122, 164; *Fasti ecclesiae Anglicanae*, vi, pp. 49, 91; *BRUO*, iii, pp. 1777–79; and for a recent discussion of Stillington's 'elusive behaviour' and responsibility for disseminating the story of Edward IV's precontract with Lady Eleanor Butler, see M.A. Hicks, *False, Fleeting, Perjur'd Clarence: George, Duke of Clarence, 1449–78* (Gloucester, 1980), pp. 163–4.

[49] Borthwick Institute, Probate Reg. IV, fo. 118; *BRUO*, iii, pp. 1692–93; P.S. Allen, 'Bishop Shirwood of Durham and his Library', *English Historical Review*, 25 (1910), pp. 445–56. John Shirwood and Thomas Langton, 'a northerner from Appleby in Westmorland', were the only two of Richard's favoured ecclesiastics for whom vacancies on the English episcopal bench could be found in his short reign (Ross, *Richard III*, p. 133). Hugh Pavy, although selected as bishop of St David's by Richard before his death, only received consecration on 9 October 1485.

involved in maintaining good relations between the Minster and Middleham, it is tempting to follow Professor Ross's example and contemplate
the career of a northern Lincolnshire clerk well known north of the
Humber, as well as being an ex-Etonian and Cambridge canon lawyer,
Master Thomas Barowe. As Gloucester's chancellor before he mounted
the throne, and as the keeper of the great seal of England and master
of the rolls thereafter, Barowe's central executive and secretarial position
in the Ricardian regime certainly deserves more attention than it has
yet received. Nor is there any ecclesiastic of the late 1470s more likely
than Barowe to have persuaded Richard of Gloucester to become a
benevolent patron towards Cambridge University in general and the
new Queens' College in particular.[50] However, Barowe too became a
canon of York (as prebendary of Langtoft between March 1478 and
his death in 1499) – by no means a purely formal membership of
the chapter for, in February 1482, he was appointed by Archbishop
Rotherham to serve as an examiner of witnesses in the archdiocesan
consistory court presided over by none other than William Poteman.[51]
How often Thomas Barowe, heavily committed to administrative work on
the duke's behalf at Middleham, was able to exercise this duty in person is
perhaps questionable; and of all the many personal links between Richard
of Gloucester and the York Cathedral clergy in the years before and after
1483 undoubtedly the most direct were those provided by a humbler but
not at all insignificant figure, Master John Harrington. The offspring of
an impoverished cadet line of a well-known Lancashire family (his father
had settled at Eastrington near Howden), John Harrington made his way
so successfully as a Cambridge-educated notary that by early 1479 he was
not only the long-standing secretary of Sir John Conyers of Hornby, but
was also serving the consistory court at York, as both the registrar and
legal agent of – yet again – William Poteman.[52] Whether or not it was
Poteman who helped to recommend John Harrington to Richard's service,

---

[50] On 10 April 1477 Thomas Barowe had been the only clerk among the four men
licensed to grant the manor and advowson of Fulmer in Cambridgeshire to Master
Andrew Doket and the fellows of Queens' College ('that they may pray for the good
estate of the king and his consort and the king's brother Richard, duke of Gloucester, and
Anne his consort and Edward their son', *CPR, 1476–85*, p. 34). For Barowe's Cambridge
connections and services to Richard of Gloucester, see *BRUC*, pp. 40–41; Ross, *Richard III*,
pp. 58, 134, 172; A.B. Cobban, *The King's Hall within the University of Cambridge in the Later
Middle Ages* (Cambridge, 1969), pp. 291–2. Cf., for Richard III as 'the most generous of
all Queens'' benefactors', C.N.L. Brooke, 'Homage to the Lady Margaret', *Cambridge Review*,
28 (January 1983), pp. 16–17.
[51] *Fasti ecclesiae Anglicanae*, vi, p. 63; *Reg. Rotherham*, i, p. 195.
[52] *Reg. of Freemen of York*, i, p. 198; *YCR*, i, pp. 175–76; *CPL*, xiii, p. 475; R. Davies,
*Extracts from the Municipal Records of the City of York during the reigns of Edward IV, Edward V
and Richard III* (London, 1843), pp. 289–304; *Documents relating to the Foundation and
Antiquities of the Collegiate Church of Middleham*, ed. William Atthill, Camden Society, old
series, 38 (1847), pp. 65, 78–9.

he certainly became one of the latter's most trusted intimates, to the extent of holding the position of clerk to the royal council by the end of 1483. Pressed by the king upon a somewhat reluctant York city council as their new common clerk in 1484, it was to be a considerable irony that during the following year Harrington proved to the indispensable agent of the mayor and aldermen in the unenviable task of winning them the good will of Henry Tudor.[53] Of all the many invaluable contact men who characterised Richard of Gloucester's rule as 'lord of the north' and, later, as 'northerners' king', Master John Harrington's links with both York and Middleham, both Archbishop Rotherham and the duke, both city council and cathedral chapter, made him the most ubiquitous of all. What more appropriate than that Richard III should eventually select him to be custodian of the records of his single greatest and most ambitious project, the college of chantry priests at York?[54]

Five years, however, before that particularly intoxicating possibility emerged, John Harrington – in the company of John Kendal, Nicholas Lancaster, Robert Booth, William Poteman and many other members of the cathedral church of York – had already become thoroughly involved in what was always to be remembered (despite its ultimate failure) as Richard's single most famous ecclesiastical foundation as duke of Gloucester.[55] Like his future and much more grandiose plans at York, and like so many of his lesser acts of religious patronage, the conversion of the rectory of Middleham into a collegiate church during the late 1470s can legitimately be used as evidence 'that Richard's interest in religion was sincere rather than cynical'.[56] But, if sincere, Richard III's religious initiatives were undoubtedly often erratic, unrealistic and even capricious, providing perhaps an accurate reflection of the personality of a king who was less the most calculating than the most impetuous monarch ever to sit on the English throne. Thus, of the two projected chantry foundations which were occupying the attention of the lord of Middleham in the early months of 1478, it was apparently to the college within the chapel of his recently acquired Barnard Castle on the River Tees that he first gave

[53] *YCR*, i, pp. 93, 109, 111, 133, 134, 142, 150, 165, 166–69; *York Chamberlains' Accounts*, pp. 183–86, 188.

[54] *British Library, Harleian Manuscript 433*, ed. R.E. Horrox and P.W. Hammond, 4 vols (Gloucester, 1979–83), i, pp. 247–48. Dr Horrox informs me that the William Harrington who held prebends at Wells and St Paul's Cathedral at this period can be proved to be John Harrington's brother.

[55] *Documents relating to Middleham*, pp. 63, 65, 66–81. For a very influential but often confused account of the foundation of the college, see C.A. Halsted, *Richard III* (1844), i, pp. 335–8.

[56] Ross, *Richard III*, p. 136. On the copious evidence, admittedly often ambiguous, for Richard's piety – as presented, for example, in P. Tudor-Craig, *Richard III* (London, 1973), pp. 23–9 – it would not be difficult to argue that he anticipated the later dynamic royal 'religious ideology' discussed in A. Goodman, 'Henry VII and Christian Renewal', *Studies in Church History*, 17, ed. K. Robbins (Oxford, 1981), pp. 116–25.

the higher priority. With its proposed complement of a dean, twelve chaplains, ten clerks, six choristers and a sacristan, to be supported by an endowment of 400 marks a year from landed rents, the college of Barnard Castle fleetingly promised to become the most ambitious late medieval chantry establishment in the palatinate of Durham.[57] By contrast, Richard's 'College within my Town of Middelham at the parrishe church there' was only intended to comprise a dean, six chaplains, four clerks, six choristers and a sacristan, for whose maintenance it was somewhat optimistically supposed that an annual income of only 200 marks might suffice.[58] At Middleham, as apparently not at Barnard Castle, Richard did however take steps to convey to his new college various rent-generating properties which may have approximated in value to the actual sum he was licensed to alienate.[59]

More interestingly still, the Middleham College statutes produced on 4 July 1478 provide the single most detailed, if at times heavily conventionalised, guide that survives to what may have been the personal religious tastes and proclivities of the future king. With their emphasis on continual residence as well as 'sufficient learning' on the part of the dean, these statutes also envisaged the future promotion to that office of suitable candidates from among the four fellows with whom Richard III had augmented Master Andrew Doket's new foundation of Queens' College, Cambridge, in the previous year.[60]

Nor, and despite Richard's somewhat unexpected preference for the Use of Salisbury rather than of York (for which special licence had to be obtained from the archbishop and chapter of York), do those statutes leave any doubt of the founder's religious as well as political identification with the north of England. Of the thirty-five annual saints' days to be celebrated by double feasts at the Middleham College (on the grounds that these were 'suche saints as that I have devocion unto'), only five had been natives of

---

[57] The licences to found the two chantry colleges of Barnard Castle and Middleham were issued by Edward IV on the same day (21 February 1478: *CPR, 1476–85*, p. 67); but the unnamed college of a dean and twelve priests which Richard had 'purposed' to endow at the parliament which had assembled in January 1478 was undoubtedly that at Barnard Castle (*Rot. Parl.*, vi, pp. 172–3).

[58] *CPR, 1476–85*, p. 67; *Documents relating to Middleham*, pp. 61–3.

[59] I owe this information, based on his careful reading of the unlisted Middleham College Deeds now deposited at the North Yorkshire RO, Northallerton, to the generosity of Dr Michael Hicks. According to Dr Hicks, it seems that Richard proposed to endow his Middleham College with many of the confiscated estates of John de Vere, earl of Oxford, granted to the duke in 1471.

[60] These statutes were printed from what seems to be the unique copy, now deposited at the North Yorkshire RO, by James Raine, 'The Statutes . . . for the College of Middleham, Dated July 4, 1478', *Archaeological Journal*, 14 (1857), pp. 160–70. For evidence that by January 1483 the archbishops of York, or their deputies as presidents of the Minster chapter, had begun to exercise their rights to confirm the election of provosts of Queens' College, see *Reg. Rotherham*, i, p. 197.

the British Isles; but of those five, St Wilfrid of Ripon and St William of York were at least obvious stars amidst the limited galaxy of northern saints. Even more significantly, the select list of four saints mentioned in the Middleham statutes as worthy recipients of principal feasts in the college's observances included not only Saints Antony and George but also the Northumbrian St Cuthbert and – most surprisingly, not least for his interesting political implications – the Scottish St Ninian.[61] As, during the late 1470s, archbishops Booth and Rotherham, canons Poteman and Booth, Masters Kendal and Harrington, as well as many others, undertook the laborious bureaucratic work of approving and licensing the emergent *collegium decani et capellanorum Ricardi ducis Gloucestrie*, they could at least be confident that the saints to be invoked there would include many who were much more central to the public image of the church of York than had been the hopelessly obscure Gloucestershire martyr St Alkelda or Arild, to whom the parish church of Middleham had been dedicated in earlier and less exciting times.

However, there were many, by no means mutually self-exclusive, reasons for founding an intercessory chantry college in fifteenth-century England; and the time has come to draw attention to the intriguing figure of the single most important clerical beneficiary of Richard's generosity, Master William Beverley, the rector and then first dean of Middleham itself. To an extent still perhaps insufficiently appreciated, this dean deserves to be remembered as both the most spectacularly rewarded and also, alas, as the most inscrutable of Richard III's 'fulle trusty clercs and counsellors'. It is certainly not at all inconceivable that William Beverley began life as a member of the prominent mercantile family of that surname in the city of York, and perhaps even as a son of Thomas Beverley senior, who had served his second term as mayor in 1472-73, eight years before his death in 1480.[62] But precisely how and when Master William Beverley came to study canon law at Cambridge and – with much greater consequence – to attract the enthusiastic benevolence of Richard of Gloucester remain highly mysterious issues. In the formal document he produced

---

[61] 'The Statutes . . . for Middleham', pp. 167–70; cf. P.W. Hammond and A.F. Sutton, *Richard III: The Road to Bosworth Field* (1985), pp. 79–80. For the similarly revealing names assigned to the college's stalls, see J.M. Melhuish, *The College of King Richard III, Middleham*, Richard III Society (n.d.), p. 7.

[62] *Documents relating to Middleham*, pp. 7, 13–14, 64–5; *Harleian Manuscript 433*, ii, p. 94. In his will of 11 August 1480 (Borthwick Institute, Probate Reg. v, fo. 184, only partly summarised in *Test. Ebor.*, iii, p. 196), Mayor Thomas Beverley bequeathed 40s. 0d. to his son William. For the blood relationships of the Beverley family of York with other members of the city's oligarchic elite, see J.I. Kermode, 'The Merchants of Three Northern Towns', *Profession, Vocation and Culture in Later Medieval England*, ed. C.H. Clough (Liverpool, 1982), pp. 18, 20. However, the surname 'Beverley' was by no means uncommon in fifteenth-century Yorkshire, and Dr Horrox notes that according to Duchy of Lancaster records, several men of that name held parkerships at Middleham in the 1460s and 1470s.

at York on 20 January 1479 to confirm his assent to the duke's transformation of his church into a college, the rector of Middleham had styled
himself simply as *capellanus* and stated that he then had no authentic seal
of his own.[63] Less than five years later, William Beverley was to find his
fortunes changed more dramatically than those of any clerk in England.
During the summer of 1483 Beverley had already been presented to one
of their Howden prebends by the obliging prior and chapter of Durham;
but it was a more important portent of things to come that within a few
weeks of Edward IV's death on 9 April 1483, and before he seized the
throne himself in early July, Richard was already embarrassing Prior
William Selling of Christ Church, Canterbury, with the unexpected request
that the prestigious rectory of All Hallows, Lombard Street, London,
should pass to the dean of his chapel; despite the wishes of the late king
and Queen Elizabeth Wydeville for an alternative pre-existing candidate
('born in our cuntre, and all the nobles of our cuntre desyrid me the
same'), Beverley was in fact to hold the rectory of All Hallows before too
long.[64] Even more magnificent prizes were to come Beverley's way during
the subsequent autumn; and on 11 October 1483 this most favoured of
the king's chaplains was appointed not only canon and prebendary of
St Stephen's Chapel, Westminster, but also dean of St George's Chapel,
Windsor. As William Beverley received a royal grant of the deanery of
the collegiate church of Wimborne in Dorset at about this time, and also
acquired the rectory of Stanhope in Weardale as well as a canonry at the
bishop of Durham's collegiate church of St Andrew Auckland, it is hard
indeed to believe that any clerk of Richard III's England was in more
urgent need of the papal dispensations to hold incompatible benefices for
which he petitioned in 1483 and 1484.[65]

The reasons for Richard III's extraordinary promotion of William
Beverley's career are no doubt always likely to be a matter for tantalising
conjecture: certainly none of the routine administrative services Beverley
is known to have performed for his master would seem to warrant

[63] *Documents relating to Middleham*, pp. 64–5. William Beverley is recorded as entering
the canon law faculty at Cambridge only in 1482–83 (*BRUC*, p. 60); but he was styled a
bachelor of decrees at York Minster by 1484 (YML, H 2 [3], fo. 180v).

[64] *Reg. Rotherham*, i, 173; cf. ibid., p. 176; *Christ Church Letters*, ed. J.B. Sheppard,
Camden Society, new series, 19 (1877), pp. 44–5. The vacancy at All Hallows had been
created by what must have been the duke's own decision to promote Thomas Langton to
the bishopric of St David's, ibid., pp. 44–5; *Harleian Manuscript 433*, i, pp. 34–6; *BRUO*, ii,
pp. 1101–2. William Beverley was presented to the church by Prior Selling and the Christ
Church chapter on 13 October 1483, Canterbury Cathedral Archives, Reg. S, fo. 328v; but
he had resigned it by the following June (ibid., fo. 333).

[65] *CPL*, xiii, p. 863; *CPR, 1476–85*, pp. 367, 373; *1485–94*, pp. 24, 472; *Harleian
Manuscript 433*, i, pp. 91, 189; *BRUC*, p. 60; *Fasti Dunelmenses*, Surtees Society, 139 (1926),
pp. 14, 183.

such exceptionally preferential treatment.[66] But of all the offices and benefices which Beverley owed to Richard, the most important for his own future proved to be a dignity in the cathedral church of York itself. On 20 December 1483 the three Minster residentiary canons, Booth, Poteman and Portyngton, assembled in their chapter house to determine a date for the admission of William Beverley as precentor of their cathedral, an office to which he had just been collated by Archbishop Rotherham; two days later it was William Poteman himself who served as Beverley's proctor at the admission ceremony, four months before the new precentor was able to appear at York to be admitted *in propria persona*.[67] A much more remarkable demonstration of the way in which the church of York was prepared – or compelled – to alter its time-hallowed constitutional arrangements in the interests of Richard III's most favoured clerk was to emerge during the course of the following summer. Until William Beverley made his entry into the York chapter in 1483, the precentorship of the Minster had always been one of the least valuable benefices or dignities the cathedral had to offer;[68] but at his palace of Bishopthorpe on 20 July 1484, and in the presence of the ubiquitous William Poteman and other members of the cathedral clergy, Archbishop Rotherham formally agreed to augment the revenues of the precentor and chancellor of York Minster very considerably indeed by annexing inseparably to those two dignities the wealthy cathedral prebends of Driffield and Laughton respectively.[69] The reasons for this last major change to the administrative structure of the cathedral church of York before the Reformation are not hard to surmise; on the death of the existing prebendary of Driffield, Master James Stanley, in the course of the following year, William Beverley was first collated and then admitted (on 25 July 1485) to that prebend, henceforward 'united, annexed and incorporated' to the precentorship he already held.[70] As it transpired, Beverley's constitutional and financial position at York Minster had been made secure in the proverbial nick of time. Systematically stripped of all his influence and many of his southern benefices in the immediate aftermath of Bosworth, he then retreated to the cathedral he had probably seen so comparatively little while his great patron was alive. From December 1485

[66] For Beverley's appointment as one of the assigns of a Norfolk manor later to revert to the collegiate church of Plessey in Essex, see *Harleian Manuscript 433*, i, p. 241; *CPR, 1476–85*, p. 509.

[67] YML, H (2) 3, fo. 180.

[68] According to the *Taxatio ecclesiastica ... Nicholai IV*, Record Commission (1802), pp. 297–8, the annual value of the York Minster precentorship was only £16 13s 4d., as compared with the dean's £373 6s. 8d., the treasurer's £233 6s. 8d. and even the subdean's £53 6s. 8d; see *History of York Minster*, pp. 53–7.

[69] Borthwick Institute, Reg. 23, fos 99v–100v, a lengthy document of which there is no attempt to calendar the contents in *Reg. Rotherham*, i, p. 96.

[70] Borthwick Institute, Reg. 23, fos 99; YML, H 2 (3), fos 184v–5.

onwards William Beverley became a regular attender at York Minster chapter meetings; and eight years later, in the summer of 1493, he even took the important step of deciding to become a residentiary canon himself.[71] But by this terminal stage of his erratic career, Beverley's good fortune had completely deserted him. It was while performing his major residence within the Minster Close in the last months of 1493 that he contracted the then prevalent disease *vocata Swetyngseknes* and died in the following January.[72] In the will William Beverley composed on his death-bed, which received probate by the cathedral chapter on 16 January 1494, there was naturally no mention of the late king to whom he had owed his meteoric rise to prominence; but in expressing a hope that he might be buried either at the Minster or the collegiate church of Middleham (where he requested his executors to arrange for a priest to celebrate masses for his soul), Richard III's favourite clerk at least made a final and valedictory gesture towards the now obliterated connection between the duke of Gloucester and the church of York.[73]

When, over ten years earlier, Archbishop Rotherham, William Poteman and their colleagues had attempted to justify their furtherance of William Beverley's financial interests by annexing the prebend of Driffield to the precentorship of the Minster, they had laid particular emphasis on their reluctance to displease

'our most Christian prince, King Richard III, who has restored the accustomed number of vicars in our said church after these had been diminished because of the poverty of their rents and possessions, and who has also founded and ordained a most celebrated college of a hundred chaplains, primarily at his own costs and expenses, in that said church of ours.'[74]

Although the archbishop and his canons were certainly correct to place special emphasis upon these two most remarkable acts of Ricardian patronage towards their cathedral, they were by no means the only ways in which the church of York benefited from the king's short reign. In the event, the Minster's most enduring memorial of Richard's long visit to York early in September 1483 proved to be an item recorded in the lengthy

[71] William Beverley is not recorded as present at the meeting of the York chapter on 3 November 1485; but he appeared at Minster chapters regularly thereafter (H 2 [3], fos 186v, 187, 191, 195v, 196v, 206r). As 'clerk of Midilham, *alias* clerk of York' he had received various pardons from Henry VII during the course of 1486, *CPR, 1485–94*, pp. 39, 126, 141.

[72] YML, H 2 (3), fo. 207.

[73] YML, Reg. Test., ii, fo. 4v. The folio on which Beverley's will was copied has been rendered partly illegible by damp; but its other most interesting feature seems to be a request that his kinsman, Thomas Beverley, should be supported 'ex bonis meis vel in universitate vel in civitate London' ad jus temporale'.

[74] Borthwick Institute, Reg. 23, fos 99v–100v.

inventory of the cathedral's precious plate and vestments compiled some twenty years later; but even that 'great cross standing on six bases . . . with images of the crucifixion and the two thieves, together with other images near the foot and many precious stones, rubies and sapphires, *ex dono regis Ricardi Tercii'*, was not to survive its donor indefinitely.[75] By a more mundane act of generosity, which parallels his now intensively studied but undoubtedly over-hasty remission of their fee-farm to the sheriffs and citizens of York, in March 1484 Richard III had also exonerated Dean Robert Booth and his colleagues, canons Poteman, Portyngton and John Hert, for life from the obligation to pay all 'tenths, fifteenths and other subsidies or aids granted to the king'.[76] At the end of that year, too, Richard's solution to the genuinely acute financial difficulties of the Minster's college of vicars choral ('th' occasion whereof is by reason of decaye of landes and revenues of the cytie of York, beyng sore in ruyne and decaye') had taken concrete form in the shape of a grant to those vicars of the advowson of the wealthy church of Cottingham in the East Riding. At the end of transactions no doubt facilitated by the fact that the existing rector of Cottingham was none other than Richard III's master of the rolls, Thomas Barowe, the York vicars had already begun to appropriate the church's revenues to themselves before the battle of Bosworth deprived them of it for ever.[77]

Richard III's abortive attempt to rescue the vicars-choral of York Minster from increasing penury self-evidently belongs to that voluminous category of the king's 'proposyd practyses' which began 'straightway to coom to naught'.[78] So too, of course, does Richard's proposed York 'college of an hundreth priests', a venture so exceptionally ambitious that it must always raise greater and more baffling problems of interpretation. It is all the more frustrating that the number of contemporary or near-

[75] *Minster Fabric Rolls*, p. 219, and cf. (for 'a blacke vestement of velvet with a grene cross, of Kinge Richard's') ibid., p. 312.

[76] *Harleian Manuscript 433*, i, p. 158; *CPR, 1476–85*, p. 378; cf. Lorraine Attreed, 'The King's Interest: York's Fee Farm and the Central Government, 1482–92', *Northern History*, 17 (1981), pp. 30–1. Not irrelevant in this connection is the unique distinction of Richard III's monarchy as the only reign in late medieval England when the northern province escaped clerical taxation completely. Accordingly, there was no meeting of the convocation of York between 1481 and 1487, whereas the less fortunate clerical representatives of the southern province met twice in Richard's reign (February 1484; February–March 1485) to grant a tenth on each occasion: see A.K. McHardy, 'Clerical Taxation in the Fifteenth Century: The Clergy as Agents of the Crown', *The Church, Politics and Patronage in the Fifteenth Century*, ed. R.B. Dobson (Gloucester, 1984), pp. 181, 188.

[77] The well-documented and complicated manoeuvres which accompanied this abortive appropriation deserve further exploration; but meanwhile, see *Harleian Manuscript 433*, i, pp. 203, 245; *CPR, 1476–85*, p. 507; *Reg. Rotherham*, i, pp. 250–1; F. Harrison, *Life in a Medieval College* (London, 1952), pp. 109–11.

[78] *Three Books of Polydore Vergil*, p. 192.

contemporary references to this college yet discovered, all of them cryptic to a degree, can be counted on the fingers of two hands. As it is, five highly abbreviated entries in Harleian MS 433 seem (at least at present) to be the only surviving traces of what must once have been a considerable crown archive relating to this extraordinary foundation at York. Paradoxically enough, it was probably Richard's own decision to instruct the clerk of the hanaper 'to delyver alle suche lettres patentes as apperteigne to the C. prestes of York unto Master John Harringtone without fyne or fee' that has deprived his later admirers of the opportunity of eulogising his most magnificent religious project.[79] Nor are the surviving records of the church of York itself much more informative: apart from three isolated allusions to Richard's college in Archbishop Rotherham's register (20 July 1484), Canon William Poteman's will (8 February 1493) and the solitary surviving Minster fabric account roll for the reign (November 1484–November 1485), the silence of the available ecclesiastical sources is an only too familiar comment on their notorious capacity to be voluminous without becoming genuinely revealing.[80] In the face of such grave evidential *lacunae*, and in the even more serious absence of a surviving copy of the college's statutes (if such were in fact ever drafted), it is impossible to determine precisely how and when the foundation began and – equally important – whether it was prosecuted very vigorously thereafter on the part of a king later and correctly diagnosed by More and Holinshed as 'somewhat above his power liberall'. Nevertheless, the fragmentary references which do survive make it sufficiently clear that although Richard intended his college to be separately endowed, at least in part from the profits of the duchy of Lancaster, he entrusted much of the responsibility 'for the leveying of almanere Rentes and duties apperteignyng to the C prestes at Yorke' to the indispensable team of Dean Booth and canons Poteman, Portyngton and Hert.[81] By at least the late summer of 1485, six new altars had been constructed within the Minster for the new *capellani domini regis*, and by the same date, too, the building of their collegiate house or *domus* must have been begun, if not completed, for some of the timbers from that soon-to-be redundant building were later to come into the possession of (almost inevitably, one might well think) Canon William Poteman.[82] Whether any at all of the projected hundred priests ever actually began to worship in the Minster before Richard's death put an end to that possibility is a good deal less than certain; and of those

[79] *Harleian Manuscript 433*, i, pp 201, 221, 242, 247–8, 267.
[80] Borthwick Institute, Reg. 23, fos 99v–100v; *Test. Ebor.*, iv, p 79; YML, E 3/30; *Minster Fabric Rolls*, p. 87. Cf. A.H. Thompson, 'The Registers of the Archbishops of York', *Yorkshire Archaeological Journal*, 32 (1935), pp. 254–7.
[81] *Harleian Manuscript 433*, i, p. 267.
[82] *Test. Ebor.*, iv, p. 79.

chaplains' proposed responsibilities nothing at all is known except that they were to celebrate masses for Richard III and his immediate kindred as well as to pray to 'God, oure lady, seint George and seint Nynyan'.[83] It is hardly likely to be coincidental that at York, as earlier at Middleham, Richard wished to glorify a Scottish saint whose successors in the see the saint had founded at Whithorn in Galloway had so often been ready to accept their subservience to the church and province of York. What interesting issues of high and metropolitan church politics, one wonders, were discussed in that intriguing *concilium* at the Minster chapter house in early September 1483?[84]

In at least some aspects of his massive chantry foundation at the cathedral of York, it would accordingly seem that Richard III knew his own mind. But did he do so in all the others? On the whole, and making due allowances for a monarch who so often made improvisation the cardinal principle of his rule, it is probable that he did. No king of his age could conceivably have remained immune from the passionate enthusiasm for spectacular chantry foundations which swept western Europe in the second half of the fifteenth century; and it might even be argued that the least controversial service Richard himself had ever performed for his own house of York was to supervise the carrying of the corpses of his father and brother Edmund from Pontefract to his family's collegiate mausoleum of Fotheringhay in the summer of 1476.[85] Even in the Yorkshire he had come to make his own Richard had not far to look – to the colleges of

[83] *Harleian Manuscript 433*, i, p. 201.

[84] Cf. the altar dedicated to St Ninian recorded at York Minster in 1483 (YML, M2 [2] c; *Minster Fabric Rolls*, p. 305). The York cathedral chapter had for the previous three centuries managed to avoid formally accepting the papal decision of 1192 that all the Scottish sees except Whithorn should be directly subservient to the papacy rather than their metropolitan church; and that the York canons tried to persuade Richard III of the validity of their stance on this controversial issue is suggested by the inclusion in *Harleian Manuscript 433* (iii, pp. 76–98) of the lengthy notarial instrument they had produced on 13 November 1464 to provide precedents for York's spiritual hegemony over the Scottish church. Richard's interest in this ecclesiastical claim to jurisdictional supremacy is hardly likely to have been diminished after Cumberland, Westmorland 'and whatever parts of south-west Scotland he might conquer' were transformed into a palatine lordship for himself and his heirs in January 1483 (*Rot. Parl.*, vi, pp. 204–5; Charles Ross, *Edward IV* (London, 1974), p. 202). A generation later, Henry VIII's first reaction to the news of Surrey's great victory at Flodden in 1513 was to write to Pope Leo X with the request that the cathedral of St Andrews should be deprived of its comparatively new metropolitan status: see R.B. Dobson, 'The Last English Monks on Scottish Soil', above, p. 133. For the (eventually successful) attempts of the late fifteenth-century archbishops of York to enforce suffragan status upon the bishops of Man, see D.M. Smith, *Guide to Bishops' Registers of England and Wales*, Royal Historical Society (1981), p. 274.

[85] Hammond and Sutton, *Richard III and Bosworth Field*, pp. 64–7. A parallel between 'the great Yorkist centre of Fotheringhay' and Richard's proposed chantry college at Barnard Castle is made in E.F. Jacob, *The Fifteenth Century, 1399–1485* (Oxford, 1961), p. 609.

Acaster Selby and of Rotherham in particular – to discover novel chantry foundations recently completed by prelates now at his own service and in his own mercy.[86] But for those who wish to undertake the hazardous business of surmising what Richard III's religious aims and objectives at York in the autumn of 1483 really were, there are two more obvious, impressive and instructive analogies still. For neither the ultimate political nor the religious purposes of the royal chapels of St George at Windsor and of Henry VII at Westminster have ever been in any doubt at all.

During the first week of September 1483, at exactly the time when Richard III was celebrating his acquisition of the English crown at York, the corpse of another famous monarch (who had expired on 30 August) was being prepared for burial at his specially reconstructed funeral collegiate chapel of Cléri on the Loire. Like Richard III, Louis XI of France was notoriously the master of the erratically unexpected; and in selecting as his final resting-place a chantry foundation one hundred miles away from Saint-Denis, he showed himself prepared to break one of the most important and continuous dynastic traditions in the history of the French monarchy.[87] During that same decade Fernando V of Aragon and Isabel I of Castile were similarly busily engaged in converting the Franciscan convent now known as St Juan de los Reyes of Toledo into an even more magnificent mausoleum for themselves.[88] Like Louis XI and the Catholic monarchs of Spain, if in very different ways, Richard III departed from some not unimportant royal conventions five centuries ago. Whether or not that monarch, 'unique among medieval English kings in the extent of his connections with the north of England',[89] might have become unique among all English kings in being buried within the 'capital of the north' remains a hypothetical and perhaps therefore illegitimate question. But when, on 15 March 1485 and only five months before the battle of Bosworth, Dean Booth and Canons Poteman and Portyngton

[86] *Rot. Parl.*, vi, pp. 256–7; *Early Yorkshire Schools*, ii, ed. A.F. Leach, Yorkshire Archaeological Society, Record Series, 33 (1903), pp. 89–96, 104–31. For Richard's own minor chantry foundations and augmentations, see M.E. Williams, 'Richard III: Chantry Founder', *Notes and Queries*, 168 (1934), pp. 23–5, and the comments in Ross, *Richard III*, pp. 129–31. Canon Poteman and his colleagues had been very involved in the creation of Dean Richard Andrew's large perpetual chantry in York Minster as recently as 1476 (*CPR, 1467–77*, p. 569); YML, L2(2)a, fos 150–1; S.E. McManaway, 'Some Aspects of the Foundation of Perpetual Chantries in York Minster' (unpublished M.A. thesis, University of York, 1981), pp. 90–101.

[87] Thomas Basin, *Histoire de Louis XI*, ed. Charles Samaran, iii (Paris, 1972), pp. 339, 363.

[88] In the event, the funeral monuments of *Los Reyes Catolicos* were transferred to the even more recently constructed Capilla Real in Granada, a salutary reminder that in the matter of choosing their terrestrial burial places, late medieval kings (not least Richard III himself) might have been wise to leave their options open.

[89] Ross, *Richard III*, p. 44.

summoned Mayor Nicholas Lancaster and the aldermen of York into the choir of the Minster to inform them of Innocent VIII's election and to convey the new pope's blessings on 'his subjects, especially our soveraine lord of the Realm, King Richard', is it not overwhelmingly most likely that they meant what they were required to say?[90]

[90] YML, H 2/2 (Memorandum Book, 1468–84), fos 12v–13v; H 2 (3), fos 183–4. I am most grateful to Dr Rosemary Horrox, Dr A.J. Pollard and Dr D.M. Smith for their helpful comments on this essay.

11

The Foundation of Perpetual Chantries by the Citizens of Medieval York

It has long been a truism that the chantry priest, rather than the monk, friar, or member of a large collegiate church, is the most significant figure if we wish to understand how organised religion affected the lives of most citizens of most medieval English towns. Miss Wood-Legh, in her *Perpetual Chantries in Britain*, has provided a detailed demonstration of the sustained interest taken by founders, prelates, parishioners and corporate bodies in the effective administration and continued welfare of the perpetual chantry. Miss Wood-Legh justifiably describes her work as the 'first detailed study in English of the chantry as an institution',[1] and its publication ought to lead to a long-overdue investigation of the exact social and economic, as well as religious, role of the medieval chantry. The hope expressed by Professor Hamilton Thompson over eighty years ago, 'that the student of chantry history may possess a more complete and compact apparatus for his work than is at present within his reach',[2] has been largely unfulfilled, not least in York itself. The detailed history of many York chantries, as well as their precise status within the religious and civic establishment of the city, still remains obscure. But the names of the great majority of individuals who founded chantries inside the walls of York are already known; and it is possibly not too soon to attempt a preliminary survey of the general patterns of perpetual chantry foundation within the late medieval city. Professor Hamilton Thompson himself stressed 'the close relation between the growth of the chantry system and the growth of the middle class';[3] and Professor Dickens has written of the multiplication of chantries 'as an aspect of the rise of a middle class: here the hard-headed and unsentimental businessmen of the middle ages had given their most impressive witness to the Faith'.[4] What are the results of applying these generalisations, however tentatively and briefly, to the singularly well-recorded example of medieval York?

When Edward VI's commissioners visited York in 1548, they recorded

[1] K.L. Wood-Legh, *Perpetual Chantries in Britain* (Cambridge, 1965), p. ix.

[2] 'The Chantry Certificates for Leicestershire', ed. A.H. Thompson, *Associated Architectural Societies, Reports and Papers*, 30 (1909–10), p. 486.

[3] A.H. Thompson, *The English Clergy and their Organisation in the Later Middle Ages* (Oxford, 1947), p. 139.

[4] A.G. Dickens, *The English Reformation* (London, 1964), p. 207.

the names of thirty-eight perpetual chantries in the cathedral (of which over a quarter were served by more than one priest) and another thirty-nine dispersed among nineteen parish churches or chapels within the city.[5] Although it is impossible to overestimate the value of the York chantry certificates for the study of the history of these foundations, it is clear that they alone, compiled on the eve of the final dissolution, are an inadequate guide to the number and importance of chantries in the fourteenth and fifteenth-century city. Several York chantries, although it would be difficult to estimate exactly how many, had decayed or been abruptly dissolved during the fifty or so years immediately preceding the two Chantries acts of 1545 and 1547: seven had been suppressed by act of parliament in April 1536 at the official request of the city.[6] More alarmingly, there is reason to believe that the Henrician and Edwardian commissioners not only occasionally confused one chantry with another, but also omitted to survey those located within several parishes altogether, possibly on the grounds that the churches in question were about, or so they assumed, to be abolished.[7] The historian of York chantries must therefore cast his net a good deal more widely than did the commissioners of the 1540s, and is immediately confronted with the extremely difficult problem of estimating the total number of foundations ever made within the city. Despite, and indeed largely because of, the extremely numerous references to York chantries in contemporary records (most notably in the archbishops' registers, the royal patent rolls, the wills of York citizens and the corporation's muniments), this is a notoriously difficult undertaking. Even the information assembled by the editor of the Victoria County History volume devoted to the city, and inserted in the accounts of parish churches within that work, can only be regarded as a provisional, if extremely valuable, guide to the number of York chantries. However it can be said with some reasonable degree of accuracy that record has been

---

[5] *Yorkshire Chantry Surveys (YCS)*, ed. W. Page, Surtees Society (1892–3), ii, pp. 428–73. An identical number of city chantries had been surveyed by the Henrician commissioners two years previously (ibid., i, pp. 5–84); but whereas Richard Wateby's chantry of St Katherine in St John's, Ouse Bridge End, was not included in the 1546 returns, that of William Langtoft in Holy Trinity, Goodramgate, failed to appear in 1548 (ibid. i, p. 53; ii, p. 459).

[6] *York Civic Records*, ed. A. Raine, Yorkshire Archaeological Society, Record Series (1939–53), iv, p. 144; A.G. Dickens, 'A Municipal Dissolution of Chantries, 1536', *Yorkshire Archaeological Journal*, 36 (1944–7), pp. 164–73. Four of these seven chantries appeared, with their incumbents, in the *Valor Ecclesiasticus* of the preceding year. The *Valor* (v, pp. 25–30) listed a total of forty chantries within York city churches and chapels but failed to survey several parishes, including two (Holy Trinity, Goodramgate and St Michael, Spurriergate) which were considered in 1546 and 1548.

[7] The York certificates recorded no chantries in the parishes of All Saints, North Street, St Martin's, Coney Street, and St Martin's Micklegate; and it would seem dangerous to assume as, e.g., in VCH, *City of York* (1961), p. 388, that the numerous chantries known to have existed within these churches had all decayed by the 1540s.

discovered of approximately 140 different perpetual chantry foundations within the city walls; and it now seems unlikely that future research will be able to add more than a very few new names to this total number.[8]

More than a third of all these York chantries were attached to the many altars within the Minster and can, from the standpoint of the York citizen, be largely disregarded.[9] Professor Jacob once likened the medieval cathedral, 'not only in appearance, but constitutionally', to 'a great ship with many decks or compartments';[10] and it seems clear that most of the inhabitants of York regarded the metropolitan church of St Peter with the same mixture of respect and indifference that the seamen of a modern trawling fleet might display towards an ocean liner. In marked contrast to its perennial and violent conflicts with St Mary's abbey, the city's official relationship with the dean and chapter of York was relatively harmonious during the later middle ages. Several York citizens counted canons and vicars choral of the cathedral among their acquaintanceship, and many others left bequests to the Minster fabric fund. But an examination of their wills leaves no doubt that the great majority preferred to express their religious aspirations through the medium of their parish churches. Remarkably few members of the ruling elite of the city were ever buried in the Minster.[11] Only four York mayors before 1500 are known to have desired interment in St Peter's cathedral, and apparently none of these contemplated the establishment of a perpetual chantry near his grave: thus John de Craven, mayor 1411–12, preferred to endow a *maison dieu* near Layerthorpe Bridge for thirteen poor; while William Selby, mayor 1385–86 and 1387–89, projected (in the event of the failure of his heirs) the endowment of two chantries at his family church of St Michael-le-Belfrey.[12] The only

[8] This estimate includes several chantries about which little or nothing is known except for the appearance of a licence for alienation in mortmain on the royal patent rolls. The York evidence therefore leads to a conclusion somewhere between the extreme view of Professor Jordan, *Philanthropy in England, 1480–1660* (London, 1959), p. 51, that 'it was quite uncommon for a chantry to survive at all for more than a century or so', and Miss Wood-Legh's statement that 'in the vast majority of cases, where there is evidence of the foundation of a chantry, there is an entry in the chantry certificates to show that it continued till the suppression', *Perpetual Chantries in Britain*, pp. 128–9.

[9] There were at least fifty-six perpetual chantry foundations in the Minster, of which all but fourteen seem to have been in existence before 1400: see *Fabric Rolls of York Minster*, ed. J. Raine, Surtees Society (1858), pp. 274–306; VCH, *York*, p. 347. Although seriously out-of-date and heavily dependent on James Torre's manuscript 'Antiquities of York Minster' (1690–1), Raine's list of Minster chantries has never been superseded.

[10] E.F. Jacob, *The Fifteenth Century* (Oxford, 1961), p. 289. See above, p. 10.

[11] R.H. Skaife collected most of the relevant information in the appendix, 'Burial Places of Civic Officials', to volume iii of his manuscript 'Civic Officials and Parliamentary Representatives of York' (York City Library).

[12] Borthwick Institute: Probate Register, iii, fo. 607; ii, fos 513–4; 'Some Early Civic Wills of York', ed. R.B. Cook, *Association of Architectural Societies, Reports and Papers*, 32 (1913), pp. 310–11; 31 (1911), pp. 323–5.

York mayor who attempted to establish a perpetual chantry within the Minster was disappointed in his ambition. Robert Holme senior, one of the greatest of all York merchants, bequeathed £400 sterling in his will of 15 September 1396 towards the endowment of a perpetual chantry, whose chaplain was to receive the handsome stipend of twelve marks per annum. If possible, this chantry was to be ordained within the cathedral; but if the chapter proved unwilling to undertake its burden, then Holme's executors were empowered to choose an alternative site in the city. This, whether or not because of the opposition of the York canons, they were eventually compelled to do.[13]

As in other English secular cathedrals, the great majority of the Minster chantries were founded by the canons of the church. Only three were apparently established on behalf of York laymen. The earliest of these was that sited at the altar of St Thomas of Canterbury and endowed in the late 1320s by Richard Tunnock, goldsmith and bailiff (1320–21) of the city.[14] Later in the same century, two perpetual chantries were founded in 1368 and 1377 for the souls of John de Stayngate, saddler, and Alan Alnewyke, goldsmith, neither of whom ever held high civic office within the city.[15] As all three men appear to have lived in Stonegate, it seems possible that they chose to be commemorated by masses within the cathedral because of their residence within the liberty of St Peter. The administration and welfare of these three foundations was never the concern of the mayor and council of York, whose only serious responsibility towards any Minster chantry was imposed upon them by the executors of Thomas Haxey, treasurer of the cathedral, who died in 1426. Haxey's chantry at the altar of St Thomas was endowed by means of a rent charge to be paid annually by the mayor and citizens of York.[16] The annual payment to the priest at Haxey's chantry was the heaviest of such charges on the common chamber of the city, and its abrupt termination in 1536 was undoubtedly the most radical feature of the municipal suppression of seven chantries and three obits in that year. No other cantarist within the cathedral was similarly at the mercy of York civic opinion; and the Minster chantry priests as a whole formed a recognisably distinctive group, many of whom received additional stipends as vicars choral, while the remainder ultimately received official recognition of their special status when St William's College was founded for over twenty of their number in 1461.[17]

[13] York Probate Register, i, fo. 102; *Association of Architectural Societies, Reports and Papers,* 28 (1906), pp. 853–7; F. Drake, *Eboracum* (1736), 318.

[14] *CPR, 1327–30*, p. 309; *York Fabric Rolls*, p. 303.

[15] *YCS*, i, p. 19; *York Fabric Rolls*, pp. 290, 303. Cf. *Testamenta Eboracensia*, Surtees Society (1836–1902), i, pp. 87, 91; M.A. Riley, 'The Foundation of Chantries in the Counties of Nottingham and York, 1350–1400', *Yorkshire Archaeological Journal*, 33 (1938), pp. 159–60.

[16] *York Fabric Rolls*, pp. 206, 304; Dickens, 'Municipal Dissolution', p. 171.

[17] *YCS*, i, pp. 7–9; VCH, *Yorkshire*, iii (1913), pp. 385–6.

The parish churches and chapels of medieval York presented an entirely different picture, for in these the great majority of perpetual chantries were always founded by York merchants and craftsmen. Occasionally, and especially during the early fourteenth century, there are instances of the endowment of such chantries by ecclesiastics: thus in 1335 Thomas de Ludham, sub-treasurer of the cathedral and vicar of St Martin's, Coney Street, founded a chantry at Our Lady's altar in his own parish church.[18] But relatively few clerks founded chantries within York city churches; and several who appear to have done so were probably or certainly acting as executors or trustees for prominent laymen. Even more infrequent was the endowment of perpetual chantries in the city by members of the Yorkshire nobility or gentry. The 'chauntre of Sir Rauffe Bulmer, Knyght', founded or refounded at St Michael-le-Belfrey in 1472 for a term of ninety-eight years, is one example.[19] More interesting is the history of the two Basy chantries in the church of St Mary, Bishophill, Senior. The first of these was founded by Roger Basy, mayor of York in the 1290s, as early as 1319; the second dated from almost a century later (1404) when Elisabeth Basy founded another chantry in the existing Basy chapel and endowed it with an annual rent of £7 from a moiety of the manor of Bilbrough in the West Riding, of which her family were now the lords. The Basies clearly belonged to that substantial group of prominent York citizens whose investment in rural property eventually led them to settle in the country, although not at the cost of severing all their connections with the town that had made them rich.[20]

The extent to which York's own citizens were themselves the founders of the large number of chantries within the city is nowhere more obvious than in the case of the two chapels on the Ouse and Foss bridges. By the later fifteenth century there were three chantries situated at altars inside St Anne's Chapel on Foss Bridge and at least another four located within the older and more celebrated St William's Chapel on Ouse Bridge. Foundation deeds of all seven of these chantries still survive and testify to

[18] *CPR, 1334–38*, p. 121. Ludham also founded at least one chantry in the Minster (*YCS*, i, p. 35; *York Fabric Rolls*, p. 293).

[19] *YCS*, i, p. 71; ii, p. 469; cf. *Valor Eccl.*, v, p. 28.

[20] *YCS*, i, pp. 68–70; ii, pp. 465–6; *CPR, 1307–13*, p. 343; *1401–5*, p. 193; VCH, *York*, pp. 391–2. Thanks to Elisabeth Basy's handsome endowment, hers was the wealthiest of all York city chantries by the 1530s (*Valor Eccl.*, v, p. 29). The migration of wealthy citizens from York into the countryside (cf. E. Miller in VCH, *York*, pp. 46, 113) inevitably reduced the number of patrons of chantries who were resident in York. Thus, by the sixteenth century, the Thwaites of North Ingelsby, Lincolnshire, had inherited the right to present to the Graa chantry at St Mary's, Castlegate; and at the same date the patronage of the junior Robert Holme's chantry in St Anne's chapel, Foss Bridge, was held by Holme's descendants at Elvington (York, St Anthony's Hall: Reg. Geo. Neville, RI 22, fos 107, 128v, 136v; Reg. Wolsey, fo. 19v). Similarly, on 22 Feb. 1464, William Salley of Saxton in the West Riding presented a chaplain to the Salley chantry in St Michael's, Spurriergate (Reg. Will. Booth, fo. 25); cf. Reg. Wolsey, fo. 51; Reg. Kempe, fo. 395v.

the full participation of the citizens of York in the late medieval vogue for bridge chapels. The early history of St William's chapel remains mysterious, but it was in use for worship at least as early as 1223, and thereafter continued to serve as York's civic chapel until its secularisation in the sixteenth century.[21] The establishment of its four perpetual chantries took place however within the remarkably short space of ten years, between 1321 and 1331, the period when the popularity of such foundations in medieval York was at its most pronounced.[22] Almost exactly a century later, a similar spate of chantry endowment followed (and may have helped to provoke) the rebuilding of Foss Bridge and the construction of a new chapel in honour of St Anne towards its northern end. The chapel can only have been completed shortly before 1424, but by 1428 three exceptionally well-endowed chantries had already been established to provide masses for Nicholas Blackburn senior, Robert Holme, senior and junior, and Alan de Hammerton, all prominent York mercers.[23] The three cantarists serving at St Anne's Chapel received their stipends from the city chamber and lived, like their colleagues in the Ouse Bridge chapel, under the direct care and surveillance of the mayor and aldermen. The latter visited the two chapels at periodic intervals in order to inspect the ornaments and vestments of the chaplains and clearly regarded the spiritual and economic welfare of these chantries as their special concern.[24]

Although the construction of two bridge chapels at York gave a few of the wealthier York citizens a limited opportunity to endow chantries therein, the latter were naturally heavily outnumbered by the similar foundations within the city's parish churches. Twenty-two York churches, slightly more than half of the total within the city's boundaries,[25] are known to have contained one or more perpetual chantries during the course of their history. The more prosperous and centrally situated parish churches contained an average of three or four perpetual chantries each. Only one York church, St Saviour's, can be credited with as many as eight chantries, six of which survived until the general suppression.[26] The large number and comparative poverty of York's medieval churches made it inevitable that perpetual chantries would be dispersed widely among the

[21] *York Memorandum Book*, ed. M. Sellers, Surtees Society, 120 (1911–14), ii, p. 68; A. Raine, *Mediaeval York* (1955), pp. 213–6. See below, pp. 274–6.

[22] York City Muniments, G. 70, nos 1, 2, 5, 8. At least thirty-six perpetual chantries were founded in the city churches between 1310 and 1340.

[23] Ibid., nos 30–2, 34, 35. Ecclesiastical licence to the mayor and citizens of York to celebrate *tres missas peculiares cotidie* at this chapel was granted on 14 Nov. 1424 (York Sede Vacante Register, 1299–1554, fo. 388v; *York Fabric Rolls*, p. 238).

[24] *York Civic Records*, i, p. 101; ii, pp. 62–3, 141–2; iii, pp. 18, 28–30, 40, 174; iv, pp. 123, 166–7. Cf. *York Memorandum Book*, ii, pp. 39–40, 51, 111–12, 134, 273–4.

[25] Thirty-nine churches within the city were assessed for a parish subsidy by York jurors in 1428, *York Memorandum Book*, ii, pp. 131–4; VCH, *York*, pp. 365–6.

[26] *YCS*, i, pp. 62–8; ii, pp. 471–3; VCH, *York*, p. 402.

parishes. No single York church could hope to rival the parish church of Newark with its fifteen chantries. At Newcastle upon Tyne, apparently the only other town in northern England where more than twenty perpetual chantries survived into the 1540s, all these were concentrated within four churches.[27] The distribution of chantry foundations within York was much more similar to that in London, where (in 1535) over 180 chantries were widely scattered among the city churches, only one (St Magnus) containing as many as eight.[28] Almost all York citizens, like those of London, endowed chantries to sustain a single chaplain. Only one York merchant seems to have been permanently successful in achieving a more impressive foundation: the two chantries founded at separate altars in St Saviour's by William Burton, mercer, in 1408 and 1409 were still extant at the beginning of Edward VI's reign.[29] Many other York merchants contemplated endowing chantries on a similar or even more handsome scale; but a comparison of their wills with the later actions of their executors shows how rarely were their ambitions realised. The executors of John Gisburn, mayor 1379–81, were instructed to found a chantry for two chaplains; but within a few years Gisburn's endowment had to be altered to apply to only one.[30]

By the time of the sixteenth-century surveys, most York city chantries were relatively poorly endowed, usually by means of messuages, tenements, cottages and shops, or fixed rents from properties within the city walls. The collection of forty original chantry foundation deeds and tripartite indentures preserved among the corporation's muniments leaves no doubt that only a minority of the founders had ever expected their chantry priests to receive an annual income larger than the statutory minimum of five or six marks.[31] The most serious feature of the situation in early sixteenth-century York was the failure of a large proportion of the city chantries to maintain even this humble level of annual revenue.

[27] *Ecclesiastical Proceedings of Bishop Barnes*, ed. J. Raine, Surtees Society (1850), pp. lxxvii–lxxxii.

[28] *Valor Ecclesiasticus*, i, pp. 378–84; similarly, at Bristol, there were thirty chantries distributed among seventeen parishes, VCH, *Gloucestershire*, ii (1907) p. 27.

[29] *CPR, 1396–9*, p. 588; *1405–8*, p. 423; *1408–13*, p. 52; *YCS*, i, p. 64, 68; ii, p. 471.

[30] *CPR, 1391–6*, p. 145; *1401–5*, p. 496. When Thomas Holme, mayor 1374–5, made his will shortly before his death in 1406 he commanded that three chaplains should be maintained at his chantries in St Mary's, Castlegate; but only one of his chantries, served by one priest, survived into the sixteenth century: *Association of Architectural Societies, Reports and Papers*, 28 (1906), pp. 870–1; *YCS*, i, p. 45; ii, p. 467.

[31] York City Records, G. 70, nos 1–40. These foundation documents impose an annual income of more than six marks in the case of only six chantries: those of Adam del Bank at All Saints, North Street; of Nicholas Blackburn and Robert Holme at St Anne's Chapel, Foss Bridge; of Thomas Nelson at Holy Trinity, Micklegate; of John Acaster at All Saints, Pavement; and of Richard Wateby, as augmented by John de Gisburn, at St John's, Ouse Bridge End. All seven men served as mayors of York.

Almost half of the forty chantries surveyed in 1535 were valued at less than five marks net per annum;[32] and although the *Valor Ecclesiasticus* undoubtedly undervalued the revenues of many English chantries, the estimates produced at York in the following decade amply confirm the general impression of financial decay. By the time of Henry VIII's reign, the economic position of the York chantry priest seems to have deteriorated much more rapidly than in many other northern parishes, whether rural or urban.[33] The chaplain who served Robert Holme's prestige chantry in St Anne's Chapel, Foss Bridge, must have thought himself fortunate to receive a guaranteed stipend of ten marks a year from the mayor and commonalty. The common practice of augmenting the revenues of decaying chantries, of uniting one poorly endowed chantry with another, and the ever-present possibility that individual priests might receive personal bequests and assistance, makes it virtually impossible to generalise with any confidence about the economic position of the chantry priests. The characteristic legacy received by one chaplain in 1406 from the wealthy widow Beatrice Sancton – of two marks per annum for six years in augmentation of his chantry[34] – could well have made the difference between extreme penury and comparative affluence. Nevertheless there is little doubt that the prosperity of most York chantries was seriously and adversely affected by the decline in urban rents and land values which was so obvious a feature of the city's economy from at least the middle of the fifteenth century.[35]

York's own economic decline no doubt provides the central explanation, if not the only one, for the fact that the fourteenth and not the fifteenth century saw the golden age of chantry foundation in the medieval city. Of the thirty-nine chantries recorded in York parishes by the Henrician and Edwardian commissioners, twenty-five had been founded before 1400, and all but seven before 1450. Even more revealing are the results of an analysis of the foundation dates of the eighty-five or so perpetual chantries recorded in sources additional to, as well as inclusive of, the chantry certificates. Only three chantries are definitely known to have existed within York parishes (as opposed to at least seventeen within the

[32] *Valor Ecclesiasticus*, v, pp. 25–30.

[33] The average annual revenue of Lancashire chantries at the Dissolution was calculated at approximately eight marks net: *History of Lancashire Chantries*, ed. F.R. Raines, Chetham Society (1862), i, p. xiii; and only two of the twenty-three perpetual chantries visited in Newcastle upon Tyne in 1548 were valued at less than five marks 'clere', *Proceedings of Bishop Barnes*, pp. lxxvii–lxxxii. The York Minster chantries were, however, considerably better endowed than those in the city churches, VCH, *York*, p. 146.

[34] York Probate Register, iii, fo. 246.

[35] The most striking example of this decline is that of the vicars choral of York Minster whose income from some 250 York tenements dropped from £160 to £100 a year between 1426 and 1456: see J.N. Bartlett, 'The Expansion and Decline of York in the Later Middle Ages', *Economic History Review*, 2nd series, 12 (1959), pp. 28, 30, 32.

Minster) before the end of the thirteenth century; but at least thirty-nine were founded between 1300 and 1350; twenty-one between 1351 and 1400; fourteen between 1401 and 1450; seven between 1451 and 1500; and only one, Sir John Gilliot's chantry at St Saviour's, between 1501 and the suppression. It is well known that throughout most of England the fourteenth century saw the climax of perpetual chantry foundation, and at first sight York's remarkably regular pattern of almost exact arithmetical decline might not seem particularly surprising.[36] However, it is noticeable that these York figures are by no means altogether consonant with those calculated by William Page, on the basis of the chantry certificates, for Yorkshire as a whole.[37] The impulse towards perpetual chantry endowment in York was not only declining long before the sixteenth century but declining much more rapidly than in most areas of northern England.[38]

This decline can perhaps be presented more vividly in other terms. The practice of perpetual chantry foundation within the parish churches of York had been originally pioneered by members of the merchant oligarchy of the city. The two citizens known to have established chantries before the close of the thirteenth century were both leading members of the urban patriciate, Robert Verdenel of the Marsh and Robert Graa.[39] During the first third of the fourteenth century similar chantries were founded to sing masses for the souls of almost all the prominent aldermanic families within the city, including those of at least six mayors: Roger Basy, Andrew Bolingbroke, Nicholas Langton, Nicholas Flemyng, Robert Meke and Richard Wateby. During the fifteenth century too, the relatively few

[36] A similar decline is evident in the Minster where only seven new perpetual chantries are known to have been founded between 1401 and 1450; six between 1451 and 1500; and one after 1500. David Palliser has been kind enough to confirm that Sir John Gilliot's bequest (in his will of 28 Dec. 1509: *Test. Ebor.*, v, pp. 12–17) of £400 'to funde a chauntre in the new chapel in Seynt Savour kirk, where my body lith, for a chauntry preist to syng for my soule' marks the close of perpetual chantry foundation within York. Several York aldermen continued to augment existing city chantries until 1529, in which year such augmentations also cease, ibid., pp. 214–5, 268–9, 270.

[37] Of the 253 dated chantry and other foundations surveyed in 1546, sixty-one were founded between 1450 and 1500 and another forty-seven between 1500 and the Dissolution, *YCS*, i, p. vii. Due to their omission of chantries which had decayed before the 1540s, all calculations based on the chantry certificates are likely to prove inaccurate; and this perhaps accounts for Miss Riley's misleading view ('The Foundation of Chantries', p. 254) that 'The custom of founding chantries was not as prevalent in the fourteenth century as it became in the later years of the middle ages'.

[38] The last Yorkshire chantry to be founded before the suppression was, according to the 1546 chantry certificates, established in the parish church of Doncaster as late as January 1533, *YCS*, i, p. 179. The collegiate church of Manchester provides an example of a parish where seven out of eleven chantries were founded after 1498: *Hist. Lancs. Chantries*, i, pp. 25–56.

[39] *Register of William Wickwane*, ed. W. Brown, Surtees Society (1907), p. 41; VCH, *York*, pp. 393, 402.

York citizens who succeeded in founding perpetual chantries were very nearly all members of the current ruling elite of the city, fellows of the mercers' fraternity (incorporated under royal charter in 1430) which dominated the social as well as the economic and constitutional life of York at the close of the middle ages. The last six citizens ever to have founded a perpetual chantry (John Carr; Sir John and William Gilliot; Thomas Nelson; Sir Richard York; and Richard Wartre) all described themselves as mercers or *mercatores* of the city, all played a prominent role in the mercers' gild and all held office for a term of one or more years as mayors of York.[40] A hundred years earlier, during the middle and late fourteenth century, the familiar names of the great mercantile dynasties of York had been supplemented by those of more obscure craftsmen. Among many possible examples are Richard Barneby, butcher, who founded a chantry at Holy Trinity, King's Court, in 1378; Robert Ampleford, ironmonger, who founded one the same year within All Saints, Pavement; and Robert Swetmouth, a tanner who joined forces with his brother William to endow a chantry in St Peter-the-Little in the 1350s. All these men were freemen of York, but not one attained the higher reaches of civic office.[41] For at least one transitory period, from approximately 1330 to 1390, the foundation of a perpetual chantry in a York church was emphatically not the exclusive privilege of the wealthy merchant and city oligarch.

It seems impossible to deny that by the end of the fifteenth century the middle ranks of the York citizenry were financially incapable of emulating the perpetual chantry endowment of their predecessors a hundred years before.[42] The decline of such endowments has often been explained by the alternative hypothesis that the orgy of chantry-foundation in late fourteenth-century England had presented the church with a problem, to use Coulton's phrase, of 'liturgical bankruptcy'. More recently, Professor Jordan has gone so far as to suggest that during the course of the fifteenth century 'the whole institution of endowed prayers

[40] York City Records, G. 70, nos 37, 38; York, St Anthony's Hall: Reg. Thomas Rotherham, pt 1, fos 129–30v; *YCS*, i, pp. 47, 62, 78–9, 83; ii, pp. 459, 463–4, 471–2.

[41] *CPR, 1350–54*, p. 5; *1377–81*, pp. 256, 285–6; *YCS*, i, pp. 49–50, 59, 77; ii, pp. 455, 457, 470. Cf. *York Freemen's Reg., 1272–1558*, Surtees Society (1897), pp. 35, 40.

[42] When John Leland visited York he thought it necessary to explain Nicholas Blackburn senior's reputation as a munificent founder of chantries on the grounds that 'This Blakeburne had very onthrifty children', Leland, *Itinerary*, ed. L. Toulmin Smith (London, 1906–10), v, p. 144. Leland's notes on the Blackburn chantries are curiously garbled and inaccurate; and the truth of his allegation seems unlikely in view of the terms of Blackburn's own will of February 1432, *Test. Ebor.*, ii, pp. 17–21. On the other hand, the childless merchant (as in the well-known case of Richard Whittington of London) was naturally especially likely to endow religious and charitable institutions: William Bowes, mayor of York 1417–18, 1428–9, left instructions in his will that the mayor and commonalty should establish a perpetual chantry for his soul only in the unlikely event of the death of all his lawful issue, York Probate Register, iii, fos 580v–583.

fell into considerable disrepute'.[43] On this issue, the evidence of later medieval York wills seems absolutely and completely unequivocal. The endowment of prayers for his soul, as compared to the endowment of prayers in perpetuity within a regular and permanent chantry foundation, continued to be the aspiration of every York merchant who could possibly afford it. Only the greatest of fifteenth-century mayors founded perpetual chantries, but almost all left large bequests (usually ranging from 30 marks to £100) to one or more chaplains for purposes similar to those expressed in the representative words of Robert Johnson, a York alderman who made his will while mayor in January 1497:

> To the exhibicion of an honest prest, to synge at the alter of our said Lady, daily, by the space of vii yeres, xxxv li. And I will that what prest that shall serve it every day, whan that he hath saide *Messe*, that he stand affore my grave in his albe, and ther to say the psalme of *De Profundis* with the Colettes; and then caste holy water upon my grave.[44]

This type of bequest naturally lent itself to innumerable variations. Most York citizens, like Johnson, preferred to monopolise the services of one chantry priest for a considerable length of time: in his will of Whit Sunday 1437 William Bowes senior made provision for the retention of a chaplain in St Cuthbert's church at 7 marks per annum for no less than twenty years.[45] Many merchants however wished to produce a more dramatic display during a shorter period: John Northby's will, completed on 13 February 1430, bequeathed £100 to ten chaplains, each of whom was to say masses for his soul (at a stipend of £5 per annum) for two years only.[46] It has sometimes been argued that such short-term endowments of prayers were regarded by fifteenth-century citizens as an alternative to the foundation of perpetual chantries of the sort favoured by their fourteenth-century predecessors. The lack of evidence for the period before the first archbishop's probate register begins in 1389 makes this a highly speculative theory. It is important to stress that the wealthiest of all fifteenth-century citizens, like the merchants Robert Holme junior and Richard Russell, endowed both temporary masses for a term of years and a perpetual chantry.

The York evidence therefore suggests (like that at London investigated by Dr Thomson[47]) that there was no serious danger of 'liturgical bankruptcy' in the late medieval city. The decline in the number of new

---

[43] Jordan, *Philanthropy in England*, p. 306.

[44] *Test. Ebor.*, iv, p. 121.

[45] York Probate Register, iii, fos 580v–583, most inadequately summarised in *Test. Ebor.*, ii, pp. 69–70.

[46] York Probate Register, ii, fo. 619.

[47] J.A.F. Thomson, 'Piety and Charity in Late Medieval London', *Journal of Ecclesiastical History*, 16 (1965), pp. 191–2.

perpetual chantry foundations cannot be crudely interpreted as evidence for a mass revulsion against the concept of the efficacy of prayers for the dead. Well into the sixteenth century relations between citizens and chantry priests continued to be close and apparently cordial. At the official level, it is well known that the mayor and commonalty took their often ill-defined responsibilities towards the city's chantries extremely seriously. The York aldermen defended the chantry chaplains against what they believed to be unjustified ecclesiastical interference and regulated such matters as the hours at which masses should be sung.[48] Even more fundamental were the personal ties which bound individual priests and citizens together. The remarkable generosity of York merchants and craftsmen towards the chantry and other chaplains of the city is one of the most striking features of their wills. The wealthier York citizens retained the services of not one but several chaplains;[49] and among the motives for the endowment of temporary or perpetual chantries was the desire to provide for the future welfare of a clerk who had long acted as a merchant's personal friend and adviser.[50] As a parishioner too the citizen had a direct interest in the effective administration of the chantries within his own church. The direct or reversionary right to present incumbents to city chantries was normally enjoyed by the rector or vicar and leading parishioners of a church; with the result that the more wealthy residents within a parish might receive the title of *advocator cantarie*.[51] No York citizen, whatever his personal inclinations, could avoid involvement in the welfare of existing perpetual chantries, and this fact in itself may help to explain the marked decline in the number of new foundations after 1450. After the middle of the fifteenth century the financial plight of existing chantries can have offered little encouragement to those who contemplated endowing chantries for their own souls. Civic opinion may have become gradually alarmed, not at the number of chantry masses, but at the number of chantry priests within the city. Thomas Bracebridge's will of 4 September 1436, with its bequest 'cuilibet Rectori ecclesiarum parochialium in Ciuitate Eboraci et suburbiis euisdem et cuilibet Capellano continue celebranti in eisdem ecclesiis parochialibus iiiid.: Ad quam summam persoluendum sufficit

[48] *York Memorandum Book*, ii, pp. 17–24, 39–40, 111–12; *York Civic Records*, i, pp. 101, 141–2; iii, pp. 40, 129–30; iv, pp. 166–7.

[49] On 10 March 1406 Beatrice Sancton, wife of a prominent York draper and future mayor, bequeathed 2s. each to six clerks 'nuper moranti nobiscum', *Association of Architectural Societies, Reports and Papers*, 32 (1914), pp. 578–9; cf. *York Memorandum Book*, ii, p. 223, for the names of three chaplains serving Thomas Nelson in 1463.

[50] As, e.g., in the will of Sir Richard York (8 April 1498) where the testator's references to his plans to augment an existng chantry close with the request 'quod dominus Thomas Gripthorp, capellanus meus, habeat pro termino vitae', *Test. Ebor.*, iv, p. 134.

[51] *York Memorandum Book*, ii, p. 100; cf. Reg. Wolsey, fos 19, 47v, 49v; Reg. Kempe, fos 392v, 402.

Summa Cs vt estimo',[52] suggests that there were then approximately 260 parish chaplains within the city. All allowances made for the factual if not legal accuracy of Mayor William Selby's famous declaration in 1388 that the city priests 'sunt speciales oratores civium, patronorum suorum et magistrorum suorum',[53] the York citizen must occasionally have thought that enough was enough. There were obvious limits to the number of chantry priests, and especially perpetual chantry priests, that a city of York's size and precarious economy could sustain. It is difficult not to believe that these limits had been exceeded many decades before Henry VIII and Somerset provided their radical solution to the problem.

---

[52] York Probate Register, iii, fo. 488.
[53] *York Memorandum Book*, ii, p. 19.

12

Citizens and Chantries in Late Medieval York

It is now a quarter of a century since Christopher Brooke drew our attention to 'one of the most notable revolutions in our history: the development of the idea of privacy, of the notion that some parts of our life at least should not be exposed to public gaze'.[1] As Brooke went on to locate that 'revolution' quite firmly in the later middle ages, his perception may offer some consolation to those recent historians of the fourteenth- and fifteenth-century English church who – despite the comparative wealth of documentation at their disposal – are so often at a loss when trying to assess the spiritual attitudes of that period with any certainty. Obviously enough, the more 'private' an individual's religion the more it is liable to be highly resistant even to the most pertinacious historian; and it is equally of the essence of such interiorised devotion that it will often be more notable for its diverse than its common features. Despite such familiar difficulties, it has undoubtedly been one of Christopher Brooke's most significant contributions to medieval studies in recent years to stimulate the present remarkable and unprecedented interest in 'popular' as opposed to a more institutionalised religion.[2] Moreover, and of more relevance to the purposes of this essay, it was also Brooke who once argued that the late medieval transformation towards a more private worship – and a more compartmentalised church design – was founded on an increasing emphasis upon 'the personal nature of the Eucharist as an individual approach by the priest to the central mysteries of the Church'.[3] Might it even be that the now much vaunted 'rise of the private life' in western Christendom during the centuries immediately before the Reformation owed its genesis less to the increased availability of a more materially

---

[1] C. Brooke, *Medieval Church and Society: Collected Essays* (London, 1971), p. 178.

[2] R. and C. Brooke, *Popular Religion in the Middle Ages* (London, 1984), although primarily concerned with the period between 1000 and 1300, is itself the most obvious example. Recent research upon late medieval English religious beliefs and practices is well represented in the lengthy bibliographies of C. Harper-Bill, *The Pre-Reformation Church in England, 1400–1530* (London, 1989) and R.N. Swanson, *Church and Society in Late Medieval England* (Oxford, 1989).

[3] Brooke, *Medieval Church and Society*, p. 181, anticipating several arguments in J. Bossy's influential article on 'The Mass as a Social Institution', *Past and Present*, 100 (1983), pp. 29–61.

comfortable environment than to a new religious sensibility within the parish church?

Fortunately enough, that difficult and perhaps even insoluble question raises problems too vast to be the subject of this essay; but it is a question, nevertheless, which immediately redirects attention to the crucial role of the chantry as the most widespread institutional expression of late medieval society's most powerful personal religious aspirations. Partly for that very reason no doubt, the English chantry foundations of the fourteenth and fifteenth centuries have attracted greater, and more sympathetic, attention during the last twenty than in the previous two hundred years. In retrospect the late Miss K.L. Wood-Legh's remarkable conspectus of perpetual chantry foundations in England and Scotland already seems less the definitive study it appeared to be on its publication in 1965 than a pioneering venture into largely uncharted seas.[4] Nor can there be any doubt that the late medieval chantry continues to pose formidable problems of analysis. As Dr Clive Burgess and others have recently shown, it will never be possible to appreciate the complex role of the perpetual chantry at all adequately until it has been placed – no easy matter – within the context of the even more diversified, and much less firmly documented, world of the anniversary, the obit and other forms of temporary provision for masses on behalf of the deceased.[5] More prosaically, the correct enumeration and identification of both perpetual chantries and their founders now appears to be by no means as simple an exercise as it once seemed. Nearly all attempts to estimate the numbers of chantries in English towns and counties are notoriously bedevilled by the fact that the two most important sources at the historian's disposal (testamentary bequests on the one hand and royal licences to amortise rents or property to a perpetual chantry establishment on the other) frequently emerge as declarations of intent rather than proofs of creation. In those rare cases where a chantry's foundation documents survive in their entirety, the processes of endowment are so often revealed in such tortuous complexity that one must assume that few such institutions were ever achieved without considerable expenditure of

[4] K.L. Wood-Legh, *Perpetual Chantries in Britain* (Cambridge, 1965). For the single most detailed reassessment of the issues – in one particular but important locality – since the appearance of Miss Wood-Legh's book, see C. Burgess, 'Chantries in Fifteenth-Century Bristol' (unpublished D.Phil. thesis, University of Oxford, 1981); idem, '"For the Increase of Divine Service": Chantries in the Parish in Late Medieval Bristol', *Journal of Ecclesiastical History*, 36 (1985), pp. 46–65.

[5] Idem, 'A Service for the Dead: The Form and Function of the Anniversary in Late Medieval Bristol', *Transactions of Bristol and Gloucestershire Archaeological Society*, 105 (1987), pp. 183–21. The remarkable range of masses and prayers for the dead available to the late medieval citizen is perhaps the most important revelation of N.P. Tanner, *The Church in Late Medieval Norwich, 1370–1532*, Pontifical Institute of Medieval Studies, Studies and Texts, 66 (Toronto, 1984), pp. 91–110.

effort and often many changes of plan.[6] A display of hesitation and even of perplexity as to whether the testator's desire to create a chantry would ever be fulfilled at all is indeed a remarkably common feature of late medieval wills themselves. More nerve-wracking still was the possibility that one's perpetual chantry might prove not to be perpetual. It may indeed have been this anxiety in particular which did more than anything else to induce among the parishioners of late medieval England the radical conviction that 'the clergy could (and should) lawfully be subject to lay control'.[7]

Such at least were the closing words of Miss K.L. Wood-Legh's own survey of the perpetual chantries in Britain a generation ago; and for that considerable scholar the propensity of the chantry to generate lay activity within the very structure of the established church was perhaps the single most redeeming feature of an institution otherwise – so she believed – not readily reconcilable with the message of the New Testament.[8] The primary purpose of this essay is to reconsider that proposition in the case of only one English town but in the light of a somewhat remarkable collection of forty-one original deeds and other documents which relate to various chantries founded in the city of York during no less than two centuries, between 1321 and 1528.[9] These records, surviving as they do neither in the York Dean and Chapter Library nor among the archiepiscopal muniments in the Borthwick Institute of Historical Research but rather within the official archives of the city of York, are in themselves an indirect testimony to a late medieval urban community's close supervision of several of the chantries, and their chaplains, in its midst. The complex web of perpetual and other chantries in the parish churches, religious houses and cathedral of medieval York have received only a very limited amount of attention since they were obliterated forever in 1548; and a detailed analysis of these much neglected documents must await the full-scale study which

[6] *The Cartulary of the Wakebridge Chantries at Crich*, ed. A. Saltman, Derbyshire Archaeological Society, Record Series, 6 (1976) provides perhaps the best documented example, a *locus classicus* indeed, of the regular – and sometimes irregular – procedures to which the founder of a perpetual chantry was so often compelled to resort.

[7] Wood-Legh, *Perpetual Chantries*, p. 314; cf. pp. 125–9.

[8] Ibid., p. 312. Miss Wood-Legh's highly representative distaste for the 'endless multiplication of mechanically performed masses' was even more pronounced in her earlier studies of the late medieval chantry, e.g. in *Studies in English Church Life under Edward III* (Cambridge, 1934) and 'Some Aspects of the History of Chantries in the later Middle Ages', *Transactions of the Royal Historical Society*, 4th series, 28 (1946), pp. 47–60.

[9] York City Archives (hereafter cited as YCA), G.70, nos 1–40. YCA, G.70, no. 13, recording Thomas Duraunt's foundation of a chantry at the parish church of St Crux in 1340, is a copy of YCA, G.70, no. 12; but YCA, G.70, no. 38, in fact comprises two quite distinct documents (one of 1485 and one of 1386) relating to the Acastre family's perpetual chantry in All Saints, Pavement. A few of the items in this collection have been known to previous scholars: but their full importance was first made properly apparent when a typescript calendar of them all (available in the City Archive Office) was prepared by Mrs Joyce W. Percy, then York City Archivist, at some time in the early 1960s.

those chantries so self-evidently deserve.[10] Here it may suffice only to observe that this was a city and cathedral so committed to the concept of the perpetual chantry that it came to house more such institutions (at least 140) than any provincial town in fifteenth-century England. Whether or not most late medieval Englishmen and Englishwomen would have accepted the York mayor and council's self-interested claim that their city was and always had been 'nomee la secounde citee du Roialme et la Chaumbre de Roy', no one at all could have disagreed with Roger Burton, its distinguished common clerk, when he observed in the late 1430s that this was 'the chief place of all the north'.[11] No doubt the intricate skeins of chantry foundation and maintenance in this 'chief place', all in all more fully documented than in the case of any other English town, were often *sui generis*; but when those skeins are finally unravelled, there can be no doubt at all that they should bear directly upon the wider issues raised by Christopher Brooke and Miss Wood-Legh.

Meanwhile the survival at York of these forty-one charters, indentures, quit-claims and letters of presentation must be seen as an unexpected bonus in the case of a city and church already well provided with an abundance of late medieval registers, accounts and wills, if not of parish records.[12] Why they should survive at all is something of a mystery: for in most cases there can have been no practical reason for their preservation, in the civic council offices on Ouse Bridge, for more than a decade or two after the dissolution of all the chantries concerned in the 1530s and 1540s. It is equally surprising, given the liability of the York civic muniments as a whole to damage by neglect, or even by occasional immersion under the waters of the River Ouse, that these chantry documents are generally in a very good and legible state of preservation.[13] None of the items in the series seems to have been produced by notaries; and the great

[10] For a brief and somewhat premature attempt to establish the general patterns of chantry foundation in the city, to which this present essay is in part a sequel, see R.B. Dobson, 'The Foundation of Perpetual Chantries by the Citizens of Medieval York', above, pp. 253–65. On the dramatic consequences of the dissolution of all the York chantries in April 1548, see especially D.M. Palliser, *The Reformation in York, 1534–1553* (Borthwick Papers, no. 40, Borthwick Institute of Historical Research, 1971), pp. 22–5.

[11] YCA, D.1 (Freemen's Register), fo. 348; *York Memorandum Book BY*, ed. J.W. Percy, Surtees Society, 186 (1973), p. 124; cf. R. Davies, *The State Swords of the York Corporation*, Yorkshire Philosophical Society Annual Report (1868), pp. 27–32.

[12] The only pre-Reformation churchwardens' accounts to survive at York are those for 1518–28 from St Michael, Spurriergate; see York Minster Library, MS Add. 220/2; *Records of Early English Drama: York*, ed. A.F. Johnston and M. Rogerson, 2 vols (Toronto, 1979), i, pp. xxxvii–xxxix; D.M. Smith, *A Guide to the Archive Collections of the Borthwick Institute of Historical Research*, Borthwick Texts and Calendars: Records of the Northern Province, i (York, 1973), pp. 39–40.

[13] YCA, K.100; W. Giles, *Catalogue of the Charters, House Books, etc., Belonging to the Corporation of York* (York, 1909).

majority take the form of tripartite indentures, of which the mayor and council's copy is of course the one to survive. In the case of the most important documents, the lists of witnesses are long and highly varied, often throwing new light on the identities of chantry chaplains, prominent citizens and civic office-holders in York. Almost all the indentures and other deeds were authenticated by seals; and it is striking, if not entirely unexpected, that from the early fourteenth century onwards not only the richer merchants of York but also its more obscure residents and chantry priests had personal seals at their disposal. These seals sometimes survive, most interestingly perhaps in the case of a letter of March 1518 presenting a chaplain to Adam de Banke's chantry at St Nicholas's altar in All Saints, North Street: this document still preserves the separate seals of the rector and four of the parishioners of that church. On the other hand, and not too surprisingly, the royal seals attached to original letters patent among the collection are now invariably missing.[14] Copies of a few of these items naturally survive elsewhere, notably Robert Holme Jr's important new ordinances of 14 February 1428 for his father's impressive chantry in St Anne's Chapel on Foss Bridge, ordinances which were also registered in one of the city's contemporary official 'memorandum books'.[15] However, it seems clear that on the whole the common clerk of York was under no compulsion to have these chantry deeds copied laboriously into his city's registers: this no doubt is the chief reason why the originals were – and are – themselves preserved.

As already implied, the forty-one documents in question are of very diverse genres and varied contents. The only common denominator is that they all relate to chantry foundations in which the mayor and council of the city of York had been assigned a direct or reversionary supervisorial role. As already mentioned, the documents range in date from 1321 to 1518; and in one or two cases the relevance of the transaction in question to a chantry, although certainly present, is not immediately apparent.[16] Four items actually relate to an obit rather than to a perpetual chantry foundation. All of these are of a comparatively late date and involved religious houses rather than parish churches in the city: they are accordingly of most interest as illustrations of the extraordinary variety of ways in which desire for vicarious intercession could be satisfied in a large medieval town, as well as of the increasing tendency for potential founders to see the mayor and commonalty of York as the most reliable guarantors that their very different religious aspirations would come to

[14] YCA, G.70, nos 9, 10, 25, 28.

[15] YCA, G.70, no. 35; copied in *York Memorandum Book BY*, pp. 149–51.

[16] E.g. a quitclaim of January 1406 whereby two parish chaplains released a tenement in Jubbergate to Thomas de Holme, possibly to support one of the several Holme chantries in the city (YCA, G.70, no. 26); 'Some Early Civic Wills of York', ed. R.B. Cook, *Associated Architectural Societies, Reports and Papers*, 28, pt 2 (1906), pp. 840–71.

fruition. Accordingly in December 1466 the prominent York merchant
and ex-mayor, Thomas Nelson, only established his elaborate obit at Holy
Trinity Priory, Micklegate ('in consideration of a certain sum of money
and of the great window at the east end of the choir newly glazed by
him'), on condition that the mayor and commonalty could distrain on the
prior and chapter there if the due services lapsed for more than forty
successive days.[17] A very similar precaution was taken by William Butler
of Selby (in January 1465) and John Gillyot Jr, alderman of York (in April
1489) when they founded their respective obits within the Franciscan and
Carmelite friaries of the city. The two stray documents which record
these endowments suggest, almost certainly correctly, that the number of
temporary chantry and other pious foundations made within the houses
of mendicant friars have been unduly neglected by recent historians of the
English town; and it is more revealing still that it was to Gillyot, albeit a
member of one of the city's most notable merchant families, that the White
Friars of York looked for the replenishment of their stock of ecclesiastical
vestments ('three copes, one chasuble and two tunicles of black chamlet
cloth adorned with the letters J and G joined together in Venetian gold').[18]
However, it may be an even more instructive comment on the increasing
reliance of the religious orders of the north upon the services of the local
laity that in 1514 it was the most prestigious civic fraternity in the city,
the Corpus Christi Guild, which undertook to found and administer an
important obit in the chapel of St Thomas Becket outside Micklegate Bar
on behalf of a monastic superior, Thomas Tanfelde, prior of Thorneholme
in Lincolnshire.[19]

With one important exception, however, all the other original chantry
documents preserved within the York civic archives relate not only to
perpetual foundations but to foundations made by members of the
city's mercantile elite within one or other of its two civic chapels or its
forty parish churches.[20] Such a conclusion is hardly surprising given the
well-known propensity of the richer – and no doubt poorer – inhabitants
of the late medieval town to direct their most urgent spiritual needs
and ambitions towards the church of the parish wherein they resided.

---

[17] YCA, G.70, no. 37; cf. Borthwick Institute, Probate Register, 5, fo. 212.

[18] YCA, G.70, nos 36, 39. Between the death of his father in 1484 and his own demise
in 1509, Sir John Gillyot was in many ways 'the most conspicuous person in York of his
time': see *Testamenta Eboracensia: A Selection of Wills from the Registry at York*, ed. J. Raine
and others, Surtees Society, 4, 30, 45, 53, 79, 106 (1836–1902), v, pp. 12–17.

[19] YCA, G.70, no. 40. Prior Tanfelde had been admitted to the fraternity of the York
Corpus Christi Guild in 1497: see *The Register of the Corpus Christi Guild in the City of York*,
ed. R.H. Skaife, Surtees Society, 57 (1872), p. 143.

[20] The civic jurors who in 1428 assessed the value of York's parish churches, *in civitate
predicta et in suburbiis eiusdem*, estimated their total number at thirty-nine: see *York
Memorandum Book*, ed. M. Sellers, Surtees Society, 120, 125 (1911–14), ii, pp. 131–4;
but cf. VCH, *City of York* (1961), pp. 365–7.

Although at least sixty perpetual chantries seem to have been in existence within York Minster at one point or another during the fourteenth and fifteenth centuries, very few indeed were ever founded by the citizens as opposed to the canons of York. More precisely, of the eight such Minster chantries established between 1400 and 1500 (during a century when the pace of such foundations in the cathedral, as in the city's parish churches, had much slackened), the only one to be founded by an individual member of the laity was that established at the altar of St Stephen by Thomas Lord Scrope of Masham in 1459.[21] For the great majority of the citizens of York, whose attitudes towards the great cathedral in their midst were often ambivalent to a degree, neither burial nor (much less) the creation of a chantry in the Minster was ever a practical or indeed a particularly looked for possibility.[22] Even the lavish bequest of £400 made in September 1396 by Robert Holme Sr, perhaps the richest of all York merchants in the prosperous 1390s, failed to ensure a chantry to perpetuate his name in the cathedral church of St Peter.[23] The citizens of York entered the metropolitan church of St Peter for a multiplicity of purposes in the later middle ages but hardly ever to observe masses being sung for the souls of their ancestors.

All the more impressive within this context is the exception mentioned above, namely the success of the powerful civic guild of St Christopher in coming to terms with the dean and chapter in order to found (on 13 December 1426) a perpetual chantry of one chaplain at the altar of St Christopher in York Minster.[24] This particular foundation, unique in York but not of course in the country, can be interpreted in many ways, most persuasively perhaps as the intrusion of what was essentially a civic institution into the *ecclesia matrix* of northern England. Although the successive chaplains were naturally to be presented to, and admitted by, the

[21] *Yorkshire Chantry Surveys* (hereafter cited as *YCS*), ed. W. Page, Surtees Society, 91–2, (1892–3), i, p. 25; ii, pp. 440–1. This elaborate Scrope chantry (for two chaplains) was apparently the single most lavish such foundation in fifteenth-century York: it is well discussed in S.E. McManaway, 'Some Aspects of the Foundation of Perpetual Chantries in York Minster' (unpublished M.A. thesis, University of York, 1981), pp. 95–9.

[22] However the wealthier inhabitants of the city and their wives were perhaps slightly more likely to aspire to interment in the nave or aisles of York Minster than is implied in Dobson, 'Perpetual Chantries', above, pp. 255–6. For some examples from the early fifteenth century, see Borthwick Institute, Probate Registers, 2, fo. 153; 3, fos 60, 287, 606, 613.

[23] The perpetual chantry eventually founded to pray for Holme's soul in Holy Trinity, Goodramgate, was undoubtedly more spacious and more responsive to the wishes of his descendants than would have been the case in the Minster: see RCHM, *An Inventory of the Historical Monuments in the City of York*, v, *The Central Area* (London, 1981), p. 5; Borthwick Institute, Probate Register, i, fo. 102; Cook, 'Civic Wills', *Associated Architectural Societies, Reports and Papers*, 28 (1906), pp. 853–7.

[24] YCA, G.70, no. 33. The then new guild of St Christopher had projected a two-chaplain chantry in the Minster as long ago as 1396 (*CPR, 1391–96*, pp. 711, 716; cf. *YCS*, i, pp. 20–1; ii, pp. 448–9).

dean and chapter, they were first selected by the master of St Christopher's
Guild and its eight longest-serving aldermen. During vacancies, the goods
and muniments of the chantry were to revert to the custody of the guild
itself; and the ordinances of 1426 leave no doubt at all that neglect of his
duties on the part of the chaplain would lead rapidly to his removal from
office – and on the initiative of the guild rather than the cathedral clergy
at that. More strikingly still, perhaps, the chaplain serving St Christopher's
altar was specifically instructed to achieve a high degree of proficiency in
both grammar and song, a requirement very rarely encountered in the
other Minster chantry ordinations of the later middle ages.[25] No doubt
only a civic fraternity with the remarkable influence of St Christopher's
Guild (largely responsible, amidst much else, for the construction of the
present York City Common Hall or Guildhall between 1446 and 1459)
could have been capable of founding a Minster chantry of such a distinctive
type; but in doing so they had undoubtedly helped to create a lay enclave
within the greatest concentration of clergy in northern England.[26] Perhaps
to make that development even more explicit, it seems that the area around
the chantry of St Christopher's Guild occasionally became an informal
citizens' preserve within the Minster. It was in close proximity to this
cathedral chantry, the only one ever recorded at St Christopher's altar,
that the mayor and aldermen not infrequently held meetings to conduct
their own highly worldly business, 'beyng togadder in counsaill behynd
Saint Christopher'.[27]

A much more obvious locale in which to have observed the mayor and
council of late medieval York in heated debate was their 'Counsell Chambre
apon Ouse Bridge', the effective centre of urban self-government in the city
until the mid eighteenth century. Although the early history of that famous
bridge and of the shops and many other buildings constructed upon it
remains problematic to a degree, it seems probable that the capacious
late Romanesque chapel of St William built near the north-west end
of the bridge preceded the appearance of a council chamber on an
immediately adjacent site.[28] However, there was already a civic prison

[25] YCA, G.70, no. 33; McManaway, 'Perpetual Chantries in York Minster', pp. 85–7.

[26] A. Raine, *Mediaeval York: A Topographical Survey Based on Original Sources* (London,
1955), pp. 134–40. The guild of St Christopher (later united with that of St George) was
one of the most influential if most mysterious fraternities in fifteenth-century York: it was
also wealthy enough to sustain one or perhaps even two maisons dieu: see VCH, *Yorkshire*,
iii (1913), p. 365; E. White, *The St Christopher and St George Guild of York*, Borthwick Paper,
72 (York, 1987).

[27] *York Civic Records*, ed. A. Raine, Yorkshire Archaeological Society, Record Series,
98–119, (1939–53), ii, p. 14; and for the location of the chantry in the south aisle of
the Minster nave see E. Gee, 'The Topography of Altars, Chantries and Shrines in York
Minster', *Antiquaries Journal*, 64 (1984), p. 347.

[28] RCHM, *Inventory of York*, iii, *South-West of the Ouse* (London, 1972), pp. 48–50; Raine,
Mediaeval York, pp. 207–22.

on Ouse Bridge by the end of the thirteenth century; and from that date to the Reformation there could never be any doubt that in effect St William's Chapel was synonymous with 'the chapel of the community of York', whose council chamber was literally next door.[29] Nowhere in York, and hardly anywhere in England, can a civic chapel have been more exposed to the close and direct scrutiny of the urban authorities; and nowhere perhaps is it easier to demonstrate the subordination of the ideal of the chantry to the attitudes and interests of a mayor and council. In the first place, it can hardly be a coincidence that within the short space of ten years between 1321 and 1331, at the very height of the fashion for chantry foundation in the city, a chapel which had apparently previously held no perpetual chantries at all came to house no less than four. The very first document to survive within the collection of chantry deeds in the York city archives is indeed the formal licence issued by the mayor and commonalty in January 1321 to enable the appointment of a suitable chaplain to celebrate for the soul of Robert of Wistow in St William's Chapel.[30] During the following year, the executors of Roger de Mar, late rector of the parish church of Whixley and succentor of York Minster, endowed another chantry at the altar of St Eligius in the same chapel; and in 1328 and 1331 respectively yet two further chantries were established at St William's Chapel in the spiritual interests of Richard le Toller, a positively prolific founder of chantries in the city, and of the chaplain John Fourbour and his benefactors.[31]

Not one of these four Ouse Bridge chantries was particularly well endowed, and none of their chaplains could expect an annual income much in excess of five or six marks. Nevertheless within a few years, and almost certainly as a result of deliberate policy rather than of the vagaries of individual benefaction, the mayor and council had equipped themselves and their city with a team of chaplains, of *oratores*, directly at their service. The value of this *équipe* for the spiritual as well as economic welfare of the mayor and council's administration of the city was to survive until the eve of the Reformation. Personal animosities within so tightly knit a group of chantry chaplains were naturally not always easy to avoid; and in 1499 the city council found it necessary to reiterate the customary admonition that the four priests should be at 'good, quiete, peciable and honest conversacion' with one another while eating their meals in common within the hall at St William's chapel.[32] Their chantries and *camerae* were subject

[29] VCH, *York*, pp. 515–16; *York City Chamberlains' Accounts, 1396–1500*, ed. R.B. Dobson, Surtees Society, 192 (1980), pp. xxi–xxii, xxviii.

[30] YCA, G.70, no. 1. Wistow's chantry survived within St William's Chapel until its dissolution in 1536 (*York Civic Records*, iv, p. 144).

[31] YCA, G.70, nos 2, 5, 8. For a fifth chantry founded in St William's Chapel, to pray for the prominent fourteenth-century Selby family, see *York Memorandum Book*, i, pp. 24–5; ii, pp. 51–2.

[32] *York Civic Records*, ii, p. 141; cf. Raine, *Mediaeval York*, pp. 215–16.

to regular aldermanic visitation; and the hours at which these chaplains recited or sang their masses were also often subjected to detailed regulation in order to suit the convenience of councillors attending meetings and of other inhabitants of the town crossing the bridge on their daily business.[33] In such and many other ways the chantry chaplains of St William's Chapel could be left in no doubt at all that it was to their services for the living, as much as to their prayers for the dead, that they owed their prominent position as perhaps the best known and most exposed chantry chaplains in the city.

Only slightly more secluded were the priests who after 1412 came to serve the three chantries located in the chapel of St Anne on the city's second most important bridge, over the little River Foss. Almost a century after the mayor and council's deliberate sponsorship of perpetual chantries on Ouse Bridge, their successors took a conscious decision to increase yet again the number of chantry chaplains in the service of the city. According to Richard II's charter of 11 February 1393 which authorised the citizens to purchase lands worth £100 per annum to maintain the bridges of Ouse and Foss, the latter was then so fragile 'that it cannot survive for long without major reconstruction and repairs'. From the very outset of these repairs, however, one of the primary motives of the civic government was to build a new chapel on the enlarged Foss Bridge, a chapel quite specifically constructed to house altars at which masses could be said for the souls of the royal family and for the mayor and citizens of the town.[34] To that extent St Anne's Chapel on Foss Bridge was even more obviously a civic chantry chapel than was that of St William on Ouse Bridge, a fact more or less explicitly recognised by the dean and chapter of York cathedral when they licensed the mayor and citizens to celebrate *tres missas peculiares* there in November 1424.[35]

As the three perpetual chantries created in the new St Anne's Chapel were initially brought into existence by an act of civic corporate will, it is therefore hardly surprising that their foundation deeds figure prominently among the original deeds in the city's archives. These deeds make it abundantly clear that in the early fifteenth century there was still no shortage of York citizens eager to respond to the civic appeal to establish chantries on Foss Bridge. As early as 1412, the executors of the late

[33] *York Civic Records*, iii, p. 18; cf. iv, p. 166.

[34] *York Memorandum Book*, i, pp. 143–5; cf. ii, p. 72. The foundation of a chantry on a newly completed or repaired bridge naturally enhanced the pious significance of both causes; and it may not be altogether coincidental that the St Anne's Chapel chantries at York were established only a few years after the endowment of the celebrated chapel of St Mary on Wakefield Bridge by Edmund, duke of York, in 1398: see *YCS*, ii, pp. 312–14; G.H. Cook, *Mediaeval Chantries and Chantry Chapels* (London, 1947), pp. 44–5.

[35] Borthwick Institute, Reg. 5A (Sede Vacante Register, 1299–1554), fo. 388v; *Fabric Rolls of York Minster*, ed. J. Raine, Surtees Society, 35 (1859), p. 238.

Alan de Hamerton, a prominent York merchant, had amassed enough lands, tenements and rents to support a chantry chaplain there at a stipend of £5 a year.[36] Much more impressive was the 'great beneficence of Nicholas Blackburn, senior, former Admiral of the King of England and Mayor of York (in 1412–13)'. As John Leland noticed on his visits to York over a century later, Blackburn was probably the most prominent of all lay founders of chantries in late medieval York; and in view of his various other projects, for instance his double chantry foundation at the York Dominican convent, it is remarkable to discover that in December 1424 he was able to assign various messuages and tenements as well as no less than 340 marks in cash to support a chaplain at the high altar of St Anne's Chapel.[37] Quite as ambitious was the third and last chantry in the Foss Bridge chapel, established in February 1428 by yet another York mercer and ex-mayor (1413–14), Robert Holme Jr. In this case Holme's initial financial grant to the mayor and commonalty was no less than 500 marks, more than enough to provide the chaplain appointed to pray for his and his family's souls with the generous (by York city standards) stipend of ten marks per annum.[38] All three of these 'prests of Fossebrygg' survived to the 1530s, receiving their stipends from the York city chamberlains and usually living in houses rented from the city's wardens of Foss Bridge.[39] Once again the chaplains in question were expected to act as a team, co-operating in acts of common worship wherever possible: Robert Holme specifically founded his own chantry on the assumption that 'the number of priests, clerks and other ecclesiastical ministers' in St Anne's Chapel would increase to the extent that his own chaplain 'should attend personally, wearing a surplice and singing'.[40] How far these ambitions were fully achieved is by no means easy to know; but there can be no doubt that St Anne's Chapel was the most impressive – and most characteristic – new 'prayer house' of early fifteenth-century York. Located only a few yards from the great and then new hall of the York mercers (now Merchant Adventurers) in Fossgate, this chapel on Foss Bridge was also a memorial to the golden age of the city's overseas *mercatores*. Few architectural disasters in the history of the city are more to be lamented by the medieval historian than the gradual dismantling of

[36] YCA, G.70, no. 30. By 1431–2 at latest, the chaplain of the Hamerton chantry had been provided with a full set of vestments (*York Memorandum Book*, i, p. 236).

[37] YCA, G.70, nos 31, 32; cf. John Leland, *Itinerary*, ed. L. Toulmin Smith (London, 1906–10), v, p. 144.

[38] YCA, G.70, nos 34, 35: the advowson of this chantry remained in the hands of the Holme family until the early sixteenth century (James Torre, 'Antiquities of the City of York', York Minster Library, fo. 745).

[39] *York Chamberlains' Accounts*, pp. 13–14, 23, 32, 62, 74, 92–3, 109, 125, 151; *York Civic Records*, iii, p. 174.

[40] YCA, G.70, no. 35.

St Anne's Chapel in the reign of Elizabeth, with the ultimate result that now 'so far as is known not one stone of it has survived'.[41]

The two bridge chapels of late medieval York accordingly provided the mayor and commonalty with a unique and eagerly seized opportunity: to control and manage not only the occasional isolated perpetual chantry but also what amounted to a couple of separate and substantial ecclesiastical establishments. In the parish churches of the city the mayor and aldermen naturally had to step a little more cautiously. Nevertheless, the twenty-five original deeds within the York city archives which relate to the foundation of perpetual chantries in those churches altogether confirm a prevailing general impression that the latter were all subjected to meticulous and at times almost obsessive lay control.[42] Naturally enough, it is the wishes of the benefactor, his executors and no doubt their advisers, which loom largest in the documents themselves. Thus in 1395 the chaplain of Robert Holme Sr's elaborate chantry foundation at Holy Trinity, Goodramgate, was required to assemble with six other chaplains on the day of the founder's obit to say the Placebo and Dirige 'with music', a ceremony to be followed by the singing of a requiem mass on the following day.[43] An even more informative example of posthumously minute control on the part of the deceased is provided by the perpetual chantry founded at All Saints, North Street, in November 1411 to celebrate for the soul of the recently deceased dyer, Adam de Banke, mayor of the city in 1405. Not only did Banke's executors require the chaplains of this new chantry to reside continuously and to refrain from celebrating pecuniary masses outside the church: they also prescribed his duties and financial commitments on the anniversary of the founder's death in scrupulous detail. Once again co-operation with the other members of the parish clergy ('wearing a surplice, to sing the canonical hours and parochial masses on every Sunday and festival with the other chaplains, clerks and ministers of that church') was essential. More significantly still, it was to be the mayor of York or his deputy who conferred the chantry on presentation by the rector and four senior parishioners; and it was also the mayor who had the responsibility of removing criminal, incontinent or mutilated chaplains.[44] Few founders of perpetual chantries in York's parish churches were quite as precisely exacting as were the executors of Adam de Banke; but the majority of the York townsmen certainly did envisage the possibility of direct and speedy intervention by the mayor and commonalty either against a negligent chaplain or against those holders of

[41] RCHM, *York*, v, p. 104; Raine, *Mediaeval York*, pp. 69–70.

[42] Cf. Wood-Legh, *Perpetual Chantries*, pp. 65–92; C. Burgess, '"By Quick and by Dead": Wills and Pious Provision in Late Medieval Bristol', *English Historical Review*, 102 (1987), pp. 837–58.

[43] YCA, G.70, no. 24.

[44] Ibid., no. 27.

urban tenements who failed to make their due rent payments towards the sustenance of the chantries in the city.[45]

In the case of several York chantries, moreover, the mayor and corporation had direct responsibility for that sustenance themselves. All the surviving civic chamberlains' accounts of the fifteenth century systematically record the payment of annual stipends to a group of chaplains who derived all or most of their income from the city government itself. Among these *salaria capellanorum* were the £5 6s. 8d. and £4 2s. 0d. paid to the two chaplains respectively serving the chantries of Adam de Banke and John Catton in All Saints, North Street; and the chaplains entrusted with commemorating the souls of Alan Hamerton, Nicholas Blackburn and Robert Holme at St Anne's Chapel, Foss Bridge, similarly received annual stipends from the city chamber at the rates of £5, £5 6s. 8d. and £6 13s. 4d. The chantry chaplains located at St William's Chapel on Ouse Bridge received most of their income directly from the wardens of that bridge but also received a supplementary payment of £2 a year for their daily celebration of Our Lady's mass in that chapel.[46] In these and several other cases, the mayor and council of York were accordingly directly responsible for the financial survival as well as the disciplinary supervision of perpetual chantries in the city. The various foundation deeds surviving in the York civic archives make it sufficiently clear that when rents and tenements were delivered to the city government as an endowment for a new chantry these were added to the revenues of the wardens of the two bridges; but when the founder of a perpetual chantry preferred to deliver a large initial cash endowment to the mayor and commonalty this too was invested in real property. Of the 500 marks provided by Robert Holme Jr, in 1428 to endow his chantry in St Anne's Chapel, it is recorded that the city council invested 100 marks in buying a tenement in Coney Street which thereafter produced a net annual rent of 6 marks.[47] In such and many other ways, the city government of York (like all founders and sponsors of perpetual chantries in late medieval English towns) became entangled in complicated speculation within the highly volatile urban property market. Indeed one of the more common if paradoxical results of the growth of perpetual chantries in late medieval towns was a reduction in the size of the parish cemetery. The now celebrated timber-framed Our Lady Row (Nos 60–72 Goodramgate, originally built in 1316) is only one of many York examples of a phenomenon which still deserves more study at a national level – the erection of two- or three-storeyed *domos rentales* on the street fronts of

---

[45] Ibid., nos 4, 5, 8, 11, 14, 15, 21, 22, 30, 32.

[46] *York Chamberlains' Accounts*, pp. 13–14, 23, 32, 62, 73–4, 92–3, 136–7, 168–9, 184–5, 202.

[47] YCA, G.70, no. 34 (the context makes it clear that the mayor and council regarded an annual return of more than 5 per cent on invested capital as perfectly satisfactory); see *York Chamberlains' Accounts*, pp. xxxv–xxxvi.

urban churchyards in a deliberate attempt to provide rents to endow and support chantries.[48] To the extent that the main trend in fourteenth- and fifteenth-century property development in the English town was towards increasing institutional ownership of urban tenements, the impact of the perpetual chantry foundation on that trend would also clearly warrant more urgent attention than it has ever received.

Not that it will ever be easy to assess the no doubt volatile economic fortunes of the York perpetual chantries – and their chaplains – in anything but a highly impressionistic manner. Even in the case of the chantries directly financed and administered by the mayor and council, the fact that their endowments were usually absorbed within the city chamber's total sources of revenue makes it impossible now to determine whether problems of insolvency were occasional or perennial. However, there can be little doubt that financial security was generally much easier to achieve in the fourteenth century, when rent values in the city often remained remarkably buoyant, than during the increasingly difficult years for urban landlords which began to affect York soon after the creation of the Foss Bridge chantries in the 1420s.[49] Waning confidence among York's townsmen about the prospects of sustaining a perpetual chantry's resources into the future still seems the most probable explanation for what came to be a sharply declining pace of chantry foundation in the city as a whole.

In very general terms (and according to a pattern fully confirmed by the surviving original chantry documents preserved in the city archives) enthusiasm among the inhabitants of York for the foundation of perpetual chantries began comparatively late and declined comparatively early. Only three or four such chantries are known to have been founded within the city's parish churches before 1300. By contrast, almost forty perpetual chantries were created in the first half of the fourteenth century, at what was unquestionably the climacteric period of fervour for such institutions; and between 1350 and 1400, during a period when perpetual chantry foundation was still occasionally within the means of York craftsmen as well as merchants, the number of new chantries was still over twenty. During the three decades between 1400 and 1430, in some ways an 'Indian Summer' of urban prosperity at York, twelve new perpetual chantries were founded in the city. However, from that date until the total suppression of the 1540s, there were only nine new perpetual chantry foundations at

---

[48] RCHM, *York*, v, p. lix. The endowment of chantries by means of rent charges on newly-built housing is one of the main themes of S. Rees-Jones, 'Property, Tenure and Rents: Some Aspects of the Topography and Economy of Medieval York' (unpublished D.Phil thesis, University of York, 1987).

[49] J.N. Bartlett, 'The Expansion and Decline of York in the Later Middle Ages', *Economic History Review*, 2nd series, 12 (1959), pp. 28–32; Rees-Jones, 'Property, Tenure and Rents', passim; P.J.P. Goldberg, 'Mortality and Economic Change in the Diocese of York, 1390–1514', *Northern History*, 24 (1988), pp. 38–55.

York, one by a Yorkshire knight (Sir Ralph Bulmer at St Michael le Belfrey in 1472) and all the others by a small handful of the city's mercantile and aldermanic elite.[50] So pronounced a fall in the number of new perpetual chantries is almost certainly less the consequence of declining respect for the ideal of the private mass than an index of the gradual contraction of the number of sizeable mercantile fortunes in the fifteenth-century city. At all social levels within the town, it is evident that chantries and their chaplains were still highly valued: as late as 1503, to take only one example, 'the parochianz of Saynt Nicholas in Mekilgate putt in a bill of peticion for the reformacion of a chaunterie in the said Kyrke called Eschton chaunterie'.[51] On this occasion, as so often in the past and future, it was the mayor and commonalty who were required to come to the rescue; and as yet there were few visible signs of any erosion in their commitment to the chantries under their official or informal care. It was only as late as 1536, when they were under increasing pressure from 'great dett' and 'great ruyne and decay', that the civic council finally accepted the financially inevitable and secured from parliament that abrupt suppression of seven of the city's chantries which now seems so clear a portent of the universal dénouement a dozen years later.[52]

In many ways of course the mayor and commonalty of a city like York never had any alternative but to be heavily involved in the remarkable spate of late medieval perpetual chantry foundations within their midst. As the collection of foundation deeds in the York city archives once again makes abundantly clear, most of the men who established such chantries were themselves ex-mayors and aldermen of the city, predestined to believe that the civic council they had once served would be the most reliable custodian or supervisor of their spiritual foundations. Nor were the responsibilities incurred by that council without some very real compensations for itself. Above all, perhaps, the mayor and aldermen – as well as prominent parishioners in each city church – were provided with the possibilities of patronage. That last, and highly prized, commodity was not otherwise immediately available even to the most substantial inhabitants of a medieval town; and there can be little doubt that the ability to influence the appointment of chantry and other chaplains in

[50] These numerical estimates, based on royal licences for alienation in mortmain and the chantry commissioners' certificates of 1548 as well as references in York records, are unlikely to be absolutely complete: see Dobson, 'Foundation of Perpetual Chantries', above, p. 261; H. Swanson, *Medieval Artisans* (Oxford, 1989), p. 159.

[51] *York Civic Records*, ii, pp. 190–1. It has been pointed out by Dr Jennifer I. Kermode that during the fifteenth century more bequests were made to augment existing chantries than to create new ones: see her 'The Merchants of Three Northern Towns', in *Profession, Vocation and Culture in Later Medieval England: Essays Dedicated to the Memory of A.R. Myers*, ed. C.H. Clough (Liverpool, 1982), pp. 24–5.

[52] *York Civic Records*, iv, p. 144; A.G. Dickens, 'A Municipal Dissolution of Chantries, 1536', *Yorkshire Archaeological Journal*, 36 (1944–7), pp. 164–73.

the city's parish churches did more than anything to bind town's laity and clergy personally together. Indeed it seems to emerge from the York evidence that one of the motives for the establishment of a chantry at all was a testator's wish to safeguard the future of a priest who had served him long and faithfully as chaplain and confessor. In 1340, for example, Thomas Duraunt founded a perpetual chantry at the church of St Crux and appointed John de Grayngham as its first chaplain, on the express understanding that he was to be under no obligation to celebrate mass or attend matins and vespers in the church 'as long as he remains in the said Thomas's company'.[53] Nearly a century later, in 1435, John Turnour, the priest appointed by Richard Russell to serve his new chantry in St John's, Hungate, was so close an intimate of this ex-mayor that he went on to act as one of his executors and also received a bequest in Russell's will (to sing masses of course) of no less than 70 marks.[54]

Nor is future research at all likely to confirm that such chantry chaplains were quite so obscure, impoverished and isolated figures as is traditionally assumed. At York at least, an increasing proportion of these priests left wills which bear witness not only to their collections of vestments and service books but also to specialist skills which enhanced their status and value in the eyes of their parishioners.[55] In 1492 the city council authorised William Insklyff, chaplain of Robert Holme's chantry on Foss Bridge, 'to fynysche and make up two books, that is to say a masse book and a cowcher' despite the opposition of the company of city textwriters. More surprisingly perhaps, William Duffield, chaplain of St Thomas's chantry at All Saints, Pavement, in 1433, was in possession of several of the books once owned by the late Archbishop Thomas de Corbridge (1299–1304); while less serious volumes, including works of history and even a mysterious 'Balletboke', could be found among the goods of other fifteenth-century chantry priests of the city.[56] The contribution of the chantry priests both to the extension of literacy and the distribution of charity in the city is likely to have been as important as it is usually obscure; but it was more important still that they were expected by the laymen of York to integrate themselves for acts of common worship into the teams of parish clergy (comprising at least an average of six or seven in each of the forty town churches) which lay at the heart of whatever popular religion

---

[53] YCA, G.70, no. 12.

[54] Borthwick Institute, Probate Register, 3, fos 439–40; *Testamenta Eboracensia*, ii, pp. 52–7.

[55] See, e.g., *Testamenta Eboracensia*, i, pp. 73, 146, 196; ii, pp. 178, 184, 202, 268, 275; iii, p. 94; iv, p. 41. Cf. the comparatively favourable judgement of P. Mackie on 'Chaplains in the Diocese of York, 1480–1530: The Testamentary Evidence', *Yorkshire Archaeological Journal*, 58 (1986), pp. 123–33.

[56] *York Civic Records*, ii, p. 78; *York Chamberlains' Accounts*, pp. 178, 185, 191, 202; *Testamenta Eboracensia*, ii, pp. 87–8, 213; cf. Mackie, 'Chaplains in Diocese of York', pp. 126–7.

in the city actually was.[57] With such numbers of priests (and private and communal masses) at their disposal, most citizens of York presumably never felt that they were in danger of suffering from serious spiritual neglect as they contemplated their progress into the next world. When, on a famous and often cited occasion in 1388, Mayor William Selby made his controversial declaration that 'the chantry priests and other stipendiary clergy of this city and its suburbs are the special orators of the citizens, their patrons and their masters', he was not in fact being at all economical with the truth.[58]

The laymen of late fifteenth-century York were accordingly not without many spiritual and other rewards for the serious financial cares imposed upon them by the scores of perpetual and other chantries within the city. However, the perpetual chantry was then – as it remains in retrospect – a highly ambiguous institution. It is a good deal easier to demonstrate that the mayor and council of York were strenuous in their endeavours to preserve chantries at a respectable spiritual level than to prove that they were always or often successful in doing so. Most arduous of their responsibilities perhaps, especially in a system of 'urban self-government by amateurs', were those presented by the complex legal, administrative and disciplinary problems which clustered round every chantry in the city.[59] A close perusal of the original foundation deeds which have provided the basis for this essay leaves one with the cumulative impression that in order for the founder of a chantry to secure some remission of purgatorial pains in the next world, his family, his descendants, his executors, and the mayor and council were often forced to undergo many purgatorial hours on his behalf in the earthly city he had left behind him. By a paradox fundamental at most levels of the medieval Christian church, the quest for one's personal salvation might all too easily add to the worldly care of one's neighbours and descendants. More paradoxically still, perhaps, enthusiasm for the private chantry made the parish churches of York and elsewhere less secluded, more vibrant with diverse religious activity, than they had ever been. As Christopher Brooke pointed out in the book cited at the very beginning of this essay, 'the bustle of chantry

---

[57] J.A. Hoeppner Moran, *The Growth of English Schooling, 1340–1548: Learning, Literacy and Laicisation in Pre-Reformation York Diocese* (Princeton, 1985), pp. 83–90; M. Rubin, *Charity and Community in Medieval Cambridge* (Cambridge, 1987), pp. 184–92. That there were approximately 260 parish chaplains in fifteenth-century York is established by a reference to bequests of 4d. to each of them in the will (4 September 1436) of Thomas Bracebridge: Borthwick Institute, York Probate Register, 3, fo. 488; Dobson, 'Perpetual Chantries of York', above, pp. 264–5.

[58] *York Memorandum Book*, ii, 19; cf. P. Heath, 'Between Reform and Reformation: The English Church in the Fourteenth and Fifteenth Centuries', *Journal of Ecclesiastical History*, 41 (1990), p. 675 ('One aspect which emerges clearly from all these studies is the growing experience shared by laymen and women of proprietorship over the church or clergy').

[59] See especially Wood-Legh, *Perpetual Chantries*, pp. 155–81 ('Chantries and the Towns').

priests and the singing of chantry masses helped to make large churches resemble vast mausolea'.[60]

However, for modern travellers in quest of the personalised religion of the fifteenth-century city, the primary objectives of pilgrimage are to be found less in the major mausoleum of York Minster than in parish churches like St Michael's, Spurriergate (the tomb of Sir Richard York), Holy Trinity, Goodramgate (the memorial brass of Mayor Thomas Danby) and All Saints, North Street (the Nicholas Blackburn window).[61] It is in such churches that even now one may occasionally encounter battered memorials to the religious proclivities of York citizens who once hoped to be remembered – and not just by the historian – for ever. Perhaps a greater reward yet may await those who visit the still surviving, if now almost totally stripped and denuded, chantry chapel of St James, founded by the powerful Holme family next to the south aisle of the nave of Holy Trinity, Goodramgate: only there perhaps in late twentieth-century York may it be possible physically to recapture what the appeal of a perpetual chantry could once have been.[62] If so, how appropriate that 600 years ago this was exactly the church and chapel in which Robert Holme Sr envisaged the frequent presence of twenty-five chaplains, not only to intercede for his own soul but also 'so that divine worship through them may be there increased'.[63] The perpetual chantries of the late medieval English town are not always easy to defend or justify; but at the least they present the most ambitious – and most costly – attempts ever made to reconcile and even merge the different spiritual needs of church and city at a deeply personal level.

[60] Brooke, *Popular Religion in the Middle Ages*, p. 110.

[61] RCHM, *York*, iii, pp. 7, 18–19; v, p. 7; VCH, *York*, pp. 370, 385.

[62] The arms of the Holme family are still visible on a shield near the entrance to this chantry chapel. Its interior is lit (much to the confusion of several architectural historians in the past and even the present) by two reused reticulated windows of the early fourteenth century inserted into the later outer wall (RCHM, *York*, v, pp. 6–7; and see above, n. 23).

[63] Borthwick Institute, Probate Register, 3, fos 100v–103v; Cook, 'Early Civic Wills', *Associated Architectural Societies, Reports and Papers*, 28 (1906), pp. 20–1.

13

Contrasting Chronicles: Historical Writing at York and Durham at the Close of the Middle Ages

'The form which historical writing took in the Middle Ages is an index of the intellectual standards of monasticism.'[1] By that severe if not altogether unpersuasive criterion, it might well be supposed that the intellectual life conducted by the major monastic, cathedral and mendicant communities of fifteenth-century England must have lacked both the excitement and the intellectual curiosity enjoyed by their predecessors. Not for nothing perhaps has John Taylor's own indefatigable interest in the medieval English monastic chronicle tended to slacken after the *annus mirabilis* of 1399; and even Dr Antonia Gransden has recently concluded her detailed survey of the last stages of the monastic tradition of English medieval historiography with the melancholy reflection that this tradition 'was all but dead well before the end of the fifteenth century'.[2] Although the gradual disintegration and final collapse of the most impressive genre of historical writing ever produced in medieval England is impossible to deny, that decline has perhaps never been altogether satisfactorily explained. No longer does it seem plausible to account for the demise of the monastic chronicle so many decades before the demise of the monasteries themselves in such general and over-simple terms as the supposed moral decline or 'spiritual rusticity' of the fifteenth-century English religious.[3] Perhaps, as John Taylor himself has done much to document, the emergence during the previous century of increasingly large numbers of secular clerks and laymen who practised the art of historical writing outside the precinct walls of England's religious houses was crucial in bringing an end to the ascendancy of the latter in this field?[4] Even so, it remains not a little surprising that so few members of

[1] J. Taylor, *Medieval Historical Writing in Yorkshire*, St Anthony's Hall Publications, 19 (1961), p. 25.

[2] J. Taylor, *English Historical Literature in the Fourteenth Century* (Oxford, 1987), pp. 174–94; A. Gransden, *Historical Writing in England*, ii, *c. 1307 to the Early Sixteenth Century* (London, 1982), pp. 342–424.

[3] D. Knowles, *The Religious Orders in England*, iii (Cambridge, 1959), pp. 456–68; H.O. Evenett, 'The Last Stages of Medieval Monasticism in England', *Studia monastica*, 2 (1960), pp. 387–419; and cf. C. Harper-Bill, *The Pre-Reformation Church in England, 1400–1530* (London, 1989), pp. 36–43.

[4] J. Taylor, 'Letters and Letter Collections in England, 1300–1420', *Nottingham Medieval Studies*, 24 (1980), pp. 65–70; idem, *Historical Literature*, pp. 14–16, 24–36.

what were still in the 1530s the most closed and self-regarding religious communities in the country should have responded to this new challenge by demonstrating a detectable interest in perpetuating the memory of either their past or their present. To take the example of the English Benedictine monk most central to John Taylor's own interests, why did Ranulf Higden of St Werburgh's Abbey, Chester, have no real successors after his death in 1363–64?[5]

It need hardly be said that so large a problem is easy to pose but impossible to answer in this short essay. Indeed a full explanation of the collapse of the tradition of historical writing in late medieval English religious houses would almost certainly necessitate a full-scale analysis not only of the well-known internal contradictions and uncertainties of purpose within that tradition, but also of the new patterns of sensibility which transformed the corporate attitudes of monasteries and cathedrals alike during the decades before and after 1400. Such at least are the conclusions which seem to emerge from the following very cursory review of what apparently happened to the practice of writing historical work within the two most important religious communities of northern England in the fifteenth century, the Benedictine community of St Cuthbert at Durham and the metropolitan cathedral church of St Peter at York. Here, if anywhere in the late medieval northern province, one would self-evidently have expected a continuing obsession with the spiritual glories of the past and the not inconsiderable material successes of the present; but at both these major *ecclesiae matrices* of the north it is hardly an exaggeration to state that by the second half of the fifteenth century the tradition of writing the history of the past, or indeed the present, had reached almost if not quite vanishing-point. Despite the extraordinary differences between the constitutional structures, the religious observances and the composition of the clergy serving these two cathedrals, they were eventually alike in failing to sustain a creative interest in the history which gave them their sense of self-identity and their international fame.[6] More ironically still, the fragments of historical composition occasionally being produced in both cathedrals at the very end of the middle ages are surprisingly similar in suggesting a final involuntary return of the full-blown flower of the English monastic chronicle to its origins, a reversion to 'annals' at times even less sophisticated than those once produced by the major Anglo-Saxon churches of the pre-Conquest church.

---

[5] J. Taylor, *The Universal Chronicle of Ranulf Higden* (Oxford, 1966), pp. 110–51. Dr Gransden makes the important point that neither Higden's many continuators nor those other 'massive histories' of the period, the *Brut* and John of Tynemouth's *Historia aurea*, tried to reproduce his own encyclopaedic and universal approach: *Historical Writing*, ii, pp. 56–7.

[6] See the surveys of the two cathedrals in G.E. Aylmer and R. Cant (eds), *A History of York Minster* (Oxford, 1977), pp. 44–108, and R.B. Dobson, *Durham Priory, 1400–1450* (Cambridge, 1973).

Nowhere in the fifteenth-century north, perhaps nowhere in England, is this contraction of historical horizons more poignant than within St Cuthbert's great religious community at Durham. For within twenty or so years of the original transformation of Durham cathedral into a Benedictine cathedral priory at the hands of Bishop William of St Calais in 1083, the monk Symeon and his contemporaries had already validated their spiritual ascendancy in the north by what amounted to the creation of a sustained historical vision of the whole of northern British history since the age of Bede.[7] This vision was of course expressed in its most lengthy and influential form within the *Libellus de exordio atque procursu istius, hoc est Dunelmensis ecclesiae*, almost certainly composed by the monk Symeon who actually witnessed the translation of St Cuthbert's remains to their new shrine behind the cathedral's new high altar in 1104. According to the *Libellus*, the fundamental key to the history of the see of St Cuthbert from its foundation at Lindisfarne by St Aidan in 635 until the death of Bishop William of St Calais in 1096, was a remarkable and at times astonishing spiritual continuity throughout the violent political vicissitudes of more than 400 years. It followed, to cite a celebrated phrase from the *Libellus* itself, that in 1083 Bishop St Calais 'was not instituting a new monastic order but restoring an old one'.[8]

Symeon provided the model which nearly all his successors at Durham were to emulate. At the centre of all the many diverse and often confusing works of history produced within or near the cathedral during the next three centuries lay the monks' continued determination to demonstrate that St Cuthbert remained the tutelary and ever-watchful protector of their community. It was no doubt for this reason above all that already by 1200 'History writing at Durham . . . tended to parochialism'. However such historical parochialism achieved some not inconsiderable successes on the banks of the Wear: few saints of twelfth-century England, for example, were as fortunate as the comparatively obscure Godric of Finchale in attracting three *vitae* at such rapid speed.[9] More obviously still, the

---

[7] T. Arnold (ed.), *Historia ecclesiae Dunhelmensis* in *Symeonis monachi opera omnia*, RS (1882), i, pp. 1–135; according to this providential interpretation of northern history, the reintroduction of the Benedictine life into St Cuthbert's own *patria* during the 1070s and 1080s was itself the direct result of the reading of *historia Anglorum* by west country monks (ibid., p. 108).

[8] Ibid., p. 11. To that extent, and somewhat unusually, the monks of Durham exploited Anglo-Saxon history to validate a post-Conquest initiative. Cf. R.W. Southern, 'Aspects of the European Tradition of Historical Writing', 4, 'The Sense of the Past', *Transactions of the Royal Historical Society*, 5th series, 23 (1973), pp. 243–63; J. Campbell, 'Some Twelfth-Century Views of the Anglo-Saxon Past', *Peritia*, 3 (1984), pp. 131–50.

[9] H.S. Offler, *Medieval Historians of Durham* (Durham, 1958), p. 13, a lecture to which this essay is much indebted. Cf. J. Stevenson, ed., *Libellus de vita et miraculis S. Godrici*, Surtees Society, 20 (1847); A. Gransden, *Historical Writing in England*, i, *c. 550–c. 1307* (London, 1974), pp. 270, 308–9.

succession of Durham monks and others who added continuations to the *Libellus de exordio* from the mid twelfth to the mid fourteenth centuries were by no means naïve in their concepts of how arguments and *exempla* from the historic past could enhance the morale and welfare of their present community. The 'domestic' histories produced at Durham by the anonymous twelfth-century continuators of the *Libellus*, then by Geoffrey of Coldingham in *c.* 1215, and, above all, by the perspicacious Robert de Graystanes (who completed his section of the history of Durham in 1336) now all urgently deserve editions less antique than those of Henry Wharton and James Raine the elder.[10] When such editions finally emerge, it may well appear that no monastic cathedral in medieval England displayed a more sustained expertise in writing genuinely local history, and in squaring some difficult circles, than did these Durham chroniclers. At one level, Graystanes and his colleagues consistently used historical evidence, and the historic past itself, against the unwelcome intrusions of bishops like Antony Bek and Lewis de Beaumont; at another, they were increasingly at pains to produce highly flattering images of those bishops in order to make the latter seem not entirely unworthy successors of St Cuthbert himself.[11]

As will be seen, this progressive tendency to write the history of the contemporary church of Durham in terms of its *Gesta episcoporum* (the title, significantly enough, by which the *Libellus de exordio* was soon to be best known) became thoroughly entrenched in the mid fourteenth century, exactly when the accounts of those episcopal *gesta* start to show obvious signs of perfunctory, excessively episodic and even banal compilation, 'an historical tradition in full dissolution'.[12] All the more remarkable was the apparently single-handed attempt by one of St Cuthbert's monks, John Wessington, to revivify the proud tradition of historical writing on the Durham peninsula. John Wessington, professed as a Durham monk in 1390 and then a student at Durham College, Oxford, before becoming sacrist and chancellor of his convent in the years preceding his election as prior in November 1416, now holds a respected place among the ranks

[10] For Raine's (excessively severe in the light of his own editorial lapses) animadversions on the 'utter worthlessness' of Wharton's 1691 edition of Coldingham, Graystanes and 'Chambre' in *Anglia sacra*, see *Historiae Dunelmensis scriptores tres*, Surtees Society, 9 (1839), pp. vii–xv, 3–123.

[11] After his death in 1311, even Bishop Bek, the source of so many of the convent's tribulations, received from Graystanes the posthumous tribute that by his benefactions 'he honoured the church of Durham more than any of his predecessors' (*Scriptores tres*, p. 91).

[12] See Oxford, Bodleian Library, MS Fairfax 6, fos vi verso, 213; MS Laud Misc. 700, fo. 14v; Offler, *Medieval Historians*, pp. 14 and n. 31, 16. The first detailed demonstration that from the pontificate of Bishop Richard de Bury onwards the Durham *Gesta episcoporum* ceases to be a coherent chronicle written by one historian was provided by N. Denholm-Young, 'The Birth of a Chronicle', *Bodleian Quarterly Record*, 7 (1932–4), pp. 325–8.

of the most learned Benedictines of fifteenth-century England.[13] Within a historical context, he fills a more exemplary role as the most dedicated northern English scholar to write at length about the past between 1400 and 1540. It therefore seems all the more ungenerous to suggest that on close acquaintance John Wessington may prove to be an example of that not uncommon late medieval literary figure, the historian who promises more than he performs. To some extent such is admittedly a provisional judgement, above all because Wessington was a prolific author in a variety of different genres. Few of his treatises and *libelli* have been analysed in detail, all the more serious a deficiency in the case of a writer who was so systematically derivative from earlier chronicles and records. Indeed his careful assembling of historical evidence for use in preparing legal or other briefs on his community's or his bishop's behalf is unfailingly impressive, even if he may sometimes cast his net too widely and irrelevantly.[14] What Wessington's large and diverse output proves beyond question is that he, and no doubt many of his fellow monks, were still thoroughly imbued with – and sustained by – the Durham historical tradition as the latter emanated from Bede. However, what it equally proves is that Wessington was largely uninterested in, or incapable of, adding substantively to that tradition.

Such a conclusion seems to emerge most clearly from Prior Wessington's most considerable literary achievement and the one most germane to the subject of this essay – his large-scale survey of the history of the see of St Cuthbert. Wessington's revised and reorganised history of the origins and development of the church of Durham (*De exordio et statu ecclesie cathedralis quondam Lindisfarnensis, post Conchestrensis, demum Dunelmensis, ac de gestis pontificum eiusdem*) was first identified by Sir Edmund Craster in his remarkable paper on the 'Red Book' of Durham; but the work has received, rightly or wrongly, virtually no scholarly attention since Craster's discoveries of over sixty years ago.[15] Of the three manuscripts of the history still known to survive, all written in the first half of the fifteenth century, the first and draft version (Bodleian Library, MS. Laud Misc. 748, fos 6–67), fills almost sixty leaves of closely-written and often interlined text, so comprising a work incomparably larger than any other associated with the prior. According to Craster's persuasive analysis, this Laud manuscript not only forms the earliest version of Wessington's 'new' history but is also itself divided into two parts, of which fos 6–47 provide a

---

[13] Knowles, *Religious Orders*, ii (1955), pp. 190–3; Dobson, *Durham Priory*, pp. 81–113, 378–86.

[14] Contemporary lists of Wessington's written works survive as DCD, Misc. Charters, 5727 (a) and (c): Reg. II, fos ix verso–x verso. Cf. *Scriptores tres*, pp. cclxviii–xxi; and for an attempt to identify all surviving tracts associated with the prior see R.B. Dobson, 'The Priory of Durham in the Time of John Wessington, Prior 1416–1446' (unpublished D.Phil. thesis, University of Oxford, 1962), pp. 580–6.

[15] H.H.E. Craster, 'The Red Book of Durham', *English Historical Review*, 40 (1925), pp. 504–19.

revised draft of the history of the see from its origins to the pontificate of Hugh du Puiset (1153–95), while fos 50–67 take the story of the bishopric of Durham from 1174 to 1356 and seem to be an original draft.[16] There is little doubt that the revised draft of MS Laud Misc. 748 was the original source of the two other extant texts of Wessington's new history, namely those to be found within Lincoln's Inn Library, MS Hales 114 (the 'Liber Ruber' itself) and British Library, MS Cotton, Claudius, D.IV. As the latter is the most handsomely executed copy of the three, decorated on its first page with the armorial shields of the see and priory of Durham as well as that of the Wessington family itself, Craster was inclined to believe that this was the final prestige edition of the history, presumably destined for the common monastic library at Durham.[17] It might be equally possible to conjecture that after Prior Wessington had instructed a scribe to complete MS Claudius D.IV for the convent's library from the first part of his original draft, he decided to have a third, rather less accomplished, copy (MS Hales 114) made for use in the monastic chancery, where it was certainly preserved in the early sixteenth century.[18] Nor does there seem any firm reason to suppose with Sir Edmund Craster that there must at some time have existed yet a fourth copy of Wessington's history, now lost but once consulted and summarised by John Leland.[19] On all the evidence available, for the rest of the middle ages Prior Wessington's revisionist history of the see of St Cuthbert circulated not at all outside the Durham cloister and perhaps not very widely within it.

Nevertheless, and despite its inadequacies, Wessington's *Libellum de exordio et statu ecclesie cathedralis quondam Lindisfarnensis* provides a unique opportunity to explore the historical mentality of an intelligent and devout Durham monk at the beginning of the fifteenth century. The first draft of the history (MS Laud Misc. 748) is of particular interest in this connection, as it seems to have been written and partly dictated by Wessington himself during his years as monastic chancellor shortly before 1416.[20] What is immediately clear is that Wessington had no intention of abandoning the traditional canon of historical work at Durham as it was represented in his community's library. Thus for the whole of the pre-Conquest history of the church of Lindisfarne, Chester-le-Street and Durham, the 'new' history relied predominantly on Symeon's so-called

[16] Ibid, pp. 508–11; MS Laud Misc. 748, fos 6–67.

[17] Craster, 'Red Book', pp. 513–14.

[18] Lincoln's Inn, MS Hales 114, fo. 1 (where Thomas Swalwell, monastic chancellor at the beginning of the sixteenth century, has written his signature); cf. *Scriptores tres*, p. ccccxxii.

[19] Craster, 'Red Book', p. 514; and for Leland's consultation of other manuscripts at Durham see his *Itinerary*, ed. L. Toulmin Smith (London, 1907–10), v, pp. 129–31.

[20] The early folios of MS Laud Misc. 748 contain instructions to the copyist (e.g. 'Nota hic processum in parvo libro ad talem signum' at fo. 52) which are probably in Wessington's own hand.

Historia Dunelmensis ecclesiae. However Wessington was at pains, for it seems to have been his major intention, to elucidate and expand from other sources Symeon's narrative whenever the latter seemed to be in danger of becoming too bare and unadorned. Thus the third book of Bede's *Ecclesiastical History* (known as *De gestis Anglorum* at Durham) and the third book of Henry of Huntingdon were cited on the very first page of Wessington's history.[21] Although Wessington's frequent insertions can sometimes spoil the simplicity of Symeon's account of the early days of the Durham church, his new arrangement of familiar historical material usually reveals a comparatively skilful practitioner of 'scissors and paste', at least for the period before the pontificate of Hugh du Puiset.

From the late twelfth century onwards, however, Prior Wessington's new history of Durham (as represented in the unrevised draft of MS Laud Misc. 748, fos 50–67) is a good deal less satisfactory. The prior's decision not to revise this section of the Laud Misc. manuscript nor to use it as the basis for a lengthier edition of a Durham history may be the result of lack of leisure after his election to the priorate in 1416; but it is quite possible that he himself realised its inadequacy. This inadequacy is all the more disappointing in that the modern historian would prefer to read Wessington's comments on this later rather than pre-Conquest period, particularly if he had taken his narrative down to his own lifetime. The prior however presumably never had any intention of continuing his composite chronicle into the fifteenth century; and to criticise him on those grounds would be to misrepresent his aims and position as a historian. There was a more prosaic reason why Wessington did so little justice to the period in Durham's history from 1174 to 1356: he left himself too little space. Within only eighteen folios (50–67) of the Laud Misc. MS, the prior made what must now seem a foredoomed attempt to combine the domestic account of events at Durham provided by Geoffrey de Coldingham and Robert de Graystanes with enlarged references to events of national or European importance. The only purpose these references now serve is to suggest what historical episodes of the preceding 200 years seemed most significant to a Durham monk writing in the early fifteenth century. It is not surprising that an English Benedictine should end his chronicle with brief accounts of the three most famous military victories of the fourteenth century (Crécy, Neville's Cross and Poitiers) as well as of the *mortalitas* of the first onslaught of the Black Death, misdated by a not untypical slip of the pen to 1368.[22] More

---

[21] MS Laud Misc. 748, fo. 6.

[22] Ibid., fos 66–7; and for Wessington's understandable interest in English humiliations at the hands of the Scots after Bannockburn see fos 61–2. For a recent important discovery of one of Wessington's sources for Border affairs during the reign of Edward III, see H.S. Offler, 'A Note on the Northern Franciscan Chronicle', *Nottingham Medieval Studies*, 28 (1984), pp. 45–59.

revealing are Prior Wessington's reserved comments on the great monastic reforming legislation of the 1330s promulgated by Benedict XII, 'qui, anno pontificatus sui tercio, pro statu monachorum constituciones edidit gravissimos . . . quas penas papa Clemens VI misericorditer commutavit'.[23] However, much the greater part of the section of Wessington's history from the 1170s to the 1350s is devoted to the internal history of his convent and especially to its notorious disputes with various bishops of Durham and archbishops of York, apparently still the main focus of local historical interest in his cloister well over a century later.[24]

As Sir Edmund Craster pointed out, perhaps the greatest fascination of John Wessington's revised *Libellus de statu Lindisfarnensis, id est Dunelmensis ecclesiae* is the unrivalled light it throws on what historical texts were actually available to a serious student of the past in close proximity to what was probably the most substantial single collection of historical texts in the late medieval north.[25] To an exceptional extent not only can the sources Wessington consulted and copied be identified but so too can the very manuscripts in which he encountered them. Thus the texts which make up at least three-quarters of Wessington's history seem to derive from two books only: the *Gesta episcoporum* (Symeon and his continuators), especially in the copy now preserved as Bodleian Library, MS Fairfax 6, and the fine three-volumed edition of the *Historia Aurea* still extant as Lambeth Palace, MSS 10–12.[26] Besides these two central authorities, Wessington naturally drew especially heavily on a variety of less substantial Durham historical works and saints' lives, far too numerous to list here. Most interesting of all Wessington's sources to the modern historian, although there is no clear evidence that he appreciated its significance himself, was the *Liber summi altaris ecclesie Dunelmensis*, skilfully reconstituted and then printed by Sir Edmund Craster.[27] Except for copious citation, as in nearly all his work, from the notorious Durham 'foundation' charters

[23] Ibid., fo. 64v.

[24] For his accounts of these most searing episodes in the recent ecclesiastical history of the north, Wessington depended primarily on Robert de Graystanes's chronicle but seems to have occasionally used, less astutely than Graystanes himself, one of the latter's own most important sources, the so-called *Annales Dunelmenses*: cf. MS Laud Misc. 748, fo. 57v; and F. Barlow (ed.), *Durham Annals and Documents of the Thirteenth Century*, Surtees Society, 155 (1945), p. 64.

[25] For a longer (but not at all comprehensive) account of historical works available in the early fifteenth-century Durham libraries than is possible here see Dobson, 'Priory of Durham', pp. 491–501; cf. Craster, 'Red Book', pp. 516–19.

[26] At least part of MS Fairfax 6 was written by 'Petrus plenus amoris' (fos vi verso, 1), conceivably the monk Peter of Durham who was monastic librarian in 1366 (DCD, Misc. Charters, 4297). Lambeth Palace, MS 12, fo. 254, has an entry inserted by John Fishburn, Prior Wessington's chancellor: for this work see V.H. Galbraith, 'The *Historia Aurea* and Sources of the St Albans Chronicles, 1327–77', *Essays in History Presented to R.L. Poole*, ed. H.W.C. Davis (Oxford, 1927), pp. 379–98.

[27] Craster, 'Red Book', 523–9.

of the twelfth century, Wessington's history made much less use of the convent's muniments than might have been supposed; but for information on more general history he was eager to exploit the respectable if not particularly voluminous collection of *Libri historiarum* preserved within the monastic cloister at Durham in the early fifteenth century.[28] Several of these volumes are now less than easy to trace; but at least it is tempting to suppose that the copy of Ranulf Higden's *Polychronicon* used extensively by Wessington may have been the one owned and eventually bequeathed to the community of St Cuthbert by Bishop Thomas Langley of Durham.[29]

Such were some of the standard sources, by no means an exhaustive list, available to the historical enquirer within the early fifteenth-century Durham cloister. They were to be pressed into service by Wessington again and again throughout his lifetime, not only to illuminate his full-scale history of St Cuthbert's see but also to document his many other tracts and treatises. Many of the latter indeed prove a good deal more lucid and coherent than the former, and in particular it might well be argued that Wessington proved more successful as a pioneering prosopographer than as a traditional monastic historian. Perhaps the most instructive of several possible examples is provided by his longest and most ambitious work on Benedictine history and theory, a treatise beginning with the words 'Quia de ortu sacrosanctae religionis monachorum plerisque vertitur in dubium' which occupies the first twenty-five folios of Durham, MS B.III.30. In this case Wessington's purpose was to provide a commentary upon a series of images or pictures of celebrated Benedictine monks, apparently painted on wood, already in place at the altar of SS. Benedict and Jerome within the cathedral church.[30] After detailed research, the biographies of no less than 148 different individuals (not all of them Black Monks) were written on parchment and attached to two or more wooden boards or *tabulae* placed in the vicinity of the altar for consultation by monks or visitors to the cathedral.[31] In this case Wessington also produced a separate list of the twenty-five authorities he had consulted in order to

---

[28] B. Botfield (ed.), *Catalogi veteres librorum ecclesiae cathedralis Dunelm*, Surtees Society, 7 (1838), where most of the 'history books' and 'chronicles' inventorised at pp. 30, 56–7, 107 still survive and can be identified. Cf. A.J. Piper, 'The Libraries of the Monks of Durham', in *Medieval Scribes, Manuscripts and Libraries: Essays Presented to N.R. Ker*, ed. M.B. Parkes and A.G. Watson (London, 1978), pp. 213–49.

[29] *Catalogi veteres*, p. 120; but (surprisingly perhaps) no copy of the *Polychronicon* now seems to survive at Durham; Taylor, *Universal Chronicle*, pp. 152–9.

[30] DCD, MS B.III.30, fos 1–25, briefly described in W.A. Pantin (ed.), *Documents Illustrating the Activities of the General and Provincial Chapters of the English Black Monks, 1215–1540*, ii, Camden 3rd series, 47 (1933), p. xiv. For the position of the altar in question see J.T. Fowler (ed.), *The Rites of Durham*, Surtees Society, 107 (1903), p. 112.

[31] As Wessington refers to 'in supremo gradu superioris tabule' (DCD, MS B.III.30, fo. 6) there seems no doubt that there was more than one of these tables or boards at the altar; for the popularity of *tabulae*, see below, n. 59, and G.H. Gerould, '*Tables* in Medieval Churches', *Speculum*, 1 (1926), pp. 439–40.

provide the biographical information he was purveying in this popular and condensed form.[32] Although this work (like several of his treatises) had the incidental polemical purpose of disputing the claims of canons regular to greater antiquity than the Benedictines, it is of even more importance in revealing how extensively, as will be seen later, the later medieval cathedral community might rely upon written *tabulae* for communicating historical knowledge. *Quia de ortu* also confirms that the painstaking compilation of biographical data constituted what was in many ways Wessington's own most successful form of historical writing.

If so, the strengths and limitations of John Wessington's work as a historian, however exceptional it seems at first sight, nevertheless still exemplify the general transformation from narrative discourse to episodic biography which forms the central characteristic of historical writing at late medieval Durham and, as will be seen, at York. It is therefore perhaps all the more unfortunate that the prior's most ambitious work should have failed to exploit the art of biography more directly. Wessington did indeed close his history of St Cuthbert's see with versions of those brief biographies of Bishops Richard de Bury and Thomas Hatfield, as well as of Prior John Fossor, which James Raine misleadingly printed as the early chapters of the misnamed Durham chronicle of William de Chambre.[33] However, in his arrangement of these biographical passages, the prior also helps to confirm the now established view that the latter were written piecemeal in the late fourteenth century and mark the more or less complete disintegration of the medieval Durham tradition of creative historical interpretation.[34] It was a disintegration which Prior Wessington, despite his creditable intentions, had been unable to arrest; but it was a disintegration too which managed to avoid becoming completely and positively terminal. For at intermittent and confusing intervals throughout the long period from the late fourteenth century until the death of Bishop Cuthbert Tunstall in 1559, new biographies of the last medieval bishops and priors of Durham were grafted on to at least a few of the copies of the convent's standard history as originated by Symeon, the *Gesta episcoporum Dunelmensium*.

Admittedly the correct interpretation of the slightly random scraps of biographical information which bring the medieval Durham chronicle tradition to its close in the early sixteenth century is no easy matter. Several of the manuscripts of the *Gesta*, like that in the library of York Minster which Raine selected as his primary copy text, actually end

---

[32] DCD, MS B.III.30, fo. 5; cf. Dobson, *Durham Priory*, p. 382.

[33] MS Laud Misc. 748, fos 63–6; *Scriptores tres*, pp. 127–42.

[34] Denholm-Young, 'Birth of a Chronicle', 326–8; Offler, *Medieval Historians*, pp. 16–17. The collapse of sustained continuity in historical writing at Durham during these years is particularly well reflected in the different hands at work within the relevant sections of Bodleian Library, MS Fairfax 6, fos 281–4.

with the death of Bishop Richard de Bury in 1345;[35] but in other manuscripts the gradual process of subsequent accretion can certainly be observed, if through a glass somewhat darkly. Most instructive of all in this regard are the later folios of Bodleian Library, MS Fairfax 6, from which were subsequently copied the identical Durham biographies in Bodleian, MS Laud Misc. 700. The late fourteenth-century compiler of MS Fairfax 6 adopted the standard Durham practice of dividing his composite account of the *Gesta episcoporum* up to the pontificate of Bishop Bury into 184 separate chapters; but by the middle of the sixteenth century his successors had succeeded in adding a further twenty-seven chapters to make a grand total of 211.[36] Although none of these chapters is of substantial length, at the very least they reveal some slight attempt to maintain a record of who the late medieval bishops of Durham and their priors actually were. In fact these 'chapters' of biographical notes are of highly uneven quality, at their most specific in the cases of Bishops Bury, Thomas Hatfield, John de Fordham and Walter Skirlaw before a more or less complete attenuation of information follows for most of the fifteenth century. Thus the one-sentence entry on Prior John Wessington himself records merely the dates of his election, his priorate and his burial, the last erroneously.[37] Only with Bishop Thomas Ruthall (1509–23) and Prior Thomas Castell (1494–1515) does there emerge a partial and final revival of what is nevertheless by now an acutely emaciated chronicle tradition.[38] As Prior Castell and his industrious monastic chancellor, Thomas Swalwell, exemplify to perfection, the last generations of Durham monks continued to be absorbed in the glories of their community's past; but that absorption no longer took the form of rewriting that past but rather of copying and recopying, with however pious an intent, historical material already in the convent's library.[39]

---

[35] York Minster, MS XVI 1. 12, fos 225v–27. As Professor Offler has shown (*Medieval Historians*, p. 24 n. 40), the late fourteenth-century continuations to the *Gesta episcoporum* are too confusingly diverse to be easily summarised – or explained.

[36] MS Fairfax 6, fos 290–6; MS Laud Misc. 700, fos 146–55v. Cf. F. Madan, H.H.E. Craster and N. Denholm-Young (eds), *Summary Catalogue of Western Manuscripts in the Bodleian Library at Oxford*, ii, pt 2 (Oxford, 1937), pp. 773–5.

[37] MS Fairfax 6, fo. 292v; MS Laud Misc. 700, fo. 149v; *Scriptores tres*, p. 147. In this entry the prior is named as 'Washington', yet another indication that these mid fifteenth-century Durham biographies must often have been written decades after the death of the bishop or prior in question.

[38] MS Fairfax 6, fos 293v–94; *Scriptores tres*, pp. 151–4. Appropriately enough, much the most valuable entry in the closing chapters of the Durham *Gesta* is the account of St Cuthbert's last celebrated medieval miracle, the healing at his shrine in 1503 of Richard Poell, one of Henry VII's servants.

[39] Perhaps the most revealing example is the collection of Cuthbertine and other historical tracts (BL, MS Harley 4843) transcribed in 1528 by William Tod, one of the last monks and first canons of the cathedral: *BRUO*, p. 570; B. Colgrave (ed.), *Two Lives of Saint Cuthbert* (Cambridge, 1940), pp. 28–9.

By one of the more curious but perhaps inevitable ironies of historical writing in the late medieval north, a not dissimilar fate befell the church of York at approximately the same period. Admittedly the metropolitan cathedral of York had never developed a sustained tradition of historical enquiry to rival that of Durham. Although the miscellaneous chronicles and associated works produced at York from the twelfth century onwards are not of course without their considerable interest, especially where the controversial issue of Canterbury's primacy over York was at stake, they failed to promote either authors of the calibre of those often encountered at Durham or an analogous sense of spiritual and constitutional development over the centuries.[40] Of the two most plausible explanations for the comparatively undistinguished late medieval historiographical tradition at York Minster – that so indisputably venerable a metropolitan 'temple' needed no historical validation for its authority over its province; and that only a small minority of the senior cathedral clergy committed their loyalties to the Minster by residing there – neither seem completely adequate. Moreover, the scarcity of interesting historical writing at the Minster seems all the more surprising when contrasted with the diverse and impressive work produced elsewhere in late medieval Yorkshire: as John Taylor has shown, the celebrated fourteenth-century monastic chronicles produced at Bridlington, Guisborough, Jervaulx, Kirkstall, Meaux, Ripon, Tynemouth and St Mary's York itself cumulatively far outweigh such historical work then being written south of the Trent.[41] Nor is it too hard to discover interesting examples (admittedly much more sporadic) of historical enquiry in fifteenth-century Yorkshire, for instance by Thomas Pickering, abbot of Whitby from 1462 to 1475, who was capable of investigating the genealogies of several armigerous families in a way not easy to parallel among the Benedictine monks of southern England.[42] Much more obviously, by the fifteenth century there was a large readership for historical work among both the senior clergy resident in the city of York and also those lay and clerical members of Yorkshire society who bought their books there. Whether or not (as seems likely) the city's

---

[40] See Taylor, *Historical Literature*, pp. 25–6. With the major exception of Hugh the Chanter's so-called *History of the Church of York from 1066 to 1127*, ed. C. Johnson (London, 1961) revised M. Brett, C.N.L. Brooke and M. Winterbottom (Oxford, 1990), nearly all the highly diverse later medieval historical literature associated with York Minster is to be found printed in J. Raine (ed.), *Historians of the Church of York* (hereafter cited as *HCY*), RS (1879–94), ii.

[41] Taylor, *Historical Writing in Yorkshire*, pp. 16–32. Thanks to the same author's own recent analysis of the highly complex composition of the *Anonimalle Chronicle*, the Benedictine monks of St Mary's, York, can also now be seen as the compilers of northern England's most ambitious, if derivative, fourteenth-century national political chronicle (*Historical Literature*, pp. 133–45).

[42] BL, MS Harley 3648, fo. 5; *DNB*, Pickering; C.L. Kingsford, *English Historical Literature in the Fifteenth Century* (London, 1913), pp. 279–91.

craft of *escriveners de tixt* themselves copied works of history for some of their customers, record has now been found of no less than thirty-five to forty bequests of chronicles or histories in the late medieval probate registers of the diocese of York.[43] The majority of these bequests are sadly unspecific; but in the case of Sir John Morton's legacy of a copy of Higden's voluminous *Polychronicon* to Robert Semer, rector of St Michael's, York, in 1431, the same volume passed from Semer to Whitby Abbey twelve years later in 1443. There can be no better illustration of an increasing appetite for similar types of historical writing among late medieval Yorkshire knights, secular clergy and religious alike, of an 'affection' for traditional history which was to survive even the Reformation.[44]

Within such a county context, the failure of the city of York itself, despite its inhabitants' proud awareness that they lived in 'une citee de graunde reputacion et tutdys nomee le secounde Citee du Roialme', to develop a genre of urban history even remotely comparable with that of the London city chronicles of the later middle ages might be thought at least slightly surprising.[45] Faced with precisely this deficiency, in 1430 Roger de Burton, the most enterprising of York's late medieval common clerks, took the highly unusual step of copying into twenty-seven folios of the city's official 'memorandum book' a copy of a *Cronica de successionibus et gestis notabilibus archiepiscoporum Eboracensium* from St Paulinus to the death of Archbishop John Thoresby in 1373. Not only does Burton's unexpected initiative prove that the history of a cathedral and its pastors could intrigue and interest a fifteenth-century city council: the *Cronica* he copied is in fact nothing more nor less than the standard history of the church of York for all late medieval readers wanting information on the topic.[46] The composite York *Cronica archiepiscoporum*, which might be interpreted as a much less substantial counterpart of the Durham *Gesta episcoporum*, is also in urgent need of more critical attention than it received at the hands of its last editor, in this case James Raine the younger. However, the latter was almost certainly correct to suggest that in its fullest, early sixteenth-century version the *Cronica archiepiscoporum* falls into three sections: the first of

[43] J.A. Hoeppner Moran, *The Growth of English Schooling, 1340–1548: Learning, Literacy and Laicization in Pre-Reformation York Diocese* (Princeton, 1985), pp. 12, 15–16, 202–3; cf. M. Sellers (ed.), *York Memorandum Book*, Surtees Society, 120, 125 (1912, 1915), i, pp. 56–7.

[44] York, Borthwick Institute of Historical Research, Probate Register 2, fo. 653v; J. Raine, ed., *Testamenta Eboracensia*, ii, Surtees Society, 30 (1855), p. 14; D. Hay, *Annalists and Historians* (London, 1977), pp. 118–19.

[45] York City Archives (hereafter YCA), York Freeman's Register (D.1), fo. 348. The only major library catalogue to survive from late medieval York reflects no particular interest in the history of the church or city there: see M.R. James, 'The Catalogue of the Library of the Augustinian Friars at York', *Fasciculus Joanni Willis Clark dicatus* (London, 1909), p. 77.

[46] The clear if not elegant hand is probably Burton's own: YCA, A/Y, fos 219v–46v; *York Memorandum Book*, ii, p. 101.

these was compiled in the early twelfth century; the second was written (almost certainly not, as Twysden and Raine supposed, by a Dominican friar called Thomas Stubbs) soon after the death of Archbishop Thoresby in 1373; while the third and final section was completed at some time in the archiepiscopate of Thomas Wolsey (1514–30).[47] Of these three parts of the York *Cronica*, the first two are much the most sophisticated; and they alone, placed together in eighty-eight consecutive chapters, form the contents of most surviving manuscripts of what became a not unpopular work. Extant texts of this late fourteenth-century version of the *Cronica* suggest that it circulated quite widely outside York Minster in attractively written quarto editions like the present Bodleian Library, MS Barlow 27, itself perhaps similar to the manuscript used as his copy text by Roger de Burton within the York city council chamber in 1430.[48]

However it is the much less popular third section of the *Cronica archiepiscoporum* which is of interest here in revealing that from the late fourteenth century onwards (and at York just as much as at Durham) there occurred a dramatic disintegration of the previous conventions of historical writing. In some ways this disintegration is even easier to observe at York Minster than at Durham Cathedral Priory because at the former no one of Prior Wessington's interests and stature as a historian ever emerged. As in the similar case of the analogous biographical notices of the prelates of Durham, those at York were composed at erratic and now unascertainable intervals in the period between the late fourteenth and early sixteenth century. Accordingly the *Cronica*'s brief descriptions of the deeds of the last thirteen medieval archbishops of York (from Alexander Neville in 1374 to Thomas Wolsey in 1514) vary considerably in interest and information. Like the Durham *Gesta episcoporum*, the biographies of these York archbishops are usually at pains to record, not always accurately, the precise dates of the pontificates in question. However, it is noticeable that at Durham it was the date of consecration but at York the date of enthronement in the cathedral which was thought most worthy of attention.[49] Thus in 1477 and 1481 archbishops Lawrence Booth and Thomas Rotherham were commended for enthronement ceremonies in the Minster accompanied by *magna convivio in palatio suo* and *magno honore* respectively; by contrast, Archbishop Thomas Savage (1501–7) was implicitly rebuked for 'being the first of his line who omitted the feasts and solemnities customary on the installation of archbishops of York'.[50] A more

[47] *HCY*, ii, pp. xx–xxvii, 312–445. Internal evidence strongly suggests that the first and second parts of the chronicle were written by, or at the instructions of, members of the senior cathedral clergy at York.

[48] Bodleian Library, Oxford, MS Barlow 27, fos 1–62, of which *HCY*, ii, pp. 422–45, provides a full and quite accurate transcription.

[49] *Scriptores tres*, pp. 144–51; MS Barlow 27, fos 47v–58v.

[50] Ibid., fos 56v, 57v, 59v; *HCY*, ii, pp. 438–9, 442.

important difference between these Durham and York biographies is that the former often include quite detailed and invariably highly laudatory accounts (especially in the case of Thomas Castell) of the cathedral priors, while at York the deans and other dignitaries of the Minster tend to be mentioned only when they were in bitter dispute with their archbishops.[51] However, both at Durham and at York, the late medieval prelate of the see (very rarely present within his cathedral community of course) was praised above all for his building enterprises. Here again there are significant differences of emphasis between the two dioceses. Whereas a bishop of Durham was most likely to be eulogised for his contribution to building works within his cathedral precinct, a fifteenth-century archbishop of York normally attracted more attention for his lavish extensions to his favourite palaces at Bishopthorpe, Southwell, Scrooby and (above all) Cawood.[52] As the late medieval prelates of the north might well have wished, it was indeed as great builders that they were most vividly remembered by the last if limited historians of their sees.

On closer examination there remains another and more revealing difference between the *Gesta episcoporum* of Durham and the *Cronica archiepiscoporum* of York. Whereas the former is invariably complimentary about the achievements of the bishops of St Cuthbert's see, the biographies of the last thirteen medieval archbishops of York are much more likely to oscillate between adulation and hostility. Not surprisingly, the extreme examples of these two very different attitudes were those provoked by the tempestuous regimes of Archbishop Alexander Neville (1374–88) on the one side and of Archbishop Richard Scrope (1398–1405) on the other. For the careers of both these politically embattled metropolitans, the biographical notices within the York *Cronica* are an important, sometimes original and often neglected source. It is naturally no surprise to learn from the latter that Neville, 'unmindful of the oath he swore to God and St Peter on the day of his enthronement', made a deliberate onslaught on the liberties and praiseworthy customs of the church of York; and in view of the cult of the martyred Scrope at York Minster itself it is even less surprising that his death was portrayed as a sacrilegious crime against an 'athlete of Christ'.[53] Much less to be expected are two other and more specific revelations: that one of Alexander Neville's greatest offences was to despatch six of York cathedral's vicars choral to Beverley Minster for over two years in the 1380s, and that it was also four vicars choral who carried, *non absque timore et tremore*, Scrope's decapitated corpse into the east end

---

[51] *Scriptores tres*, pp. 152–4; MS Barlow 27, fos 48, 59v.

[52] *Scriptores tres*, pp. 145, 146, 155–6; MS Barlow 27, fos 47v, 54, 55v, 58v.

[53] MS Barlow 27, fos 47v–49; *HCY*, ii, pp. 422–5; cf. R.B. Dobson, 'Beverley in Conflict: Archbishop Alexander Neville and the Minster Clergy, 1381–8', in C. Wilson (ed.), *Medieval Art and Architecture in the East Riding of Yorkshire*, British Archaeological Association (1989), pp. 152–4.

of the cathedral choir on the day after his execution.[54] In a quite different and happier context, neither Archbishop Thomas Arundel's consecration of a stone altar in the vicars' chapel within their Bedern nor Archbishop William Booth's appropriation of the church of Nether Wallop to their college was allowed to be forgotten.[55] But then the more closely one examines these miniature biographies of the late medieval archbishops of York, the more clear it becomes that it was the latter's benevolence towards the Minster's college of vicars choral which tends to be warmly appreciated and carefully recorded. If so, what are the possible implications for the vexed issues of the composition and authorship of the last section of the *Cronica archiepiscoporum*?

More than a century ago James Raine the younger hazarded the 'conjecture' that the author of this third and final section of the chronicle of the archbishops of York might have been William Melton, chancellor of the Minster from 1498 to 1528. It now needs no urging at all that there could be few more implausible candidates for such a role than this sophisticated Cambridge-educated disciple of Erasmus, tutor of John Fisher and reader of Thomas More's *Utopia*.[56] In the writing of brief conventional lives of English prelates, William Melton – like Erasmus and More – can have had little interest at all. Indeed it now seems necessary to direct attention towards an altogether different element within the cathedral clergy. Is it not most likely that by the early sixteenth century the duty of sustaining the decaying tradition of medieval historical writing in the mother church of the northern province had passed to the Minster's vicars choral – among the most obscure rather than the most distinguished servants of St Peter at York? Perhaps not altogether coincidentally, a highly similar development seems to have occurred at another of the church of York's minsters, Ripon, where one of two surviving metrical chronicles of the see was begun by a vicar and chantry priest of the 1370s, John de Alhalowgate, and completed by a *simplex presbyter* of Ripon in the next century.[57] In all these cases, as at Durham, the compilers of the biographical sketches also often reveal their local origins by displaying a knowledge of the epitaphs then to be read on the tombs and effigies of recently deceased pontiffs within their cathedral churches.[58] More significantly still, and in Yorkshire as well as at Durham,

---

[54] MS Barlow 27, fo. 53; *HCY*, ii, pp. 428–33. Not surprisingly, the circumstances of Richard Scrope's execution made him the only fifteenth-century archbishop of York to stimulate a minor outburst of hagiographical and biographical literature: see *HCY*, ii, pp. xix–xx, 292–311; J.W. McKenna, 'Popular Canonization as Political Propaganda: The Cult of Archbishop Scrope', *Speculum*, 45 (1970), pp. 608–23.

[55] MS Barlow 27, fos 49v, 55v; *HCY*, ii, pp. 425, 436.

[56] *HCY*, ii, p. xxv; *Testamenta Eboracensia*, v, Surtees Society, 79 (1884), pp. 258–9; Aylmer and Cant, *York Minster*, p. 73; B. Bradshaw and E. Duffy (eds), *Humanism, Reform and the Reformation: The Career of Bishop John Fisher* (Cambridge, 1989), pp. 25–6.

[57] *HCY*, ii, pp. xxviii–xxx, 464; Taylor, *Historical Writing in Yorkshire*, pp. 23, 32.

[58] E.g., MS Barlow 27, fos 50–1, 56v; *HCY*, ii, pp. 427–8, 437–8; *Scriptores tres*, pp. 133–4, 145, 148, 149–50, 154.

these miniature biographies of prelates seem not infrequently to be related to – and perhaps derive from – what a late medieval visitor to a major church would have been able to read for himself on boards or *tabulae* as he wandered through the nave, transepts and aisles.[59] Here too the writing of history at England's two great northern cathedrals seems to have come full circle. As the most distinguished and scholarly monks of Durham and canons of York in the late middle ages lost interest in producing historical work themselves, so what historical writing there was perhaps came to be increasingly addressed by the lesser cathedral clergy to the pilgrim and the tourist. If so, this melancholy story of medieval northern historical writing in decline may not, after all, be without a cautionary moral to impart for the future of the English historical profession in the 1990s.

[59] For the view that the historical narratives fastened to the two surviving late medieval *tabulae* at York Minster were designed to instruct and edify pilgrims and visitors to the cathedral, see Aylmer and Cant, *York Minster*, p. 108 n. 227; cf. a paraphrase of these narratives in J.S. Purvis, 'The Tables of the York Vicars Choral', *Yorkshire Archaeological Journal*, 41 (1967), pp. 741–8; and for their use by the cosmographer, John Foxton, at the close of the fourteenth century, see J.B. Friedman, 'John Sifferwas and the Mythological Illustrations in the *Liber cosmographiae* of John de Foxton', *Speculum*, 58 (1983), pp. 391–418. The use of such 'tables' to provide historical information is very evident at Ripon (*HCY*, ii, pp. xxviii, 446) and Durham (see above n. 31 and, for a life of Bishop Bury on a *tabula pensilis*, Denholm-Young, 'Birth of a Chronicle', p. 326). As the examples recently collected in Gransden, *Historical Writing*, ii, p. 495, suggest, the role of *tabulae* as an important agency for the transmission of historical knowledge in the later middle ages deserves much more attention than it has ever received. I am grateful to both Dr Gransden and to Dr David Smith for their generous assistance during the writing of this essay.

Index

York) 168, 178–9; as chancellor of York 168; university education of 169; archiepiscopal election 170–1; relations with Edward I 170–1, 180; consecration of Antony Bek as bishop of Durham 175–6; relations with Durham prior and convent 176; death of at Pontigny 176

Wilfrid, St (of Ripon) 29; cult of 220, 243; Life of by Eddius Stephanus 29

William (bishop of Ostia) 128

William I (king of England) 34, 35, 38, 40–1; conquest of England 29, *and see* Conquest; foundation of Battle Abbey 36n., 40; foundation of Selby 37–41; endowments to Selby 42; royal foundation charter to Selby 34n., 35, 37, 38–9, 40

William of Malmesbury, *Gesta regum Anglorum* 45

William Rufus 42–3

William of St Calais (bishop of Durham) 24; foundation of Durham Priory 32; as bishop of Durham 287

William of York, St, cult of 243, translation of relics to high altar of York 174–5; miracles of 175

Wilton, John 210

Wilton, Stephen (residentiary canon of York) 210, 218n., 219, 221, 222, 223n.; as a royal clerk 212, 213

Wimborne (Dorset), collegiate church of 244

Winchelsey, Robert (archbishop of Canterbury), relations with Edward I 168, 171

Winchester 43n.; bishops of 184

Windsor 250; St George's Chapel 212, 244

Wistow, Robert (of York) 275

Wodham, John (residentiary canon of York) 198n., 218n., 219, 220

Wolsey (Cardinal) 231, 298

Wolveden, Robert (residentiary canon of York) 210n., 222

Wren, Thomas (titular prior of Coldingham) 123

Wressle Castle (East Riding) 97

Wycliffe (North Riding) 56

Wydeville, Queen Elizabeth 229, 244

Wykeham, William of 89

York, archbishops of xi, 3–4, 6, 10, 23, 24, 30, 35, 38, 39, 41, 42, 204, 205, 213, 214, 298, 299, 300–1; relations with Canterbury 178, 296; relations with Durham 176–7, 189, 216, 226n., 292; relations with Scotland 90–1, 179–80; relations with canons 5, 208, 213, 231; relations with deans 231, 299; relations with king 37–8 (William I) 41, 42, 230–2 (Richard III), *and see* Richard III; and the crusades 172; registers of xi, 9, 10, 12, 165, 166–7, 263; residences of 299 (Southwell, Scrooby); at Cawood Castle 193, 299; at Bishopthorpe 7, 299; role of in royal government 191; vicars-general of xi; visitations of 202n.; *and see* Lawrence Booth, Thomas Rotherham

—, archbishops of, in reign of Edward I: 164, 165–84; registers of 165, 166–7; relations with Edward I 170–3; relations with Durham 176–7; conflicts with Canterbury over right to carry primatial cross 178; loss of metropolitan supremacy over Scotland 179–80; limited economic resources of 180–3

York, archdiocese of ix, xii–xiii, 135, 138, 164, 177, 179–80, 196, 197, 214, 249n.; consistory court 240; early history 4, 177, 179

York, cathedral of, canons x, xi, 1, 3, 8, 11–12, 23, 30, 141, 168, 169, 174, 175, 181, 206, 212, 221, 228, 255, 298n.; relations with archbishops 5, 6, 7, 170, 181, 182, 187, 198, 225, 231, 238; conflicts with Archbishop Alexander Neville 186–8, 191–2, 193; relations with York aldermen 215, 255, 273–4, 276; relations with gentry and magnates 21; involvement in royal government 182–3, 191, 192, 195, 205, 229, 239; relations with Richard III 225–46 (*and see* Richard III); numbers of 51; university education of 23, 169

—, residentiary canons (in the fifteenth century) 195–6, 296; university